UNEVEN DEVELOPMENT IN THAILAND

Uneven Development in Thailand

Edited by
MICHAEL J.G. PARNWELL
Centre for South-East Asian Studies
University of Hull
England

Avebury
Aldershot • Brookfield USA • Hong Kong • Singapore • Sydney

Published by
Avebury
Ashgate Publishing Limited
Gower House
Croft Road
Aldershot
Hants GU11 3HR
England

Ashgate Publishing Company
Old Post Road
Brookfield
Vermont 05036
USA

British Library Cataloguing in Publication Data

Uneven Development in Thailand
I. Parnwell, Michael J.G.
330.9593

ISBN 1 85972 085 4

Library of Congress Catalog Card Number: 95-83043

Typeset by Michael J.G. Parnwell
University of Hull

Printed and bound by Athenaeum Press, Ltd.,
Gateshead, Tyne & Wear.

Contents

List of figures and boxes

List of tables

Contributors' institutional affiliations

Dr Daniel Arghiros, Research Fellow, Centre for South-East Asian Studies, University of Hull, England.

Dr Peter Bell, Social Science Division, State University of New York, USA

Prof. Philip Dearden, Department of Geography, University of Victoria, Canada.

Dr Chris Dixon, Department of Geography, London Guildhall University.

Prof. Chris Garforth, Agricultural Extension and Rural Development Department, University of Reading, England.

Dr Philip Hirsch, Department of Geography, University of Sydney, Australia.

Assoc. Prof. Suranart Khamanarong, Department of Social Sciences, Khon Kaen University, Thailand.

Prof. Leedom Lefferts, Department of Anthropology, Drew University, USA

Dr Mike Parnwell, Centre for South-East Asian Studies, University of Hull, England.

Dr Johannes Drasbaek Schmidt, Research Fellow, Department of Development and Planning, Aalborg University, Denmark.

Dr Jean-Christophe Simon, French Scientific Research Institute for Development/Asia Centre, Grenoble University, France.

Dr Paiboon Suthsupa, Department of Agricultural Extension, Chiang Mai University, Thailand.

Mika Toyota, Ph.D. Student, Centre for South-East Asian Studies, University of Hull, England

Dr Guy Trébuil, International Rice Research Institute, Los Baños, Manila, The Philippines.

John Walton, Centre for South-East Asian Studies, University of Hull, England.

Dr Peter Williamson, Department of Geography, University of Sydney, Australia.

Dr Wathana Wongsekiarttirat, Faculty of Political Science, and Social Research Institute, Chulalongkorn University, Thailand.

1 Introduction: Uneven development in Thailand

Michael J.G. Parnwell and Daniel A. Arghiros

Hyperbole and reality

To judge by the epithets and metaphors which have been liberally used to describe Thailand's economic 'miracle', the Kingdom is well on its way to joining the world's economic 'superleague'. Variously seen as 'Asia's Fifth Tiger', an 'Emerging Superstar' and the 'Cinderella of Asia', the widely held impression is of an outstanding economic success story. This is not without good reason: since the 1960s, and most particularly the boom years of the 1980s, Thailand has consistently posted among the highest rates of economic growth in the world, averaging around 7-8 per cent per annum during this time and on occasion reaching double figures. As Hewison (1989b, p.1) has noted

> [t]ourism has boomed, manufactured exports have skyrocketed, and economic growth statistics are regularly being revised upwards.

Thailand is seen as a dynamic and optimistic country which has benefited significantly from a changing international division of labour.

Behind this very substantial façade lies the other of the 'two Thailands' (see *Far Eastern Economic Review*, 14 April 1994), where change is much slower, improvement less obvious, and prospects less bright. The benefits of the boom have not affected everyone and everywhere to an equal extent. Many have been left behind, and even marginalised, in the scramble for self-improvement. The 'other' Thailand is found away from the economic heartland of Greater Bangkok and the country's Central Region (see Figure 1.1), in the hamlets, villages and small towns of the country's periphery which are less accessible and far less attractive to the investors who have fuelled Thailand's economic boom. Glimpses are also to be found among the slums and squatter settlements, the scavengers and street-vendors of the capital city - areas and people who suffer directly the environmental and social externalities of rapid and largely uncontrolled economic growth. As Hewison (1989b, p.2) observes

> [w]e can see the modern, 'rational' factories and the sweatshops and pollution; a burgeoning service sector and hundreds of thousands of prostitutes; a rapidly developing middle class and workers and peasants

> struggling grimly to reproduce themselves and their families; urban growth and rural marginalisation; and so on.

Viewed from this perspective, Thailand is less a 'tiger' and more a 'sheep in wolf's clothing' (Parnwell, 1993d, p.53 *et.seq.*).

So, as Dixon notes in this volume, Thailand's designation as a near-NIC has more the character of a Newly-Industrialising City than Country, so comprehensively does Bangkok and its hinterland dominate the country's spatial economy. Nearly four-fifths of Thailand's manufacturing value-added emanates from the capital city and, as we shall see later in this chapter, the regional distribution of income is heavily skewed in favour of the economic core. There is also evidence that income disparities have increased during, and as a consequence of, the boom years (Grandstaff, 1992; Hewison and Brown, 1994). Consequently, as Chai-Anan and Sukhumbhand (1993, p.124) note

> the overall picture of Thailand is that of a dynamic country that has been able to take advantage of the growth of the world economy and at the same time to cushion itself from the worst vicissitudes arising therein, but also a country faced with problems of equity and distribution, of poverty and lack of opportunities for advancement for many of its own people.

Thus, whilst not wishing to deny or decry the Kingdom's undoubted economic, social and welfare achievements, the notion of 'success' and the accomplishment of 'development' have both to be qualified. Thailand is as striking an example of uneven development as it is of economic achievement. It is with the context and form of uneven development that this volume is mainly concerned.[1]

Uneven development

Uneven development is the manifestation in space (i.e. between places, sectors and people) of the problem of unequal access to natural, social, political and economic resources (O'Connor, 1989). The word 'access' is used advisedly here because it introduces connotations of fairness and justice (Lummis, 1992), as opposed to simple patterns of distribution, and thus has an influence on how uneven development is seen. Uneven development may be a predominantly economic phenomenon, but it is not essentially an economic problem: the 'problem' rests with society, and particularly the disadvantaged areas and peoples who tend to be left behind or overlooked as development proceeds. It may be an "endemic characteristic of capitalist societies" (Hudson, 1988, p.484), and its antithesis - a perfectly even pattern of development - may be impossible to achieve, but if it is viewed in value rather than factual terms, its existence and persistence is harder to accept (Lummis, 1992, p.38). Value and factual judgements of uneven development also lead to significantly different planning responses: the latter necessitates a quest for greater spatial-economic homogenisation and integration, whereas the former requires confrontation of rather more fundamental and deep-rooted social and political differentials. Thus there is no simple answer to the question "is uneven development undesirable"? An economistic empirical perspective would yield a negative or at best a non-committal response, whereas a humanistic value judgement would lead to an affirmative reply, linked to the social immorality of personal and territorial welfare differences.

Uneven development can partly be explained by inherent factors such as geography and the environment - i.e. differences in climate, resource endowments and accessibility. However, uneven development is much more complex than the simple product of natural factors. It also involves historical, socio-cultural, economic and political explanations. It is thus largely a socially determined process - for it is not places that exploit other places, it is people. Muscat (1994, p.237) claims that structural factors have reinforced 'natural' development imbalances, and thus the role of the state, including both its explicit spatial policies and the spatial consequences of other major initiatives, must also be examined in seeking to explain the existence and persistence of uneven development. As we shall see shortly, the implementation of successive five-year plans has tended to reflect the priorities of powerful groups in Thai society. Development has served the urban élite at the expense of the rural majority, the urban poor and the environment. Thailand's integration into the global economic and political system has also had a strong influence on the nature and magnitude of uneven development.

It is important to emphasise that uneven development is not a static phenomenon but an on-going, dynamic process.

> uneven regional development is not a simple and static reflection of the geographically uneven distribution of productive forces within a particular social formation. It is rather a dynamic process, acquiring various forms and intensities, depending on the specific historical conjecture in the social formation under question (Hadjimichalis, 1987, pp.85-6).

Smith (1986, p.99) argues that

> uneven development is not an extraneous process which swoops down on static geographical blocks; rather it is the continual struggle of opposed tendencies toward differentiation and equalization.

In the case of Thailand, it appears that this is itself a very unequal struggle. The 'natural' tendency towards disparity has tended to be reinforced by the various forms of intervention, public and private, which have taken place over time. In contrast, there has been no countervailing <u>tendency</u> towards equalisation. However, as the following discussion and chapters will show, the mal-distribution of productive enterprise and the spoils of economic growth has gradually contributed to the emergence of a more critical assessment of how best to 'do development' in Thailand, driven as much by the imperatives of an over-heating economy as the pressing needs of a disadvantaged and marginalised populace.

The following discussion will look at some of the factors which can be used to explain the emergence, extension and entrenchment of uneven development in Thailand. Our choice of factors to be considered is necessarily selective, and includes the context and direction of development planning, the prioritisation of development paths, and the internationalisation of the Thai economy. We start with a brief assessment of the contribution of geography and environment to the regional pattern of development.

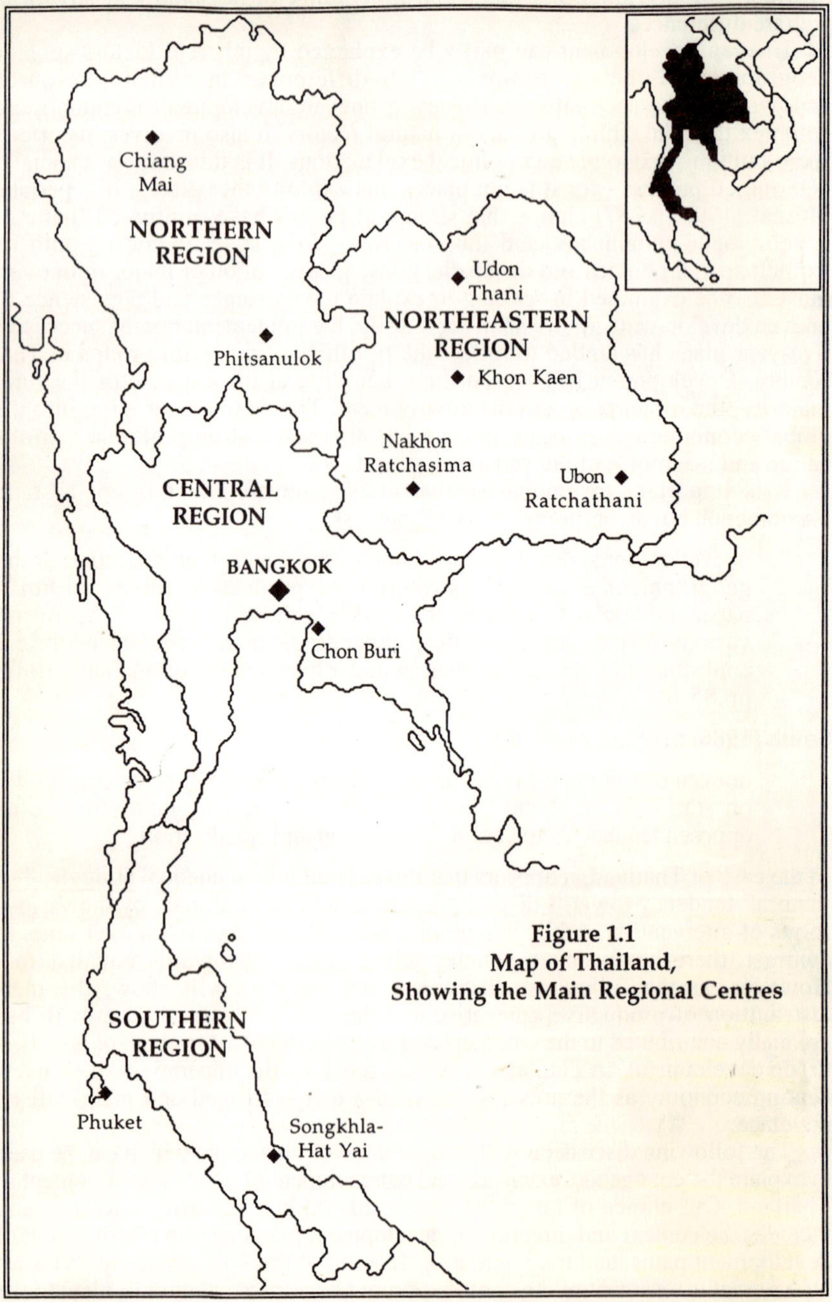

Figure 1.1
Map of Thailand,
Showing the Main Regional Centres

Some explanations for uneven development in Thailand

Geography and environment

Geographical location and environmental factors explain some of the imbalances in Thailand's development process. Differentials in regional agricultural productivity and, consequently, regional income disparities can be explained, to a certain extent, by variations in soil fertility, drainage, rainfall patterns, climate and topography.

Thailand is usually divided into four geographical regions: the Central Plain, the North-East, the North and the South (see Figure 1.1). The Central Plain is the most prosperous region of the country. Its rich alluvial soils, flat terrain and good water supply are favourable factors for extensive rice production. Consequently, irrigation facilities and cultivation for export have been overwhelmingly concentrated in this region. Arbhabhirama *et.al.* (1988, p.106) note that the irrigation systems of the Central Plain constitute almost 55 per cent of the country's total irrigated area. As a result, the initial ecological advantages of the Central Region have been compounded. In addition, the region's close proximity to Bangkok, the Kingdom's major domestic market and centre of international trade, further promotes its advantageous position over the North-East, the North and the South.

The marginality of the Northeastern environment is often used to explain the poverty of the region (Parnwell, 1988). The infertile, sandy soils and extensive periods of both severe drought and heavy flooding in the North-East make it the least favoured region in the country. These factors have been cited as the principal reasons for poor agricultural productivity and consequently very poor per capita income which stands at 40 per cent of the national average (Arbhabhirama *et.al.*, 1988, p.20). By way of example, average yields of rice between 1985/86 and 1990/91 in the North-East were less than 1.5 tonnes per hectare. In the Central Plain yields averaged 2.3 tonnes per hectare (more than 50% higher) over the same period (Ministry of Agriculture and Co-operatives, 1989, pp.18-19; 1991, pp.18-19: cited in Rigg, 1993, p.214).

The Northern region comprises a series of steep mountain ranges incised by steep valleys and rivers. It is characterised by alluvial soils, a fairly reliable rainfall pattern and a well developed irrigation system which facilitates upland crop production. Its agricultural productivity enables the population to maintain a better standard of living than the Northeastern region but which is not as high as that in the Central or Southern regions.

The Southern region enjoys a tropical climate with the highest average regional rainfall (Arbhabhirama *et.al.*, 1988). Nevertheless, the region is not a major rice-production area due to unsuitable soils and topography. The ample water supply makes the region conducive for the planting of rubber. In addition, horticultural crops, fisheries, favoured tourist locations, and rich mineral deposits provide wealth for the population of the region.

Planning context

Responsibility for drafting Thailand's national development plans has long been the preserve of established technocrats located mainly in the capital city,

Bangkok. These plans have been executed by government agencies and private entrepreneurs (Chamarik, 1993, p.230). There have been criticisms that the development strategy implemented by these groups has impoverished the rural majority for the benefit of a wealthy élite. London notes that decisions about the allocation of resources are made on the basis of principles of social and spatial dominance, such as "building on the best" (London, 1980, pp.80-1). As a result, scarce resources have been allocated more often to élites than the masses, Bangkok rather than the provinces, Bangkok élites rather than Bangkok masses, and provincial élites rather than provincial masses.

The country's national planning body is the National Economic and Social Development Board (NESDB) founded in 1957. The national development plans formulated by the NESDB provide general guidelines which require support from the various sectoral government agencies. As a result of the independence of the various departments within the Thai bureaucracy, the NESDB has little influence over the line agencies which implement the plans. Tambunlertchai (1989b) notes that these agencies are not required strictly to adhere to plan specifications. Furthermore, the implementation process is characterised by widespread duplication of institutions, overlap of responsibilities and lack of co-ordination. As a World Bank study, cited in Demaine (1986, p.107) states:

> There is little evidence that Thailand's development plans systematically guide or govern the actions of departments...in the day-to-day conduct of government affairs. Although national development plans should never be treated in mixed economies as binding and inflexible statements of government intentions, the frequency and extent to which development plans appear to be disregarded in the allocation of financial and administrative resources and in the introduction of new policies, programs and projects is indicative of a lack of full commitment to the concept of development planning.

There is thus often a wide gap between rhetoric and reality.

The national development plans implemented in Thailand in the 1960s and 1970s were predominantly concerned with promoting rapid growth in GNP through capital-intensive industrialisation. As they were based upon *laissez faire* policies and concerned with efficiency and aggregate economic growth, these plans had disappointing results in terms of the distribution of benefits. They produced very uneven growth and increased spatial imbalances both geographically and interpersonally. As a result, development by-passed many people and regions. In 1975/76 the income share of the top 20 per cent of the population was 49.2 per cent of the national income; this figure had increased to 51.47 per cent by 1980/81. Comparable figures for the lowest 20 per cent of the population were 6.05 and 5.41 per cent respectively. In 1970 rural-urban income differentials in Thailand were among the highest in the world at 3 to 1 (Panayotou, 1983; cited in Hirsch, 1990, p.11).

In the late 1970s the Thai government progressively became more concerned with personal, sectoral and regional equity. It was realised that if a determined effort was not made to remedy spatial inequities, the imbalances could result in economic stagnation and political instability in the peripheral areas. To rectify these problems the Thai government embarked upon a spatial approach to development planning in the Fourth Five-Year Plan (1977-81) to enable larger numbers of people to participate in and benefit from economic growth (Keokungwal, 1992, p.43). The central element of this approach was the straightforward application of the growth pole strategy of concentrated urban-industrial decentralisation (see Demaine and Malong, 1987; Hansen, 1981; Douglass, 1981; Richardson, 1984).

Despite the government's attempts to encourage new industrial investment in peripheral areas and to discourage new investment in the Bangkok Metropolitan Area (BMA) relatively little change in regional distribution has occurred (Pakkasem, 1981). As a result of the low level of purchasing power within the regional areas, difficulties in serving widely scattered small markets, lack of supporting infrastructure and skilled labour, and anxiety about regional political stability, private investors and entrepreneurs have been reluctant to invest in the regional growth poles (Kaothien, 1991). Industries have been more inclined to establish themselves on the periphery of Bangkok to take advantage of the fiscal incentives which have been offered to industrial units that locate outside the BMA (McGee and Greenberg, 1992). The few industries which have relocated to the regional growth poles have generated few linkages with the rural sector and the 'spread' effects which appeared so enticing in theory have not taken place to any meaningful extent in practice. Not only have the growth poles failed to produce 'trickle down' benefits but the 'backwash' effects have tended to exceed the spread effects. Wong and Saigol (1984) argue that the growth poles have drained their rural hinterlands of resources, capital and productive manpower. The growth poles have thus become islands of dynamism surrounded by stagnating rural hinterlands. The development of regional growth poles has therefore created at a regional level exactly the same problems that they had been created to combat at the national level.

Thus, the top-down, concentrated decentralisation policies tied to the development of urban-based industrialisation have had little impact on uneven development in Thailand. Bangkok has been unable effectively to guide such development due to the fact that most top-level officials based in Bangkok lack the experience and knowledge of local conditions in the peripheral regions.

Hardoy and Satterthwaite (1986, pp.5-6; cited in Jones, 1993, p.67) note that more attention needs to be paid to "modifying the social, economic and political forces which seem to be the major causes of existing spatial trends ... not spatial mechanisms such as diverting investments to 'growth centres' or 'new towns.'" Jones (1993, pp.68-9) reinforces this view

> Policies with more chance of success would be those stressing the elimination of 'metropolitan biases' in tariff structures favouring import-substitution industrialization and in other manufacturing development strategies, elimination of subsidization of rice prices for urban consumers, introduction of 'full-cost pricing' for public transport, electricity and other Bangkok services, and more generally, increasing the taxing power of the Bangkok government, and reducing the 'Bangkok bias' in the provision of higher education and other government facilities.

Pernia (1991, p.118) notes that "explicit dispersal policies have been rendered largely ineffective by the profound spatial biases of macroeconomic and sectoral policies, including trade, industrial and agricultural policies." Thus, in essence, efforts to redress spatial economic imbalances in Thailand are unlikely to amount to much more than a 'public relations exercise' without a fundamental challenge to the prevailing growth-driven top-down orthodoxy. It is towards these two phenomena - centralised decision-making and a 'growth at all costs' philosophy - that we will now briefly turn our attention.

Centralist approach

Since the administrative reforms undertaken by King Chulalongkorn in 1892, decision-making in Thailand has become extremely centralised. Centralisation was used to strengthen national unity and to increase central control over local activities at a time when Thailand was threatened by colonialism. As the central government administrative system is located in Bangkok this has major consequences for the way in which articulation with the rural hinterland is organised. Ramsay (1976, p.17) defines centralisation as "the increasing ability of a central government to determine who is recruited to office at lower levels of government, how decisions are made at these levels, and to what purposes the capabilities of these governments are put." Decisions and policies thus emanate from the centre to the rural areas and provincial cities - programmes and projects are imposed in a 'top-down' manner on the peripheral regions. Officials located in Bangkok tend to perceive and define problems and needs according to their own urban background.

Chamarik (1993) argues that as a result of this centralisation it is mainly the minority urban population who have participated in the growth process and consequently it is this group who has benefited to a far greater degree than the rural majority. He notes (1993, p.259) that

> The widening urban-rural disparities are in themselves a manifestation of failure of the 'top-down' strategy which simply takes for granted that increases in national income will automatically and sufficiently trickle down to the rural masses and thus solve all outstanding social and political problems.

Vienne (1989, p.43) notes that the centralised structure of decision-making and the implicit resultant competition between participating agencies is more often committed to serve the best interests of their superiors rather than the remote rural dwellers themselves (see also Rigg, 1991b). It is clear that there is a need for decentralisation since both the wide range of resources and needs means that the centralised model of development is not sufficiently sensitive to local factors.

Hirsch (1994, p.326) identifies a general thrust towards decentralisation both within and beyond the bureaucratic system in Thailand. He cites as evidence of this proposals to give *tambon* (sub-district) councils more powers and legal status to make decision-making on development programmes more participatory. However, the provincial and district authorities would retain the ultimate power of veto, rendering the *tambon* council an extension of the bureaucracy rather than serving as an independent body. Girling further observes (1994, p.310) that only the wealthier councils would be eligible to sign contracts and raise funds for development purposes.

Thus, in reality, the general situation in Thailand is one of deconcentration (the central government posts employees at the local level) and delegation (central government delegates its powers to the local level) but not much devolution (central government cedes power to local decision-makers). Whatever its rhetoric with regard to decentralisation, the government appears unwilling to cede its considerable powers to the local level, where choices will thus continue to be significantly constrained.

Growth-oriented development

The Thai government's emphasis on engendering efficiency and rapid economic growth, whilst underpinning the euphoric epithets with which we opened this chapter, has not resulted in equal welfare distribution and social justice among people and regions. Infrastructure and other basic facilities have in the past been provided principally in areas with high growth potential. As a result, the fruits of economic growth have benefited those areas already well endowed with infrastructure and already experiencing growth. As Hewison and Brown (1994, p.484) note "Thailand's economic performance does sparkle, but it does so for some more than others."

Chamarik (1993, p.230) suggests that the policy of promoting growth at the expense of distribution and equity was deliberate, noting that

> Opportunities to earn profits', an operative ideal inherent in the growth perspective among 'neo-classical' Thai economists, have been energetically taken and have been politically well-protected...

Meyer (1988, p.465) claims that it is still widely held among Thailand's economic managers that rapid economic expansion will 'outgrow' economic and social problems. He cites the 1986 World Bank study *Thailand: Growth with Stability - A Challenge for the Sixth Plan Period* as urging the Thai government to adopt a more growth-oriented strategy. Meyer challenges the validity of the thesis that Thailand's current social, environmental and distributional problems can be 'outgrown'.

Since the Fourth Five-Year Plan (1977-81) the government's rhetoric has shifted from growth *per se* to growth with equity. But, despite the conceptual shift of emphasis from growth to equity and thus from uneven to balanced development, "the commendable intentions of the planners are not matched by an equally commendable plan of action" (Oey Meesook, 1978, pp.1-2; cited in Chamarik, 1993, p.249). The Sixth Five-Year Plan (1987-91) argues that to remain internationally competitive investments must be concentrated in areas with comparative locational advantages - i.e. the Bangkok Metropolitan Region (BMR). In addition, given that the Eastern Region is the wealthiest sub-region outside Bangkok and enjoys close proximity (80-150 km.) to the capital city, it is likely that the promotion of the Eastern Seaboard (ESB) Project will widen regional disparities by creating a large BMR-ESB conurbation area (McGee and Greenberg's (1992) archetypal Extended Metropolitan Region), while the North and North-East lag increasingly behind.

It should already have become clear that we are dealing here with inter-related, not isolated factors which explain the emergence and persistence of uneven development in Thailand. Thus, for instance, the earlier-mentioned features of Thailand's geography, allied to the country's geo-political situation, have had a profound impact on the historical pattern of the Kingdom's development. Thus created, differentials of dynamism and relative stagnation have themselves had a strong influence on the subsequent pattern and pace of development. Constant throughout this cumulative process, particularly since the mid-19th Century, has been an inexorable internationalisation of the Thai economy which, itself, has bestowed or reinforced locational advantages and disadvantages within the spatial economy.

Although Thailand was the only country in South-East Asia to escape colonisation it did not escape the influence of colonialism and was effectively colonised in economic terms (see Dixon and Parnwell, 1991). The Kingdom was forced to sign a number of unequal treaties, starting with the Bowring Treaty between Britain and Siam in 1855, in order to retain its political independence. These treaties required Thailand to allow free trade between private traders rather than the former state monopoly in trading, to keep tariffs at or below 3 per cent and to limit export duties (Robinson *et.al.*, 1991, p.5). The treaties also indirectly provided opportunities for foreigners to accumulate more wealth than the local population. Pramuanratkarn (1979, p.11) notes that

> Since the nineteenth century Thailand has been put into a status of a peripheral state, serving economic interests of the core area of the world economies.

Thus Thailand was as affected by its dependent position in the world-system as other South-East Asian countries.

Meyer (1988, p.10) argues that the unequal economic trade between Thailand and the West fundamentally changed the country's production structure and the control and value of land. He notes that it also increased interpersonal and regional inequality. Export production was concentrated in the Central Plain and products were shipped to the West through the port of Bangkok. A new commercial economy was thus opened up which drew the resources of capital and labour from the outlying regions to the Central Plain. At the same time imports penetrated the peripheral regions and undermined some local industries (Meyer, 1988, p.20). International demand resulted in an increase in rice production for export and, later, an increase in other agricultural products. Thailand changed from a self-sufficient economy to one specialising in rice production. However, the benefits of free trade were not evenly distributed, nor was there an adequate mechanism of redistribution, or even a realisation of the inherent undesirability of such a situation. The increase in production benefited foreign merchants and élites based in Bangkok rather than rural Thai farmers (Pramuanratkarn, 1979, p.45). Thailand's peripheral position in the internationally stratified economic system also resulted in an uneven urban structure, featuring an exceptionally high degree of urban primacy.

Thailand's emerging position within a New International Division of Labour (see Thrift, 1986) has compounded some of the consequences of the earlier internationalisation of the Thai economy. Transnational corporations (TNCs: mostly Western and East Asian) have taken an increasing interest in Thailand as a locus for investment and the export of certain low-technology production functions - a means of reducing production costs and maintaining margins of profit. As a result of these recent changes in the global division of labour Thailand has, since the early 1980s, experienced a large in-flow of Foreign Direct Investment (FDI) towards export-oriented industries. The volume of FDI increased from 1,127.5 million baht in 1979 to 62,516.3 million baht in 1990 (Apibunyopas, 1993, p.97). Between 1986 and 1989 - the peak of the economic boom - annual FDI in-flows and exports more than doubled (Rock, 1994, p.27).

TNCs have been attracted to Thailand by, *inter alia*, the availability of low-cost labour and raw materials and the economic liberalisation and deregulation policies adopted by the government in the late 1980s. Douglass (1992, p.10) also notes the following factors which explain why FDI has been targeted towards the ASEAN-4 (Thailand, Malaysia, Singapore and Indonesia):

> stable supplies of nonunionized labour, lower environmental regulation, 'flexible' land-use regulations and lower land prices, and the relative absence of well-organized middle-class social movements demanding improvements in and greater regulation of the built environment.

Charoenloet (1991, pp.32-3) notes that workers in TNC exporting industries are subjected to 'double exploitation' - they have to work longer hours and are paid much less (5 to 10 times) than workers in the West. The internationalisation of capital and the growth of the world market have also strengthened many existing forms of women's subordination and introduced new forms of exploitation.

Beyond its social impact, flows of FDI have also had a clear influence on Thailand's spatial economy. The flow of FDI has been heavily concentrated in the Bangkok Metropolitan Region, and there have been few linkages between TNCs and local small-and medium-scale industries (Apibunyopas, 1993). Wong (1994, p.12) notes that virtually all Japanese investments in Thailand are located in the Bangkok metropolis despite the government's decentralisation policy. Thus, the over-concentration of FDI in Bangkok is exacerbating the already highly uneven spatial pattern of development. Moreover, the distribution of FDI by economic sector is also highly uneven. The tertiary, secondary and primary sectors accounted for 46.3%, 41.5% and 12.2% of total inward FDI respectively during the 1970-88 period (Apibunyopas, 1993, p.100). On a geographical basis, the Northeastern, Northern and Southern regions respectively received 5.7%, 7.5% and 8.5% of total FDI in 1990 (calculated from Apibunyopas, 1993, p.101).

Power and politics

In Thailand all crucial decisions regarding development have been taken by the privileged few. The greater economic power of élites enables them to control the political process. The vast majority who have little power in the economy rarely receive benefits from the policies imposed by these élites. London and Anderson (1985) argue that élites make decisions which disproportionately benefit the economic and political interests of their class - i.e. benefit both central and local élites rather than the 'public interest' of the masses. They argue (1985, pp.236-7) that

> as a result, policies implemented tend to create and/or perpetuate regional economic inequalities, through intra-national exploitation and neglect of the periphery by the center.

During the Fifth Plan period (1982-86) state power penetrated every village (Chai-Anan, 1989). The influence of the central government élite on local governments and their budgets means that they control the delivery of services and the posting of personnel. Atkinson and Vorratnchaiphan (1994, p.156) note that the financial dependence of municipalities on the central government in the early 1980s was about 70 per cent and rising.

London and Anderson (1985) argue that the distribution of public resources in Thailand reflects the interests, decisions and policies of central élites. However, the power of central élites is not absolute. They are thus forced to maintain close ties with local élites in peripheral areas. Thus, provinces with greater concentrations of local élites are more successful in demanding central government expenditures for infrastructure development. Furthermore, the presence of élites often accentuates economic inequality in an area. To maintain order they protect their interests by employing additional social controls, such as the provision of development resources and services - leading to higher overall expenditure levels in the province.

Nakata and Dhiravegin (1989) argue that social culture plays an important part in shaping political culture and encouraging the reproduction of existing inequalities (see also Rigg, 1991b: 1993; Hirsch, 1993). The basic philosophy and pattern of interaction is superior-subordinate relationships, characterised by dyadic, hierarchical personal and reciprocal ties. These relationships are often referred to as patron-client ties. As a result of the traditional belief in differential rights, status and power, politics came to be seen as the prerogative of the ruling élite rather than a fundamental right of citizens. Girling argues that

> Consciousness of power on the part of the bureaucratic elite accompanied by consciousness of lack of power by the rest were the twin norms of Thai politics (Girling, 1981b, p.164).

The above social values enabled the powerful to accumulate wealth at the expense of the powerless. Jacobs (1971) argues that it is the patrimonial nature of Thai society that has enabled the country to achieve a level of modernisation but not development. Patrons and clients possess resources which the other needs. Patrons exchange material rewards for the loyalty and support of their clients. As a result, there is a high probability that state resources will be used by élites for élites. Patrons benefit via the consolidation of their power and the accumulation of wealth, while clients benefit materially. As patron-client relationships exist throughout Thailand, the control of state expenditures is heavily biased towards the higher strata in both rural and urban areas. Authors note that the bulk of rural resources are allocated on the basis of patron-client reciprocity. District officials favour development projects which are personally advantageous in terms of promotion, profit etc. Village élites/clients request projects from the district officials which serve their immediate self-interest.

Some aspects of uneven development in Thailand

The foregoing discussion has shown how complex and deeply entrenched in the Thai context the process of uneven development is, and thus how difficult will be its amelioration. We now turn our attention briefly to the identification of uneven development in some of its multifarious forms. We will then round off this introductory discussion by attempting to draw out some of the themes and issues which will be addressed elsewhere in this volume.

Regional disparities

Although it tends to generalise a highly complex reality, the geographical region has been widely used as a means of identifying the spatial dimensions of inequality in Thailand. On this basis we find that the distribution of economic activity, income and public utilities is highly uneven. Ayal (1992) has suggested that Bangkok and the Central Region stand out like a newly-industrialising economy set within an underdeveloped country, so disproportionately has the capital region benefited from government policy measures *vis à vis* other parts of the country. Whilst true in aggregate terms, such a generalised depiction tends to overlook significant pockets of economic dynamism in the peripheral regions (e.g. the regional cities and zones of intensive commercial agriculture), and also downplays the extent of differentiation within the dynamic core. None the less, it is difficult to argue with some of the following figures.

Regional differentials in production are very sharp. In 1988 the Bangkok Metropolitan Region (BMR) contributed up to 50 per cent of Thailand's Gross Domestic Product, even though its share of the country's population was only 10 per cent (Kaothien, 1991, p.1027). The BMR produced 62 per cent of Thailand's gross domestic industrial output in 1986; by 1989 this had risen to 76 per cent (Ichikawa, 1991, p.65; Muscat, 1994, p.252). According to factory registration data, at least 50 per cent of all factories in Thailand were located in the BMR in 1989 (Ichikawa, 1991, p.65). Furthermore, 12 of the country's 23 industrial estates were in the BMR and Board of Investment figures show that the BMR's 5 inner provinces attracted the bulk of approved projects (Ratanakomut, Ashakul and Kirananda, 1994, p.205). In stark contrast the North-East, with one-third of the country's population, accounted for only 5 per cent of manufacturing value-added (Tonguthai, 1987, p.190), and less than 12 per cent of Gross National Product (Brown, 1994, p.171).

Not unexpectedly, a similar situation appertains in relation to the distribution of income and the provision of infrastructure. Average per capita income in Bangkok was more than double the national average in 1988 (Rigg, 1991a, p.156), and was approximately nine times greater than that of the North-East in 1988, having risen from a factor of 7.2 in 1984 (Kaothien, 1991, p.1028). A report in the *Bangkok Post* (5.6.1988) noted that the regional gap in income and living standards is widening every year. Under the Sixth Economic and Social Development Plan (1987-91) the BMR attracted almost 92 per cent of total investment in infrastructure and 96 per cent in transport (Ratanakomut, Ashakul and Kirananda, 1994, p.206). Bangkok also has the highest concentration of universities, hospitals, doctors, industries, financial organisations, telephones and private cars (Rigg, 1991a, p.156; see also *The Economist*, Oct. 31 1987, p.15; Douglass, 1992, p.19), and receives approximately seventeen times more public utility services than the population in all other provinces combined (Tonguthai, 1987, p.190). Oey Meesook (1978, p.90) has argued that

> regional disparities in large part are a reflection of the urban-rural disparity. The more urbanized a changwad (province), the higher its income, the better its standard of living and the better its provision of social services to the population (cited in Chamarik, 1993, p.238).

Rural-urban disparities

Thailand had a population of 56 million in 1990, of whom around 30 per cent lived in urban areas (defined as municipal areas and sanitary districts) and the remainder in rural areas (Ratanakomut, Ashakul and Kirananda, 1994, p.212). The urban sector has gained by far the larger portion of the fruits of development. It has also benefited to a greater extent than the rural sector in terms of the provision of infrastructure, financial services, educational and health facilities, etc. Accordingly, Lewis and Kapur (1990, p.1365) argue that Thailand presents "an extreme, albeit complex, case of rural-urban dualism." The resultant and widening disparity between the rural and urban populations is reflected in the major social and economic indices - income distribution, employment, public services, health care and education.

In 1988/89 about 23.7 per cent of the population lived under the poverty line. Some 29.4 per cent and 6.7 per cent respectively of the population living in rural villages and municipal areas was classified as poor (Bhongmakapat, 1990, p.165). As a result of rapid economic growth urban poverty fell rapidly during the 1980s, whereas the decline in the countryside was far less dramatic (*ibid.*, p.165: however, this is challenged by Ratanakomut, Ashakul and Kirananda, 1994). Grandstaff (1992, p.123) notes a growing disparity in the purchasing power of households in urban and rural areas. On the basis of an analysis of Gini coefficients, Ratanakomut, Ashakul and Kirananda (1994, pp.207-8) argue that inequality between rural and urban areas was much more serious than inequalities among urban and rural households.

Similar patterns can be observed in relation to the provision of education facilities. A significant proportion of those enrolled in secondary education are in urban areas, particularly Bangkok (Hirsch, 1994, p.324). Only an estimated 14 per cent of rural children continue beyond compulsory primary education compared with 80 per cent in Bangkok (Fairclough, 1993, p.25). The bias is even more extreme in the tertiary sector: 75 per cent of university applicants live in Bangkok (Economist Intelligence Unit, 1995, p.10). In all cases, disparities in access to education lead in the longer-term to a widening income gap between rural and urban areas, and also contributes to rural-urban migration (discussed below). Duggan (1991, p.145) reports that the previous emphasis on providing higher education within and around Bangkok was recognised in the late 1980s as a factor inhibiting more even regional economic development. In response, a greater emphasis has been placed on expanding education provision in regional centres as a means of assisting regional development. However, he notes that a rural-urban gap remains since rural education is of a lower standard than education provided in urban areas. Furthermore, the standard of rural education is declining as more resources are concentrated in urban centres.

In seeking to explain rural-urban differentials, attention initially focuses on government policies. Tonguthai (1987) notes that the pattern of development in Thailand conforms to the urban bias model of development in which the development decisions of the government reflect the interests of the urban élites. Rural areas, particularly in the 1960s and 1970s, were neglected by a state élite which systematically allocated resources to urban areas, particularly Bangkok, because of the greater efficiency of resource use which was expected to occur here. The government's pronounced emphasis was on large-scale industries that concentrated around Bangkok and the Central Plain. A service-led growth strategy further accelerated the expansion of Bangkok as a primate city. Prayong Netyarak, a Thammasat University economist, notes that

> Government policy relating to rural development [has] failed to achieve its objectives because it [has] been determined in an urban context. The government [has] spent very little on rural development - some 6% of the entire national expenditure budget - and [has] enforced policies which effectively brought down the income of farming families and further widened the gap between rural and urban populations (*Bangkok Post*, 4.5.1988, p. 3; cited in Gohlert, 1991, p.21).

The benefits of such development have not 'trickled down' to the rural hinterland. Rather, the economic vulnerability of peripheral rural areas has tended to increase (Brown, 1994).

Intra-rural disparities

Disparities exist not only between rural and urban areas but also between the 'haves' and 'have-nots' in both areas. Richards (1982) argues that intra-rural income disparities reveal pockets of intense absolute poverty which are not highlighted in aggregate poverty statistics. Meanwhile, Douglass (1981) points out that uneven development in Thailand does not mean that the benefits of development policies accrue solely to Bangkok and Bangkok élites. Certain rural/local élites have substantially benefited from policies which provide patronage and subsidies for provincial élites. Turton (1989, p.82) argues that village élites, district level officials and traders have 'local powers'. He argues that the structural position of these élites is enhanced by their 'linkage' role

> above all through relations which enable them to accumulate (or be the first stage in the accumulation of) village surplus through wages, commodity dealing, retail prices, rent and interest.

Village élites are able to control state-initiated committees, associations, development projects, etc. They also reinforce their politically and economically dominant positions through various forms of non-economic patronage which enables them to benefit from more traditional-derived forms of relationship.

Bruneau (1983) argues that there is increasing antagonism between the majority of villagers and an emerging class of rich villagers who have formed an alliance with government officials. He notes that development policies favour the rich by providing them with loans, seed, fertilizers and tractors.

Consequently, the gap between rich and poor widens. Gohlert (1991, p.21) points out that only the well-off farmers and middlemen stand to benefit from the government's Paddy Price Support Programme which is ostensibly intended to enable farmers to postpone the sale of their rice when prices are low through the aid of low-interest loans. The problem is that the loans are dependent on the availability of rice for sale. As a result of periods of severe drought in the North-East many small farmers do not have any rice to mortgage and therefore they do not qualify for the low-interest loans. It is problems such as these which tend to reinforce existing levels of intra-rural differentiation, however well-intentioned may be measures to help the rural poor.

Hirsch (1994), Falkus (1991), Muscat (1994) and Lewis and Kapur (1990) all note that inequalities within rural society are not a new phenomenon. They existed long before national integration or government intervention had become important economic forces. Hirsch (1989) notes that, following frontier settlement in the Lan Sak district of Uthai Thani province, land was unevenly distributed. The influential early settlers exchanged parcels of land for a combination of payment and help in land clearance. Muscat (1994) notes that differentiation in ownership of quality land arose among Laotian migrants settling on virgin land in the North-East. Those who arrived first settled on land with the best soil and water conditions. He notes (1994, p.245) that rural differentiation also arises through "accidents of misfortune and the unequal distribution of normal variations of individual ability and motivation." However, all of the above argue that rural differentiation has increased with the intensification of the cash economy, commodification of land and other rural resources, and increased levels of indebtedness. Hirsch (1989, p.308) claims that

> Extended commercialisation and increased use of capital in agriculture, national strategies of diversification that result in local specialisation, and shortages of new agricultural land point toward increasing inequality at the village level.

Urban structure

The pattern of urbanisation (the increase in the proportion of the total population living in urban areas) in Thailand has been highly unbalanced. The low level of urbanisation of only 23 per cent stands in stark contrast to the country's spectacular urban primacy (Pernia, 1991, p.119). Bangkok, standing at the apex of the national urban hierarchy is frequently cited as one of the world's outstanding examples of urban primacy (Keokungwal, 1992, p.39). The capital city dominates both the rural hinterland and all other centres in the urban system. Its share of the country's urban population is 27 times larger than Nakhorn Ratchasima, the second largest city (Ratanakomut *et.al.*, 1994, p.205). The Economist Intelligence Unit (1995, p.9) notes that the BMA is more than 50 times the size of the regional capitals of Chiang Mai and Haad Yai. Bangkok's population is projected to exceed 10 million people by the year 2000 (Jones, 1993, p.59). There has already been a significant 'spillover' of Bangkok's population into the 5 surrounding provinces as corridors of development have radiated outwards from the metropolitan area to form an

Extended Metropolitan Region (McGee and Greenberg, 1992). Thus not only is Bangkok "a central place it is the central place in Thailand" (Pramuanratkarn, 1979, p.4). An ESCAP report (1982) notes that, "in many ways Bangkok was ...and still is Thailand" (cited in Singhanetra-Renard and Prahudhanitisarn, 1992, p.159).

In seeking an explanation for Thailand's remarkably unbalanced urban structure, and in particular the extreme primacy of Bangkok, we need to consider a combination of historical, geographical, cultural, economic and political factors. Pernia (1991, p.118) notes that

> Historical and geographic parameters, internal and international market forces, macroeconomic and sectoral policies, and explicit spatial policies all have direct or indirect associations with spatial development and human settlements.

Falkus (1991) notes the following historical factors which explain how Bangkok's primacy became established:

(i) Since the 1850s Bangkok's population growth increased at a greater rate than that of the population as a whole;

(ii) The provisions of the Bowring Treaty (1855) only applied to a thirty mile radius surrounding Bangkok;

(iii) The early development of Bangkok as an international port, location of European business houses and centre of Chinese migration; and

(iv) The measures taken by the government in the 1870s, and more recently, to centralise political and financial power in Bangkok.

Added to these circumstances in Thailand's modern history are a variety of geographical or locational influences which have made it prosper as a centre of trade. Jones (1988, p.148) notes that the high degree of primacy may be due to "geographic 'facts of life', particularly Bangkok's nodal location and national port function." Hussey (1993) adds that Bangkok's location in the agriculturally rich central plain has further contributed to its geographical advantages, and reiterates Jones's assertion that, as a port city with access to the Gulf of Thailand, transportation costs to external markets are much lower in Bangkok and the surrounding provinces than elsewhere in Thailand. Hussey (1993) also sees Bangkok as the spiritual centre of Thailand, wherein are found the most important Buddhist temples and the main residence of the Royal Family.

The economic influences on Bangkok's spatial dominance have already been well rehearsed in this chapter. Bangkok is the main domestic market and centre of international trade. The major industry, banking and trade establishments are also located in the metropolis. According to Pernia (1991, p.119), Bangkok's urban primacy "has been nurtured by the concentration of economic activity in the metropolis." Hussey (1993) notes that utilities, water and power, in addition to being cheaper in Bangkok, are also more reliable. Labour productivity is higher in Bangkok because the labour force has greater industrial experience and is better educated than in the peripheral areas. Transaction costs (banking, services and governmental licences and permits) are also lower in Bangkok. During the period of import-substitution industrialisation Bangkok, as a port city, was the optimal industrial location due to its international trading facilities. The concentration of industrial activities in and around the capital city has led to agglomeration economies which, in turn, have encouraged the further concentration of industrial activity and population settlement. Ichikawa (1991, p.66) notes that the primacy of Bangkok was not reduced by the shift to export-oriented industrialisation since accessibility to the port and other infrastructure remain important factors in the locational decision-making process of export-oriented investors.

Some of the political factors we have already examined in relation to uneven development in Thailand as a whole are also relevant to the context of Bangkok's primacy. The Thai government is highly centralised and Bangkok is the centre of decision-making power. This has tended to result in an urban-biased, or more precisely, a Bangkok-biased, development policy. Biases in macro and sectoral policy have promoted the growth of Bangkok. Measures such as agricultural pricing policy, the over-valued exchange rate, investment in (and subsidisation of) urban services and infrastructure, and the government's emphasis on Bangkok as the country's industrial centre have accentuated the primacy of Bangkok. Korff (1989b, p.50) argues that

> Because the strategic groups are city-based, or more precisely, Bangkok-based, given their interests and strategies, they create a Bangkok-based state, which necessarily has the prime objective to stabilize and strengthen the role of Bangkok in society, politics, and economy.

Bangkok's dominance of the country's urban system and its over-rapid development have not been without problems. As we have already seen, the growth of Bangkok has increased inequalities between urban and rural areas, especially between the metropolis and the rest of the nation. The wide and persistent rural-Bangkok income disparities and rapid economic growth in the metropolis have triggered extensive in-migration to Bangkok. London (1980) argues that Bangkok is parasitic, extracting wealth and surplus value and inhibiting the growth of the less developed hinterland. However, Korff (1989b, p.51) notes that while it is true to a certain extent that Bangkok is parasitic, it is also true that "the opportunities available in Bangkok are a base for the reproduction of rural society." He points to the importance of circular migration to Bangkok and the remittances sent to rural families which enable the latter to remain in the village. In addition, while the heavy concentration of investment in Bangkok has resulted in a high level of development it has also led to problems of inertia, congestion, environmental degradation and the lack of adequate urban infrastructure and employment provision. Motor vehicle registrations are 3.5 times higher in Bangkok than the national average (Suwarnarat, 1993, p.68). A study by the Japan International Co-operation Agency in 1990 claimed that the costs of Bangkok's jammed roads may amount to 60 per cent of the capital's regional product (JICA, 1990; cited in McGee and Greenberg, 1992, p.40). The severe traffic congestion results in unacceptably high levels of air pollution. Carbon monoxide levels are 32 microgrammes per cubic metre (exceeding the 20 microgrammes critical level) and the amount of lead pollution is estimated at 6.2 microgrammes per cubic metre which grossly exceeds the acceptable limit of 3 microgrammes (Pernia, 1991, p.129). Douglass and Zoghlin (1994, p.172) note that sewerage services exist for only 2 per cent of Bangkok's population, and inadequate drainage facilities have resulted in flooding and water pollution.

Sectoral differentials

During the past three decades the Thai economy has undergone a structural transformation in terms of changing sectoral balances. In 1960 agriculture was the most significant sector of the economy. However, the role of agricultural production versus non-agricultural production has declined considerably. Manufacturing, services and finance have become dominant. Indeed between 1970 and 1980, manufacturing grew more than twice as quickly as agriculture (Tonguthai, 1987, p.185). As a consequence we find widening gaps between average per capita incomes in the agricultural and non-agricultural sectors.

In 1990, only 12 per cent of Thailand's Gross Domestic Product and 23 per cent of exports came from agriculture, compared with 40 per cent and 91 per cent respectively in 1960 (Hirsch, 1994, p.321). The share of agriculture in real value added declined from 27 per cent in 1970 to 16 per cent in 1989, whilst that of industry increased from 25.6 to 35 per cent during the same period (Bhongmakapat, 1990, p.162). Since the early 1970s manufactured exports have expanded at a rapid rate and in 1986, for the first time, exports of manufactured products exceeded those of agricultural produce (Falkus, 1991, p.59 - although Rock (1994, p.27) and Meyer (1988, p.468) set the date at 1985). Manufactured goods, which made up only 1.2 per cent of exports in 1960, were 28.3 per cent in 1980 and 40.2 per cent in 1988. Hewison and Brown (1994, p.483) claim the latter figure had risen to about 75 per cent by 1990.

One of the principal problems associated with this dramatic structural transformation of the Thai economy has been that it has applied mainly to value added and not employment, and thus it has been associated with increasing problems of unemployment (although this is challenged by Muscat (1994, p.255) who claims that, as non-agricultural employment rose by an average of 7.1 per cent a year in 1987-89, and total employment by 3.6 per cent, recent job creation has probably exceeded growth of the labour force which is estimated at 2.75 per cent). Pubbawesa (1989), Grandstaff (1992) and Krongkaew (1988) note that despite its relatively large size the manufacturing sector has not been able to generate enough employment for the rapidly expanding labour force. This is primarily because it emphasises capital-intensive techniques. Grandstaff (1992, p.121) suggests that increased income disparity is caused by the failure to restructure employment with a massive transfer of labour from the agricultural to the manufacturing and servicing sectors. Krongkaew (1988, p.74) notes that the overwhelming proportion of the population (72.5%) is still engaged in agriculture.

In seeking an explanation for the decreasing relative importance of agriculture in national value added, we again need to consider government policy. We have already seen that certain government development efforts have been biased towards the urban-industrial sector, which has clearly had a detrimental effect upon agricultural production. The price distortion on agricultural products (e.g. through a government-imposed premium and duty on rice exports, rice reserve requirements, rice export quotas, export taxation on other agricultural products etc.) lowered the terms of trade between agricultural production and other sectors. As a result, resources were transferred from agriculture to industry (Bhongmakapat, 1990). Tonguthai (1987) notes that the

ag. decline but now great is activity...

above policies encouraged capital and entrepreneurial ability to flow out of agriculture and into the urban-industrial sector. This contrasts sharply with widespread government protective measures towards the industrial sector, which has benefited from various kinds of investment and tax incentives, over-valuation of the Thai currency, and protection from foreign competition.

As we indicated earlier, Thailand's economic transformation has also been influenced by the internationalisation of the Thai economy. In the present context, the collapse in world commodity prices has also had a strong influence on the relative dynamics of the agricultural and industrial sectors. World prices for Thailand's 5 major export crops declined considerably between 1981 and 1986 (Akrasanee and Wattananukit, 1990, p.375). Chintayarangsan (1989) notes that although yield improvement has been achieved in most crops, it has not been sufficient to off-set the decline in prices.

Gender differentiation

Finally, we look at uneven development as it manifests itself in a non-economic manner (although, of course, there is a close association with the various forms of economic disparity which we have been considering). Because of limitations of space we shall look at just one aspect, gender differentiation.

In addition to an urban bias in national policy we might contend that there is also a gender bias. Furthermore, the development process has differentially affected women in various socio-economic classes. Tantiwiramanond and Pandey (1991) note that it has had a positive impact upon upper-class women by giving them opportunities to pursue education and careers, but an adverse effect upon women from the lower-classes. They also note (1991, p.19) that

> The occupational stratification of women in both urban and rural areas has further differentiated them especially in terms of income and status into subsets of the advantaged and the disadvantaged. Consequently, although all women share the common problems of social and economic discrimination, their specific problems vary within each of the two subsets.

Thai values confer on women a social position which is inferior to that of men (Tantiwiramanond and Pandey, 1991). Buddhism (to which 95 per cent of the population adhere) undermined the esteem in which women were held as a result of the high value placed on motherhood by denying them the right to become monks (Bunnag, 1973). The concept of the accumulation of merit and the Law of Karma justified the exploitation of women. Being born a woman revealed that one had an inadequate store of merit in previous lives; consequently women were viewed as inferior to men. The subordinate position of women in Thai society is summed up in the popular expression, "men are the front legs of the elephant, women the hind legs" (Odzer, 1990, p.15).

Effect of development on rural women

Women in pre-modern Thai peasant society enjoyed equal economic status with men as they played an important role in agricultural production. In addition to their productive roles women also bore the main responsibility for reproductive activities such as cooking, washing and child-care. However, it is important to note that the processes of production and reproduction were seen as a unified activity. Thus, in economic terms the position of women in relation to men was complementary rather than subordinate (Tantiwiramanond and Pandey, 1991). However, despite the high level of participation of women in productive activities, at the political and ideological level they were generally subordinate to men (Ratanakul, 1990; Omvedt, 1986).

Phongpaichit (1982) notes that the prominent role and status of Thai women in the traditional agricultural economy has been eroded and transformed with the incorporation of Thailand into the world capitalist system and the subsequent introduction of cash crop production for export and agricultural mechanisation. In addition, rural development programmes have tended to by-pass, and often adversely affect, women. These processes have led to the marginalisation of women in agriculture.

Rural development in Thailand has been directed at increasing agricultural productivity, and consequently farm income, through the introduction of modern farming methods and institutions in the rural sector. As a result of the patriarchal orientation of development planning it is men rather than women who are targeted to achieve the objectives of rural development. The assumption was that development that benefits men will automatically benefit women. As the Brandt Commission (1980) states:

> Plans and projects are designed by men to be implemented by men on the assumption that if men, as heads of households, benefit from these projects, the women and the children in those households will benefit too. Women's problems still tend to be regarded as separate, rather than as facets of the culture and structure of all societies.

The disappearance of the subsistence economy and the introduction of cash crops has negatively affected the position of women. Men did not emerge as the main income-earners of the family until cash crops were introduced. Cash crop production was directed at men as they were assumed to be the heads of households and central to agricultural production. Consequently, credit and assistance were directed at and monopolised by men. Cash crop production reduced both the amount and the quality of land available for subsistence production which progressively fell upon the shoulders of women.

Increasing agricultural production under the 'Green Revolution' introduced in the 1960s in Thailand has had an enormous effect on rural women. This policy of intensifying food production through the introduction of double-cropping with the utilisation of hybrid high-yielding varieties of rice demanded extensive irrigation and increased mechanisation as well as the use of fertilisers and pesticides. The inputs required by Green Revolution agriculture are usually beyond the economic reach of rural women - they rarely have access to capital or credit to invest in machinery, hybrid seeds or chemicals. Although mechanisation has resulted in an overall decline in demand for labour, the effect has been greater for women than for men since it was men who were taught to use tractors and other farm machinery (Sookasame, 1989). The introduction of mechanisation has seen a reduction in the importance of female labour in rice production which has become increasingly a male preserve. A process of masculinisation of agriculture is thus occurring with a concomitant decrease in women's knowledge about rice production and technology. The exclusion of rural women from agricultural production results in a lowering of their status in communities; has made them more economically dependent on men; and has excluded them from the public sphere. However, it is not technology *per se* which determines the extent of female participation in mechanised agriculture but the nature of the existing social and gender relations under which technology is introduced. As Agarwal (1985, p.112) argues

> More often than not, the problem cannot be located in the technological innovation per se, since what is often appropriated about the innovation is not its technical characteristics but the socio-political context within which it is introduced. This gives the innovation its specific class and gender bias and mediates the distribution of costs and benefits from its adoption.

Thus, as a result of village and state patriarchal biases rural women have lost out in the wake of technological progress despite the fact that technology itself is not gender specific.

As top-down rural development planning structures in Thailand have traditionally been male dominated they have neglected the interests of rural women (Tantiwiramanond and Pandey, 1991). However, since the United Nations Declaration of International Women's Year in 1975 and the subsequent pressures created during the Women's Decade (1975-85) for development "to bestow benefits on all", there has been a spate of development projects aimed at "integrating women into development." The problem is that these projects are segregated and are mere appendages of larger development schemes targeted at men. They are thus peripheral to the thrust of mainstream development planning (Sookasame, 1989). For example, the Department of Agricultural Extension has set up a Home Economics Programme for rural women which offers courses on model home-making, nutrition and family health (Sookasame, 1989). Programmes of this nature do not necessarily meet the specific and immediate basic needs of rural women (Sirisambhand and Gordon, 1987). Tantiwiramanond and Pandey (1991, pp.37-8) note that the village women of Ban Thung Yao "were exasperated by pointless, officially imposed activities such as Chinese cooking in areas where nobody eats Chinese food, or attempts to teach dressmaking or artificial-flower making skills." The supplementary nature of projects for women reinforces the idea that women's domestic roles are primary (Pongsapich, 1988, pp.32-3). Further development along such lines will only serve to reinforce the stereotyping of gender roles. It is also important to note that agricultural extension agents are generally male. Mitchell *et.al.*'s (1979) evaluation of women-oriented programmes of sericulture found that men dominated the positions of trainers and managers.

In the attempt to 'integrate' women into development, marginal and tokenistic women's organisations have been established which emphasise and institutionalise rural women's reproductive functions. These piecemeal efforts to 'integrate women in development' based upon conventional notions of women's roles serve further to undermine women's already disadvantaged position. Thus, rural development programmes often appear to have enhanced gender differentiation. The problematique is the nature of women's integration into the development process, for the relations through which this integration occurs appear to be part of the problem rather than part of the solution. Until rural women are seen as agents of development rather than as objects of development, and their rights to equitable participation in the decision-making process are recognised, a major reversal of the *status quo* is unlikely.

Education, employment and political participation

Women's education continues to lag behind that of men, particularly in rural areas. Most rural women have less than four years of schooling. Singhanetra-Renard and Prahudhanitisarn (1992) note that the traditional bias among parents in favour of educating sons beyond the compulsory level (lower elementary) continues to exist. As a result, rural women are less educated than their male counterparts. In 1988 the number of women aged 11 years and over with no education was 2,148,900 compared with 1,028,700 men. The illiteracy rate among women is 25.2 per cent compared with 11 per cent among men (Sookasame, 1989, p.205). The male bias in education limits rural women's potential as they experience lower social status and face fewer opportunities in rural labour markets than men. Their lack of education and skills training also restricts both their access to employment opportunities in urban areas and the political arena (Tantiwiramanond and Pandey, 1991). They thus remain as secondary status workers in both rural and urban labour markets.

The rate of participation of women in the labour force is high - 46 per cent of the total (Tantiwiramanond and Pandey, 1991, p.14). However, women are under-represented in high rank positions and the majority continue to hold low-paid, low-status unskilled jobs with little security (Odzer, 1990). Tantiwiramanond and Pandey (1991,p.14) note that only 8 per cent of women are employers, in contrast to 13 per cent of men. Pongsapich (1988, p.95) notes that only 7 per cent of judges and prosecutors in 1987 were women. The average wage earned by women is much lower than that of men. Meesook (1978, p.8) notes that "close to one-third of employed women do not earn sufficient income for their basic needs." Omvedt (1986) notes that women have been systematically discriminated against in terms of wages due to the widespread view that their income merely represents some kind of family 'extra'.

Women, particularly rural women, continue to be under-represented in the political sphere. In 1986 there were only 12 women out of a total of 347 members in the national parliament and 5 women out of 260 members in the senate (Pongsapich, 1988, pp.84-5). The number of women's positions in local administration is still much smaller than men's. In 1985 only 0.13%, 0.52%, 0.32%, 0.30% and 0.37% of sub-district chiefs, assistant sub-district chiefs, village chiefs, assistant village chiefs and sub-district doctors respectively were women. It is clear from the above that, as Tantiwiramanond and Pandey (1991, p.14) argue, women are "under-represented in terms of economic ownership and excluded from the decision-making processes in society at large."

Migration

Many rural women have migrated to urban centres as a result of the lack of opportunities available for them in the rural sector, and the concomitant growth of industry, services and commerce in the urban sector. Tantiwiramanond and Pandey (1991) note that female migrants out-number the number of men migrating to Bangkok: in 1988, the proportion of women among the total number of migrants to Bangkok was 62.2 per cent (Singhanetra-Renard and

Prabhudhanitisarn, 1992, p.165). Some of these rural migrants find employment in factories, others find employment in massage parlours and as prostitutes.

There is considerable debate as to whether female factory wage-labour provides an expansion of opportunities for women, and also the effect that it has on gender relations. It could be argued that, rather than challenging gender divisions which subordinate women, female factory employment is based upon precisely this subordination which guarantees a supply of cheap and docile female labour. Women's secondary status is thus reinforced. However, on the other hand, migration to urban areas and factory employment offers women some autonomy, earning power and may thus loosen the bonds of a patriarchal family. A similar picture exists with respect to prostitution by which means an estimated 2 million women in Thailand earn their living (*The Nation*, 1.7.1989, pp.1-2). While it reproduces the restrictive traditional values with respect to female sexuality, prostitution also allows women some social and economic autonomy (Hantrakul, 1988).

Women's development and the national plans

The United Nations Decade for Women (1975-85) had a major impact on the visibility of women and their incorporation into development planning. Women were not mentioned in the First and Second National Economic and Social Development Plans (1961-66 and 1967-71). Women's issues received attention for the first time in the Third Plan (1972-76). However, interest in women was focused on family planning issues only (Pongsapich, 1988, p.31). Women's development was mentioned in the Fourth Plan (1977-81) but only in terms of other social development programmes - education, health and labour. The Fifth Plan (1982-86) had women's development as an autonomous heading. Two national women's development plans were produced with short-term (1982-86) and long-term (1982-2001) goals. However, the Sixth Plan (1987-91) did not differentiate target groups by their needs - in other words women's development was not separated out from overall development activities. Tantiwiramanond and Pandey (1991) note that, as a result, the plan was criticised as regressive because it reflected a lack of understanding on issues of women's development.

Although women have received attention in certain national plans this seems to have amounted only to lip-service being paid without any real attempt to tackle the fundamental problems involved. As Tantiwiramanond and Pandey (1991, p.34) note

> The commitment to women's causes ... is demonstrated by more than just the presence of an advisory commission or a written promise. It requires implementation and enforcement of the policy.

Overview

The aim of this volume is to help raise awareness of the characteristics of uneven development in Thailand, and of the various social, political, economic and structural forces which have contributed both to its existence and persistence. The contributors are all specialists on Thailand, and have used their wide experience of research in the Kingdom to provide an insightful and locally-informed view of what uneven development means for people in many walks of life in Thailand. It is this locally-informed, realist approach which provides the volume's most distinctive and, we hope, valuable contribution to an increasingly important field of study.

The book follows a consistent line of enquiry which moves from macro to micro, or from wide to narrow. The first three chapters take a broad look at the context of Thailand's dramatic economic transformation, focusing on aspects of the Kingdom's spatial and political economy and the machinations of the political system. Chris Dixon sets Thailand within the wider international context. He shows how economic liberalisation and deregulation, occurring largely at the behest of the World Bank and the International Monetary Fund in the form of structural adjustment measures, have contributed to the Kingdom's economic boom. At the same time, however, they have weakened the central government's autonomy and power to control the pattern and process of Thailand's subsequent economic transformation. This theme is taken up by Peter Bell, who looks rather critically at the negative social and economic consequences of the intensified internationalisation of the Thai economy. He draws attention to some of the contradictions associated particularly with export-oriented economic growth, not least for Thai labour, women, environment and life-style, and which underpin his notion of 'maldevelopment'. Johannes Schmidt also emphasises the weakening of state control over the development process, contingent on internal as well as external economic and political influence, both of which have grown as a consequence of increasing state liberalisation. On the domestic front this centres on the growing power of Thai business and the continuing power of the military to influence the direction of economic policy-making, and with it the extent to which pressing social needs can be addressed. He uses this situation to challenge the superficial but widely portrayed view that the state's shifting alliance from the military to business is a sign of growing democratisation which, in turn, may be seen as an essential first step in the amelioration of uneven development.

The following five chapters deal broadly with industrialisation, which is viewed from a wide variety of perspectives. Jean-Christophe Simon focuses on the industrialisation process as it is presently unfolding, especially in the country's industrial heartland centred on Bangkok metropolis. The context of his analysis, which is informed by in-depth empirical research, is Thailand's relatively late arrival as an industrialising nation. His discussion identifies the principal factors and actors which lie behind the industrial boom. The chapter by Daniel Arghiros and Wathana Wongsekiarttirat also focuses on Thailand's economic heartland, but in this instance it is the so-called Extended Bangkok Metropolitan Region which provides the back-drop to their assessment of the political context and consequences of social and economic change occurring in an area which is being rapidly transformed largely because of its close proximity to the capital city. The brick-making industry provides the central focus of their study. Meanwhile, John Walton's paper examines the process of and constraints on industrialisation in one of Thailand's economically backward, peripheral regions, the North-East. He casts an economist's eye over the hurdles of regional industrialisation, and uses this to explain why the Thai government's industrial decentralisation policies have met with only limited success. The theme of industrialisation in the North-East is also taken up by Leedom Lefferts, in his anthropological assessment of continuity and change in the region's (and Kingdom's) textile industry. His viewpoint is informed by a detailed examination of the historical importance of Thai textiles, both as an item of trade and as an important manifestation of Thai material culture. He also asks whether the kinds of changes which have taken place during the course of the last century, and especially the last few decades, should necessarily be interpreted as constituting 'development'. Finally, Mike Parnwell and Suranart Khamanarong explore the potential role to be played by the rural industrial sector in underpinning *in situ* means of promoting economic development and diversification in the North-East. One among many advantages of such an outcome would be to stem the tide of migration from the region to Bangkok which, they argue, brings different but distinct disadvantages to both areas, and to the unevenness of the development process more generally.

The third grouping of chapters deals with another of Thailand's dynamic economic sectors, tourism. Peter Williamson and Philip Hirsch's enquiry is set on what is simultaneously one of the Kingdom's most picturesque and most rapidly despoiling islands, Koh Samui. The tourism boom has had a major impact on the coastal environments of the southern provinces, and also a sharply differential impact on the people of these coastal zones. Williamson and Hirsch show how a restricted cohort of islanders and, mostly, outsiders has largely controlled the process and rewards of tourism development. Others, lacking capital, land, contacts and opportunity, have, instead, been largely obliged to endure the myriad environmental, social, economic and cultural effects which have come to be associated with the industry. This theme, of the differential distribution of costs and benefits from tourism development, is further explored by Philip Dearden in his assessment of trekking tourism to hill-tribe communities in northern Thailand. His cost-benefit analysis, informed by systematic field-research in the region, identifies an optimal stage in the evolution of the trekking business, where benefits to the communities, tourists and agents of tourism are roughly evenly distributed. However, for reasons which he identifies, the inexorable momentum of tourism expansion, as with so many other forms of 'development' in Thailand, sees the optimum stage rapidly passed, and with it a shift in the balance of benefits away from the hosts and, in the longer term, guests, and towards the commercial brokers of the tourism boom. Finally, Mika Toyota takes an in-depth look at some of the specific effects of trekking tourism for one hill-tribe community in the northern Thai province of Chiang Rai. She looks in particular at three aspects of the impact of tourism: the way in which the encouragement of opium-smoking as a 'thrilling adventure' for trekkers is helping to perpetuate, or even extend this practice within the study community, with serious social and economic consequences for those involved; the socio-political impact of the tripartite encounter between tourists, guides and hosts which tourism engenders; and the impact of tourism on Akha self-identity and the way that this hill people are seen by outsiders. Toyota uses her intimate familiarity with the community in question to challenge a number of popular stereotypes and misconceptions concerning the Akha people.

The last two chapters in this volume focus on the process and consequences of changes which are taking place in Thailand's agricultural sector which, although it has not displayed the same degree of dynamism found in the industrial and commercial sectors, none the less continues to provide an important source of livelihood for the majority of Thailand's population. Guy Trébuil shows how the rationalisation of the agricultural sector in the interest of engendering efficiency has yielded clear 'winners' and 'losers'. His analysis of a cross-section of study communities reveals clear patterns of farmer differentiation. His research also helps us to understand how such patterns emerge and, importantly, how they might be reversed by the promotion of farming systems which are at once in tune with the needs of efficiency, equity and community - a formidable task. Finally, Chris Garforth and Paiboon Suthasupa explain how agricultural development measures which are ostensibly implemented for the principal benefit of the weakest and most disadvantaged groups of farmers often unconsciously pass them by. Using the example of agricultural extension through the grassroots medium of rural people's organisations, they show that there is sometimes a wide gap between the principle of grassroots action and its effectiveness in practice. They also identify inherent weaknesses in the design and implementation of agricultural extension programmes in Thailand, and offer a range of policy measures which might overcome them, in the process helping to encourage the spread of development benefits to the areas and social groups which need them most,

Each of the authors was originally asked to address the question "who has benefited from recent processes of economic, social and political transformation in Thailand?" As the following chapters clearly show, the resounding response is "many, but far from all." More to the point, several authors show that some have benefited at the cost of others and that, more generally, a minority has enjoyed the lion's share of the spoils of growth. In identifying these and other aspects of uneven development in Thailand we hope that we may help to raise awareness of the consequences of unbridled economic growth, its meaning for those whom the boom has largely passed by, and what steps might be taken in the interests of building a fairer, more equitable society whilst maintaining the current momentum of economic growth. This latter point is picked up again in the concluding discussion in Chapter 15.

Notes

1 The authors would like to express their gratitude to Miss Claire Yeatman for her help in getting materials together for this chapter.

2 Thailand's rapid economic growth: Causes, sustainability and lessons

Chris Dixon

Introduction

The rapid economic growth and structural change that Thailand has experienced since the mid-1980s has attracted a great deal of attention from the international and regional development agencies, transnational corporations, development planners and policy-makers. It is widely considered that if, during the next few years, the Kingdom's recent pattern of development is sustained and consolidated Thailand's experiences will have important lessons for the rest of the Developing World (Castells, 1991, p.iii). For, at first sight, Thailand appears to have much more in common with other countries of the Developing World than was the case with the four Asian NIEs (Newly Industrialising Economies), Hong Kong, Singapore, South Korea and Taiwan. Not only has Thailand's recent rapid growth taken place in a radically different context but it also appears to have been promoted by a very different balance of factors. For some observers the differences in context and process are sufficient to form the basis for new models of development.

Thailand's industrialisation has been associated with a much greater involvement of foreign investors and transnational corporations than was the case in Taiwan and South Korea, and a much lower degree of state intervention and direction than was the case in Singapore, South Korea and Taiwan. Indeed, the Kingdom's rapid economic development has been associated with deregulation, liberalisation and a reduction in the economic activities of the state which have facilitated the activities of foreign investors and transnational corporations. These developments have been presented as providing a new 'model of development'. Handley (1991, pp.34-5) has summarised this view:

> Economists, development agencies and international development specialists are already starting to forsake their hallowed Japanese, South Korean and Taiwanese models of development for a new one: the Thai model. To them, Thailand's four years of double digit growth represents the success of a decade of deregulation and the honing of investment codes to produce one of the most user-friendly investment environments among developing countries.

Such a 'deregulation' model of economic growth is very much in line with the current 'neo-liberal' development orthodoxy promoted by the international agencies and enshrined in the World Bank and IMF structural adjustment programmes. Given that Thailand was subject to formal agency based adjustment programmes during the period 1981 to 1986 it is perhaps not surprising that the Kingdom is represented as one of the two most successful cases of structural adjustment (the other is Chile;[1] see World Bank, 1988 and 1991).

For the international agencies, in particular, the 'Thai economic miracle' is seen as primarily the result of the application of the 'correct' government policy. As with the euphoria that accompanied the emergence of the Asian NIEs, the historical development and the particular national, regional and international circumstance are treated as residual to matters of policy. While this view of the Asian NIEs has been substantially dispelled since the mid-1980s (see Deyo, 1987; White, 1988) it has re-emerged with respect to the three dynamic ASEAN economies - Indonesia, Malaysia and Thailand (see for example World Bank, 1993). Thus little attention has focused on the antecedents and wider regional and global circumstances of these countries' recent rapid economic growth.

It is the purpose of this chapter to examine the validity and implications of the deregulation and policy-orientated views of Thailand's recent development through a review of the nature, origins, impact and sustainability of the Kingdom's present pattern of growth. Finally, the wider lessons of the Thai experience are examined.

The Thai economy before the 'boom'

During the 1950s and 1960s Thailand established a pattern of growth dependent on Import Substituting Industrialisation (ISI) and the expansion of agricultural production. Increased agricultural production resulted principally from the extension of the cultivated area. While there was significant diversification into export crops such as maize, cassava and kenaf (upland jute) there was little intensification of production (Feeney, 1982). This was a reflection of the comparative abundance of uncultivated land and unreliable rainfall (Dixon, 1976). The availability of land and ease of access to it enabled a much higher proportion of the population to remain in the agricultural sector than would be expected from the rising level of per capita GDP.[2] The sustained growth of the agricultural sector supplied rising export earnings and steady growth of GDP with little direct investment, simply by the application of labour to land. At the same time the state extracted considerable surplus from the agricultural sector in the form of taxation of, in particular, rice exports.[3] The agricultural sector was thus the Kingdom's main engine of growth and a major source of government revenue. The ISI sector grew out of a programme of 'state capitalism' initiated during the 1950s and was typically protected (Ingram, 1971, pp.284-8).[4] In 1959 the Board of Investment was established with the brief of promoting domestic and foreign investment in the 'modern sector'. The promotional measures were progressively enhanced as were the levels of protection. In addition, the tax on rice exports depressed the domestic price of rice and hence the level of urban-industrial labour costs. With these advantages a substantial industrial base was established by the early 1970s. This was dominated by a number of major Thai-Chinese industrial groups with close links to the military and the bureaucracy (Elliott, 1978, pp.118-23; Riggs, 1966, pp.258-64). Indeed, the promotional scheme gave little incentive to either small concerns or technical innovation and tended to encourage the growth of large, often inefficient undertakings with considerable over-capacity (World Bank, 1980a).

The limited size of the domestic market and concerns over the Kingdom's long term political stability may have been expected to have discouraged foreign investment and transnational activity (Dixon, 1991a, p.172). However, because of its geo-political situation Thailand was the recipient of considerable American economic and military 'aid' - US$1.13 billion between 1950 and 1970 (Caldwell, 1974, p.63; Elliott, 1978, p.131). In addition, the presence of American personnel [5] generated a high level of expenditure, the expansion of the service sector and the growth of urban centres adjacent to major military bases (Elliott, 1978, pp.129-33).[6] The scale of American aid was far short of that received by South Korea and Taiwan during the key periods of their growth.[7] However, Caldwell, (1974, pp.63-9) concluded that American aid to Thailand had an impact out of proportion to this volume because of the 'targeting' of 'bottlenecks' in the economy.

The USA promoted and largely paid for a number a major highway projects. While these were primarily strategic they opened up new agricultural areas, increased access to markets, particularly in the North-East, and gave an important boost to the domestic construction industry.

Overall, the involvement of the USA, as in South Korea and Taiwan, both supplemented foreign investment and boosted the confidence of investors. In consequence, and despite concerns over security, a number of TNCs established operations in Thailand during the 1950s and 1960s (Hewison, 1985, p.273). As a result a number of key areas of the economy became dominated by foreign capital, notably textiles, motor vehicle production, petroleum and tin.[8]

While Thailand's development during the 1960s was remarkably 'low key' the average annual rate of growth of GDP was 8.3 per cent. This compared very favourably with Taiwan (9.2 per cent), Singapore (8.8 per cent) and South Korea (8.6 per cent). However, unlike those economies Thailand's growth was not driven by the manufacturing sector. The Kingdom remained a producer of a comparatively limited range of primary products. In 1970, 85 per cent of export earnings were from the primary sector, principally rice, rubber, tin, maize and kenaf.

From the early 1970s the pattern of growth based on primary production and ISI was reinforced by the growth of the tourist industry and remittance income from overseas workers. These were to provide important 'cushions' for the Thai economy during the increasingly difficult international trading conditions that prevailed during the 1970s. By 1980 the earnings from tourism were second only to those from rice exports. Thailand, like other economies heavily dependent on energy imports, experienced a serious shock from the 1973 oil price rise. The problems resulting from the substantial increase in the energy bill and subsequent period of global recession and inflation were compounded in a number of ways; perhaps most significantly by the run-down, and eventual withdrawal in 1976 of the USA military presence. The impact of the loss of American military aid was magnified by the Khmer Rouge takeover of Cambodia, the subsequent Vietnamese invasion, and an escalation of rural insurgency within Thailand. In total these events resulted in a substantial increasing of Thailand's defence budget and a reduction in funds available for development and economic management. The increasingly difficult economic conditions were accompanied by political uncertainty. There were violent changes of government in 1973, 1976 and 1978, and, particularly after 1976, increased rural insurgency and state repression. Many commentators, including some Thai officials, were making extremely pessimistic pronouncements, predicting escalating economic and political turmoil culminating in violent revolutionary change within two or three years (Dixon, 1979, p.1072). The political instability and weakness of the governments of the 1973-80 period combined with the severity of the economic problems to undermine the effective management of the economy. To a degree there was a retreat from the conservative financial policies which had long dominated Thai economic management. During the 1970s policy makers were increasingly faced with crisis management (Muscat, 1994, p.132; Aboonyi and Bunyaraks, 1989, p.30). Further, Muscat (1994, p.132) has concluded that the weak governments were reluctant to undertake potentially unpopular measures. In the face of increased economic difficulties after 1975 policies became expansionary rather than focused on establishing economic stability. At least in part these problems reflect deficiencies in the mechanisms available for managing serious long-term adjustment of the Thai economy (see World Bank, 1980b).

Despite the economic and political problems that faced Thailand during the 1970s the economy grew at an annual average of 7 per cent - low compared to the Asian NIEs but high, and consistently so, compared to global and Third World trends. However, behind this growth there were serious long-term problems. The balance of payments current account, adverse in almost every year since 1953 (except 1955 and 1956), rose from an average of 1.6 per cent of GDP during the first half of the decade to 5.2 per cent in the second. The deficit was increasingly covered by short-term borrowing as a result of which overseas debt and, more significantly, the debt service ratio rose rapidly. In addition, the annual inflation rate averaged more than 10 per cent between 1973 and 1980, far more than the Kingdom's main trade partners (Akaransee *et.al.*, 1991, p.4).

To a degree the growth of the Thai economy during the latter part of the 1970s could be described as 'debt sustained', with the established pattern of growth and attendant policies being maintained, at least in part, by overseas borrowing. However, the economic expansion of this period also reflected a very dynamic export sector, which despite domestic inflation and an over-valued currency[9] achieved a doubling in the volume of exports. This was reinforced, as has already been noted, by the rapid growth of tourism.

During the 1970s there was very limited structural change in either the domestic economy or the composition of exports. Indeed while the share of primary products in export earnings had fallen to 70 per cent by 1980, and there had been an expansion of manufactured exports, particularly textiles, this change was greatly exaggerated by the fall in the prices of primary products.[10] Similarly, the slight shift in the structure of GDP - the share of agriculture falling from 28 per cent to 25 and that of manufacturing rising from 16 per cent to 20 - reflected relative price movements.

In 1980, despite policy statements in favour of export orientated manufacturing and the introduction of various incentive measures from 1972 onwards,[11] Thailand could be characterised as a country in which the majority of the population was rural and engaged in agriculture and in which economic growth and government policy remained centred on primary production and ISI. However, with the benefit of hindsight it is apparent that while cyclical changes in the global economy were creating major difficulties for the Thai economy, structural changes in the global economy and in the Thai economy itself were making the past pattern of growth and attendant policies outmoded. Indeed, Muscat (1994, p.216) has suggested that the cumulative economic problems faced by Thailand during the 1970s reflected the failure to adjust to the changed conditions that followed the 1973 oil shock.

The crisis of the early 1980s and the introduction of structural adjustment

The serious economic problems faced by Thailand at the end of the 1970s were magnified into a major crisis by the 1979-80 oil price rise, the subsequent collapse of non-oil commodity prices and sharp rises in interest rates. The terms of trade declined by 22 per cent, the current account deficit widened to 6 per cent of GDP and the debt service ratio rose to 20 per cent. The deteriorating economic situation was exacerbated by the question marks over the Kingdom's long term political stability. There had been a substantial loss of confidence on the part of both domestic and foreign investors. A survey of 65 Japanese corporations conducted during 1979 concluded that the investment situation was 'hopeless' (cited in Tasker, 1991, p.49). During 1979-80 the Thai government initiated an austerity programme aimed at curtailing inflation, easing the balance of payments deficit and checking the growth of overseas debt. Key measures included the raising of fuel prices and increasing government revenues. In addition, moves towards longer-term structural change were incorporated into the draft Fifth National Plan. However, these measures and proposals were insufficient to change the pessimistic views of investors or the international agencies. In addition, the implementation of austerity measures, particularly the proposed increase in energy prices, sparked off considerable public protest which undermined the already weak government of Kriangsak Chomanand, contributing to its fall and increasing fears of further political disruption.

The depth of the economic problems prompted approaches to the World Bank and IMF for funding. The World Bank initiated a series of studies of the Thai economy and late in 1980 produced an economic review of Thailand (World Bank, 1980b). In essence the World Bank concluded that the Kingdom's economic problems were long-term structural ones. The impact of external shocks - oil price rise, fall in commodity prices, contraction of tourism and markets for manufactured exports - had merely exposed deep seated contradictions of the development process and the failure of previous governments to adjust to changed economic circumstances. To correct the situation a five year programme of 'structural adjustment' was advocated, the proposals for which followed the broad outline that became the norm during the 1980s (see for example Dixon *et.al.*, 1995). For Thailand, specific recommendations included:

- the raising of domestic energy prices to the international level (they were 20 per cent below and were a key element in the subsidisation of the industrial sector);
- the ending of other fuel and transport subsidies;
- reduction of government expenditure;
- ending the import substitution policy for industry;
- placing emphasis on export-orientated industry;
- reducing import taxes;
- removing all export restrictions and taxes;
- substantially reducing foreign exchange controls;
- imposing strong deflationary monetary and fiscal policies;
- privatising state concerns; and
- reforming the taxation system to increase efficiency of collection and yields.

Overall, these recommendations were aimed at establishing the economy, opening it more fully to international capital, and substantially reducing the state's developmental role to matters of policy. Further, the World Bank saw structural adjustment as necessary in order "to shift the pattern of growth from one based on the extension of land under cultivation and on import substitution to one based on increasingly intensive use of land and industries producing for domestic and export markets under competitive conditions" (World Bank, 1980b, p.19).

The Thai government accepted the World Bank's analysis and proposals, incorporating them as an integral part of the Fifth National Plan (1982-86). More significantly, the implementation of the recommendations was made a condition of two Structural Adjustment Loans (SALs), the first in March 1992 for US$150 million and the second in April 1983 for US$175.5 million. The World Bank did not, as was more usual, require Thailand to undertake a series of measures before the first SAL could become available. It was accepted that the policy statements contained in the Fifth Plan, the commissioning by the government of a series of studies of key areas, the imposition of austerity measures and some limited reforms during 1980 and 1981 were indicative of a positive attitude towards structural adjustment and could be regarded as a 'down payment' (Sahansakul, 1992, pp.13-15).

Measures implemented during 1980 and 1981 before the first SAL became available included the liberalisation of restrictions on agricultural exports,[12] a rise in energy costs, increases in the charges made by state enterprises (notably the Bangkok Metropolitan Transport Administration), the establishment of an export draw-back procedure and the 10 per cent devaluation of the baht in September 1981. The last two measures were by far the most significant.

However, in so far as they boosted exports and relieved pressure on the balance of payments they appear only to have prevented further deterioration (Table 2.1)

In addition to the SALs, which were geared to the longer term adjustment of the economy, agreement was reached with the IMF on appropriate shorter term policy responses. These were aimed in particular at the restructuring of demand, reducing the public savings-investment gap, and limiting the growth of foreign debt (Panayotou and Sussangkarn, 1991, p.6). To support these policies the IMF agreed standby credit arrangements for the period 1981 to 1983 of SDR 814.5 million.[13] Critical to the whole question of structural adjustment was the Fifth Plan. It has been described as a 'milestone document' in Thai development planning (Muscat, 1994, p.180). There is no doubt that, compared to its predecessors, the Fifth Plan was extremely comprehensive, the product of wide consultation, and set out a clear view of the Kingdom's situation and the key problems that needed to be addressed. With respect to its implementation the differences with its predecessors are far less marked. Inevitably resources fell well short of those necessary, thus conflicts and weaknesses in the decision-making process both within the planning bureaucracy and the government were rapidly exposed. The plan comprised two distinct areas: growth and structural adjustment; and equity, social and rural development. In the event these two areas proved incompatible. While considerable concern was expressed, in particular by the then Prime Minister, Prem Trinsulanonda, over the inequitable distribution of wealth, rural-urban differentials and the uneven pattern of national development, little was done. The questions of growth and adjustment came to dominate the implementation of the plan.

The implementation of structural adjustment

The implementation of the structural adjustment programme proved to be extremely problematic. Successive Prem cabinets[14] encountered serious problems in implementing the World Bank recommendations. As with the earlier moves under the Kriangsak government, attempts to reduce fuel and transport subsidies coming on top of the recession and government austerity measures sparked a series of mass public protests. Similarly, the public sector unions were instrumental in organising public campaigns against privatisation proposals. In addition, there were powerful domestic and foreign interest groups which reacted against the prospect of being adversely affected by many of the measures, most significantly the raising of energy and utility prices, the reduction of tariff barriers and the removal of the tax on rice exports. Given the very close and complex interrelations between the bureaucracy, military and domestic capital (see also the chapter by Schmidt in this volume) there was considerable pressure to hold back on the reforms. In addition, the removal of tariff barriers and the rice export tax would have deprived the government of much-needed revenue at a time when the recession was reducing tax yields. Thus Thailand, like a number of South-East Asian economies was "caught in a bind and could engage in only a very limited degree of restructuring" (Robison *et.al.*, 1987, pp.11-12). In consequence, between 1981 and 1985 a variety of reforms was introduced which gave the impression of great activity in implementing structural adjustment, but few were of real significance.

Table 2.1a
Key Features of the Thai Economy, 1970-1990

Year	Growth of GDP (%)	Inflation Rate (%)	Openness Ratio	Current Account Balance GDP (%)	Debt/ GDP (%)	Exchange Rate	Government expenditure as % of GDP
1970	6.6	0.8	27.7	-3.5	10.3	20.9	19.8
1971	5.0	0.4	28.2	-2.4	10.7	20.9	19.9
1972	4.1	4.8	30.8	-0.6	11.0	20.9	18.5
1973	9.9	15.6	33.0	-0.4	8.4	20.6	16.0
1974	4.4	24.3	40.2	-0.6	8.5	20.4	16.2
1975	4.8	5.3	35.9	-4.1	9.1	20.4	18.4
1976	9.4	3.8	38.0	-2.6	9.5	20.4	19.0
1977	9.9	7.6	41.3	-5.5	10.1	20.4	16.9
1978	10.4	7.9	39.5	-4.8	11.5	20.3	17.8
1979	5.3	9.9	46.7	-7.6	14.8	20.4	17.9
1980	4.8	19.7	48.9	-6.4	17.7	20.5	19.1
1981	6.3	12.7	48.2	-7.4	20.5	21.7	19.0
1982	4.1	5.2	42.7	-2.8	23.3	23.0	20.4
1983	7.3	3.8	41.7	-7.3	24.1	23.0	19.9
1984	7.1	0.9	42.7	-5.1	26.0	23.5	19.6
1985	3.5	2.4	43.9	-4.1	34.1	27.1	21.1
1986	4.9	1.9	3.6	0.6	33.8	26.3	20.4
1987	9.5	2.5	51.1	-0.7	2.3	25.7	19.2
1988	13.2	3.8	59.8	-2.8	25.8	25.3	16.7
1989	12.2	5.4	64.8	-3.7	23.5	25.7	14.7
1990	10.0	6.0	68.8	-6.0	23.2	25.6	14.7
1970-75	5.7	10.6	34.6	-2.0	9.6	20.7	18.2
1976-80	7.8	8.9	44.1	-5.7	12.7	20.4	18.1
1981-85	5.7	4.4	44.3	-5.4	25.6	23.6	20.0
1986-90	9.9	3.8	60.3	-3.1	27.7	25.7	17.1
1970-90	6.7	7.2	51.2	-4.0	18.5	22.5	18.3a

Notes:
1 Openness ratio = % (export+import)/GDP
2 Stock of debt includes only long-term debt
3 Exchange rate = baht per US dollar

Table 2.1b
Key Features of the Thai Economy, 1970-1992

	Terms of trade 1987=100	Budget deficit as a % of GDP	Gross domestic capital formation US$m	Foreign direct investment US$m	Exports US$m	Manufactured exports US$m	Primary exports US$m
1970	178.9	n/a	119.0	48	710	76	629
1971	160.0	n/a	119.6	39	827	113	706
1972	151.5	-4.8	120.6	68	1039	190	863
1973	176.1	-3.2	132.7	77	1527	343	1201
1974	168.3	+0.1	132.4	189	2402	422	2002
1975	141.2	-2.0	131.5	22	2162	397	1784
1976	132.6	-4.9	148.7	79	2950	572	2398
1977	131.7	-3.2	184.3	106	3451	683	2803
1978	141.8	-3.6	204.6	50	3996	1039	3042
1979	134.9	-3.7	212.7	51	5207	1402	3879
1980	123.1	-4.9	220.5	187	6369	1886	4579
1981	108.9	-3.6	230.5	288	6849	2019	4978
1982	94.7	-6.5	226.1	189	6797	2014	4914
1983	100.1	-4.0	255.1	348	6275	2058	4284
1984	97.3	-3.5	283.0	400	7279	2583	4780
1985	90.6	-5.4	268.0	162	7056	2800	4221
1986	104.3	-4.5	256.6	261	8786	3944	4820
1987	100.0	-2.3	296.4	182	11629	6125	5446
1988	98.2	+0.7	361.0	1081	15902	8192	7068
1989	94.4	+2.9	483.9	1726	19976	11453	8377
1990	91.6	+4.5	664.4	2303	23002	14796	8014
1991	91.7	+4.7	780.9	1847	28324	18903	9138
1992	91.2	n/a	845.5	1979	34473	21672	10477

However, in terms of macro-economic indicators the progress was sufficiently rapid during 1981 and 1982 for the World Bank to agree the second SAL. The fall in the level of inflation, the reduction in the current account deficit and the growth of GDP were considered satisfactory. The same could not be said of the budget deficit or the level of government expenditure (see Table 2.1). The view of the World Bank appears to have been that the progress of structural adjustment had been overtaken by the continued, changing nature and intensity of the international recession. Thus a longer period of adjustment than that originally envisaged was necessary (Muscat, 1994, p.188). However, the progress under the second SAL continued to be slow with respect to reforms, the budget deficit and the level of government expenditure (Table 2.1). As a result the World Bank's (1984) review of the progress of the structural adjustment programme was extremely critical of the limited progress.[15] The Bank was particularly concerned over the size of the budget deficit. This had expanded to 5 per cent of GDP instead of contracting to 3.5. The growth in the budget deficit reflected both the failure to reduce government expenditure and shortfalls in government revenue; the latter a product of slower growth and associated lower tax yields.[16] Relations between the World Bank and the Thai government deteriorated. During 1985 Thailand began to turn to commercial sources of finance and plans for further SALs were abandoned. Thailand was, however, able to reach agreement with the IMF over a two-year funding package of US$586.6 million. In December 1986 an IMF review was also extremely critical of the lack of progress of structural adjustment, particularly with respect to the size of the budget deficit. Subsequent negotiations broke down and Thailand abandoned the IMF funding having drawn on less than half of it.[17]

By 1986 very limited progress had been made towards implementing the main World Bank and IMF recommendations. Many of the structural adjustment related targets for the Fifth Plan (1982-86) were not achieved, notably the debt service ratio, the budget deficit and government expenditure. Indeed, these only began to show significant decline in 1988. Sahansakul (1992) reviewed the SALs and concluded that in general they had a beneficial impact on the economy, but the impact was a very slight one. Panayotou and Sussangkarn (1991, p.9) concluded that while it is extremely difficult to quantify the impact of the SAL programmes

> Nevertheless, it can probably be said that with the serious attention of the government on the structural imbalance problems, supported by the World Bank and the IMF, and the adoption of generally prudent monetary and fiscal policies, the Thai economy avoided getting into serious difficulties during the structural adjustment period. When the world economy recovered, and beneficial changes occurred in the world economic environment, Thailand did not have a serious overhang from the structural adjustment period, and was in a position to take advantage of the changes that occurred.

Muscat (1994, pp.184-222), in an appraisal of the structural adjustment period, comments on the limited progress made in such areas as institutional development, agriculture and export promotion and concludes that

In some important areas, the adjustment objectives were achieved only partially, or were totally frustrated, due to a combination of adverse external economic circumstances and weak government resolve. Three outstanding cases were tariff reform, industrial restructuring and state enterprise privatisation.

Despite limited progress and the continuing economic problems of the early 1980s the Thai economy maintained growth rates that where by international standards extremely respectable. More significantly the abandonment of the formal IMF and IBRD programmes in 1985 and 1986 was accompanied by signs of economic recovery. To a degree the improved global trading situation, falling oil prices and the expansion of export earnings gave the Thai government the confidence to forego funding from the international agencies. However, the commitment to structural adjustment was not abandoned with the programmes. The Sixth Plan (1987-91) reiterated the commitment to structural adjustment-like reforms, though not directly by name. Since 1986, and more especially 1988, a significant number of the original recommendations have, at least in part, been implemented.[18]

The elimination of the rice export tax had been delayed because of its importance to government revenue and the fear of reaction to increased living costs and increased cost of labour. The low level of prices that prevailed during late 1985 and early 1986 together with the evidence of economic recovery gave the opportunity to remove the tax. The removal was expected to raise farm incomes and stimulate rice exports. Initially the removal appears to have had little impact on domestic prices, principally because of the very depressed state of the international rice market. However, with a partial recovery during 1987 and 1988 retail prices in Bangkok rose by 60 per cent. The removal of the tax took place with little reaction on the part of employers or consumers (for a discussion of the possible reasons for this see Siamwalla, 1989, p.29). However, the impact of the removal of the tax on cost of living, farm income and labour costs has received little attention. It is tempting to conclude that this, like other aspects of adjustment, was only implemented when it could be done with the minimum of disruption and protest. For the rice tax, which for decades was a highly contentious issue, to have been removed with such apparent ease suggests that its role had become an insignificant one. A similar cautious and gradual approach occurred with respect to fuel and public transport subsidies. These were progressively removed between 1986 and 1988. In addition, price controls and import controls on a wide range of minor items, such as certain drugs, cosmetics and toothpaste, were removed during this period.

In the key area of industrial tariff protection progress was extremely slow. Despite some reduction and simplification of tariffs under the first SAL the average level of protection rose between 1985 and 1988, principally in order to increase government revenue.[19] Indeed, tariff levels only began to decline from October 1990 when the duty on imported machinery was reduced from 35 per cent to 5 per cent. In the following July duty on computers fell from a range of 20 to 40 per cent to 5 per cent, and for components from 40 per cent to 1 per cent. Other reductions still provide a considerable measure of protection, notably for motor cars where the duty on vehicles of over 3000cc has been reduced from 300 per cent to 112.[20] Overall, by 1995 there had still been no substantial across-the-board reduction in the levels of tariff protection. There was a similar long delay in reducing foreign exchange controls. While some simplification of procedures took place there was no effective relaxation until May 1990, when the Board of Trade announced a three-stage programme which effectively removed all restrictions by early 1992. Privatisation made no progress until the late 1980s when three small enterprises - the Bangkok Jute Mill, the Gunny Bag Factory and the Wire Diffusion Company - were liquidated and the small Thai International Shipping Company sold. Since 1990 there has been a more concerted effort with regard to the privatisation of the remaining sixty state enterprises. This was marked by the sale of 15 per cent of the holdings in Thai International early in 1991. However, the Thai public sector is by no means a drain on public expenditure. In 1990 the state concern employed 260,000 people, had a turnover of US$11.7 billion and returned pre-tax profits of US$1.8 billion, or 14.7 per cent of revenue. Only five concerns made losses, the largest of which was the Bangkok Metropolitan Transport Administration, followed by the Thai State Railway. The post-structural adjustment pressure for privatisation has come from the inability of the concerns (and unwillingness/ inability of the government) to finance the much-needed expansion of the Kingdom's infrastructure. While by 1995 little progress had been made in privatising state concerns, a variety of measures implemented from the early 1980s onwards had increased control over their budgets and investment programmes.

During the early 1990s a series of other adjustment-related measures was introduced, notably the deregulation of the financial markets, the floating of oil prices and the revamping of the tax structure. The level of personal income tax was reduced from 35 to 30 per cent and an across-the-board 7 per cent value added tax imposed. These measures were aimed specifically at simplifying the structure and increase the level of yield. Thus a range of 'home grown' structural adjustment measures was implemented well after the boom was under way. Indeed, only with renewed economic growth, political stability and the reduction of the political influence of the ISI sector was it possible to implement some of these policies at all. Thus the reforms may be viewed as sustaining the boom rather than initiating it. As Muscat (1994, pp.216-22) has suggested, the Thai pattern of adjustment was an extremely gradual one. Measures appear in general to have only been effectively implemented when they would cause limited disruption and protest. In part this reflects the weak governments of the 1980s and their need to serve a variety of often conflicting interests. Perhaps more significantly the gradual approach reflects the cautious, light-handed and conservative approach to economic development and management that has characterised Thailand since the late 1950s.

The causes of the boom

It does not appear possible to relate the rapid economic growth that Thailand experienced after 1986 to the limited progress made in structural adjustment by that date. The acceleration of growth was closely related to the expansion of manufactured exports, initially textiles and later electronic products. There are, however, two questions here: firstly, what caused the initial acceleration of exports; and secondly, what has sustained the growth? In attempting to answer these two questions it is important to consider Thailand in its broader regional and global context. As has already been noted Thai policy and attitudes remained firmly ISI oriented in 1980. Subsequent liberalisation has not dismantled the protective structure that supports ISI. Indeed, Akrasanee *et.al.* (1991, p.17) in a review of Thai commercial policies concluded that:

> Thailand's recent economic success appears to have been attained despite, rather than because of, the evolution of trade and commercial policies. Commercial policies have been of the classical import-substitution and anti-export nature and have become increasingly so in the second half of the 1980s.

The liberalisation that has taken place since 1990 has almost certainly had a positive impact on manufactured exports and foreign investment. In addition, the various measures for simplifying and streamlining export and investment procedures implemented since the early 1980s undoubtedly sent the right messages to both Thai and foreign export-orientated firms. As Muscat (1994, pp.194-6) has noted, these measures are indicative of a fundamental change in attitude on the part of successive administrations in favour of manufacturing. Like other measures aimed at attracting foreign investment it is often the 'message' that their implementation sends that is of greatest significance (ESCAP, 1983). However, even in 1995, that change in attitude was by no means fully reflected in policy.

During the early 1980s the value of manufactured exports grew extremely slowly, accelerating during 1984-6 and entering a period of spectacular growth in 1987 (Table 2.1). The devaluation of the baht during 1984, reinforced in 1985 as the baht declined substantially with the US dollar, improved the competitiveness of Thai exports. During the late 1970s and early 1980s there is little doubt that the over-valuation of the baht had operated against exports. However, while the devaluation must be considered a factor in the expansion of exports, as Muscat (1994, p.194) has stressed, it can not be considered to have been solely responsible.

The acceleration of economic growth was based on the export of labour-intensive manufactured goods, initially textiles. It is apparent that some producers were beginning to become more export orientated during the early 1980s despite the less than conducive policy environment. Thai producers were able to expand markets for such products during a period of relatively rapid growth in the global economy when the Asian NIEs were beginning to lose their comparative advantage in such activities. From the early 1980s onwards, Thai exporters were remarkably successful in expanding sales, particularly in new markets outside of the increasingly restricted EU and North American areas.

The acceleration of the rate of growth of exports appears to have taken place with little increase in domestic investment (Table 2.1). Thus the initial stages of the export expansion reflected the ability of the Thai manufacturing sector to expand production with little additional investment. There is indeed considerable evidence of over-capacity in Thai manufacturing during the early 1980s. For example, in 1984 the Thai Textile Association reported that there was serious over-capacity in the industry which neither the Government nor the trade association was capable of reducing. It was also revealed that as much as

30 per cent of the capacity was illegal (Dixon, 1991b, p. 1035). The excess capacity had resulted from the over-expansion of heavily protected and privileged sectors exacerbated by the recession and the contraction of the domestic market. It was this excess capacity that was utilised by a dynamic export marketing sector in the initial stages of the boom.

Once the rapid growth of manufactured exports had started, a major factor in its continuation and acceleration was that, from 1987, Thailand became a major destination for Japanese and Asian NIE investment in labour-intensive manufacturing operations. As the Asian NIEs lost their competitive position in these activities they sought alternative, stable, low cost locations within the Pacific Asian region. The flow of Taiwanese investment into Thailand and later other parts of South-East Asia after 1987 is particularly striking. Overall this relocation is giving rise to a Regional Division of Labour between the Asian NIEs and the ASEAN Four of which Thailand is a key element.

However, it is important to stress that while there is no doubt that foreign investment has played a major role in the rapid expansion of the Thai manufacturing sector, the onset of the period of spectacular growth of exports appears to predate the influx of foreign investment (Table 2.1). In the period 1985-7 foreign investment's share of net domestic capital formation showed little change, averaging 1.9 per cent. The share rose sharply to 7.5 per cent in 1988 and peaked at 9.5 per cent in 1989, subsequently falling to 5.8 per cent in 1992. Further, as Akrasanee *et.al.* (1991, pp.22-3) have argued, given the normal start-up time for factories, the 1987 investment could not have been making any significant contribution to exports before 1988.[21] Thus, however important foreign investment became to the Thai economy, the critical early stages of Thailand's accelerated growth "were overwhelmingly Thai supplied and financed" (Akrasanee *et.al.*, 1991, p.23). The attraction of Thailand for Japanese and Asian NIE labour-intensive manufacturing investment was two-fold. Firstly, in the mid-1980s Thailand had one of the lowest levels of industrial labour cost in ASEAN,[22] and the devaluation and realignment of the baht[23] had substantially improved the competitiveness of exports. Secondly, the receding of the economic crises and the appearance of relative political stability[24] gave the Kingdom an advantage over the rest of the ASEAN Four. Economic and political crises in the Philippines, question marks over economic and political stability in Malaysia, and the persistence of high levels of control over investment in Indonesia all contributed to the attractiveness of Thailand for foreign investors. The importance of Thailand's political stability during the critical periods of the 1980s is deserving of much fuller attention. Prime Minister Prem Tinsulanonda was in power from March 1980 until July 1988: this was the longest parliamentary premiership in Thai history.[25] His period of government saw two attempted coups (in 1981 and 1985), three general elections and five cabinets, but gave an air of continuity, robustness and stability rare in the Kingdom's history. This had two important consequences. Firstly, as was noted above, Thailand's investment rating was dramatically revised. Allied to this was the belief that the days of successful coups and direct intervention in the government of the Kingdom were over (the events of 1992 were of course to prove that this view was premature). As Amsden (1989) has concluded more generally for Pacific Asia, late industrialisation was being accompanied by late democratisation.

Secondly, during the critical phases of recession, adjustment, recovery and accelerated growth and structural change there was considerable continuity of government policies. This is not to say that there were not considerable divisions within the cabinets over public investment and development objectives. There is little doubt that this also contributed to the confidence of both domestic and overseas investors. The confidence that stemmed from the apparent establishment of stable and at least quasi-democratic government, was give a substantial boost following the July 1988 elections with the appointment of an premier (Chatichai Choonhaven) and a full cabinet who were all elected. Neher (1988) summarised well the view of Thailand held by many internal and external observers

> the capacity of the government to cope is high, the future is bright for all segments of the nation, democracy is flourishing (at least compared to other developing nations), and the remarkable stability of the Kingdom is constant. Those agreeing with this interpretation note the rapid and consistent economic growth, the manageable debt, the end of communist insurgency, the extraordinary fact that no successful military coup has taken place for ten years.

Once the manufacturing-based export boom was under way it was reinforced in two ways: first, by the expansion of primary exports (Table 2.1); and secondly, by the promotion of tourism. Muscat (1994, p.197) goes as far as to suggest that tourism was the "single most important export policy success" of the 1980-88 period. He sees the promotion of tourism, centred on the 1987 Visit Thailand Year, as instrumental in raising receipts from US$1 billion in 1985 to US$3 billion in 1988 - c.15 per cent of income from the export of goods and services, and substantially reinforcing the Kingdom's rapid rate of economic growth. Overall, during the 1980s both the economic and political situation in Thailand changed radically and the Kingdom became regarded as politically and economically stable and an investment 'hot-spot'. However, there is in all this a clustering of favourable global and regional circumstances that Thailand was able to take advantage of rather than any particular policies or strategies that could be isolated and applied elsewhere.

Conclusion: sustainability and lessons

During the late nineteenth and early twentieth centuries the Thai state took a lead in promoting reform, establishing a modern legal and bureaucratic system and constructing infrastructure, notably rail and telegraph links. Between 1932 and 1957 the state actively promoted industrialisation through direct participation in production and protectionist policies. Subsequently, however, successive Thai governments have been the least interventionist of any in South-East Asia. The developmental role of the Thai state was increasingly restricted to one of fostering domestic and foreign private enterprise. The government provided infrastructure and attempted to create a secure and attractive environment for investment. The establishment, since the early 1960s, of planning structures at all levels gives the impression that development is highly co-ordinated and regulated. In practice Thai planning has proved singularly ineffective (see for example Demaine, 1986; Siamwalla, 1993). Since the late 1950s Thai development policy has relied heavily on conservative monetary and fiscal policies to control inflation and manage the balance of payments (Booth, 1993, p.3). Until the late 1970s these policies were comparatively successful in maintaining a stable economic environment. However, the external shocks of the late 1970s and early 1980s revealed significant weaknesses in the macro-control of the economy particularly with respect to fiscal matters and the control of credit (World Bank, 1980b).

While the level of government expenditure has been substantially lower than that of Malaysia, it has been markedly higher than in Indonesia and the Philippines. However, unlike Malaysia, and to a lesser extent, Indonesia, Thai governments have not found it necessary to devote significant resources to redistributive policies with respect to either personal wealth or the spatial pattern of economic growth.

Since 1960 a series of national plans has been drawn up and implemented under the auspices of the National Economic and Social Development Board (NESDB). Despite this there have been few signs of any co-ordinated development strategy (Siamwalla, 1993). In part the lack of co-ordination is rooted in the comparative independence, within budgetary constraints, of the various government departments, ministries and agencies. However, beyond the general favouring of industrial growth and a neglect of the agricultural sector there has been little evidence of any clear sectoral policies. There has been no question of the state following the Asian NIE pattern of 'picking winners' and actively promoting them.

It is perhaps not unfair to characterise Thai development from the late 1950s onwards as the product of limited state intervention, with little overall co-ordination and direction, and weak and generally ineffective planning mechanisms at all levels. Since the early 1980s a degree of liberalisation and reduction on the role of the state's developmental role has occurred. It seems likely that these developments have made successive Thai governments more light-handed and less effective in managing the economy and directing development.

For the World Bank (1980b) a corollary of liberalisation and the reduction of the role of the state was the development of institutions and decision-making mechanisms of the state. There is little evidence that these aims have been achieved in any way (see Muscat, 1994, pp. 189-93 for a discussion), the Thai government and bureaucracy apparently remaining singularly ineffective at decision-making. On the broader front of economic policy, while since the early 1980s various attempts have been made to improve and streamline decision-making processes, they have met with limited success (Muscat, 1994, pp.177-9). A series of interministerial committees was set up (or revitalised) to oversee particular aspects of economic policy, for example the Export Development and Debt Committee and the National Economic Steering Committee (this to oversee the structural adjustment programme). With a view to improving relations with the business community the Joint Public Sector Private Sector Consultative Committee was established. In addition, a number of *ad hoc* bodies was set up to deal in the shorter term with a range of priority areas such as tourism. However, while again these developments sent the right general messages to investors the fragile coalition governments of the period were ineffective in making major decisions on such critical issues as major infrastructural projects. This is perhaps most clearly seen in the protracted debate over the development of the Eastern Seaboard. Beyond the consistent growth and adjustment framework set out initially under the Fifth Plan and the streamlining and relaxing of certain procedures and the positive attitude towards investment and enterprise, both domestic and foreign, it is difficult to identify specific developmental measures which 'explain' Thailand's sudden acceleration of growth.

By the mid-1990s the Thai economy had become closely linked to the fortunes of the Pacific Asian and wider global economies. This is a direct result of economic liberalisation and the rapid growth of the export-orientated manufacturing sector. The situation contrasts markedly with that which prevailed during the 1970s, when Thailand's low degree of integration with the global economy provided a degree of insulation from the prevailing unstable trading conditions. While the opening of the Thai economy has been both a contributing factor to, and a consequence of, the re-orientating and sustaining of economic growth, it has made the Kingdom far more vulnerable to external 'shocks'. There is no evidence to suggest that the Kingdom has become any more able to deal with such events than it was during the late 1970s and early 1980s.

The growth and structural change of the Thai economy since 1986 has been spectacular by any standards. The World Bank's (1980b) aims of opening the economy more fully to international trade and finance, and shifting the balance of growth from the primary sector to manufacturing, have been substantially achieved. The critical question is whether these developments are sustainable in the long run. The growth and even more the structural changes have been heavily concentrated in the Bangkok Metropolitan Region. This has exacerbated the Kingdom's already remarkably uneven pattern of development. It is not unreasonable to suggest that the recent growth has largely by-passed the majority of the population who remain rural in residence and engaged in agriculture. The heavy concentration of growth in the BMR has created major problems of congestion and pollution. It may well be that the conditions created by the boom will eventually come to discourage both foreign and domestic investors. In addition, growth of income disparities, the low income-generating capacity of agriculture, the failure of industrial employment to grow fast enough, and serious shortages of housing, services and welfare provision, may well generate major social tension and political unrest. The events of April and May 1992 give added weight to this prediction. The congestion, lack of infrastructure, rising costs of land and labour, and signs of skilled labour shortage are beginning to discourage foreign investment. The faltering of Thai growth in the face of the above problems reflects the lack of the long-term investment in infrastructure and training that has characterised the development of the Asian NIEs (McGee and Lin, 1993). Moves towards substantial upgrading of infrastructure only took place once the situation had become critical. The long heralded mass-transit system is unlikely to be completed before 2000. There are signs that foreign investment which has become a major element of Thai growth is beginning to falter. The out-flow of investment from East Asia has slowed. There are moves towards automation of labour-intensive processes and the retention of these operations rather than exporting them (*Asian*

Business, December 1990, pp. 50-2). This in addition to the diversion of investment into the EU and North America in anticipation of increased protection, and into China and Vietnam. Faced with the loss of comparative advantage in labour-intensive manufacturing activities the NIEs were able to move to more skill- and capital-intensive activities. The prospects for the Thai economy following this line of development appear to be extremely limited. A major constraint is the lack of skilled labour. In consequence Thailand is now confronting a major contradiction: wage levels are becoming too high for the labour-intensive sector, while the lack of skilled labour is limiting the move into higher labour cost activities.

The developmental problems facing Thailand in the mid-1990s are closely related to the long-term minimalist developmental position adopted by the state. The sustainability of the present pattern of growth is being threatened by the lack of effective planning controls and the lack of the long-term investment in infrastructure and training that has characterised the development of the Asian NIEs and facilitated their moving into higher technology production.

The limited economic role of the Thai state is now presented as a virtue and a major factor in the Kingdom's recent economic success. Such a view appears to ignore the consequences of uncontrolled economic growth with limited central planning. Additionally, they overlook the very different pattern of development experienced by the NIEs. For them the direct and substantial involvement of the state was critical to the sustaining of economic growth and structural change.

It is becoming increasingly apparent that the current problems facing the Thai economy can only be dealt with by the state taking a far more overt role in the economy. Indeed there are signs of increasing political pressure for this (Booth, 1993, p. 3). The Seventh Plan (1992-96) and more recent government policy statements may herald a change. The degree to which a major increase in the role of the state will prove economically or politically expedient remains very much a moot point. Further, it may well be that even rapid and radical transformation of the Thai state will not be able to recover the situation.

If Thailand's growth does not significantly falter and NIE status is achieved, are there any lessons for other Developing Countries? Firstly, while Thailand is at first sight a more 'typical' Third World country than the Asian NIEs, its particular non-colonial form of articulation (Dixon and Parnwell, 1991), relative abundance of land, geo-political situation and the related involvement of the USA combine to produce a very special background for development. Secondly, the review of development policies suggests little that is transferable. The Thai economy grew consistently and comparatively rapidly until 1979 with a high level of protection and a low level of integration into the world economy. While there was a range of subsidies and market controls both planning controls and macro-direction of the economy remained weak (World Bank, 1980b). Once the boom was well under way there was a degree of deregulation of the economy. Indeed in the early 1990s Thailand conveys the impression of largely uncontrolled growth. Thus in some ways Thailand is beginning to conform to the model of development that for so long was incorrectly attributed to the Asian NIEs, i.e. unfettered *laissez faire* capitalism. However, it is difficult to envisage this as a new 'model of development'. Like the Asian NIEs it is the product of a particular set of international conditions and internal economic and political structures. Certainly Thailand is not the model for 'successful' structural adjustment.

Notes

1 This resource-rich country contrasts profoundly with Thailand in terms of past patterns of growth and in the situation under which structural adjustment was implemented. Chile's rapid growth since the mid-1980s has been based on the export of primary produce. The only significant growth of manufacturing as been related to processing. For a detailed review see Gwynne (1992).

2 In 1992, according to the World Bank, Thailand had a per capita GNP of US$1,840 and 23 per cent of the population was classed as 'urban'. Only 12 countries were recorded as having a lower level of urbanisation, and those were amongst the poorest countries in the world.

3 From 1955 until 1986 the Rice Premium, effectively a tax on rice exports, kept the domestic price of rice up to 35 per cent below the prevailing international level. This levy depressed the income of rice farmers, kept down the cost of living for urban dwellers (and thereby the level of wages) and became a major source of government revenue.

4 However, until the late 1970s the level of protection was lower than that prevailing for most Third World ISI sectors. In 1978 the average percentage levels of tariff protection in ASEAN were:

Indonesia	33.0
Malaysia	15.0
Philippines	44.2
Singapore	5.6
Thailand	29.4

Source: GATT, 1980.

5 The number of American troops stationed in Thailand was:

1966	6,500
1967	34,400
1968	44,400
1969	47,600
1970	44,100
1971	36,100
1972	30,200
1973	43,500
1974	35,000

Source: Elliott, 1978, p.131.

In addition after 1964 Thailand became the main 'R and R' location for troops stationed in Vietnam.

6 The main bases in the North-East were at Nakhorn Ratchasima, Ubon Ratchathani and Udon Thani.

7 Between 1946 and 1978 American economic and military aid to South Korea amounted to US$13 billion and to Taiwan US$5.6 billion: Cummings, 1987, p.76).

8

Sector	Per centage foreign owned
Vehicles	55.5
Textiles	54.7
Oil	96.0
Tin	90.0
Soft drinks	65.0
Detergents	60.0
Milk products	60.0
Steel	20.0

Source: Hewison, 1985, p.274.

9 From 1955 until 1978 the baht had a fixed nominal exchange rate with the US dollar. This resulted in the long-term over-valuation of the currency which was substantially paid for by the agricultural sector (Jitsuchion, 1989, p.43).

10 During the 1979s there were violent fluctuations in commodity prices. However, the overall trend was a steep decline. The World Bank's composite index of non-oil commodity prices fell from an average of c.120 in 1968-70 to c.95 in 1978-80.

11 Provision was made under the 1963 Industrial Promotion Act to exempt exporters from the taxes on imported machinery, raw materials and other intermediate products. In 1972 additional incentives were made available to exporters and the Export Promotion Act gave exporters full tax exemption on imported goods. There were further relaxations of tariffs and increases in incentives in 1974 and 1977.

12 These were principally connected to the establishment of private sector slaughter houses for the export of beef and pork, and the removal of restrictions on rubber exports. None of these measures was of major consequence.

13 Special Drawing Rights, the equivalent in the period of US$936 million.

14 There were five between 1980 and 1988.

15 For a detailed review of the implementation of each of the proposed structural adjustment measures see World Bank, 1986, Annex 2.

16 Tax yields had in recent years repeatedly fallen below target, a reflection of cumbersome and inefficient revenue systems. This was an area that the World Bank had highlighted for reform.

17 The Government was reluctant for the break with the IMF to occur, for despite being able to borrow funds on the international market at a lower rate it wanted IMF approval for its economic policy (Sricharatchanya, 1986, p. 122).

18 For a tabulated comparison with the situation described by the World Bank in 1986 see Sahasakul (1992, pp. 20-27).

19 The average level of tariff protection rose from 29.4 per cent in 1978 to 40 per cent in 1988. Elsewhere in ASEAN tariff levels fell during this period leaving Thailand with the highest level in the group. In 1988 the average per centage levels of protection were:

Thailand	40.0
Indonesia	20.1
Malaysia	13.3
Philippines	28.3
Singapore	5.6

Source: GATT, 1990.

20 The delay in reducing tariff levels also reflected their importance as sources of government revenue. Earlier cuts would have exacerbated the already problematic budget deficit.

21 Since writing this it has been suggested to me that for some plants the 'start up' time can be very short indeed. However, this does not detract from the main point that acceleration of the growth of manufacturing exports pre-dates the sharp increase in foreign investment.

22 Hourly wage rates in the electronic sector (USA=100):

Indonesia	4
Thailand	5
Philippines	8
Malaysia	10
South Korea	14
Hong Kong	16
Taiwan	16
Singapore	19

Source: Scott, 1985.

23 The baht was devalued by 8 per cent in 1981 and by 14.8 per cent in 1984. More significantly, the 1984 devaluation established a managed fixed exchange system which tied the baht to a 'basket' of the currencies of the Kingdom's major trading partners. This not only made Thai exports more competitive but also allowed more flexibility in responding to changes in trade and exchange rates (Jitsuchion, 1989, p.41).

24 Despite attempted *coups d'état* in 1981 and 1985 there was only one Prime Minister between 1980 and 1988. This contrasted markedly with the conditions that prevailed during the 1970s.

25 This needs to be qualified in so far as Prem himself was appointed rather than elected and his cabinets all contained some unelected members.

3 Development or maldevelopment? The contradictions of Thailand's economic growth

Peter F. Bell

Development or maldevelopment?

Export-oriented growth and maldevelopment

The phenomenon sometimes referred to as 'NIC fever' has created a euphoria among economists that Thailand will soon become the 'fifth tiger', another Newly Industrialised Country joining the ranks of the 'four Asian tigers' (Hong Kong, Singapore, South Korea and Taiwan). This euphoria is not grounded on a careful analysis of the limitations of export-led growth, nor is it shared by those who look at the social consequences of this development process. If Thailand is a success story, it is a highly problematic one. A careful examination may reveal that it is, rather, an exemplary case of 'maldevelopment'. Maldevelopment refers to a pattern of development with strongly negative socio-economic consequences in terms of inequality, unevenness, cultural fragmentation, and a negative impact on women and the environment. Economists who tout Thailand's success are often using the narrow measure of growth in Gross National Product as their criterion. The United Nation's Human Development Index, while it includes only two additional measures (life expectancy and literacy), suggests a broader definition, but still not broad enough. This chapter will examine the Thai development process in terms of three important values: efficiency, equity, and democracy.[1]

Thailand serves as an excellent case study of many of the contradictions of the current development policies which are being practised on a global level. One difficulty of exposing this model lies in the widespread use of terms like 'country', and 'national development', which suggest that development policies have no class bias but serve everyone; that industrialisation was brought about either by inevitable 'progress' or by the value-free choices made by ideologically neutral state planners. 'Development' in this light appears to be the result of a collective will of the people. In reality capitalist development expresses strong class interests or, as one author has put it "the will of capital" (Hamilton, 1983, p.37). It is necessary to penetrate this ideological veil in order to reveal the actual content of development, and to address the questions of for whom it has been, and to whom it should be, directed.

The term 'development' may appear to be value-free but is in fact a highly ideological one. Development does not occur in a vacuum. The development model which has dominated in Thailand since the 1960s emerged from three main influences: American advisors (especially in the 1960s); American-educated Thai technocrats; and the desire of the Thai state to promote vigorously a capitalist class. While the overall importance of the impact of the United States on Thailand since 1950 is not contested, writers disagree about its positive and negative consequences.[2]

If the development policies adopted reflected external influences, it will not be surprising that the outcome is not necessarily the best economic model for raising the standard of living of the majority of Thai people. Export-Oriented Growth fails on the grounds both of equity and general human welfare. It also diminishes the autonomy of the Thai people to determine their own economic outcomes. Integration into the world economy entails:

(i) the dominance of production methods with a bias towards labour-saving technology;

(ii) an orientation of economic resources to the needs of external markets;

(iii) the subordination of labour to a highly competitive world market for manufactured goods; and

(iv) the domination of a particular lifestyle and model of consumption which necessitates the commodification of everyday life.

The contradictions of development

In the case of Thailand, rapid growth has been built on contradictory political-economic relations. The Export-Oriented Growth model requires a particular conjuncture of political and class forces central to which is class and gender inequality and the dominance of the business class. This conjuncture includes:

(i) *Control over labour:* a cheap and malleable labour force; limited legal constraints such as the enforcement of labour laws including those governing minimum wages and safety; limited and not too militant unionisation of labour; extensive use of female and possibly child labour;[3]

(ii) *The transfer of savings from the agricultural sector for urban and industrial development:* this has led to the relative underdevelopment of agriculture and of the rural population. Such a process promotes what economists have called 'an unlimited supply of labour' which can move from rural to urban employment;

(iii) *A political climate which favours capitalists* and their right to accumulate resources without impediment such as regulation (e.g. pollution control); tax policies which favour both capital accumulation and the wealthy; and the absence of expensive government regulations and social policies. These factors prevent wages from rising too rapidly, and they also permit the unimpeded exploitation of natural resources. These in turn require that the 'social structures of accumulation' (the relations of capital to capital, labour to labour, capital to labour, and government to economy) promote capital accumulation;[4]

(iv) *Abundant foreign capital and technology:* this entails a high degree of dependency on important intermediate goods and means the implementation of economic policies to integrate Thailand further into the global economy. These are generally policies favoured by the International Monetary Fund and the World Bank: liberalisation of tariffs, freedom to repatriate profits, capital mobility, promotion of free market policies and the end of government subsidies and public enterprises (see also the chapter by Dixon in this volume);[5]

(v) *Global markets for manufactured goods,* which are open and relatively free from protectionism. The global markets for manufactured goods are highly competitive, and shifts in comparative advantage, or changing tariffs, can have a profound effect on export demand.

The present conjuncture in Thailand is fragile and, as the 1990s have shown, these elements can easily be disrupted by external changes, such as a shift in the direction of capital flows, and internal political instability, such as military coups. Export-Oriented Growth is both vulnerable to changes in the world economy and contradictory in its impact. The conditions required for growth may cause structural imbalances, such as environmental destruction and income inequality, which may distort and even limit the possibility of growth in the future, making it non-sustainable.

The Export-Oriented Growth model is associated with, if not directly the cause of, many features of maldevelopment: the destruction of the environment, and relative neglect of the rural population in favour of urban, manufacturing-based projects. Since manufacturing replaces more labour-intensive activities with rising capital-labour and capital-output ratios and thus does not provide sufficient employment for the population, the model generates both intra-personal and inter-regional inequalities of income. The disproportionate employment of young women in export-oriented industries may have strengthened the sexual division of labour. Reliance on tourism, the largest single export in recent years, as the source of foreign exchange to pay for the technology needed for industrialisation has stimulated the growth of the sexual services industry. Like other aspects of the growth model, this too is highly vulnerable in the light of both political instability and the rapid transmission of the AIDS virus.

Integrating the country further into the world economy through both the flows of commodities and investment has led to increasing reliance on world markets and foreign capital. Export-Oriented Growth also subordinates the population to Western corporate planners who structure not only investment, technology and production but also consumption, and through this both culture and lifestyle. In short by placing growth as the central social goal, the model concentrates economic decision-making in the hands of a small élite, and to the impersonal forces of the world economy, subordinating Thai society to the hegemonic influence of Western consumer culture.

export-oriented growth ≠ expansion for sex ind.

Westernization

Capitalist development in Thailand

The sources of capitalist accumulation in Thailand

As Thailand comes close to the magic status of becoming a NIC, economists of different political persuasions refer to it as an exemplary case of economic development. Its economic success supports, perhaps ironically, the views of economists on both the right and the left. The NICs have been called the "trump card" of orthodox economists (Hamilton, 1983, p.35) as they appear to validate neo-classical economic theory, especially the alleged benefits of open economies and free market policies. For others this development reveals the success not of the market but rather of rational state planning. Some theorists stress the critical role of foreign, especially Japanese, investment in recent growth (Unger, 1991). The latter view is consistent with Suehiro's (1985) analysis of the fundamental role played by foreign capital in the historical development of Thai capitalism. For the more orthodox Marxists, and critics of dependency theory, the model appears to vindicate the view that capitalist industrialisation is possible in the Third World. Others have argued that this capitalist growth is autarkic and that Thailand has an independent 'national' bourgeoisie (Hewison, 1989).[6]

The perspective of this chapter is that capitalism arose historically from the symbiotic relationship between Chinese merchants, Thai bureaucrats, Thai landowners and foreign capital. The form of capitalist development reflects both internal and external class forces, which have shaped the particular character of the surplus extraction process, including foreign capital and US foreign policy.[7]

Factors underlying recent development

Thailand has made the transition from a primary commodity export economy to an industrialising one in the last thirty years. In 1986 the value of manufactured exports exceeded those of primary commodities for the first time. This structural transformation was achieved, however, not through the free market, but rather through systematic government policies which favoured the development of a manufacturing sector, and a capitalist class. These policies occurred in two distinct stages: Import-Substitution Industrialisation in the 1960s, and Export-Oriented Growth since the 1970s.

Although the growth of GDP has been uneven, reflecting the country's vulnerability to internal and external political and economic forces, the overall trend of the last thirty years has generally been of economic expansion. During the period since 1965, Thailand has experienced one of the highest growth rates (in terms of GNP) in the world. After the recession of the early 1980s, the growth rate of the late 1980s was quite dramatic, with an average annual increase in GDP of 11.1 per cent from 1987 to 1990. The rate fell to 8.2 per cent in 1991 and 7.5 per cent in 1992, but rose again to 8.8 per cent in 1995. This growth was primarily in the areas of manufacturing and services. In general, agricultural growth was one-third to one-half the rate of growth of manufactures, and fluctuated a great deal more. In 1995 the principal sources of growth in the economy were manufactured exports, industrial production and, to a much lesser extent, agricultural production.

The rapid growth of the 1980s was fuelled by specific forces: large in-flows of foreign investment, vigorous private domestic investment, and a boom in manufactured exports and tourism. The principal investors in the 1980s were Taiwan (which invested primarily in labour-intensive activities) and Japan (primarily capital-intensive investments). In the three years 1986-89, for example, 40-50 per cent of the investments approved by the Board of Investment were for projects which would export 80-100 per cent of their output. Requests for Board of Investment promotion fell dramatically in the early 1990s, which officials attributed to a decline in the Japanese economy, and to competition from Southern China and other ASEAN countries for investment funds from Taiwan and Hong Kong.

Continuous balance of trade deficits arising from capital imports were made up by receipts from tourism and other sources, leading to a balance of payments surplus in some years (approximately US$4.5 billion in 1989 and 1991, and a deficit of over US$7 billion in 1994-95). Foreign reserves have grown continuously over many years to a level of US$0.8 billion, and there has been a reduction of the debt:export ratio which fell from 20.1 per cent in 1986 to 13 per cent in 1991.

A little observed but significant shift in Thailand's internal pattern of production occurred in 1993 as high-technology exports (computers, electrical appliances, etc.) overtook labour-intensive exports (textiles, clothing, jewellery, etc.). This structural change, while signalling a maturing of the Thai economy, also indicates a new source of vulnerability. Thailand serves as the assembly point for foreign-designed and developed technology products, thus there is an ever-present danger of loss of competitiveness (*Bangkok Post Year End Review*, 1994, p.11). Economists have argued also that multinational investment has not led to high or desirable levels of technology transfer (Prasartset, 1988). This shift towards higher technology production also points to a problem in the educational system: by 1996, 72 per cent of the labour force will still not have gone beyond primary education and will, as a result, be undereducated for employment in the higher technology industries.

Compared to other South-East Asian countries, Thailand had several important economic advantages in the shift from Import-Substitution Industrialisation to Export-Oriented Growth during the 1970s. These included:

(i) abundant agricultural commodities which could be exported (leather, wood, fruit, fish): natural resource-based exports accounted for 27 per cent of total exports in 1993 compared to over 60 per cent in 1980;

(ii) Thai industry enjoyed a relatively low level of protection, which generated fewer economic inefficiencies than other countries; and

(iii) the relatively large size of the economy permitted economies of scale to be enjoyed (Jansen, 1989).

The contradictions of export-oriented growth

While the Export-Oriented Growth model has been adopted globally, it nevertheless has a number of fundamental theoretical contradictions:

(i) It has *a built-in need for imported capital goods and technology* for industrialisation, and thus an imminent balance of payments problem created by the difficulty of earning sufficient foreign exchange to pay for these imports. In most countries this has led to permanent balance of payments problems and in many to higher levels of external debt. In Thailand it has led to reliance on tourism and the export of workers overseas whose remittances contribute to the balance of payments;

(ii) *Low labour absorptive capacity*, and thus an inability to provide work for the population; it is characterised by rising capital-labour and capital-output ratios in manufacturing (the latter rose from 1.6 in the early 1950s to around 2.3 in the mid-1980s: Ikemoto, 1988, p.29);

(iii) *The displacement of agricultural labour* leading to landlessness and underemployment. Many of these rural workers end up in petty services (e.g. hawking) in Bangkok, while others work overseas, for example in the Middle East. There were also an estimated 200,000 Thai women working in the sexual services industry in Europe alone in the 1980s (Karnjanauksorn, 1987). Thai women are reportedly working in night clubs and sexual service outlets in Japan, New Zealand and Australia. Meanwhile 25 per cent of the population lives below the poverty line, swelling the slums of Bangkok. Implicit in these conditions is the threat of social violence. A prominent Thai government official voicing concern said: "If those 15-16 million people lose their hope, they will not stay with the system. They could do something violent";

(iv) The relative *neglect of agriculture in favour of urban-based manufacturing projects.* The development model in Thailand has long been premised on the extraction of agricultural surplus for use in the urban areas (Bell, 1990a). In the early years of development the rice tax served as a regressive resource transfer from rural to urban areas, accounting for, by some estimates, 60 per cent of the transfer of resources from rural to non-rural areas in the years 1953-63 (Feeny, 1982, pp.113-14: cited in Hirsch, 1990, p.54). The rural areas have continued to provide a large surplus by transferring resources to urban areas. This transfer amounted, according to one estimate, to around 23 per cent of agricultural GDP in the second half of the 1970s, and perhaps 15 per cent in the early 1980s (Siamwalla and Setboonsarng, 1986). This is a continuation of the historic pattern resulting from the particular structuring of the fiscal system, pricing policies, and trade policies. Banks have maintained a consistently urban-biased policy. The banking system transferred through voluntary deposits around US$280 million per annum in 1975, and around US$1,400 million in 1982 from the rural to urban areas (Jansen, 1989, pp.8-9). The aim of these policies was to shift resources to the corporate sector for the creation of an export-oriented industrialisation.

(v) *Export-Oriented Growth requires relatively cheap labour to compete in the highly competitive world markets* for manufactured goods; this pushes down the wage rate below minimum subsistence. This means that workers are forced to rely on other sources to feed, clothe and house themselves at minimum levels; this often takes the form of relying on family income outside of work, and so forth. This intensifies efforts to subordinate labour through divisions of the class based on the wage hierarchy, gender divisions, etc.[8] Export-Oriented Growth promotes the oppression of women through both low wage manufacturing and the sexual services industry. Data show that 90 per cent of rural children (about 72 per cent nationally) do not enter secondary school, and many form part of the 1.5 million child labour force (aged 11-14) which is highly susceptible to abuse. Over 2,500 of these children are estimated to be child prostitutes (Komin, 1989, pp.69-70).

Problems facing the Thai economy in the 1990s

Beyond these fundamental contradictions, there are a number of specific economic weaknesses which are very evident in Thailand in the 1990s:

(i) Industrial investment has necessitated a surge in capital goods imports, leading to rising trade deficits (amounting to between US$7-10 billion in the 1990s, depending on the year). This gap has been met by capital in-flows, but the suspicion is that a fairly large proportion of these in-flows is attracted by speculative (short-term) gains, and can easily be withdrawn. Indeed, the IMF pointed to Thailand as one of several possible danger spots for capital flight following the collapse of the Mexican economy in 1994;

(ii) Tourism accounted, until a downturn in 1991-92, for about 12 per cent of total export value, and Thai workers' remittances from abroad another 7 per cent of the total. After many years of dramatic growth in which numbers grew by over 20 per cent in 1988 and almost 14 per cent in 1989, the years 1991 and 1992 saw very sharp declines in the number of tourists, from over 5 million a year to 3.6 million. There has been a recovery since 1993 (5.7 million) and a projection of over 7 million by 1996. Tourism is in any case expensive: according to one estimate, the imports necessary to support the tourist industry accounted for more than 50 per cent of the income which it generated in 1987 (Wuttithep *et.al.*, 1989);

(iii) Increasing inflationary pressures were seen in the late 1980s, resulting from supply side constraints: rising land prices (85-100 per cent rise, per year, in Bangkok in recent years); rising wages (minimum wage raised 15 per cent; public sector wages up 10 per cent in 1990); and a tightening of the labour market for skilled workers and professionals. The rate of inflation has hovered in the 4-5 per cent range in the 1990s, on average, caused largely by international trade prices (especially for oil and agricultural goods). Infrastructural constraints such as inadequate roads, ports, communications, and energy supplies endanger future levels of growth, although major infrastructural investments once they are made may be important sources of future growth, rivalling that of exports;

(iv) Agricultural exports vary from year to year. There is continuous pressure for increases in the minimum wage to both farm labourers and urban workers. The latter generally earn twice the wage of their rural counterparts (see also Chapter 1);

(v) Corruption in Thailand is rampant at every level of society, including the government. It is a phenomenon which consumes the energy of the political system as different factions seek access to the spoils through political power. Corruption feeds off and strengthens the pre-existing social inequality. Low incomes encourage graft and corruption. An article in the June 29 1995 issue of the *Far Eastern Economic Review*, entitled "The Tension Within" described the corruption of the 1995 elections. Lacking substantial political differences between the parties, candidates win votes through patronage and money. The bridge between the rural basis of many candidates' voters and the different expectations of urban voters is a source of possible political instability. Rural voters want their elected officials to siphon money into their areas for improved services which the development model has neglected;

(vi) After the bloody military suppression of pro-democracy forces in 1992, there has been a return to political stability and the emergence of a relatively stable political centre. The lessons of 1992 to outside investors was the constant danger of military intervention. But since that time the military has taken a back seat to civilian rule although much of its power and behind-the-scenes influence has diminished. Certainly the emergence of a new class of business people and technocrats has changed public perception and perhaps also the balance of political power.

The historic existence and importance of an over-blown military has its roots in the international class forces at work in the 1950s-1970s which led to the U.S. channelling large amounts of military and economic aid to Thailand in the context of the Vietnam War.

Export-Oriented Growth in theory and practice

It may seem at first glance that the shift to an Export-Oriented Growth model was a result of the application of the dominant economic paradigm of comparative advantage. The neo-classical arguments which favour increased trade and an export orientation are well known. Trade tends to stimulate growth, the division of labour, and promotes greater international and domestic equality through factor price equalisation, thus making more efficient use of world's resources. Neo-classical theory assumes perfect competition, and the complete mobility of resources - conditions which do not exist. The theory also ignores both the fundamental role of the state in managing the development process and also the negative effects of integration into the world economy through markets, capital flows and technology. Nevertheless the Export-Oriented Growth strategy attracts wide appeal to orthodox economists (see for example Belassa, 1981) and is central to the policies imposed on debtor nations by the IMF and the World Bank.

Another important political factor in the shift to Export-Oriented Growth has been the influence of international organisations such as the World Bank and IMF, which both advocate free trade and liberalisation, including the lessening of state intervention, opening the country to foreign investment and reducing tariffs. Although the shift to Export-Oriented Growth began in the 1970s, with the Third Plan (1972-1976), it received a bigger push in the 1980s, especially with the Fifth Plan (1982-1986). In the early 1980s the World Bank issued two reports which urged the Thai government to adopt an export-led industrialisation strategy.[9] The 1984 World Bank Report, *Thailand: Managing Public Resources for Structural Adjustment*, advocated a 'structural adjustment programme' along these lines to reposition Thailand within the world economy (for a fuller discussion of Thailand's structural adjustment programme, see the chapter by Dixon in this volume). The programme argued for the classic liberalisation and pro-foreign investment policies. However influential such recommendations might have been in the minds of Thai policy-makers, export-promotion was not fundamentally linked in Thailand with a free market philosophy, but rather with selective government intervention: fiscal, monetary and trade policies, investment incentives, and so on.

This is also the case with the existing NICs. A comparison is instructive. The conditions which favoured the emergence of the other Asian NICs were as follows:

(i) All four NICs either had established industrial bases (Taiwan and South Korea) or trading and financial networks (Hong Kong and Singapore);

(ii) Each received substantial in-flows of foreign investment (South Korea received US$12.5 billion in economic and military aid from the United States alone in the years 1950-70). In the period 1952-1962, in South Korea and Taiwan, U.S. loans and aid funded 70 and 85 per cent of imports and 80 and 38 per cent of domestic capital formation respectively (Robison*et.al.*, 1987,p.373). By contrast Thailand received $3.3 billion of U.S. aid from 1946-1988 (two-thirds military and one-third economic: Muscat, 1990, pp.37). Thailand benefited substantially from the spill-over of the U.S. in Vietnam in the late 1960s;

(iii) The industries which spear-headed export growth in the 1970s and 1980s had their origins in the import substitution industries of the 1950s and 1960s which were carefully developed through government policies (tariff protection, etc.);

(iv) The shift in production in the developed capitalist countries, in which industries such as textiles, automotives, electronic assembly, engineering, etc. were increasingly moved to Third World countries. This provided the new markets needed by these emerging NICs;

(v) In every case (except Hong Kong), the state played a leading role in both generating and co-ordinating industrial growth (Robison *et.al.*, 1987, p.373). Rather than adopting *laissez faire* policies, state intervention was redirected e.g. by tariff manipulation, infrastructural investments, export credits, and the suppression of organised labour;

(vi) The absence of political and social factors which might impede governments in adopting Export-Oriented Growth policies permitted them to move rapidly. In Taiwan traditional opposition had been weakened by land reform, and in South Korea military regimes were able to impose their policies with ease. No popular resistance movements emerged to challenge these until the 1980s; and

(vii) Other factors favouring the push towards Export-Oriented Growth were: (a) the desire to escape from the capital import dependence of Import Substitution Industrialisation, and an orientation towards consumer goods production; and (b) the saturation of domestic consumer markets (Hewison, 1985).

The relative slowness of South-East Asian countries in adopting Export-Oriented Growth, when compared to the other NICs, was the result of two main factors:

(i) The so-called New International Division of Labour (NIDL) was very different in the 1980s from that of the 1960s and 1970s, when the NICs began their export-based growth orientation. Important changes include the fact that China now serves as a cheap labour economy, and there have been changes in both technology and labour costs in rich capitalist countries which have made it possible for industry to be relocated back in the capitalist centres; and

(ii) In Indonesia and the Philippines, the policy of Import-Substitution Industrialisation was stronger and moves towards Export-Oriented Growth were resisted by bureaucratic capitalists who depended upon the protection of ISI which the state afforded (e.g. under the Marcos regime). In Indonesia, domestic capital was dependent upon the state; in the Philippines, the primary product export sector was maintained through active state intervention.

The Thai case

The foreign exchange constraint arising from the import of needed capital goods has led to the growth of tourism as an official development strategy. It has become the largest single export. The socio-economic consequences of this are profound: accelerated land speculation, displacement of farmers, the invasion and commercialisation of traditional cultures such as the hill-tribes, intensification of prostitution, and an adverse environmental impact. Not all of these factors are directly attributable to Export-Oriented Growth but the model intensifies all of them.

The Export-Oriented Growth model is predicated on the employment of female labour which has led to greater levels of exploitation of labour in general, as wages are driven low by intense international competition (e.g. in textiles and electronic assembly). An intensification of the sexual division of labour in Thailand has occurred through the entry of a large number so young women into factory work. In the ten largest export commodities, women accounted for 80 per cent of total employment in the late 1980s. This intensification has occurred also in the sexual services industry, which is partially, but by no means completely, a response to tourism. The Bangkok sex trade is highly significant in terms of foreign exchange earnings. The importance of tourism is shown by the data that in 1988, tourist receipts amounted to US$3 billion while the largest imports, such as mechanical equipment and parts, were US$3.5 billion, and electrical equipment and parts US$2.3 billion (Bell, 1992). Clearly industrialisation is heavily dependent upon tourism, of which a significant component is the sexual services industry (around 65-70 per cent of tourists are single males).

Because of the high prevalence of extra-marital sexual relations, Thailand has an almost perfect network for the transmission of the AIDS virus. The AIDS epidemic, by even optimistic scenarios, will affect perhaps 2 million Thais by the year 2000; it will cost US$500 million to 1 billion in lost earnings and will account for one-third of all deaths in Thailand. Some estimates predict as many as 4 million people will be infected with HIV by the end of the century.[10]

There are also increasing levels of foreign ownership of the economy and foreign control over economic decision-making, and with it the attendant impact on modes of consumption (marketing) and consumerism (foreign products). The advertising industry meanwhile grows by 20-25 per cent per year. The total expenditure on advertising in 1989 was US$400 million, and had reached over US$1 billion by 1993 (Thailand in Figures, 1994, p.150).

The neglect of the agricultural sector is a further factor. Agriculture continues to be extensive rather than intensive, so that productivity rises very little. There is a growing differentiation among farmers in terms of income, land ownership, and so on. Also, Export-Oriented Growth in agriculture means less attention is given to subsistence crops while producing more (e.g. fruit, plantation crops) for the export market. Multinational corporations are heavily involved in the processing and marketing of agricultural goods.

In Thailand 25 per cent of the land has been affected by severe soil erosion (Hirsch and Lohmann, 1989). Environmentalists have revealed that the existing pattern of growth is non-sustainable in terms of the existing resource base and the way it is utilised (*ibid.*, p.441). Environmental struggles are connected to struggles over the distribution of resources and the direction of development. Recent struggles over the environment include the following: bans on logging; struggles against dam projects; protests against salt-mining; attempts to reclaim national forests and beaches, and to protect islands from tourism. The environmental and rural development movements are represented by a broad coalition of forces: students, academics, NGOs, some of the middle class, and local grass-roots citizen groups with regional and international linkages.

Although official data are unreliable (putting unemployment at less than 7 per cent of work force), unemployment will intensify in the future due to rising capital-output and rising capital-labour ratios. This is a normal part of capitalist accumulation based on modern manufacturing. This process also creates a dualism in the urban areas, with a modern manufacturing sector, employing relatively few workers, existing alongside a traditional, more labour-intensive small firm sector. The result is a swelling of the underemployed, particularly in the service sector, which consists of street vendors, touts, prostitutes, scavengers, servants, etc. A fundamental contradiction is that the wealth of the few in the cities has at its opposite pole the relative poverty of the many in the slums and in the rural areas, where unemployment results from the very mechanism which generates industrialisation.

The future maturing and likely unionisation of the urban labour force, and the end of the rural farm to which workers can retreat, will transform industrial relations and the prospects for future control over labour, and thus wages. Thailand may be caught in the 'wedge' between the NICs with rising wages and the low wage economies which surround it, such as China and Indonesia. In addition the growth of agri-business in the rural areas will mean that few farmers will own land and the need for agricultural labour will fall dramatically (one estimate is that only 40 per cent of Thai people will live in rural areas by the end of the century).

There is a growing dominance of business in politics (Laothamatas, 1989; Phongpaichit, 1992); business has asserted its own independence, and growing involvement in politics, a process which was accelerated by the abortive military crackdown in 1992.

There have been growing levels of social and regional inequality (Krongkaew, 1985). In the ten-year period 1975-85, the share of the richest fifth of the population rose from 49.3 per cent to 55.6 per cent of aggregate income. The rural:urban income gap is estimated at 1:10. The Bangkok Metropolitan Region generated about 58 per cent of all income in non-agricultural growth and 50 per cent of all growth in the period 1970-83 (Komin, 1989, p.21). This is revealed by newspaper headlines which read: "Millions miss out as Thai economy booms" (*Bangkok Post*, July 12 1990) and "500,000 homeless children in Bangkok" (*Bangkok Post*, July 16 1990). Concern for the absolute level of poverty has prompted an economist at the Thailand Development Research Institute, Dr. Chalongphob Sussangkarn, to argue for a negative income tax to raise the poorest to the poverty line. He also has warned repeatedly about the problem of social inequality and the danger of social unrest which it breeds. The slow rate of growth of the agricultural sector makes amelioration of this problem unlikely.

The Thai economy was aided in the 1980s by the fall in oil prices (50 per cent of the level prior to the Iraq crisis); also (in 1989) by a realignment of world currencies which cheapened Thai exports. The economy was also boosted in the late 1980s by the recovery of primary exports (especially the prices of rice and raw sugar), and by the construction boom. Many of these circumstances have disappeared in the 1990s. Most dramatically, perhaps, there was a collapse of the speculative boom in the construction industry which slowed from rates of growth of 21-23 per cent in the years 1988-1990 to around 8 per cent in 1992. Enormous gaps in public infrastructure remain to be filled, or even started, most dramatically the problem of traffic (and public transportation) in Bangkok itself.

"The values and world views of the Thai people, founded on century upon century of Buddhist principles are shattered", observes an article in *Thailand 2010*. Many Thai observers lament the replacement of the values of the community with those of the individual and capitalist market place, yet others see it as the inevitable result of rising living standards. There seems little doubt that the transition to capitalist and market-oriented values is transforming personal relations and unseating traditional culture. Many see an exacerbation of this problem in the social polarisation which the development model has brought about, threatening social violence.[11]

Conclusion

Export led development in Thailand "concentrates development in industrial and commercial sectors using the resources of the vast rural sector and its environment" (Hirsch and Lohmann, 1989, p.445). There is no mechanism which ensures that the benefits of development are spread evenly. As in previous phases of Thai economic history, the majority of the Thai people - even though many have experienced a rise in their standard of living - are treated as secondary to a process which favours a small but growing middle class in the cities.

The foregoing analysis has suggested some of many ways in which capitalist development in Thailand is unstable and tending to a pattern of non-sustainable social and economic development. An alternative development strategy would involve a number of elements impossible to imagine in the current political economy conjuncture. These reforms would include much less reliance on exports as an engine of growth, and would involve income redistribution, production based on labour-absorbing processes, and an output mix aimed more at domestic markets where increased local demand could partially replace export-led demand. A much higher priority would have to be placed on the provision of increased resources for agriculture, of development programmes to alleviate rural poverty, including services, infrastructural development, and so on. Efforts to increase the productivity of the agricultural sector would focus on rural income redistribution, the development of new technology, and the retaining of savings for use in the agricultural areas. Few commentators expect government policies towards agriculture to change dramatically in the future

A more radical view of development would call for a non-patriarchal development pattern which would respect the environment, Thai cultural values, and which would not use tourism and the exploitation of women as a lever of development. There are many voices in Thailand raised in opposition to current development patterns. These include environmental groups, womens' groups, human rights groups, and NGOs. So far their voices have not been as powerful as those of the business community, but by the year 2010 the imminent contradictions of this pattern of development may force such a radical shift.

Notes

1 All indices contain implicit values about what it is important to measure. For an elaboration and definition of these values in political economy, see Bowles and Edwards, 1993, chapter 2.

2 For very different assessments of the role and impact of the United States on Thailand, see Bell, 1978; 1982; 1991; and Muscat, 1990.

Muscat's assessment of the aid programme justifies the U.S. impact, which he documents in great detail, in terms of the concept of "regional stability".

3 The minimum wage in Bangkok in 1993 was US$5 a day (US$4 in much of the countryside outside the larger towns); this is up from US$2.50 in 1980, not adjusting for inflation.

4 For an elaboration of this framework, see Bowles and Edwards, 1993.

5 For a debate on these policies, see the chapters in this volume by Chris Dixon and Johannes Schmidt.

6 This ideological debate is of significance in that it colours the views not only of political activists but also of policy-makers. Its significance becomes clearer in discussions about alternative development models and how to bring about social change.

7 See Bell, 1978 for an extended examination of this influence.

8 See Bell, 1988 for a discussion of how these mechanisms fit into the global economy. See Deyo, 1990 for a discussion of different forms of labour control in the East Asian economies.

9 See Laothamatas, 1992.

10 Estimates by Dr. Weerasit Sittitrai of the Thai Red Cross, cited in "Apocalypse Soon", *Thailand 2010, the Nation's Mid-Year Review 1993*.

11 The outlines of this debate among Thai academics are provided in the article "A Farewell to Tradition" in *Thailand 2010, the Nation's Mid-Year Review 1993*. Those that share this concern are Nidhi Aeusrivongse (Chiangmai University), Paiboon Wattanasiritham (Rural and Social Management Institute) and Amara Pongsapich (Chulalongkorn University). Those opposed include Ammar Siamwalla of the Thailand Development Research Institute.

4 Paternalism and planning in Thailand: Facilitating growth without social benefits

Johannes Drasbaek Schmidt

Introduction

As the end of the century draws close, Thailand continues to surprise. Despite a political system marked by coups, instability and rapid change, Thailand has managed to succeed economically. The Kingdom now has the second-largest market economy in South-East Asia in terms of GDP, and an economic growth rate which in the late 1980s was among the highest in the world.

At the time of writing (early 1995), the Leekpai government had placed top priority on income distribution and the spread of prosperity. Prime Minister Chuan headed a coalition consisting of the four so-called 'angelic parties' which emerged from the election that followed the May 1992 incident, when a popular up-rising toppled the military and its supporting 'devilish parties'. One of many features which distinguished the Chuan administration from its predecessor, the military-installed technocratic government of former Prime Minister Anand Panyarachun, was the objective of its economic policies, in particular attempts to socialise the content and implementation of Thailand's five-year development plans. Anand's approach had been clear-cut and simple: the goal was to reduce the government's role and create rules to induce more participation and competition within the private sector. The Chuan coalition government was more concerned with adjusting Anand's free-market approach towards one with social and distributional criteria more to the fore. This is not an easy task: the government is faced with the task of navigating between the interests of industry and agriculture in a country where about 70 per cent of the population still resides in rural areas.

Due to the shortcomings of past economic policies there are growing problems in educational provision and achievement, environmental damage, poverty, uneven income distribution, a growing contradiction between Bangkok and the rest of Thailand, the unplanned, traffic jammed sprawl of Bangkok, and deficiencies in the provision of infrastructure in general. The economic policy shortcomings which have given rise to these failures appear to be based on a lack of co-ordination and co-operation between ministries and departments at a time when policy-formulation and implementation are becoming more complex and comprehensive. Another explanation points to factors external to the domestic context: "a cynic might ask if the function of national planning has arisen merely to justify asking for more loans." (Wonghanchao, 1988, p.15).

The specific dimensions of economic policy-making and planning have received a lot of attention in the South-East Asian context during the past five to ten years. A vast literature has sought to explain the determining political factors behind major shifts in economic strategy, policy-making and industrial policy in Thailand (see e.g. Dhiravegin, 1992; Laothamatas, 1992b). Among the explanations, there are claims that Thailand has entered a new era where the ability of business to influence and affect government policy has been enhanced. This process became evident during the 1980-88 Prem period and in particular in the 1988-91 period of the Chatichai administration. Organised business associations became significant players in the conduct of government, thus suggesting that Fred Riggs' (1966) model of a bureaucratic polity is no longer valid (Laothamas, 1992a; Pongchaipit, 1992a).

In Riggs' model the rotation of power between sections of the bureaucracy - the civil servants and the military - is the most salient characteristic of Thai regimes (Riggs, 1966: see also Wilson, 1962; Siffin, 1966). Riggs saw the state as an arena where

> the failure of formal political institutions to achieve control over the bureaucracy has not meant the elimination of 'politics' and the achievement of an 'administrative state'. Rather, it has meant that the arena of politics, the focus of rivalry, and the struggles for power, wealth or other public values have moved within the bureaucracy itself. (Riggs, 1966, p.197)

Regarding the regimeform, his categorical conclusion was that "the Thai political system ... may be classified on a scale measuring power distribution between democratic and totalitarian extremes." (Riggs, 1966, pp.379-80).[1]

However, more than a decade ago, John Girling criticised this highly Euro-centric and functionalist description: "Riggs overstates the purely factional content of political rivalry. National politics is simply a struggle for power and advancement of interests among factions and cliques, by overemphasizing factional struggles he neglects the social changes" (Girling, 1981a, p.10: see also Girling, 1981b).

This chapter also questions the validity of the argument that the pressures creating change in economic strategy in Thailand intersect with a 'new' trend in political alignment - from military domination towards greater democracy with increased business influence. Pongchaipit (1992a) for instance suggests that, instead of being insulated from the pressure of local business and external factors, the Thai government is vulnerable to all kinds of pressures from interested parties. "In particular, the dynamic business sector played a key role in pushing for reforms which favoured export growth" (Pongchaipit, 1992a, p.12). The pressure from internal and external forces created a policy climate of unbalanced planning and uneven development.

Considering these assertions it is important to note the following:

(i) Thai policy-makers have never been insulated from exogenous pressures. Actors and institutions have played a determining role in major policy shifts in Thailand, especially in relation to external events;

(ii) the business sector has always had a degree of influence on sectoral policies in Thailand.[2] According to World Bank documents, even the first national plan was designed to implement a 'market-based industrialisation strategy'. This was not only a matter of timing but a conscious attempt by the state to support the domestic private sector because "the Thai state has sought to promote the interests of the most 'progressive' capitalist forces: both productive capital (industrial and more recently agrarian capital) and the dynamic financial sector dominated by banking capital, making for a powerful and rapidly developing capitalist class. All of this has been seen by many state managers to be in the 'national interest'. In essence the 'national interest' is best served by what is best for capital" (Hewison, 1989, p.213). On the other hand, macro-economic policy-making in Thailand has, for the most part, not been politicised;

(iii) monetary, exchange and other macro policies have been pragmatic and non-ideological. This partly explains why Thailand has been able to achieve remarkable success in economic growth compared with other developing countries (Chai-Anan, 1990b, p.182).

This chapter attempts to argue that in terms of economic policy-making and regimeform it is appropriate to term the role of the state in Thailand 'paternalistic and developmental' with a high degree of capacity and autonomy (Crone, 1988; Ng, Suedo and Crone, 1993; Schmidt, 1993b). Most scholars today agree that the impressive growth performance of East Asia urges a new focus on the political bases of development rather than the previous preoccupation with underdevelopment (Doner, 1992, p.398). It is also the case in the recent literature on the new institutional economics (NIE) perspective on NICs and on the political economy of stabilisation, which suggest that institutional arrangements, including regime type, the government's role in organising interest groups, and the internal structure of the policy-making apparatus, help to account for variations in policy choice, and thus economic performance (Haggard and Kaufman, 1989; Haggard and Chung-In Moon, 1990).

The view from within needs to be complemented with a neo-mercantilist and international political economy (IPE) perspective which goes beyond the differences between neo-classical theories and their latest application, NIE and public choice theories on the one hand, and statist contributions on the other. It emphasises the internal or external forces behind growth in Thailand and attempts to give examples of how international institutions - e.g. the IMF, World Bank, transnational corporations, and core states - influence economic policy-making.[3] To illuminate the applicability of the IPE and neo-mercantilist perspective in an empirically grounded argument, the analysis uses industrial, trade and investment policies as examples on national responses to changes in the international order.[4] Though international pressures weigh heavily on developing countries, the ability of such countries to formulate coherent responses is contingent on institutional arrangements and capabilities, among them the nature of economic decision-making structures and the policy instruments available to political élites.

To enhance understanding of the politics of intervention and regulation, Haggard (1990, p.43) suggests that the following factors should be taken into consideration: (i) there is a need to focus more squarely on the political organisation of business through peak associations, links to political parties, and informal political ties to the state itself: in short, to focus on the political capabilities of business; and (ii) there is a need to look at foreign investment and the politics of regulation. Such analysis provides the broader political context within which the domestic private sector operates in supporting or resisting the entry of foreign firms. Three dimensions of the state as an institutional and legal structure bear on the ability of political élites to realise their interests. The first is the degree of insulation from societal pressures, which in turn is a function of the institutional arrangements linking state and society. The second is the cohesiveness of the decision-making structure itself. The third concerns instruments that are available to state élites in pursuing their political and substantive goals. Variations in these institutional characteristics and structures, internal as well as external, influence policy choice and implementation.

The Japanese and NIC experience

In 1975 the Japanese economist Kojima explained some of the main features of the rise of Japan to core status as based on xenophobia and a specific pariah-relationship with the United States. The American security umbrella - *Pax Americana* - provided Japan with unusual preferences. On the other hand, Japan has been a reluctant host to foreign direct investment (FDI). "This follows directly from the long tradition of Japan's suspicion of foreigners and wish to be independent of foreign control" (Krause, 1972, p.162; see also Kojima, 1977, p.46). Instead of FDI, Japan was successful in stimulating the massive in-flow of foreign technology which in eighteen years between 1950 and 1968 represented about 10,000 contracts and payments in excess of US$1.4 billion. Technology in-flow permitted the modernisation of old and the creation of new industries under extremely favourable conditions (Kojima, 1977, p.36). In fact, until 1969 all FDI had been subject to case-by-case screening by the Japanese authorities (Sekiguchi, 1983, p.237). When the contracts were regarded as too restrictive, the government often intervened to modify the terms by means of administrative guidance. Many licensing agreements were accompanied by restrictive marketing provisions.

Comparing with the experience of Thailand it is striking to note that she has been highly dependent on FDI. But it remains unclear how effective the transfer of technology has been. In fact, there is no effective screening process in Thailand and this sort of information is not published in most of the ASEAN countries.[5]

In the words of Chalmers Johnson (1986, p.565; see also Johnson, 1982) neo-mercantilism in the Japanese-type capitalist developmental state has four fundamental structural features:

(i) stable rule by a political-bureaucratic élite that does not accede demands that would undermine economic growth or security

(ii) co-operation between public and private sectors unde guidance of a pilot planning agency;

(iii) heavy and continuing investment in education for everyo with policies to ensure the equitable distribution of national income, a

(iv) a government that understands the need to use and respect methods of intervention based on the price mechanism.

Each of these fundamental features exists in the Japanese, South Korean and Taiwanese context, although with differing weight, patterns of historical evolution, and trade-offs arising from emphasising one element more than others. This is not the case in the ASEAN-4, where the capacity and autonomy of the state has severe external constraints which limit its room of manoeuvre, However, it is possible to discern both similarities and differences in relation to the four points noted above:[6]

(i) the importance of political stability and insulation of planners and policy-makers from domestic forces interference in Thailand equals the Japanese experience;

(ii) the evidence shows that the role of a pilot planning agency, NESDB, in Thailand has the same function as MITI in Japan. However, the effects of policy implementation are different;

(iii) none of these special features has been successfully replicated. The overall literacy rate is very high, and primary school enrolment was at a satisfactory level of 97 per cent in 1985, thanks to budgetary allocation to the primary level. With regard to the training of scientists and engineers needed for industrialisation, Thailand produced only 4.8 persons per 10,000 population, the second lowest figure for Asian countries (Komin, 1991, p.122). As Table 4.1 indicates, poverty has increased during the 1980s, and income distribution in particular has tended to become more disproportionate (Robinson *et.al.*, 1991, p.6). As the *Economist* has commented: World Bank officials have no pat answer for why there has been so little trickle-down in Thailand. Some say it is because the boom has concentrated on Bangkok. Only 15 per cent of the population lives in the Bangkok area, which accounts for half of GDP. Income levels are nine times higher than in the northeastern part of Thailand, where one-third of the population lives (*The Economist*, May 15 1993). This is in part due to discrimination against agriculture, and the lagging expenditures in social welfare despite large fiscal surpluses in the 1990s;

(iv) on this particular point Thailand has tried more or less successfully to intervene in the market place through the price mechanism and guidance at the macro-economic level. Furthermore, there has been continued government support for private-sector investment policy throughout various regimes.

Table 4.1
Poverty and Income Distribution, 1975-88

	1975/76	1980/81	1985/86	1988/89
Poverty incidence*				
Overall*	30	23	30	24
Urban*	13	8	6	7
Rural	36	27	36	29
Income distribution				
Top 10 per cent	33	35	39	38
Top 20 per cent	49	51	56	55
Bottom 20 per cent	6	5	5	5
Gini coefficient	0.43	0.45	0.50	0.48

* Measured as the percentage of households below the poverty line.

Source: David Robinson *et.al.*, 1994, *Thailand: Adjusting to Success: Current Policy Issues,* Washington D.C.: International Monetary Fund.

Domestic political stability, economic efficiency and receptiveness to FDI have made Thailand among the most internationally competitive and attractive to investors in recent years. The importance of FDI to economic growth in Thailand compared with its South-East Asian neighbours is discerned from the pattern of FDI flows described by Dixon in this volume (see also Tambunlertchai and Panachet, 1990, pp.59-91).

Like other developing economies Thailand has little influence over the international and regional forces that affect her competitiveness and attractiveness to foreign investment; but as earlier mentioned, government policy can be crucial in shaping this competitiveness and attractiveness. It is thus appropriate to discuss some of the common features from the NIC experience which Thailand has used in her own growth strategy towards becoming a NIC.[7] The basic elements are sustained high economic growth, rising average income, rapid industrialisation (led mainly by exports), and an increased role in world trade. Thailand has already joined the established NICs in becoming a prime target of trade protectionism in Western markets with tough market-opening pressures from the United States and the multilateral institutions.

ASEAN or the recently suggested free trade area, AFTA, have not played any significant role in Thailand's growth strategy. On the contrary, it might even be claimed that the most appropriate response to the regionalisation of the world economy with increasing trade blocs like the EC and NAFTA, seen from

South-East Asia, has been a strengthening of state capacities and capabilities. This is illustrated by the extremely high rates of investment in physical capital. In this respect, the region's countries have been following the path trod earlier by Japan. As a general rule, countries are able to sustain a brisk expansion if, after their per capita income levels climb above US$1000, their fixed capital investment (the combined investment by the private and public sectors) remains in excess of 30 per cent of GNP. Such a high level of investment carries with it the risk of faster inflation and a deteriorating balance of payments, but it enables a dynamic pattern of development. It is noteworthy that, in 1989, fixed capital investment as a per centage of GNP was 37.3 per cent in Singapore, 34.7 per cent in Indonesia, 31.0 per cent in Thailand and 29.6 per cent in Malaysia, compared with 31.6 per cent in South Korea. Looking at the rate of effective import protection, Thailand is second only to Indonesia in South-East Asia. The estimated effective protection rate was 51 per cent in Thailand and 59 per cent in Indonesia, compared with 20 per cent in the Philippines and 23 per cent in Malaysia (World Bank, 1993, p.16).

The important role of state policies is also clear from the high priority which is afforded growth-related objectives, such as increasing productivity and competitiveness. The degree of state intervention in orchestrating export-led growth is particularly evident in the specific relationship between state and civil society, especially the dominance of the technocrats over business. In sum, it would seem that the Thai state has accorded the highest priority to economic growth but at the expense of welfare and social justice.

Formulation of policies, development planning and implementation: indicative or a show case?

Development planning in Thailand is a recent phenomenon. The First National Economic Development Plan was formulated in 1961 covering a five-year period up to 1966. In the first 15 years of planning, problems were considered mainly from economic viewpoints and with the principal objective of fostering economic growth. Emphasis on support to a free enterprise system was the prime concern of the Thai planning agency until the adoption of the Fourth National Economic and Social Development Plan (1976-1981) when, as can be seen, social issues were given some attention.

Implementation of plan policies, however, reflects the priorities of powerful groups in Thai society. These sectional interests have been such that various social issues, such as increasing living standards of poor farmers, have been neglected in the past (Buckley, 1982; Khan, 1988). There are other indicators showing that Thai development policy in general, and rural development policy in particular, has actually contributed to rural impoverishment. As noted in Table 4.1, Thailand's skewed curve of income distribution illustrates this failure: 60 per cent of the people receive 25% of the national income whereas 10 per cent enjoy 38%. Damrong Thandee (1985, pp.14-15) noted that the participation, influence and mutual interests of the military-bureaucratic leaders, the landed aristocracy and the indigenous bourgeoisie have moved Thailand's political economic development towards a policy favouring private investment based on a technocratic model of development.

Figure 4.1
Organizational Structure of the Public Sector in Thailand

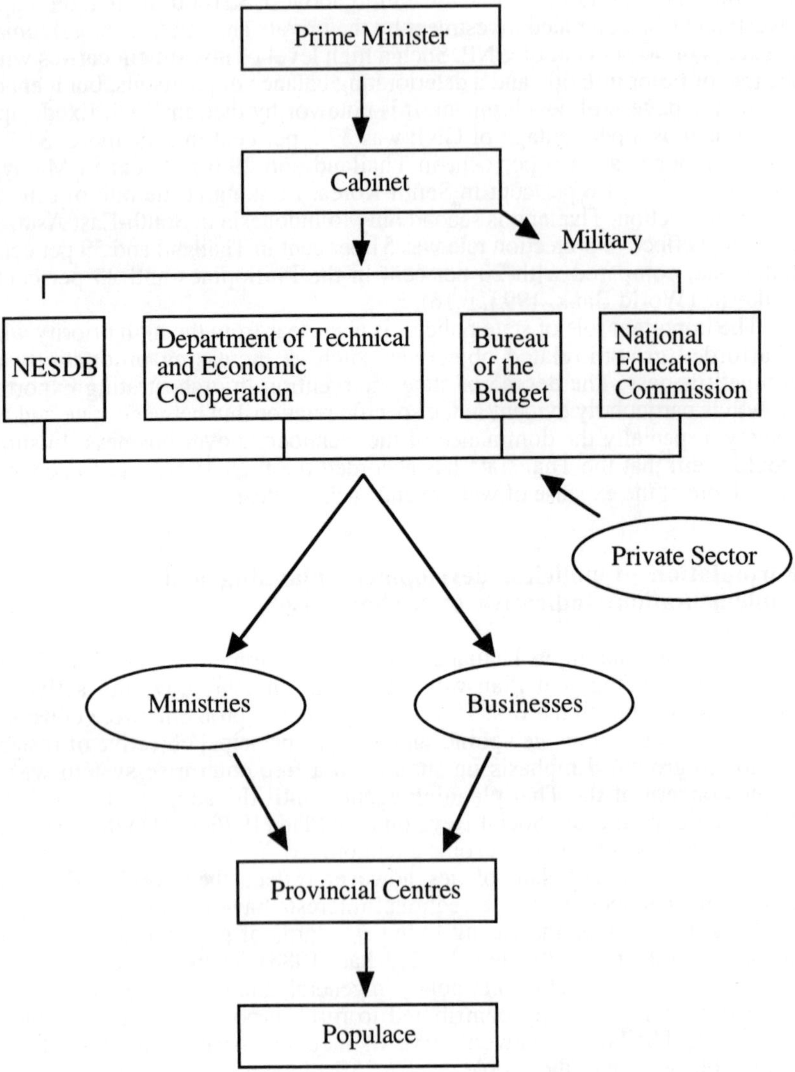

Figure 4.2
Linkages to Planning and Budget Organisation

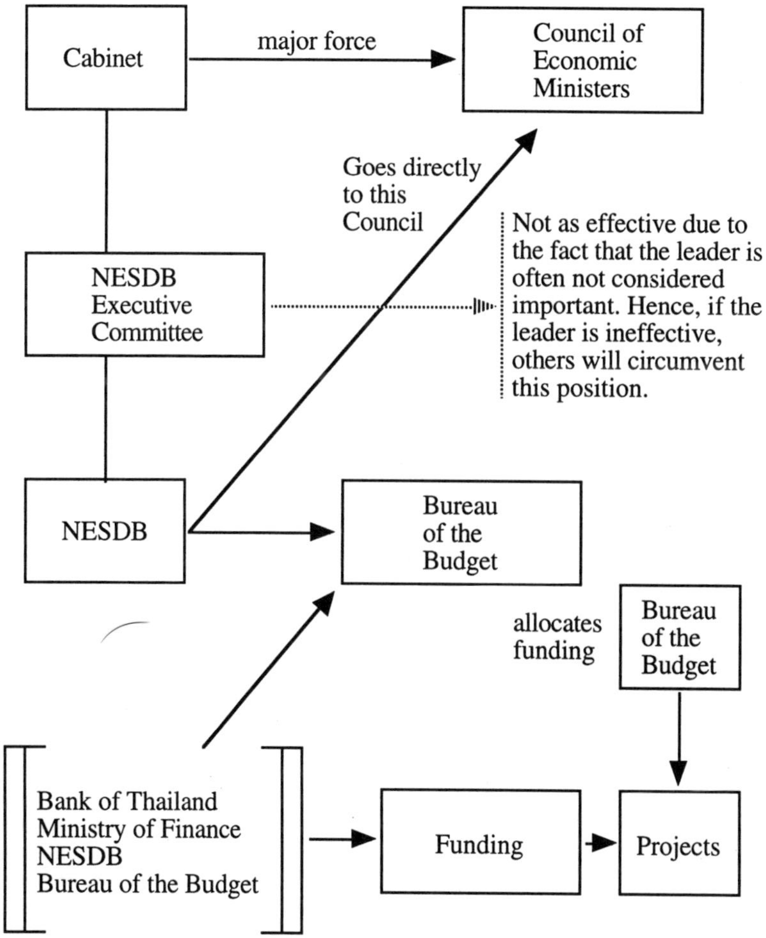

The decision-making process is characterised by one responsible agency, the National Economic and Social Development Board (NESDB), which is charged with the formulation of policies and formal planning (see Figure 4.1). Planning is done on a macro-level, while implementation is undertaken by the various sectoral government agencies at the micro- or operational level. The NESDB is essentially an instrument of the Prime Minister, who utilises it to push ahead his programmes and *vice versa*. But in the end it is the Cabinet which decides final policy. Hence, decision-making and policy planning processes are very different, but the role of the NESDB is one of steering and monitoring those agencies responsible for implementing plans (see Figure 4.2 which, like Figure 4.1, is derived from Wattanasiritham *et.al.*, 1988, p.38). However, in addition to the NESDB, the Bureau of the Budget (BOB) and the Fiscal Policy Office (FPO) also play a significant role. Above these agencies, located in the bureaucracy, the Council of Economic Ministers (CEM) in 1982 replaced the former Economic Policy Committee. As the top decision-making structure, the CEM is a highly insulated policy body, and the technocrats' response to a rapidly changing socio-economic and political situation, while the parliament as an institution does not have any strong influence upon national development planning or the decision-making process concerning plan objectives.

Political parties and public interest goups appear able only indirectly to influence the planning process (Prasith-rathsint, 1987, pp.34-5). Businessmen may play some role in planning through the Joint Public and Private Sectors Consultative Committee (JPPCC), especially those aspects which are concerned with export policy or tax structure. But it seems that the JPPCC represents an attempt by the state to maintain and exert its autonomy towards big business groups in society (Wattanasiritham *et al*, 1988, p.199). This aspect will be further touched upon below.

To be sure, the role of the three sets of international actors and institutions - transnational corporations and banks, core states, and especially the World Bank, IMF, GATT and such regional development organisations as the Asian Development Bank - have had a tremendous influence on historical and current patterns of policy-formulation in the Thai context. In the late 1960s and the 1970s the debate concerning economic policy-making centred on Import Substitution Industrialisation and Export-Oriented Industrialisation strategies, with the Ministry of Industry supporting the former and the Board of Investment the latter. In the 1980s, however, much of the debate has revolved around the measures required to handle the economic crisis, and much of this has had to do with the IMF and World Bank's recipes for the economy.[8] The World Bank and IMF have been closely associated with Thai development policy since the early 1950s and still they exert some pressure indirectly through specific policy recommendations and through locally-funded think tanks such as the Thailand Development Research Institute (Puntasen *et.al.*, 1992). The World Bank has placed some US$4.375 billion in Thailand since the early 1950s; US$1.8 billion more is promised. Critics say that these funds have exacerbated deforestation, together with the misery it brings to ordinary villagers, not just through a few careless projects or neglect of the forest sector, but through an entire pattern of investment and economic policy undertaken in collaboration with the country's past military rulers who saw foreign capital as a way of shoring up [their] rule. The Bank first began helping to open up the country to overseas investment and the world economy in the 1950s. Since then, it has encouraged the government to subsidise, rather than compete with big firms; to keep labour costs low; and to make alliances with members of the local élite who could benefit from industrialisation, export promotion, and rural development. By providing loans for power stations, pipelines, and communications, it has forced ordinary people to underwrite the overhead costs of big business. World Bank projects and advice have succeeded in pulling Thailand into a world economic game in which it remains at a perpetual disadvantage in terms of trade, bargaining power, and ability to protect itself through subsidies and tariffs (Lohmann, 1992; cited in Wuliger, 1992, p.8).

The military's role in economic decision-making is complex and reflects its powerful role within the Thai state structure. According to Pongchaipit (1992a, p.3), the military is a major player in the political process, a dependent of the state, relying on allocations from the government budget. Also, the military is a major corporate presence in the economy. Over the years, the military has built up significant assets in land and commercial businesses. This means that the military has corporate interests affected by the government's economic policies.

Depoliticisation of the planning and economic policy-making process in the domestic context occurred in the 1970s when the Communist Party of Thailand challenged the state and the existing system. According to Chai-Anan (1990b, p.185), changes resulting from social and economic modernisation have not strengthened the growth of civic organisations because the transformation of economic power into political power has been delayed by the relative autonomy of the state in policy-making matters. The Thai bureaucracy has been able to transform itself during the process of economic growth by actively promoting economic development and co-opting first the technocrats, and then the private sector. Since 1961, while military factions fought each other and took turns in 'ruling' the country, it has been the technocrats who have actually steered the ship of state (Chai-Anan, 1990b, p.196). The bureaucracy has, so to speak, made it possible for the government to allow the financial-business community to participate in some areas of the decision-making process under terms of reference determined by the state at a time, in the mid- to late-1970s, when the business sector expanded rapidly. This process of co-option has meant that the latter does not present a real challenge to the bureaucratic-activist, technocratic state but strengthens it because the state's decision-making capacity is enhanced by the private sector's participation as a source of information, expertise and, ultimately, legitimacy. Moreover, once the private sector is given the channel, the <u>need</u> for the financial-business community to seek alliances with political parties in order to influence policy decisions is lessened (Chai-Anan, 1990b, p.189).

Significantly, the Fifth Plan, drafted by civilian and military bureaucrats in close collaboration with one another, identified as the main objective of Thailand's development strategy the achievement of national stability. The guidelines for the Sixth Plan period also relate to the need for maintaining economic stability.

In the first three plans, co-ordination with the private sector was never acted on. The same laws from 50-100 years ago still apply today even though Thailand is in a different stage of growth altogether. Laws provide a convenient source of power and Thai officials do not want to change their power status. According to a convincing case study presented by Chai-Anan, the purpose of the JPPCC is to be used as a mechanism created and utilised by technocrats to arrange relations between the state and the private sector. It is a vehicle or a non-political body used by the technocrats, not only to establish a constructive alliance with industrialists, bankers and businessmen, but also to put pressure on the bureaucracy to initiate policy reforms. In this sense the technocrats are taking the role of reformers as well as guardians of the 'national interest' (Chai-Anan, 1990b, pp.193-4).

The Sixth Plan, like its predecessors, in essence consists of sets of policy statements, providing a very broad framework for the government agencies to follow. Being broad, lacking operational content, devoid of statutory enforcement, and unbinding of budget allocation, it provides much lee-way to the line ministries to interpret and exploit the plan as a useful reference only when they find it beneficial to do so. The overall direction of the Sixth Plan is to make structural adjustment and to solve problems by not creating them. According to the Plan, it aims to accomplish national development with efficiency, to attain the overall targets and to achieve an integrated system for government operations. This is to avoid duplication and lack of co-ordination within the public sector and to improve the efficiency of existing development instruments, the quality of government services, and co-operation between the public and private sectors. The latter, especially, is emphasised (Government of Thailand: NESDB, 1987, p.12).

Two major shifts became manifest in the Fifth and Sixth National Economic and Social Development Plans (1982-1986 and 1987-1991). These were:

(a) the initiation of a large-scale industrial development plan - the Eastern Seaboard Development Programme (ESDP) - following the discovery of natural gas in the Gulf of Thailand; and

(b) the protection granted to heavy industries producing intermediate and capital goods (Komin, 1991, p.115).

The implementation of these two plans required a stronger degree of intervention from the state than previously, and will undoubtedly strengthen regulative policies towards the entry of foreign investors and an increasing level of substitution to local business conglomerates.

Another recent example of the clash between ISI and EOI protagonists is the case of the automotive industry. The state's strategies to rationalise the auto industry took a new turn in the early 1980s, following the World Bank's advice regarding an industrial restructuring programme. The goals of the restructuring programme were to dismantle inefficient ISI industries and to embark upon export-oriented industrialisation (EOI). Since then, the state has been sharply divided into opponents and proponents of ISI. The resulting fragmented state caused a delay in policy-making during the early- to mid-1980s. Without strong leadership in the ISI coalition, the NESDB, backed by the World Bank, took control over the direction of the auto industry and declared a total freeze in 1983 without strong opposition from local parts firms, mostly due to the economic recession of the early 1980s.

The ISI coalition fought back when Ob, a nationalist with strong suspicions towards the Japanese, took office in 1983. His nationalist policy was strongly opposed by foreign assemblers as well as by other (EOI) government officials and technocrats, including his own deputy. Nevertheless, Ob's increased localisation programme was adopted in 1984. However, its unprecedented political influence was short-lived because of Ob's departure and a newly emergent political coalition in 1985. Ob's resignation ushered in a new political coalition which was a compromise between the ISI and the free trade technocrats. This case parallels the clash between the technocrats such as Phisit Pakkasem, of the Council of Economic Ministers, who indicated that it was necessary to accept IMF discipline, while others such as the then Bangkok Bank president, Boonchu Rojanastien, argued that "the government should not let the IMF control us" (Hewison, 1987, p.70).

Trade, industry and investment policies: between protectionism and deregulation

The Thai government runs a conservative monetary policy but an expansionary fiscal policy with large public sector deficits which, after a period of heavy external borrowing in the late 1970s and early 1980s, are now financed mainly by domestic borrowing. The savings rate was low and there was a large gap between savings and investment, resulting from an imperfectly developed capital market. However, as noted above, due to financial policies the gap has been considerably narrowed. Although the formal banking system is closely held by a few Thai-Chinese family business conglomerates, strong government guidance compensated for a distorted capital market and achieved a high degree of monetisation of the economy in 1988.

NESDB support to industries has been implemented through sectoral ministries regulation, direct intervention and substitution. Industries have been

> exempted from import tariffs, sales taxes, corporate income tax or reduction in the prices of water and electricity, which means a loss in government revenue ... [but] ... among the more important objectives that industrialization is expected to bring forth: employment generation, regionalization and export promotion, only the last objective has been met. The biggest failure of the Thai manufacturing sector is in its inability to absorb labour (Kaosa-ard and Israngkura, 1988, p.157).

Thailand's trade policies have been adjusted generally in response to developments in the balance of payments and in accordance with various government financing requirements but not formulated in the context of a clear-cut or enduring economic strategy (see OECD, 1992, pp.131-2). During the Third Plan period, from 1972-83, the import substitution policies that were put in place in plans of the previous period were joined by new export promotion policies. A number of conflicting policies in the early 1970s created a deteriorating balance of payments. These policies included the imposition of controls on interest rates and selected prices, and later combined with an expansion in government expenditure financed by accelerated foreign borrowing and domestic credit creation; increased protection of import competing industries, yet the parallel introduction of export incentives. By 1983, the fiscal and trade balances had worsened sharply, external debt had begun to build up, and growth had slowed. The government's subsequent reaction was to tighten monetary policy and to raise import restrictions.

The fourth period, from 1983 to the present, has been marked by the beginning of a commitment on the part of the state actively to promote exports. The decision of the policy-makers taken in the early 1980s to encourage an outward orientation to economic growth was motivated by economic difficulties stemming from external shocks, earlier policy mistakes, and the diminishing potential of Thailand's previously reliable engine of growth, agriculture. As earlier noted, the policy élite's strengthened interest in promoting exports was also underpinned by the possibility of creating employment for an expanding labour force.

Despite pressure from the World Bank, IMF, GATT, and the EOI technocrats, bureaucrats implemented tariff reforms that lowered marginally the overall nominal average tariff but reduced the dispersion of effective protection for the manufacturing sector. At the same time, however, in order to raise revenues, policy-makers introduced a general import duty surcharge that largely off-set the effects of the tariff reform. In late 1984, in a renewed effort to correct domestic and external imbalances, credit policy was tightened significantly, tax reforms were introduced, and the long-standing practice of fixing the baht to the U.S. dollar was abandoned. Instead, the baht was substantially devalued and pegged to a basket of currencies of Thailand's major trading partners. This devaluation was a major factor behind the improvement of international competitiveness in Thai industries which further increased in 1987 due mainly to the value appreciation of the Yen, the Korean Won, and the Taiwanese Yeun against the Dollar.

Investment incentives were also extended to encourage investment in EOI and labour-intensive industries. However these incentives were generally ineffective. Both the system of export financing and the network of investment incentives were highly concentrated on particular industries. In addition, export incentives were directed at firms exporting the near totality of their production, leaving practically no incentives for industries producing primarily for the domestic market to shift some of their production to exports, retarding both employment growth and the development of inter-industry linkages. Despite the intention towards deregulation on the part of the technocrats in the NESDB and their counterparts in the multilateral institutions, the bureaucrats in the line-ministries and domestic business succeeded in preserving the high protection rate of domestic industries.

By 1986, the structure of protection was essentially the same as it had been before the attempted reforms except that the revenue-generating power of the tariff structure had been strengthened considerably. The combination of external influences, a more flexible exchange rate policy, the absence of restrictions on foreign capital, the new (albeit targeted) EOI investment incentives, and the overall cautious attitude of the government seem to have overridden, during favourable times, the bias against exports in the tariff structure, which, in less propitious circumstances, had been the principal binding constraint (OECD, 1992, pp.132-3).

Impact of state intervention and regulation in Thailand

Taking the welfare dimension as a parameter for a successful investment strategy, several studies suggest that the effect has been limited. According to the investigation by Wonghanchao and Pongpissanupichit (1987, pp.245-6)

> The most important ... [finding is] ... that a large percentage of the promoted manufacturing firms in the sample, both foreign and local, are undesirable from the standpoint of welfare, despite the inclusion of the positive indirect social income effects. *This is to be expected as many of them are in import-competing industries, which usually exist and survive only with heavy protection from the government.* (my emphasis)

Furthermore, as earlier mentioned, "Thailand still lacks an effective system of screening, negotiating, registering and monitoring U.S. or any FDI activities" (*ibid.*, p.250).

Another problem with the EOI strategy is well described by Kaosa-ard and Israngkura (1988, p.193): "while the possibility of Thailand approaching NIC status has been hailed by foreign observers as well as some Thai technocrats and bureaucrats, it is important to remember that such a status is not the primary objective of development. Nor does it reflect the quality of development. Thailand cannot be considered as successfully moving ahead if the bulk of its population remains in the relatively low-income, stagnant agricultural sector." What is needed, not as a replication of the Japan and NIC experience but as a matter of up-grading the status of the rural population, is emphasis in economic policies on a non-urban-alternative.[9] The problem with the current policies is a need for stronger support by the state to enhance welfare in the rural areas: a revolution in private farming and marketing is needed; 'free trade' and market incentives are incapable of producing this by themselves. Private enterprise needs government support. So extended government intervention and expenditures on a massive scale in agriculture is essential. The basic question is: will the Thai government give the priority for finding and allocating the requisite funds? And, probably more important, will it be courageous enough to do this in opposition to the World Bank's orthodox dogma of 'privatising' at all costs? (Wonghanchao, 1988, p.7). The essential problem is the lack of land reform which was crucial in the success of Japan, Taiwan and South Korea. "To permit and facilitate these changes in agricultural production, changes in the social structure and tenure patterns must occur. Most of Thailand's farmers do not own their land and therefore, do not qualify for the bank loans necessary to stimulate these developments." (*ibid.*, p.7).[10] About 40 per cent of rural labour are still waiting on a solution to property rights to the land they claim (DANIDA, 1990, p.10). A related problem concerns the large number of rural poor because, "when world commodities experience price slumps as was the case in 1986, the proportion of people under poverty line increased to 29.5 per cent. With subsequent improvements in world commodity prices in 1989, this proportion again dropped to 23.7 per cent, clearly confirming that world commodity prices are crucial in determining rural poverty conditions in Thailand." (Government of Thailand: NESDB, 1992, p.99). Another paradox inherent in the EOI strategy is the fact that "[f]oreign investment has less contributed to employment expansion than local investment, because their firms are more capital intensive than the local ones" and "industrial investment will strengthen rather than lessen unemployment problems in Thailand in the next decade" (Chiengkul, *et.al.*, 1984, pp.113-4).

In short, the costs of EOI and the efforts of attracting FDI are seriously exceeding the benefits. Thailand's competitive edge is determined by stable supplies of non-unionised labour, low environmental regulation, 'flexible' land-use regulations and low land prices, and the relative absence of well-organised middle-class social movements demanding improvements in and greater regulation of social, economic and environmental problems. The outcome of this process is recognised by NESDB planners. Growing disparities in income and prosperity widened sharply but no detailed policy instruments or operational framework are provided in the Seventh Plan, suggesting that nothing has changed (Government of Thailand: NESDB, 1992, pp.99-163).

The 1974-1976 democratic experiment was easily overturned partly because its efforts to help farmers hurt Bangkok. This experience, together with the infamous Black May incident in 1992, undoubtedly forced the Chuan administration to rely on the bureaucracy when it came to implementing decentralisation. Gubernatorial elections, more power to local administrative bodies and the making of the *tambon* (commune) councils into juristic entities ended up with giving the Interior Ministry even more power than it had before. Several mass protests by villagers in 1993 over land rights and dam construction marked the inefficiency of implementation and the vested interests of the alliance between the bureaucracy and capital. Democratisation and decentralisation of decision-making power appears to be almost impossible in a country where disparities between urban and rural areas have widened during the last three decades. Average incomes in the Isan provinces of North-East Thailand were 2,961 baht/household in 1988 compared with an average household income for Bangkokians of 7,793 baht.[11]

According to the East Asian experience, "[t]he periods of greatest economic growth in Japan coincide with periods of growing authoritarianism, not with periods of democracy, as Western theory suggests." (Johnson, 1989, p.66). The pre-conditions for this specific authoritarian regimeform is the differentiation between reigning and ruling: "[r]eigning is a very specific activity: it involves creating genuine political stability, correcting excesses committed by the bureaucracy, promoting entrepreneurship, and avoiding the usual consequences of state intervention in economic affairs - namely, bureaucratism, corruption, and a misallocation of resources." (Johnson, 1986, p.563). But, it is precisely these problems which characterise Thai policy-making and they are inherent in the symbiotic relationship between business and line-ministries.[12]

Conclusion

Despite a history of instability in the regimeform, Thailand ranks high compared with her South-East Asian neighbours in terms of growth and macro-economic parameters. Thai policy-makers maintain a significant level of stable conservative performance in macro-management of the economy and continue to implement cautious fiscal and monetary policies and a flexible exchange rate policy. The Seventh Five-Year Development Plan (1992-1996) differs from earlier plans in its main target, which is improvement of income distribution, whereas formerly the objective was solely based on economic growth and stability. However, the global retreat of the welfare state towards what could be called the competitive state means a reduction of public spending and public sector borrowing, for they drive up interest rates and displace investment. The current polity and ideology in the contemporary world economy is mercantilist, not minimalist or liberal. Yet it is not clear that Thailand is well-placed to move on to the next step of economic development. A recent World Bank study of six East Asian countries concluded that Thailand was the only one that had failed to make significant in-roads into poverty and social inequity. Through the 1970s, 1980s and the beginning of the 1990s, some 9 million were classed as 'absolute poor'. As the bank noted, "in 1990 Thailand's incidence [of poverty] was as high as Indonesia's, even though its average GNP per capita was 2.5 times higher." (World Bank, 1993, p.8).

In this setting the basic developmental objective is the military establishment's assertion of a virtual entitlement to control the executive. Thailand's present regimeform has been labelled various ways: semi-democratic, bureaucratic authoritarianism with limited pluralism, mandarin oriental capitalism, and a bourgeois praetorian political system. However, as noted above it does not make any sense, because the regimeform is able to change from one day to the other, but the bureaucracy remains intact. Thus, the paternalistic developmental state is a more accurate term. It is difficult to find any evidence indicating a change in the attitude of the private sector towards state authoritarianism. Direct and indirect repression continues to rule the relationship between capital and its intermediary, the state, and on the other side labour and peasant organisations. The chance for Thailand turning into a NIC seems premature since about 70 per cent of the total labour force remains dependent on agriculture and in the stagnation of rural poverty.

Concluding this chapter, it is apparent that Thailand has followed a neo-mercantilist policy approach to cope with its integration into the world economy. Despite pressure from the multilateral peak organisations - the World Bank, the IMF and the technocrats in the Ministry of Finance, NESDB and the Central Bank - the alliance between bureaucrats from the line-ministries and local business has had some success in avoiding the worst trappings of readjustment. Thus protectionism, nominal tariffs and non-tariff barriers continue to be a salient feature of Thai industry and trade policies.

What is new about the 'new' theory of business as the vanguard of democracy is difficult to comprehend. The comparative advantage of Thailand's business sector has been and continues to be the exclusion of labour, whether rural or urban, from participation and social benefits. This is further confirmed by the indicative and related approach to planning which brings considerable doubt as to whether any welfare improving implementation will take place at all.

Technocrats and state managers have a firm grip over macro-economic policy-making and the process of formulating and implementing plans. When it comes to sectoral policies, the interest of business does not indicate a renewed focus on democracy, participation or a deliberate state-guided distribution of welfare. The major influence of business is reduced to getting state subsidies in various sectors and protection based on low labour costs and no trade union activism. On the other hand, external events and actors still play a considerable role, direct and indirect, through various instruments and pressures on policy-making. At the moment the multilateral advice is to introduce income distribution and the reduction of poverty in planning. But it remains to be seen if the ideology of 'trickle-down' is still part of that advice, or whether a genuine policy recipe and a framework for implementation will arise.

Notes

1 The characterization of the political system then was: "... a government having a secularized and functionally specialized bureaucracy, staffed by career officers but not subject to control by extrabureaucratic political institutions, would have the characteristics of a 'bureaucratic polity'. Such a polity was defined in terms of the domination of the official class as a ruling class, even though formal constitutional charters and ceremonial doctrines of government might give lip service to modern ideas of popular sovereignty or traditional concepts of royal and divine sovereignty." (Riggs, 1966, p.396).

2 The shift to export orientation in the 1970s reflected "[t]he increased influence of big capital within the Thai Political Economy" (Hewison, 1987, p.57). In his 1989 work, Hewison defines an early symbiotic relationship between Thai big capital and the state in the following way: "This is not to suggest that either the state or capital is dominant in theoretical terms, but rather that both have particular roles determined by the nature of class relations" (Hewison, 1989, p.213). This symbiosis is manifest: "there are significant linkages between state officials, both past and present, and the capitalist class; indeed there is considerable overlap between the two groups" (1989, p.206).

3 For an application of this theoretical framework on economic policy-making in the ASEAN-4, see Schmidt, 1993b.

4 Neo-mercantilism is a complex phenomenon grounded in developmentalist nation- and state-building and survival. It goes beyond traditional efforts to protect domestic production through tariffs or other restrictions; it includes dumping, export subsidies, certain types of industrial policies, as well as so-called voluntary export or import agreements, monetary nationalism, and various forms of 'beggar-my-neighbour' policies. But the basic question is concerned with the objectives and instruments of trade policy: are latecomers to industrialization and thus liberalisation reaping too many benefits from free trade and the opening of new markets?

5 It still remains unclear how trade in technology is performing and how government institutions intervene when the case is judged unfair (see Sueo Sekiguchi, 1983, p.14n; p.24).

6 See also Mackie, 1988. However, Mackie (p.290) dismisses the Japanese model as useless in a South-East Asian context: "What is most striking about this analysis, however, is the fact that <u>none</u> of the four

elements in Johnson's explanation could be said to be strongly evident in any of the ASEAN Four countries."

7 The OECD in 1979 defined the four following characteristics of NIC status as: (i) they are pursuing an outward-looking policy (which means the promotion of growth through exports; (ii) they are increasing their share of industrial production and exports; (iii) domestically, they are increasing the share of manufacturing industry in total production, total exports and total employment; and (iv) they are rapidly reducing the gaps in per capita income (real GDP) *vis-à-vis* the industrialized countries (OECD, 1979).

8 For a good account on the heavy involvement of these two agencies in Thai policy formulation see: Hewison, 1987, pp.69-79; also Sahasakul, 1992.

9 The daily media covers other suggestions and a broad-based debate on this issue. See for instance "Do we want to be a NIC!", *The Nation*, 30 August 1988; and Thanong Khanthong, "Buddhistic Economy: Happiness for Everyone", *The Nation*, 5 September 1988.

10 For a good case study pointing to the failures of plan implementation in rural development see Charoensin-o-larn, 1988.

11 For other indicators of the extreme primacy of Bangkok versus the rest of Thailand - the so-called 'diseconomies of scale' - see Jonathan Rigg and Philip Scott, 1992, p.106. See also Chapter 1.

12 See also Turton, 1989, pp.72-74. He is in line with the arguments of Girling and Hewison, but adds the autonomy of the military as an important dimension which enjoys "...a momentum of its own somewhat hybrid, parasitic, 'secondary complex of predatory interests'" *ibid.*, p. 73.

5 The Thai manufacturing sector: New patterns of expansion

Jean-Christophe Simon

Introduction

The gradual emergence of manufacturing activities in Thailand over the past twenty-five years has brought about a situation that is both promising and full of challenges. From a relatively narrow base in the early 1970s, the manufacturing sector has grown to the present structure that is both much larger (in terms of companies and employment) and wider (in terms of range of products, skills and activities). The dynamics of industrial expansion have also brought substantial qualitative changes:[1]

(i) The recent acceleration of industrial expansion has made industry the engine of growth of the past decade, with a dramatic pattern of diversification of manufacturing activities. A characteristic feature of sectoral development is (a) the combination of internal market and export orientation, (b) the gradual up-grading of activities, and (c) increasing linkages between them. These new trends at the macro-level are reflected in the new manufacturing export mix and determine the international competitive advantage of the country;

(ii) At the micro-level, the impact on the social scene is also of particular significance: sub-contracting between formal and non-formal producers, webs of traders and manufacturers, and emerging groups of companies, are elements that hold promises and problems for the future. Challenges are also present in the workplace, as the first waves of industrial wage earners have been characterised by low qualifications, and high mobility. Current issues are increasing management capability (recruitment, experience) and training of labourers (formal and on-the-job) to allow industries' maturation and progress;

(iii) Institutions have changed too: industrial policy has re-focused its priorities in the 1980s on most issues ranging from incentives and trade promotion, regional targets, technology acquisition and labour educational improvement, as part of the strategy to keep up the momentum of industrialisation, and keep abreast of the new wa South-East Asian NICs.

One of the key elements brought forward by Amsden (1989) in her study of industrialisation in South Korea, is that late-comers among the industrialised nations have benefited from both existing state-of-the-art technologies to enable them to expand their manufacturing sector and compete with more advanced nations (e.g. in the automobile industry), and from a holy alliance of the business sector and bureaucracy aimed at selecting the appropriate strategies to assert the national position among the leading economic powers in the world economy. The late 1980s have shown that Thailand in her turn has put these forces into motion. The gradual opening up of the Thai economy has indeed allowed the participation of foreign capital and introduction of state-of-the-art technologies for considerable widening of the industrial base (particularly in the petrochemical and electronics sectors).

Thailand's industrialisation has also benefited in two ways from the experience of the East Asian NICs themselves:

(i) The influx of industrial investment from South Korea and Taiwan during the late 1980s, following adjustments in monetary policy, brought a substantial transfer of capital, and to a lesser extent experience and know-how, as most of the new industrial ventures were labour intensive;

(ii) During this period there were also many occasions for the country to reflect upon the experience of its predecessors on the industrialisation path as many seminars and expert meetings held in Thailand emphasised the comparison between the Asian groups of NICs.[2] This source of inspiration clearly also influenced the business community, the economic press and the public policy-makers.

In this context, there are several distinctive features that make the emergence of manufacturing activities in the Thai case original when compared to the East Asian NIC experience:

(i) Firstly, the manufacturing sector was slow to emerge as a driving force in the economy. This late burgeoning can be attributed to the abundance of natural resources, the tapping of which generated enough wealth to sustain the economy for several decades, from the 1950s to the 1970s. Primary products were considered a key asset for a developing economy until the closing of the rural frontier. The processing of natural resources (agro-food, marine and forest products) remained the basis of manufacturing activities until the mid-1980s, and is still a major component of production. The attitude of Thailand towards its neighbours indicates that this strategy is likely to be pursued further;

(ii) The recognition of industry as a national priority was only occasionally stated until the beginning of the 1980s. Few local entrepreneurs were keen to invest in industry, as a wide range of other activities provided, and still provide, good opportunities for investment - ranging from agricultural diversification, construction and tourism to land and property. The recent industrial diversification has brought together the initiatives of local entrepreneurs and foreign investors (including a large number from East Asian NICs), creating many joint-ventures between them (which was not the case in South Korea at a comparable stage of development);

(iii) In a similar manner, the state lacked the determination to set clear priorities, mobilise resources, establish strong incentives or supporting measures, as had earlier been the case in South Korea; this was partly due to a lack of vision, and also to a reliance on agricultural diversification to enable the country to pursue rent-seeking strategies for several decades. The government nevertheless succeeded in keeping the fundamentals of the economy on track through strict macro-economic policies (and occasional adjustment), thus offering industrialists both mild protection and stability.

Industrialisation and the emergence of manufacturing activities

A steady process of industrial development

In Thailand the process of industrial development was steady but took a long time to gain impetus, and it would thus be wrong to speak of a quick industrial miracle. The manufacturing sector (excepting rice and timber mills) consisted of just a few companies in the 1950s and there was no 'big push' of industries as occurred in South Korea or Taiwan. As Isarankura (1969, p.266) puts it

> even if it were granted that the government could command adequate resources to carry out a 'big push' programme, there would still be serious obstacles due to supply and demand limitations.

The comments of Charoenloet (1971, p.5), who wrote about the early years of development during the 1960s, explain that the process was slow to take off because the starting point was so low:

> one of the major obstacles to industrial growth in Thailand is the smallness of the home market. Another factor which limits the growth of industries is the lack of natural resources - fuel and energy, inadequate transportation. An equally serious deterrent to industrial development is the lack of capitalist entrepreneurship. People who have higher incomes and wealth tend to use their resources in relatively unproductive ventures.

The industrial base, although weak in both size and dynamism, was already firmly established in the early 1970s. The manufacturing sector consisted mostly of food processing and textiles, plus machinery and chemicals (see Table 5.1). Industrial expansion went through several stages: in particular, the development of import substituting activities in the 1960s and the first wave of the manufacturing export boom of the mid-1970s. It took about two decades to achieve a substantial level of manufacturing activity: in 1975 agricultural production had a clear lead over industry (25% and 20% of GDP, respectively);

during the late seventies and early eighties, agricultural and manufacturing activities had a similar weight in the gross domestic product (around 20-22%). Thereafter, the expansion of the manufacturing sector was impressive, as is clearly shown in Table 5.2. The growth of manufacturing value added during the early seventies (averaging 8% per annum from 1971-75) is comparable to the beginning of the present decade (7.5 % p.a. in 1990-93).

Table 5.1
Contribution of Selected Industrial Sectors to Manufacturing Value-Added

	1980 (%)	1990 (%)
Food, beverages	31.9	25.5
Textiles, leather	26.4	27.5
Furniture, wood products	3.4	1.7
Paper, printing	1.9	2.6
Chemicals, petroleum, plastics	12.3	10.4
Minerals, metals	3.9	5.7
Machinery, equipment	14.3	16.2
Others	5.8	10.5

Source: NESDB data.

Even at the beginning of the 1980s, Tambunlertchai (1983, p.1) could not anticipate the strong acceleration of the industrial sector's expansion that took place in the middle of the decade

> the shift from domestic sales to exporting is not a smooth process and usually only a few industries in a country can be successfully moved from import substitution to export expansion.

In fact, the transition from the import-substitution phase to a new export-oriented drive was already well on its way at that time, but the bulk of industry in Thailand was still geared towards the domestic market (see also Ariff and Hill, 1985). Manufacturing development accelerated in the late 1980s[3] when the country passed though the threshold of the industrial age, or 'graduated' as an NIC: in 1987, the manufacturing sector's share shot above the 25 per cent benchmark which in fact was barely enough to justify the 'NIC label' fashioned by the popular press. The manufacturing sector's share is now about 30 per cent of GDP. More interestingly, manufacturing contributed to a 40 per cent increase of GDP during the period 1990-93, while agriculture contributed only about 6.5 per cent.

Table 5.2
Growth in the Contribution of the Manufacturing Sector to GDP

	1971-1975	1976-1980	1981-1985	1986-1990	1990-1993
Mean Share of GDP (a)					
Agriculture	25.4	22.2	20	16.8	13.1
Manufacturing	18.9	21.6	21.4	23.3	28.8
Trade	16.8	16.8	16.5	17.2	17.8
Average Annual Growth (b)					
Agriculture	2.9	2.8	3.8	2.9	2.9
Manufacturing	8	6.7	3.4	11.6	7.7
Finance	4.7	8	7.1	23	9.8
Largest Share in GDP Growth (c)					
Agriculture	16.6	10.6	17.8	5.6	7.1
Manufacturing	31.8	23.8	16.4	30.8	41.1
Trade	19.2	16.9	12	20.5	14.1
Finance	2.7	3.5	4.5	10.2	12.1

Source: NESDB data.

Notes: all the above figures are per centages, based on value added at constant 1972 prices. The last period, 1990-93, is based on the new series at constant 1988 prices, in order to reflect new structural changes in the economy.

(a) relative share of largest sectors in GDP, with average for each period.

(b) average annual growth for the sectors with the highest performance in 1992.

(c) contribution of each sector to the growth of GDP for the given period - i.e. the relative share in the increase of value added.

Table 5.3
Employment in Industry

	1970	1980	1992
Labour force	15,600,000	23,000,000	30,000,000
Participation rate	44%	49%	52%
Wage labour in manufacturing (a)	42%	49%	57%
Industrial employment	1,950,000	2,650,000	3,600,000
Export zones (b)	0	2,800	35,000

Sources: National Statistical Office; (a) NESDB; (b) I.L.O.

Throughout that period, and until now, manufacturing development has had little employment effect as the bulk of job supply was, and still is, in the agricultural sector (see Table 5.3). A considerable number of jobs classified as manufacturing are in 'informal' activities rather than the formal wage earning category: according to the official Thai ascription, non-registered plus self-employed. The persistence of seasonal labour migration is reflected in employment variation according to the slack dry season, when there is excess of labour in the fields, and the peak season, when many people leave factories, workshops and city jobs to go back to rural activities.

Table 5.4
Sectoral Share of Manufacturing Value-Added

%	1975	1980	1985	1990	1994
Agro-based	32	31	32	19	17
Textiles	23	24	24	21	22
Emerging	13	16	18	25	29

Source: NESDB/ADB.

Note: Agro-based refers to food- and fish-processing, beverages, tobacco, rubber.
Textiles refers to textiles and garments.
Emerging groups includes electronics, automotive, etc.

Considering the role of agriculture in overall growth, it is not surprising that the first two decades of manufacturing expansion were agro-based to a large extent: post-harvest processing of basic agricultural products, such as rice and sugar mills, kenaf or cassava processing, accounted for the majority of registered plants in the period 1960-70. But progressively, new activities such as fruit- and fish-canning and poultry-breeding have emerged thanks to rapidly expanding foreign markets. They were followed later by production geared to the affluent urban markets, such as the manufacture of milk products, soft drinks and instant foods. Many of the food processing activities are still small-scale plants, province-based to serve a large local and regional population. This explains why the relative weight of all processing activities related to agriculture and fisheries remained strong until the mid-1980s: about one-third of manufacturing value added was directly related to fisheries and agricultural activities. The agro-food sector represents just 17 per cent of manufacturing value-added today, and an extra 8 per cent is derived from wood products and rubber processing, and from light engineering directly related to agricultural equipment and implements (see Table 5.4).

This feature gives justification to those Thai economists who coined the concept of "NABIC" or Newly Agro-Based Industrialising Country (see Santikarn, in Ikemoto and Wonghanchao, 1988, p.192) in order to acknowledge the agricultural component and linkages with the expansion of manufacturing activities. Their point is particularly strong for the period until the early 1980s, with expanding acreage generating several hundred new rice mills in northern and northeastern provinces, and new plants for the processing of sugar, cassava and edible oils. They also rightly forecast the on-going decline in the use in industry of natural inputs produced in the country (marine products and timber, imports of which are increasing, and natural fibres, where production is in decline). Furthermore, the current rapid diversification is changing the industrial development pattern, with a contraction of the relative share of the agro-food sector and the processing of natural primary products. In that respect the current balance between agricultural and industrial inputs as a base for manufacturing activities in the country is not likely to last unless a more even pattern of growth between primary - mostly agricultural - and industrial growth can be restored.

Diversification of sectors and multiplication of enterprises

The last decade has been a turning point in the diversification of the industrial sector. This could probably be explained by the conjunction of two phenomena:

(i) National development policy, and entrepreneurs' strategies, have shown an increasing awareness of the potential for new forms of production for both the internal and export markets; and

(ii) A host of new foreign or joint-venture manufacturing firms started operations in 1986-89. This reflects the relocation of direct investment from East Asian and, to a lesser extent, European countries and the USA (Lall, 1990).

All sectors have grown at a fast rate, ranging from the production of most consumer goods to a growing variety of intermediary and equipment goods, and regardless of whether their production is geared towards the domestic market or to exports. This development is epitomised in the expansion of sectors such as petrochemicals or electrical goods: the petrochemicals sector was boosted by the exploitation of natural gas resources, and has now developed a comprehensive structure of up-stream and down-stream activities in addition to oil refining (see Tingsabadh, 1987).

A combination of export orientation and domestic market boom

The manufacturing boom has undoubtedly been market-driven: it has benefited from both the widening of the local consumer market (and particularly the demand emanating from new urban consumers) and the newly-acquired international position of Thailand as a manufacturer supplying world markets.

Table 5.5
Relative Share of Manufactured Exports, 1970-1994

	1970	1975	1980	1985	1990	1994
Trade Opening [(a)]	30	37	47	44	68	69
Export ratio [(b)]	10	15	20	19	29	31
Share of Agro-Food Products.	49	60	47	46		25
Share of Non-Food Manufacturing Products	15	20	32	41		66

Source: Thai Customs data.

Notes: (a) Exports plus imports in relation to current GNP;
(b) Exports/ G.N.P

The new domination of manufactured exports is in line with the opening up of the economy: the ratio of exports plus imports to GNP was 28 per cent in 1970, 48 per cent in 1980 and about 70 per cent in 1994 (see Table 5.5). During the same period the share of manufactured exports (excluding food products) grew from 15 to 66 per cent of all exports (see Table 5.6). This structural change is also reflected in the mix of products found in the new export pattern: in 1993, eleven out of the top fifteen export products were manufactured goods. In addition to the change in the ranking of the top ten, it is interesting to note that the ten items amounted to 75 per cent of exports in 1970, but represent only 45 per cent of all export products now. This is evidence of the much wider spectrum of products that is presently exported. There are, however, differences in the performance of the major manufacturing products, as Brummit *et.al.* (1992) show: "three sectors alone accounted for about 75% of the increase in the 1980s - machinery and electrical products, cloth and leather, and canned goods." The measurement of comparative advantages also shows that newly exported products have shown the highest growth rate over the period 1985-92: these are computers and electrical goods, leather and garments, and plastic products. In this context exporters of manufacturing products have benefited from both increased market diversification, and privileged access to markets in the USA and Europe through such mechanisms as the System of Preferences (Chirathivat, 1988).

Table 5.6
The Top Ten Exports of Thailand, 1970-1993

1970		1980		1993	
Rice	17	Rice	15	Garments	9.5
Rubber	5	Tapioca	11	Computer	6.5
Maize	13	Rubber	9	Jewellery	4.3
Tin	11	Tin	9	Plastics	4.2
Tapioca	8	Maize	5	Prawns	4
Jute	5	Garments	4	Rubber	4
Beans	2	Cut stones	2	Integrated Circuits	3.8
Prawns	2	Sugar	2	Rice	3.5
Tobacco	1	Prawns	1	Footwear	3
Timber	1	Canned fruit	1	Caned seafood	2

Source: Thai Customs data (% of total exports).

Local markets have created the pull factor for a wide range of products. The production of construction materials and standard consumer goods (beverages, toiletries, home appliances) has grown steadily over the past decades to satisfy an ever-widening market in rural and urban areas. Most industrial conglomerates have started and then thrived on a local market basis (see Box 5.1): Saha Union in the textile business, Charoen Phokpand in the processing of animal feed and foodstuffs, Saha Pattana in consumer goods (from garments to household products), not to mention myriad family-controlled companies in the automobile, chemical, basic metal and textile sectors. This deepening of activity geared to the local market was at the centre of the debate about a second phase of import substitution and industrial restructuring in the early 1980s (Akrasanee *et.al.*, 1987) and the 'adjustment crisis' in 1985-86 was further evidence of the importance of internal sales for local industries.[4] Contrary to common belief, the rate of exports of industrial sectors is still limited, when measured in global terms - although obviously a product-based analysis would give different results. At present only about one-third of the production of durable consumer goods such as refrigerators, air conditioners and washing machines is exported.

Box 5.1
Diversification of an Industrial Giant:
The Siam Cement Group

The diversification of manufacturing production is epitomised in the recent transformation of the Siam Cement Group (SCG) from a national producer of cement and construction material into a conglomerate at the forefront of the new phase of manufacturing initiated in the 1980s.

The historical sources of Siam Cement lie in a monarchy-sponsored industrial company, established in 1913, and open to foreign collaboration. The Siam Cement Group is still under the controlling influence of the Crown Property Bureau (with a share of about 25%), but has embarked on an ambitious strategy aimed at gaining a leading position in several sectors of strategic importance for the future of the country.

Since the mid-1980s, in addition to an ever-increasing position in the cement, refractory and construction material business, SCG has expanded its capacity in the pulp and paper industry, and initiated projects in the chemical sector (synthetic latex, polyethylene). The group is also famous for equipment and machinery activities that have been considerably diversified over the past years, such as engines and parts (with Japanese partners), tyres (with Michelin from France), compressors, and so on. Beyond these fundamental sectors SCG is now also active in trading and consumer goods production (e.g. TV tubes and assembly with NEC from Japan), and to a limited extent in the food processing sector (also with Japanese partners). To serve some of these development it has developed its own industrial estate, north of Bangkok, and also has plants on the two public estates of the Eastern Seaboard.

After having maintained an exclusively national base, the group is now also seeking opportunities for export sales mostly in neighbouring countries (cement), but also on world markets (TVs, sanitaryware), and for investment in South-East Asia (especially Indonesia and the Philippines).

For a company whose activity had been limited to construction material for almost half a century, this evolution can be viewed as a challenging turn-about. Nonetheless, there is considerable basis for optimism about the future: SCG is famous for its management abilities, market appraisal and cautious policies. It can mobilise financial resources easily, and its stock is one of the few industrial blue chips of the Securities Exchange of Thailand. It has been careful to seek alliances with local companies and major foreign partners in order to limit capital exposure or to acquire the best technology and know-how. In addition, the group has undertaken a revamping of its top management structure, and promoted an ambitious internal training scheme to make sure its staff are up to the new tasks.

The textile and garment industry

The textile and garment industry is an obvious case of rapid sectoral development that is based on local and export markets: it is well known that it developed first as an import substitution industry and then increased its export-orientation in the mid-1970s, when garment exports increased rapidly. Product diversification and the multiplication of businesses resulted in a comprehensive industrial structure that was large, and in most cases nationally controlled and operated. Garments only emerged as one of the ten major export products in 1973 when, together with other textile products, they accounted for a mere 3 per cent of exports by value. By 1984 this proportion had reached the 10 per cent mark, and the sector has maintained its position thereafter.

However, the textiles sector cannot be said to be typically export-oriented: data computed from the NESDB (1985, p.28) show a global rate of export for the entire textile industry shifting from 10 per cent in 1975 to about 14 per cent in 1980 (passing a peak of 18% in 1978). The agglomeration of the various sub-sectors hides the fact that some activities, like garment production, are much more export-driven than others. Nowadays, the up-stream companies (cotton and artificial fibre-spinning) target most of their production to the local weaving mills (25% only of these two categories of product are directly exported); these mills in turn supply a garment sector that exports officially between 50-65 per cent of its production. This does not take into account a substantial amount of invisible and border trade exporting that is assumed to be in the range of 10 per cent of total volume in the case of garments. The local market presents increasing possibilities to sell higher-grade textiles - good quality material for fashion garments is in demand. In this way production has become market- and competition-driven (as opposed to relying on stable bulk orders for cheap products).

Small and large companies have demonstrated their mastery of three major skills: one is the flexibility to adapt their production to a wider range of customers in order to conquer new markets (children's clothes for Europe, the Middle East and Japan differ widely!); another is awareness of potential benefits to be gained from diversification and quality improvements (see Boxes 5.2 and 5.3); and thirdly, the ability to exploit fully connections to foreign markets, either through buying agents from regional hubs such as Hong Kong or through the local trading companies that play a key role in the industry.

In our survey we found that a significant proportion of the garment companies that we visited between 1990 and 1992 have based their development strategy on this dualism of markets by selling to both the local and export markets (see Tables 5.7 and 5.8). Many companies in the garment sector were initiated in the late 1970s to supply the local market only, and then managed to find an outlet in exports: only a few (about 30%) did so directly, the remainder operating through trading companies (45%) or under sub-contracting arrangements with local manufacturers (25%). Among the non-exporting firms are those that chose to sell to the local market (e.g. department stores) or had acquired licenses to produce fashionable international brands. Most exporters showed an ability both to expand into new markets (e.g. the Middle East and Africa) and even to deal with restrictive import practices (either by perverting the control procedures or by diverting exports through intermediary markets). A limited proportion of companies benefited from government promotion or assistance, but the majority of surveyed entrepreneurs declared that personal networks were more conducive to the expansion of export markets.

Box 5.2

From Sweat and Noise to Industry

Many of the agricultural machinery plants - commonly found in major towns of the Central Plain but also increasingly in major cities of Isan - certainly qualify for the 'sweat-shop' and even 'noise-shop' label, as they consist of units or assembly lines where pieces of metal are cut, pressed, welded, and integrated with components such as gearboxes, engines and electrical apparatus, to make equipment ranging from simple carts and tube pumps, to small tractors or even small combine harvesters for paddy fields. The entrepreneurs have benefited from the expansion in the market for agricultural implements, together with the changing cultivation techniques. The local paddy combine harvester is a good case of adapted technology meeting the new needs of farmers at a time of scarce labour.

A plant surveyed in Nakhon Pathom province showed that mechanical engineering ventures are most frequently based on the personal initiative of an experienced mechanic (some of them came from the transport sector, or even tin-dredging activity). The entrepreneur also needs an acute sense of commerce to attract customers, provide reliable maintenance and consider improvements to the machines. This is frequently achieved through 'imitative innovation', based on ingenuity, without support from a licence or a larger company, and no formal technical or financial support from a public institution.

Box 5.3

An Entrepreneur in the Garment Boom

A typical garment producing firm, the case study enterprise was founded in the Phaya Thai district of Bangkok in 1970 by a former shop employee. In the beginning only 10 sewing machines were enough to produce clothes sold to stores and wholesalers in the local market. Expansion in the following decade brought the capacity to 50 machines with 80 workers employed in the peak season, and the firm's size then doubled in the following decade. At the beginning of the 1990s more than 300 people were working in the factory, which is now under a limited company established in 1986 to facilitate exports.

The entrepreneur declared that his previous work gave him experience about garment types, quality, and production networks, and confidence that he could initiate his own business to serve customers whose demand was increasing in a prosperous country. He had enough funds from his savings and family contributions to start and expand the company.

Sales management was crucial for the expansion of the company: the entrepreneur developed strong connections with local trading companies and then directly with a customer from Japan. Through his requirements, this customer contributed to improvement of quality and production, and even offered to initiate a large garment producing joint-venture. But the entrepreneur declined because of the large financial commitment and he preferred instead to establish a new textile printing business for his son.

Table 5.7
Characteristics of Selected Entrepreneurs in the Export Sector

% of respondents	Toys and Handicrafts (b)	Canning Industry (a, b)	Garment Industry (a)
Venture created for exports only	95	90	80
Established company from start-up	100	95	65
Family funds in capital	–	–	75
Promotion from Board of Investment	90	75	35
Assistance from Ministry of Industry or Commerce	–	25	15
Collaboration with professional network	10	40	45
Collaboration or joint-venture with foreigners	80	75	25
Work with local trading company	–	25	45
Work with sub-contractors	15	–	25
Exported to new markets over past 5 years	80	85	85

Source: (a) Author's survey with ORSTOM-CUSRI, 1990-93; (b) Federation of Thai Industries, 1992.

Table 5.8
Results of a Survey of Manufacturers in Six Thai Provinces

% affirmative responses	Garments	Engineering	Food processing
A single manufacturing company as main business	85	95	95
Profitability within 3 yrs of start-up	90	100	80
Family collaboration to start firm	85	55	25
Entrepreneur's education level up to secondary	95	65	70
At least two executives educated to university level	25	35	15
Production for local market	55	100	45
At least 20% export sales	65	0	75
Family collaboration to run firm	85	35	25
Member of professional association	20	15	55

Source: Author's survey with ORSTOM-CUSRI, 1990-93, based on 62 interviews with founder/entrepreneurs or factory managers.

Manufacturing development and leading actors

Late industrialisation and state intervention to promote manufacturing industry

The role of the state in manufacturing development has been rather limited: it is a characteristic feature of Thailand that government intervention has been focused more on general macro-economic policy, with less energy and fewer resources devoted to the direct support of firms (see also the chapter by Johannes Schmidt in this volume). As a new-generation NIC, the country has certainly benefited from the experience of the East Asian countries in regard to to some of the policies which were implemented in the late 1980s.

The vigorous expansion of manufacturing activities was not anticipated in the early 1970s, and neither was it deliberately programmed over the subsequent span of 20 years. In reality, public policy on industry was vague, with few targets, restrictive administrative ambitions, little means to intervene and, above all, a lack of vision about the prospects for industrialisation. Evidence of a growing awareness of the increasing importance of manufacturing activities and the need for a new impetus for industrial growth was to be found mostly in the new policies of the early 1980s:

(i) The 'Thai Inc.' policy, promoted by the Deputy Premier Minister Boonchu Rojanasatien in the early 1980s, put a clear emphasis on new large-scale industrial investment, backed by public infrastructure and an increased openness to international companies. A heritage of this short-lived policy was the Eastern Seaboard Development Programme;

(ii) The 1982-86 economic stabilisation period was marked by efforts to reorganise the public enterprises, and to improve the international competitiveness of the manufacturing sector. For example, the NESDB sponsored studies and meetings to encourage industrial restructuring and to encourage a greater capacity for manufactured exports (NESDB, 1985).

A constant feature of the institutional framework was the weakness of the Ministry of Industry. It was, and still is, ranked low in the government posts hierarchy (relatively to the 'majors' such as Interior, Agriculture, Finance, Commerce, Defence and Foreign Affairs). Therefore it failed to attract the attention of ambitious politicians in need of a launching pad for their career, or brilliant civil servants for whom co-ordinating or financial public bodies had more appeal. Its budget is limited and it does not have a great deal of control or scope for initiative over manufacturing exports policy (which comes under the Ministry of Commerce), foreign investment selection (under the Board of Investment), or technology improvement (under the Ministry of Science and Technology). In addition, the public manufacturing enterprises (distilleries, sugar or paper mills) have never been at the forefront of industrial activity: they were too small compared to those under other ministries (such as Transport and Communication). In the 1980s, the inclusion of the new companies of the rapidly-growing petroleum sector has changed this picture slightly in favour of the Ministry of Industry, but it has occurred at a time when technocrats have to bargain with politicians and businessmen to discuss industrial priorities and share spheres of power and interest. This was well demonstrated in the changes which occurred at the top of major public enterprises such as the Petroleum Authority of Thailand or the Industrial Authority of Thailand.

In the national plans, the dimensions of manufacturing development were broadly taken into account as part of the general orientation of the economy - whether to increase exports in the late 1970s, or restructure and adjust to constraints in the early 1980s. The plans did include specific targets of expected growth, employment or exports, and were vague in terms of priority policy measures which were most appropriate in order to reach these targets. Continuity of policies and policy evaluation were also weak throughout the period (Tambunlertchai, in Warr, 1993). The Sixth Plan (1987-91) was more specific in terms of the targeting of sectors such as agro-industry and engineering, or regional and medium-sized industry, but came up with no particularly fresh policies to support these industries at a time when the private sector had a free hand to initiate all sorts of activities. The most distinctive feature of industrial policy, particularly that enunciated in the the Seventh Plan (1992-1996), is its submission to the general economic policy of expansion, liberalisation and a controlled opening-up to the global economy. The underlying assumption of public policy is that a growing and open economy will be a stimulus for industrial development independently of public sectoral policies that would in any case be difficult to implement given the low administrative capability and the high bargaining and entrepreneurial power of the private sector (Muscat, 1994).

A central issue of industrial development is the role of public policies to protect the emergence of local activities: this was illustrated by the recent debate created by the World Bank report about the success of East Asian experiences of industrialisation, and also conflicting views about the respective roles of the state and private sector. The World Bank itself considers that industry in Thailand has evolved from a protected to a more competitive status. Protection was increased to its maximum in the 1970s and "consumer goods and transport equipment emerged with the highest effective protection rates by the end of the decade" (World Bank, 1983). Although this policy was altered in the 1980s - with increasing import-content regulation, protection for basic industries (such as chemicals) and reduction of import tariffs on equipment - this resulted in a lack of backward linkages for many consumer goods industries, and demands for continued protection by many industrialists. In addition to this biased protection, the promotion of industry has mostly benefited the larger companies and conglomerates that were in a position to negotiate privileges for the expansion of their activity. Our field surveys highlight the fact that most entrepreneurs in middle- to small-size businesses emerge and thrive without incentives from the public sector.

The country, having coined the motto 'dynamic society, open economy' following the political upheaval of 1992, seems to consider itself at the forefront of the modern and forward-looking states of South-East Asia. This tells us a lot about the changing ideology of the State and the new confidence of business strategies. One could easily assume too that the most substantial changes of the past decades can be found in the relationship between public and private economic élites, rather than through a renewal of the principles of industrial policy. Recent history has shown that the government has chosen to concentrate on macro-economic adjustment rather than invest in industry (see Box 5.4 below), and that incentives and co-ordination are mostly aimed at horizontal policies - e.g. skill and technology acquisition, infrastructure development, overall trade and investment promotion, liberalisation and administrative reform.

Box 5.4

The Eastern Seaboard Development Programme: Industrial Blooming and Spatial Chaos

The Eastern Seaboard Development Programme, initiated as a state-promoted endeavour, survived the stabilisation period of the mid-1980s, but lost much of its original spirit and some government-backed projects too. The largest industrial components were not retained as mostly state-backed ventures (e.g. the fertiliser project, soda ash plant), and the whole growth pole concept was diluted by the spill-over of eastern Bangkok into the development region. The major infrastructural components, such as the container terminals at Laem Chabang and the railway line, were built between 1988-94 but were slow to start operations in order to serve the export boom. The public industrial estates took a lot of time to get off the ground, providing excellent opportunities for several private ventures to tap the booming market for industrial serviced land in the three Seaboard provinces.

Nevertheless the two industrial target zones, Laem Chabang in Chonburi province and Map Ta Phut in Rayong province, are now well-established industrial locations: the former is almost fully built with large plants such as tyres, TV tubes and auto parts; in the latter, most of the country's petrochemical activities are concentrated, ranging from the gas separation plant that was the initial springboard of the project, to basic chemicals and plastics, and other intermediary product industries.

The public planning part of the programme remains a black spot: co-ordination between government agencies has been slack for the past decade and conflicting goals and policies have contributed to the patch-work situation. The lack of tools to control the location of industrial plants and hazardous activities has resulted in the dispersion of industries. Resource management for water and power is also a serious issue. Social planning has been disappointing too: the 'new town' concept did not materialise and employees are to rely on services provided by the private sector (such as lodging, new housing estates, private hospitals) in neighbouring districts. Naturally the traffic and commuting flux have increased tremendously.

Instead of the industrial growth centre that was in the minds of its promoters, the Eastern Seaboard symbolises the failure of coherent public planning, and has simply facilitated the expansion of the Bangkok conurbation along a stretch of 100 miles through to Rayong province.

Changing attitudes of entrepreneurs in industry

Local entrepreneurial abilities have been widely discussed in past years, and in the industrial sector they were frequently considered weak and mostly based on rent-seeking or oligopolistic activities geared towards a protected local market (Suehiro, 1985; also see McVey, 1992 for a good summary of the various theses). But it seems that in Thailand, the recent period has marked a turning point. Opportunities were so numerous and risks so limited that entrepreneurial attitudes could be observed at all levels of society: they were behind the expansion and diversification of all kinds of activities from agriculture (shrimp-farming, fruit, vegetable and essential oil production) to services (tourism, trading) and industry (from large-scale petrochemical plants to small garment workshops). McVey (1990, p.31) interestingly sketches the change of mood capturing the "materialisation of the Southeast Asian entrepreneur" as she puts it: "in the end, as with most human undertakings, it may come down to something of a spirit: a feeling, part inspiration, part contagion, that great things may be gained and that the moment must be seized."

In the manufacturing sectors, particularly, there has been a transformation in entrepreneurs' behaviour - a change that could be related to the specificity of enterprise generation in the manufacturing sector over the past fifteen years. The organisation of industry in particular presents a dualistic structure: "on the one hand ... the cottage industry model with its system of co-operation, supervision in industrial workshops ... and on the other hand a taylorized system" of formal factories (Pongsapich *et.al.*, 1994, p.4).

A survey of medium- and small-sized manufacturing companies in a mix of sectors gives interesting clues about this:

(i) The majority of respondents indicated that their factory is their main business and their major source of income, which can explain the commitment they show to make it prosper. This is particularly true for the new generation of entrepreneurs who started a business in the boom period (1975-81) and who are deeply committed to the success of their family-based venture: it is their passport to social progress as, with limited formal education, they have reached a desirable social status and access to affluent consumer society. Many of them see the survival of their business as the key to the future of their children. This contradicts earlier statements in the literature about lack of entrepreneurial abilities or aspirations among local élites. The new sino-Thai generation in particular seems able to put the same dedication and energy in industry as their fathers - or grandfathers - put into trade a few decades ago;

(ii) A majority of entrepreneurs also stress that they reached profitability (in a broad sense) in less than two years, and three-quarters of them in less than three, which is quite rapid by general standards. Local industrial capitalists had obviously to limit their short term speculative ambitions as returns in manufacturing activities generally cannot match those drawn from trade or land speculation. But quick profitability has certainly encouraged the imitative strategies and the multiplication of ventures in sectors such as garment or plastic parts production;

(iii) The findings also suggest that family collaboration seems to play a large role, either in company initiation or operation. It is frequently identified for informal financing support for the start-up of the business, hence the limited support required from official public institutions such as banks or administrative offices.[5] Very commonly members of the family are also employed in the performance of daily tasks in the firm such as accounting or marketing - this was the case in 75 per cent of plants we surveyed.

Qualitative surveys have also identified the role of network co-operation between industrialists: either on the basis of informal peer groups or through formal associations (professional or ethnicity-based), through which the entrepreneurs up-date their market information and their technical knowledge, as well as seeking financial support for the diversification of activity.

Alliances with foreign entrepreneurs or international companies cover a wide spectrum of situations. They range from the very large joint-ventures (e.g. in the Eastern Seaboard industrial estates, or the automobile industry) to smaller grassroots companies of garment manufacture and food-processing. Not only do they mobilise substantial finance capital through official or informal channels (e.g. from Hong Kong or Taiwan), but they also contribute in various ways to technology acquisition. This was the case in the early stages of manufacturing development (Suehiro, 1985) and is still very relevant at the present stage.

Joint ventures have benefited from the economic boom, which can explain the low rate of failures and the willingness to pool resources even though legal protection is quite limited. In that respect Thailand's industries have been more open to foreign collaboration than, for instance, South Korea's.

One of the current challenges facing industrialists is the maturation of their ventures. Depending on the size and dynamics of their activity this may require changes in business strategies and company organisation to adjust to new opportunities, market evolution or simply family transformation.

(i) Large conglomerates have started or accelerated their diversification. The general trend is in favour of strategic alliances between major companies - particularly between industrial, service and commerce based groups - to control the fastest-growing markets. The involvement of several of the major conglomerates (such as Siam Cement Group, Charoen Phokpand, Metro) in the petrochemical projects of the Eastern Seaboard is evidence of the willingness to get involved in strategic industries. Several conglomerates are also seeking expansion overseas: this is true for C.P., with its numerous ventures in China, but also Boon Rawd, the major beer manufacturer seeking business in Asia and even Europe. As a result of their diversification strategies, many large-scale companies have revamped their internal structures - in some cases family rows over strategic decisions have resulted in majors rifts in the company (for example at the well known car manufacturer, Siam Motors).

(ii) The family-owned companies are in many cases faced with two sets of difficulties: one is to integrate the various attitudes of the various members, and particularly the new generation. The second is adapting to the new business environment, requiring professional management, adaptation and diversification of production - beyond mere rent-seeking strategies. This is in line with McVey's observations (1992, p.21 and p.24) that "nowadays, requirements for capital, political connections, and broad international operations make for an opening-out in terms of finance, business organisation and social style. Family firms have become family controlled corporations and these in turn have increasingly included outsiders in their direction." In that respect the assets are unevenly distributed: large family conglomerates can still muster considerable support from family-controlled banks, mobilise human resources, and lobby for government support, whereas smaller and emerging family companies still suffer from an institutional bias towards large firms.

(iii) Entrepreneurs in small- and medium-size companies have to choose strategies: either to explore new areas of diversification or to show continuing flexibility to adapt to market opportunities and changes. A badly documented question is to assess whether they are ploughing back their profits for the development of the venture. The entrepreneurs' current commitment to manufacturing activity is crucial in terms of national competitiveness, but also in terms of keeping a substantial labour absorption capacity. If a rent-seeking attitude were to arise among small- and medium-size enterprises in several labour-intensive sectors the future would be bleak, as companies would rather reduce activity than take the hard path of productivity increases and new investment.

At a lower level, in terms of size, but concerning a far greater number of cases, is the issue of whether the small workshops can be seen as the basis for lasting activities. Many single owner-family-based firms may not have the stamina to evolve into larger companies; others will remain like sub-contractors whose future is determined by traders or bigger corporations, in Thailand or overseas. For small business, and particularly for those quasi-cottage industries working as sub-contractors, survival prospects seem to be bleak: they are heavily dependent on buyers/traders giving orders, and they try to keep their costs low by cutting down labour wages, as Charoenloert shows in the Bangkok garment sector (cited in Pongsapich *et.al.*, 1994, p.135; see also Bunjongjit and Oudin, 1992): "in recent years we have seen the proliferation of these small producers in the informal sector, competing for a limited number of orders, and in this process, driving down the price they can charge. The aim of the informal sector is not to maximise profit as one would find in the formal sector but rather to survive."

New dynamics of manufacturing activities

Emerging rural industries

Over the past two decades many political statements have been expressed and policy measures outlined to encourage 'rural industrialisation' as a way to limit poverty in the countryside (see e.g. Parnwell and Khamanarong, 1990; and also their chapter in this volume). It did not materialise as expected, largely because of weak policies, but above all because of an inadequate economic environment in the provinces at the time. The current general prosperity of the country has

Box 5.5

Grassroots Industry in the North-East

A textile workshop in Kamalasai district of Kalasin province, surveyed in 1993, is owned by a resident of the village. Previously he worked in a Bangkok plant, and then became a trader of cotton threads which were bought by women for their traditional weaving activities. He bought some second-hand spinning machines from a Bangkok factory and had a small plant built, with his own funds (he declared investing 400,000 baht from his savings plus loans from friends). At first he only employed two persons but now, two years after he started, eight persons, in addition to his wife, are working on the premises (production capacity also doubled, from 2 to 5 tons per month). The cotton yarn is bought monthly from Bangkok spinning mills. He sells to traders from the same province, but also occasionally to neighbouring provinces. Trade is brisk because peasants are still keen on doing their own home weaving; even in irrigated areas where the intensity of agricultural work is higher, women can afford 2-3 days off for cotton-weaving to make material for clothes or household goods. But the small workshop also sells (approximately 10-20%) of the yarn to the house next door where another new rural entrepreneur manufactures knitting material, on three machines, to supply Bangkok garment manufacturers. Local connections also include sub-contracting to neighbouring houses.

Having prior industrial experience, the entrepreneur can do his own machine maintenance, or find local mechanics to assist. He is already thinking about dyeing yarn himself, expecting to increase present quality levels in the process. He complains about the infrastructure (bad roads, no telephone) but has his own mobile phone. He is satisfied with village labourers and envisages expansion, possibly with support from the Department of Industrial Promotion.

Small enterprises are also finding a niche for sport and plastic shoes production: with more than 100 million feet running around in the country, there is ample need to supply the local market alongside the larger companies working under license from major international brands, mostly for export. Interestingly some segments of production are moving closer to markets up-country. We surveyed such a workshop in Kalasin province.[6] Buying inputs (foam sheets, plastic parts) from Bangkok-based suppliers, a former shoe-trader established a small workshop in a vacant house, employing only eight people from the village, to prepare and assemble shoe-parts. Manufacture required very little capital and almost no equipment, while the products are supplied to local shops in the province and wholesale traders. This type of endeavour can be seen as part of a new wave of cottage industries in Thailand - a type of cottage industry that complements well-known traditional handicrafts or the production of household goods.

resulted in a spill-over of manufacturing activities into the rural areas (see Box 5.5). Although off-farm activities have always been a regular part of rural life, and often contribute a substantial component of farmers' income (Pampiemras, 1987; Pongsapich *et.al.*, 1994), they have not generated substantial manufacturing transformation at the provincial level in Thailand - contrary to Japanese or Taiwanese models of rural industrialisation where proximity of manufacture and agriculture, induced by both geographic and social factors (limited space, increasing labour supply), resulted in a blooming of rural industries and an increased density of industrial establishments in the countryside.

Recent studies have highlighted the factors behind changes taking place in the provinces (see in particular the 1990 series of reports by Biggs and Tambunlertchai for the TDRI): "the important factors responsible for determining the degree of provincial industrialisation included provincial income level, size and density of population, availability of an adequate infrastructure ... degree of financial development and distance from Bangkok" (Tambunlertchai *et.al.*, 1990, p.5). The persisting rural-urban divide of Thailand (in fact the Greater Bangkok conurbation-other provinces divide) that was the hallmark of the spatial structure of manufacturing production, is now, slowly, being transformed. The Bangkok conurbation industrial network is now being extended to about ten neighbouring provinces within a radius of more than 100 kilometres from central Bangkok, but the past five years have shown that distant provinces can also attract substantial manufacturing activities.[7] Regional rural areas, next to major centres such as Khon Kaen, Songkhla and Chiang Mai, are now encroached upon by industrial plants that increase the off-farm income component of rural people. It is expected that peripheral development will be strengthened further by increased relationships with neighbouring countries (e.g. along the banks of the Mekong, and in the Malaysian and Cambodian borderlands).

The major sources of this dynamism appear to be spatial transformation (the closing of the rural frontier, and the development of infrastructure) and a dual structure of industries geared towards the local market and those located in the province as a production base for distant customers (large urban centres, exports: cf. the cushion-making industry discussed by Parnwell and Suranart in this volume). This is a consequence of both push and pull factors:

(i) On the one hand, industries are looking for sources of raw materials (fresh produce for canneries, oil and sugar mills), cheap labour, or even simply land and water. The new frontier is not in the congested and overpriced suburbs of the Bangkok metropolitan region but in those provinces with active markets and communications;[8]

(ii) On the other hand, the relative stability of farming, plus diversification, backed by additional transfer incomes (from off-farm activities, wage labour in cities, overseas employment) created a substantial demand for industrial goods, some of which can be produced efficiently at the regional level (from agricultural equipment to household goods).

The question of sustainability of the rural industrialisation trend has also to be raised, as there seem to be several major weaknesses in the current dynamism (see also the chapter by Walton in this volume):

(i) Start-up of many entrepreneurial initiatives is based on the cheapness of resources. They are very vulnerable to changes in the availability of raw materials and local labour. Those working for the local market probably do not anticipate productivity problems and forthcoming increased pressures from more advanced trading networks such as department stores and large manufacturers willing to benefit from provincial markets. Export-oriented companies in the fruit- and vegetable-canning business have made little effort to strengthen their linkages with farmers, and some plants have had to close down or move to other regions because of supply problems;

(ii) Entrepreneurs, in spite of low education levels, are making the most of their individual experience. Some have developed activities closely linked to their past working experience, being sub-contractors for larger manufacturing or trading companies in Bangkok they know well; this concerns formal and informal activities for labour-intensive production of garments, stone-cutting and handicrafts (see also the chapter Parnwell and Suranart in this volume). The stability of these links is still open to questions as rural entrepreneurs have no bargaining power and can survive only as long as the cost structure enables them to compete with other industries in need of wage labour;

(iii) Lastly, surveys suggest that keeping the dynamism of entrepreneurial initiatives in the provinces is less dependent on well-focused policies (such as industrial promotion, training, or financial support) than overall improvement of the regional standing in terms of services and transport infrastructure and cross-border links that enhance the attractiveness of the region at the national level (thereby catching the attention of investors). In that context, continuing efforts will be needed to ameliorate the institutional bias against the provinces in order to maintain their contribution to local economic progress and social cohesion.

Labour in industry: experience and skill acquisition

At the present stage of manufacturing development two issues are widespread in all sectors and forms of activities: qualification and mobility of manpower. They are very closely related to the social structure of Thailand, with a low level of secondary, technical and university education, and high propensity of rural residents to double activity. On the one hand labour mobilisation in labour-intensive industries was made easy by the willingness of rural migrants to get a poorly-qualified job: in many sectors, such as garments or fruit- and marine-product canning, the labour intensity and the low qualification admittedly did not offer much scope for qualitative improvement. This is nothing original in terms of the history of industrialisation as industries have always been the starting level for the integration of workers in the labour force. But in Thailand more skill-intensive industries are emerging and their demand for quality labour is higher.

On the other hand high mobility of labour between activities has deterred the training efforts of many companies: this may threaten qualitative changes in manufacturing production and the overall productivity of industry. In the manufacturing sector the mobility of labourers is related to structural factors, as stated above, and to intense competition from factories to attract workers. A marked reluctance towards in-house training has been observed by surveys (see Table 5.8, and also Thienchai, 1987) and generally admitted in interviews by many factory managers of both local and foreign companies. The reason put forward is that job-hopping is too widespread under the current economic boom. Interestingly, it is more frequently expressed in the factories of the Bangkok metropolis, and in the larger industrial areas of Pathum Thani, Ayutthaya and the Eastern Seaboard region, whereas in the more distant provinces, industrial employment opportunities being narrower, managers can expect more stability although they occasionally complain about absenteeism related to rural activities and festivities. These problems are still overwhelmingly characteristic of industries in Thailand. But at the same time one can identify elements that suggest a way out of the human resource crisis - new behaviour of industrialists and a maturation of labourers' skills. The responses of companies to these issues are diverse: some, mostly small-sized, accept the constraint as part of their daily life, although they regularly complain about it;[9] others try to implement measures in order to base productivity improvement and quality of production on industrial manpower up-grading.

The managerial level is crucial at a time when most ventures have just completed their take-off and rapid expansion, and are in search of adequate structures and forms of production to cope with productivity improvement. For promotion of human resources at the managerial level, two elements are to be considered:

(i) Firstly, in many manufacturing companies, the firm's founder has been at the same time the chief engineer and the general manager, while other members of his family assist him for administration, sales, etc. These entrepreneurs now tend to bring in members of the new generation, frequently having a university training. Bridging the generation gap may, however, still be an issue for the future as far as many small companies are concerned.

(ii) Secondly, managers are a scarce resource: many companies have to rely on mechanisms of internal promotion. Those that can recruit fresh specialised university graduates are usually in the upper tier - i.e. the modern medium- and large-size ventures. Because of the scarcity, the manager/employee ratio is rather low, which seems to be detrimental to a more forward-looking attitude in some companies. In spite of this difficulty, the managerial culture is taking root in a context that is favourable to the melting pot approach (Bailes and Tabtieng, 1993), mixing many elements including Japanese influence and American education.

For workers in industry new skills have to be learned and new technologies experienced and mastered: for many Thai workers, this is indeed a new approach to knowledge as the education system still places a large emphasis on repetitive learning, passive absorption of knowledge, or diplomas as an end rather than a pathway to gaining genuine experience.[10] Skills for industrial work are generally broadly defined at the recruitment stage, but according to managers it is internal training that matters more: all freshly-recruited workers need to adapt to the new environment, and in any case they consider that the qualifications of new workers from the technical education/vocational college are rather low, and that few curricula are suited to industrial work.

Our interviews with managers of foreign companies also showed a contrast with previous observations about instability and lack of flexibility of manpower and analyses of workers' attitudes (for example, as described by Thientai, 1987, or the Bank of Thailand annual survey):

(i) Some of the surveyed companies show a concern for a stable employee structure in order to guarantee quality of output, and therefore prefer to adapt their wage and training practices accordingly.

(ii) Several medium-size companies (over 150 workers) have developed links with formal education institutions; for production of jewellery, garments and electrical goods they accept short-term trainees from vocational schools and technical colleges, thereby helping to bridge the gap between the world of formal education and the world of industry. Many industrial activities from garment and textile articles to jewellery and light engineering actually require a well-trained and dedicated workforce that cannot be mobilised at short notice.

The particular case of workers in the gem-cutting and jewellery production sector shows both the expansion of a traditional form of craft and also the establishment of a new group of highly-qualified workers: in some of the modern factories manufacturing jewellery for export, young people are acquiring skills that are similar to those mastered by fellow craftsmen in Europe - and, according to a factory director, they are even quicker to learn than trainees of a parent company in France. Many of them have not been offered a high education, and few have technical college training prior to their recruitment, but on-the-job training seems quite a satisfactory solution in the medium term.

Conclusion: emerging challenges for the manufacturing sector

Several issues from the early 1980s no longer represent limitations for the future expansion of industrial activities in Thailand - namely the diversification of sectors and export markets, the multiplication of small companies, the strengthening of private initiative, and even the acceleration of manufacturing expansion outside the Bangkok area. Nevertheless, beyond the easy times of rapid industrialisation that have taken place during the past decade, challenges ahead for the manufacturing sector can chiefly be identified at the level of international competitiveness and workers' aspirations.

In the area of trade and international relations, the new manufacturing activity has brought a well accepted connection to the world economy and a new regional standing. It is a major economic strength that the range of industrial products and market destinations are so diversified as these can reduce considerably the industrial sector's vulnerability to economic downturns. It also maximises the experience gained by both workers and entrepreneurs. External investment and trade are no longer seen as foreign dimensions to the country and even manufacturing prospects in co-operation with neighbouring countries are now well recognised (e.g. role of the Board of Investment in promoting activities in Vietnam). At the same time, policy-makers have recognised that the new international context brings new challenges: for example, increasing competition from ASEAN countries including, now, Vietnam, and even more so from China; also, a new capacity to play a role in the world trade system,[11] and the necessity to contribute to the debate on freer/fairer trade in the world trade system.

In spite of so-called globalisation, the national policy will have to be up-dated to maintain competitiveness and contribute to the pursuit of new orientations for manufacturing activities. Porter (1990, p.682) interestingly argues that nations matter more in the current era of increasing competition, and he also recognises the potential conflicts related to evolution of industries, maturation and construction of competitive advantage. For Thailand, the industrial future may require more skills and commitment from all actors.

Looking at the situation in the factories, one comes out with a picture that may have far-reaching consequences for the future: about two million people are acquiring wage-earner habits, consumption patterns and new skills, but also new social roles and expectations, through their work in industry. It is doubtful that many of them would trade their current employment for their previous job in agriculture, or for self-employment. Social positions and connections are being restructured, and many wage-earners probably feel they have a right to prosperity and well-being. Many non-wage earners or low-paid workers are also aspiring to obtaining better jobs (hence the high turn-over). These attitudes could, during times of economic down-turn, be converted into a higher demand for equity. Modern institutions and tools for social regulation are needed: it seems obvious that in Thailand material progress has out-paced public institutional improvements - this can be seen in the slow emergence of social security and rapidly-growing demand for private health care, insurance or education.

In this respect, there is no straightforward recipe for success, or typical ‘Asian industrial miracle’ feature to be found in Thailand, beyond the key elements of regional prosperity and stability, individual dynamism, open markets and devoted capitalists. Many entrepreneurs have indeed demonstrated their capacity to combine local and foreign resources, to adapt to shifting world conditions, to comply with set standards, and up-grade their technology. On the other hand, labour force mobilisation was easy at a time of prosperity that could be shared, however unfairly, between rent-seekers, capitalists, wage earners and self-employed.

These elements are the basis of the industrial manufacturing dynamics of Thailand which presents an interesting combination of flexibility and diversity, both inward-looking, regionally-focused and export-oriented, with the intervention of local and foreign entrepreneurs, a large mix of products, and a diversity of industries and skills. The obvious benefit is to rank the country among those that constitute the world networks of manufacturing production, and to establish Thailand as one of the emerging manufacturing powers of South-East Asia.

Notes

1 The chapter draws examples from sectoral and entreprise level case studies of selected manufacturing activities in Thailand. Published and unpublished reports have been used together with data derived from surveys and interviews collected between 1986 and 1993, mostly with entrepreneurs/factory managers, in most of the sectors constituting the industrial mix of the country - ranging from textile/garments to metal products, jewellery, food processing and chemicals, in both export-oriented and local market enterprises. Major reference works are mentioned in the bibliography, but quotations have been kept to a minimum.

2 In this respect, the IMF-World Bank meeting held in Bangkok in 1991 came as a sort of graduation ceremony for Thailand as a NIC, replicating the conference held in Seoul in 1989 which marked the first consecration of the 'Asian development model'.

3 It must be recalled that the expansion of the manufacturing sector was sustained over more than three decades: it took place in a context of global regular quantitative growth of the domestic product, a middle path of growth, whereby the rate of GDP growth was never inferior to 4 per cent per annum from 1965, which is certainly remarkable compared to the average for developing countries (around 2 per cent for 20 countries of the same category). Thailand never experienced negative growth as in other Asian NICs, such as South Korea in 1980 or Singapore in 1985, and only recently suffered from the 'double-digit growth fever' that used to be the characteristic of some East Asian economies.

4 The stagnation of agriculture and the public sector's austerity measures led to a restriction of sales of industrial goods and a negative growth for the whole manufacturing sector in 1985 (see Tambunlertchai, 1993, p.121). The sales of small tractors, for example, were halved between 1981 and 1985.

5 This might be a feature of the past as its seems that industrialists are no longer reluctant to borrow funds from private financial institutions, such as the Industrial Finance Corporation of Thailand or the promotional funds from the Ministry of Industry.

6 It was selected out of a sample list of manufacturing activities of Khon Kaen and neighbouring provinces as identified by the Department of Industrial Promotion.

7 In the engineering, garment and food-processing sectors about 80 per cent of the 48 plants we surveyed in 1990-93 in Khon Kaen, Ayutthaya, Chon Buri and Chachoengsao provinces, in a sample based on registration with the Ministry of Industry, excluding rice mills, were less than six years old.

8 In regional surveys of entrepreneurs a striking feature is the role attributed to transport and telecommunication (their improvement over one decade in remote provinces, and their contribution as a factor of

production). At the grassroot level the Thai entrepreneur highly values movement and flow of information.

9 See for example the Bank of Thailand's annual Survey of Business conditions *Production, Investment and Employment in Manufacturing, Trade and Construction.*

10 Evidence of this new attitude towards technology training can be found in the recent burgeoning of private technical education.

11 Thailand, along with the other emerging industrializing nations of South-East Asia, has joined the earlier NICs in the list of countries that have a slot in the world trade system: accounting for about 1 per cent of word exports, which is slightly less than the level enjoyed by Malaysia in 1992. In comparison, South Korea and Taiwan both have a 2 per cent share of world exports.

6 Problems of regional industrial development in North-East Thailand

John Walton

Introduction

Since 1970 Thailand has experienced sustained economic growth averaging 7.9 per cent per annum. Although the double-digit growth of the late 1980s (12% annual average between 1987-1990) focused international attention on the dynamism of Thailand's economy, recent growth of 8.4 per cent in 1994 and a slightly higher growth forecast for 1995 convey a continuing picture of economic success. A sectoral break-down of overall GDP growth rates supports the popular view that recent growth is largely the result of industrialisation. Between 1970 and 1990 the growth rate of value added in industry increased at approximately 11 per cent per annum whereas the corresponding increase for agriculture was only 3.5 per cent (Asian Development Bank, 1994).

The nature of economic growth, especially the more recently export-led manufacturing boom centred around Bangkok, has heightened interest in the long-standing debate over increasing regional and income disparities in Thailand. The Seventh Plan (1992-1996) notes that "income disparities among households of different socio-economic status and between rural and urban areas has increased to an alarming level." In terms of income distribution the top 20 per cent, or the wealthiest group of households, increased their share of aggregate income from 49.3 per cent in 1975/6 to 54.9 per cent by 1987/8, while the share of the bottom 20 per cent declined from 6.1 per cent to 4.5 per cent. The Seventh Plan also indicates a growing disparity in the regional contribution to national income, with Bangkok's contribution increasing from 42 per cent in 1981 to 48 per cent in 1989, while other regions experienced a relative decline, with the North-East's share declining from 14.7 per cent to 11.4 per cent.

The Seventh Plan claims, however, that the incidence of poverty was reduced from 30 per cent in 1976 to 23.7 per cent in 1988; however, this is challenged by Krongaew *et.al* (1992) who, using adjusted poverty lines, conclude that 48.8 per cent of the people were living in poverty in 1988, with a poverty incidence of 55.7 per cent in rural areas representing about 22 million people, and a poverty incidence of 31 per cent in urban areas representing 4.8

million people. The North-East region, which accounts for about a third of the total population, had the highest poverty incidence at 67 per cent compared with 14.7 per cent for Bangkok.

In April 1993 the Board of Investment (BOI) announced a new set of policies and criteria for investment promotion which was specifically directed at provincial development and industrial decentralisation. These new policies appear to be more positive and far-reaching than previous attempts at promoting regional industries, and it is the intention of this chapter to examine these proposals in order to assess their likely impact on regional development. For instance, do they represent a dramatic change in policy, and are they likely to be more successful than previous initiatives which have been criticised as ineffective?[1]

In this context the North-East, as the most backward and impoverished region, is taken as a case study. Before examining the new policies and their implications for the North-East, a brief summary of some of the theoretical or conceptual issues relating to regional development is undertaken, followed by an outline of previous regional policies.

Decentralisation and regional development

Since the 1960s there has been a growing and lively debate on issues of decentralisation and regional development. This has come about as a result of the disappointing lack of achievement in regional development, and increasing recognition that earlier models of economic development, presumptive of a 'trickle down' effect, have failed to promote implied linkages, or multiplier effects to the rest of the economy (Todaro, 1989, p.65; Arndt, 1983, p.1).[2]

Demaine and Malong (1987, p.10), noting the weakness of linkages, and indeed the possible negative effects of urban-industrial growth models, argue that planning for and the implementation of development cannot satisfactorily take place within these 'top-down' frameworks, and that decentralisation is required to address the complex problems associated with rural development. However, as far as Thailand is concerned decentralisation of the planning process has consisted only of local planners being able to choose from a 'menu' of projects offered by central authorities, thus ensuring that decision-making at the local level is severely constrained.

As with many development issues the decentralisation debate has taken on a wide range of issues and invited commentary from different ideological camps (for opposing views see Slater, 1989; and Rondinelli, 1990b). Samoff (1990), taking a somewhat more balanced approach, dismisses extreme views and suggests that there is no absolute value in either central direction or local autonomy: both are important and must co-exist. Rondinelli (1990b, p.492) makes the critical point that "decentralisation as an organisational concept is inevitably a political issue" and that it can be used for a wide range of political, economic or social purposes, and for good or ill depending on the motives and intentions of political leaders. In attempting to clarify definitions, Samoff (1990, p.515) notes different meanings attached to decentralisation, including "deconcentration (spatial relocation of decision making), delegation (assignment of specific decision making authority), and devolution (transfer of responsibility for governing understood more broadly)." He concludes, however, that the use of similar terms for sharply different meanings has rendered effective dialogue nearly impossible.

If we concur with Samoff that effective dialogue in relation to decentralisation is nigh impossible, and also accept Demaine's view that little effective decentralisation has occurred in Thailand, the approach adopted by Douglass (1990) to summarise the main economic or economic geography theories may provide a more satisfactory background to understanding regional inequalities, or uneven development in Thailand. Douglass suggests at least three opposing paradigms of thought have emerged: (a) modified neo-classical economics; (b) socio-political-cum-economic theories of polarisation (cumulative causation); and (c) political economy explanations of uneven spatial development reaching from the local to the world scale. While acknowledging important differences between neo-classical and polarised models, Douglass (1990, p.8) identifies commonalities, especially the points "that urban-industrial growth initiates powerful forces of concentration which can only be overcome in the longer-term, if at all. [Also] the two dimensional, core-periphery image of the world, with development impulses only moving in two possible directions; toward the core or 'reversed' toward an undifferentiated periphery." Given these commonalities, Douglass reminds us that the major point of disagreement arises in policy prescriptions to correct inequalities, with the neo-classical school advocating the free play of market forces while the polarisation theorists firmly opt for state intervention and planning, arguing that market forces are too slow, or ineffective in bringing about desired change. He notes, however, that differences have narrowed with the emergence of growth pole theory which guided government intervention in a manner which, rather than spreading resources evenly over space, concentrated them in a handful of cities and industrial estates as a means of capturing both efficiency and equity concerns with one single regional development policy. The conclusion is that "[d]espite a number of daunting theoretical and practical problems associated with growth pole theory it remains the dominant policy in Asia in the 1990s" (*ibid.*, p.9). Douglass, however, points to the danger of growth poles, because of a lack of linkages, becoming "cathedrals in the desert" (*ibid.*, p.9).

With regard to the view of the political economist that capitalist development is inherently uneven, Douglass likens this to a game of chess with neither a unidirectional spatial pattern nor tendencies toward a steady state. Moreover, with the growth of transnational corporations and increased international industrial mobility, uneven spatial development takes on yet another dimension with the new international division of labour.

Whether analysis is conceived within the wider decentralisation theory or perhaps more specifically economics oriented theory, the principal actor still appears to be the state and its level of intervention in the planning process. Thailand presents an interesting case not only because of its wide regional and income disparities, but also because it has attracted high levels of foreign investment, especially the relocation of industries from East Asia, which appears to have been an important reason for the widening domestic spatial inequalities, with foreign investors clearly favouring Bangkok and its supporting port facilities in their promotion of export-led manufacturing industries. Just how important government intervention, as opposed to natural comparative advantage, has been in attracting foreign investment into Thailand is difficult to assess, although promotional privileges have tended to match, if not better, similar policies elsewhere in the region.

Frequent changes of government and implied political instability tend to deter foreign investors. However, in the case of Thailand, despite frequent changes, successive governments have generally chosen not to diverge significantly on industrial policy (see also the chapter by Schmidt in this volume). Furthermore, the lack of continuity and fragility of government probably allowed the World Bank to strengthen its long-standing pervasive influence on economic policy. In this sense the level of state involvement would be minimised within an essentially neo-classical, market-oriented philosophy. It is also likely that the frequency of government change has created indecision, or delayed decision-making. For instance, this seems to be, at least partly, the reason for the slow implementation of infrastructural development to overcome traffic congestion in Bangkok.

Industrial development and regional policy in Thailand

Existing industrial development policies stem from the change of government in 1958 when General Sarit assumed power. Despite earlier attempts in the 1950s to move away from the previous policy of state-owned industries, the first serious efforts originated with the Sarit Administration, culminating in the 1962 Industrial Promotion Act which incorporated a package of fiscal incentives and tariff protection typical of then contemporary import-substitution policies. The Board of Investment (BOI), established in 1959, has been the main instrument in determining the preferential allocation of industrial investment. The criteria adopted by the BOI appear to have been directed at maximising economic growth irrespective of any regional considerations, although in 1972 extra incentives to encourage regional industrial development were introduced. However this met with little success since the vast amount of promoted industry continued to gravitate toward Bangkok.

Over-valued currency and preferential access to credit encouraged the growth of capital-intensive, import-substituting industry which preferred to locate in urban areas. Furthermore the rice premium, which effectively imposed a heavy tax on the agricultural sector to subsidise low urban rice prices, strongly biased the internal terms of trade against the rural sector. The overall effect of such measures was to negate any specific regional initiatives and generally maintain the bias toward urban areas.

The Pearson Report (Commission on International Development, 1969, p.334) suggested that the rice premium had played a significant part in stimulating industrial development by creating or sustaining a low wage environment. Whilst this may have supported urban-based industry, its net effect by penalising the rural sector was to reinforce regional disparities.

Since it appears that broad development policy has worked strongly against specific regional policies, it is worth examining in more detail regional development policy, especially as it is has been, since the early 1970s, the declared intention of the government to disperse industrial activity away from Bangkok into the provinces.

The First and Second Five Year Plans between 1961 and 1971 mainly concentrated on national development issues and prime consideration was given to the establishment of basic infrastructure, including roads, power supply and irrigation, while industrial promotion policies were designed to create an atmosphere conducive to private sector investment.

The Third Plan (1972-76) continued with the broad objectives of previous plans but acknowledged that the achievements of the 1960s had been narrowly distributed, and that little trickle-down effect had accrued to the regions. It did little, however, to redress regional imbalances and development expenditure, for most part, remained firmly concentrated within Bangkok and the Central Region.

The Fourth Plan (1977-81) marked a more determined effort by the government to address itself to the problem of regional development and essentially espoused a basic needs philosophy. Proposals for regional development were based on a decentralised urban growth strategy following a polarised growth model whereby specific urban areas were singled out for rapid development, the main premise being that the concentration of growth activities within designated regional centres would eventually filter through to their rural peripheries, thus modifying regional production structures. Agro-processing industries were identified as offering the most potential whilst the up-grading of regional infrastructure and increased provision of education, health and other public utilities was seen as a way of supporting and stimulating local economic activity.

The need for decentralisation continued to be emphasised in the Fifth Plan (1982-1986) with additional incentives offered for small- and medium-scale labour-intensive industries locating in provincial areas. To overcome the limited spread effects of first-generation growth centres, the government identified further regional growth targets. In the case of the North-East, while Khon Kaen and Nakhorn Ratchasima were retained as the main regional urban growth centres, Udon Thani was classified as a second-generation regional urban growth centre while Roi-et, Surin, Sakon Nakhon and Ubon Ratchathani were identified as other 'low-order' regional urban growth centres.

Dixon, in his chapter in this volume, observes that in the Seventh Plan (1992-1992) the hierarchical 'growth pole' approach has been replaced by a more 'mixed approach'. In essence, policy seems to have moved much closer to the type of strategies advocated by Douglass which require more emphasis on rural-focused regional development rather than urban-centred region development. However, Dixon also notes that, while the Sixth and Seventh Plans contain specific policies aimed at encouraging the dispersal of manufacturing away from Bangkok, the mechanisms for achieving this remain weak and unclear.

Fiscal incentives administered by the BOI and monetary measures formulated by the Bank of Thailand have been the main mechanisms to implement regional industrial development policies incorporated in national development plans. First introduced in 1972, additional privileges include a reduction of up to 90 per cent of business taxes on sales of products for a period of not more than five years, a reduction of 50 per cent on corporate income taxes for an additional five years, and twice the costs of transportation, electricity and water supply allowed to be deducted from taxable corporate income. In addition to normal depreciation allowance, up to 25 per cent of the cost of infrastructural facilities installation is allowed to be deducted from taxable corporate income at any time within a period of ten years from the date of earnings (Board of Investment, 1978, p.24).

Despite the additional incentives detailed above the superior economic attractions of Bangkok have continued to influence strongly the location of industry toward the centre. In many cases industries took advantage of the additional incentives by merely locating at strategic positions within newly designated investment zones, which in practice led to clusters of industry being located just beyond 50 kilometres from Bangkok on the two major highways leading to the North and North-East. The Fifth Plan proposed restrictions on the establishment of new industry in Bangkok but this policy was not implemented, possibly because of the fear that in a highly-competitive international environment seeking foreign investment, potential investors would be deterred from locating in Thailand.

Following on from the 1972 incentives, the BOI announced a series of regional investment incentives throughout the 1970s and 1980s, mainly variations on the initial theme but which unfortunately have led to confusion and ambiguity. In a critical analysis of BOI promotional incentives Lohaunchit (1990, p.164) makes five criticisms:

(i) Too many and too frequent changes in policies and measures;

(ii) The BOI tried to promote too many conflicting objectives at the same time;

(iii) Because of the number of directives the system has become complex and cumbersome to handle;

(iv) Extra regional incentives were based mainly on business and corporate tax exemption. However, provincial industries often evade taxes and it is therefore doubtful whether such incentives promote provincial industrial development; and

(v) There is no clear focus on whether the BOI wants to promote large modern provincial industries, which would be funded by investors outside of the provinces, or to promote indigenous local industries, which would be mainly small-scale industies.

Lohaunchit's conclusion is that, despite the theoretical provision of incentives to areas outside of Greater Bangkok, in actual practice the promotion of provincial industries has been neglected by the BOI's preoccupation in meeting other objectives, especially the promotion of large-scale import-substituting industries in the 1960s and 1970s, and the promotion of export industries in the 1980s.

On the monetary side there has been a concerted effort to channel increased flows of credit into rural areas. In 1975 the government announced a regulation requiring commercial banks to direct at least 5 per cent of their total lending to the agricultural sector, either directly or through the Bank for Agriculture and Agricultural Co-operatives (BAAC). By 1979, the amount of total compulsory credit to be directed to the agricultural sector had been increased to 13 per cent, of which two per cent was earmarked for agribusiness. This policy was gradually broadened to become a rural credit programme in 1987 in which 20 per cent of total commercial bank lending was to be allocated to rural areas, including small-scale rural industries that were not necessarily specifically agriculture related.

Also in 1975, in an attempt to stem the reverse flow of funds to Bangkok, the Bank of Thailand initiated a policy whereby the provincial banks were required to lend at least 60 per cent of their deposits within their own catchment areas, with at least one-third of this lending to be channelled to farmers. Lohaunchit (1990, p.80), however, questions the effectiveness of the provincial credit measures by suggesting that commercial banks reclassified their operational areas, thus credit extended by bank offices in the Greater Bangkok area, which was previously classified as Bangkok, was subsequently reclassified as 'provincial' credit.

In 1991 the central bank further relaxed regulations by broadening the definition of agricultural credit to include wholesaling and exporting of agricultural products, while at the same time dividing the total credit area into nine major regions, rather than individual provincial bank catchment areas as previously. These measures were designed to create greater flexibility and to encourage the establishment of more commercial bank branches in provincial areas.

In the same year that regional incentives were introduced, 1972, the BOI also introduced measures to promote export manufacturing industries which clearly favoured Bangkok as a locational base. The 1973/4 OPEC oil price increases directed further attention to the importance of exports to correct balance of payments problems, with the second round of OPEC increases in 1979 creating further difficulties which undermined regional development expenditure. Although Thailand's economy weathered the global economic down-turn in the first half of the 1980s better than its ASEAN neighbours, the government was nevertheless preoccupied with maintaining national economic stability (see the chapter by Dixon in this volume for a review of World Bank and IMF structural adjustment programmes). The Sixth Plan (1987-91) was conceived in a period of economic uncertainty but later revised as economic growth accelerated from 1987. Krongkaew (1988, p.90) suggests that the success of the export sector in the late 1980s diverted the attention of public authorities from the promotion of provincial and rural small- and medium-scale industries, one possible explanation being that the export promotion strategy produced quick results which it was hoped would, through a trickle-down effect, redress industrial imbalances.

The North-East

According to the 1994 Statistical Yearbook of Thailand the North-East region covers an area of 168,900 kilometres accounting for one-third of the country's total land area. In 1993 the population was estimated to be 20.2 million, or 34.6 per cent of Thailand's total population of 58.3 million. The North-East is estimated to have the highest amount of agricultural land in the country accounting for 46 per cent of total agricultural area, but only contributes one quarter of the total agricultural product, due mainly to poor soil fertility, erratic rainfall and a lack of irrigation. For instance yields of rice, the principal crop, are usually lower in the North-East than other regions - in the 1992/3 crop year the yield was estimated at 274 kg/rai in the North-East, compared with 348 kg/rai for the national average and 487 kg/rai in the Central Region (see Dixon, 1977).

Aggregated data on the North-East itself can be misleading, however, since there are significant differences between provinces. For instance, the poorer changwats such as Si Sa Ket, Surin, Yasathon and Roi-et, with per capita gross regional products in the 11,000 to 13,000 baht range, are much worse-off than Nakorn Ratchasima, Khon Kaen and Loei, which lie in the 19,000 to 21,000 baht range (Statistical Yearbook of Thailand, 1994).

Agriculture is the mainstay of the North-East's economy and accounts for 27 per cent of Gross Regional Product. Because of erratic rainfall agriculture is primarily based on a rain-fed monocropping system. Nearly two-thirds of cultivated land is under rice, while cash crops including cassava, maize, kenaf, sugar cane, mungbeans, soybeans, groundnuts and cotton make up most of the remainder. The most significant change in the North-Eastern agricultural scene over the last two decades or so has been the expansion of the higher-value cash crops, although this has been accomplished through extending the margin of cultivation rather than encroachment of paddy land which also continued to expand. Expansion has been mainly at the expense of forested land which declined by nearly 20 per cent in the 1980s and in 1993 accounted for only 13 per cent of the region's land area. Apart from ecological concerns this land frontier is now exhausted, and future gains in output will necessarily have to come through more intensive cultivation.

Most economic activities in the North-East are related to the agricultural base. Agro-based industries such as cassava processing, rice and sugar mills are the main manufacturing activities and these in turn create important linkages to other economic activities, especially transportation. Historically poor transport links and communications kept the North-East isolated. The construction of the Friendship Highway in the late 1960s significantly overcame one of the major infrastructural bottlenecks and opened up the region to market forces, stimulating the growth of cash crops such as cassava which has become a major export commodity.[3]

A closer examination of the industrial structure of the North-East clearly identifies the dependency of industry on the agricultural base. Moreover the pattern that emerges is strongly influenced by such factors as weight loss and perishability - where these are not present the tendency is for industry to locate nearer to Bangkok either for its superior market potential or its port facilities for export.[4] For example, the final dry product of cassava represents just over one-third of the original root product, thus almost two-thirds weight loss is involved in its processing. With the 1992 production of cassava in the North-East amounting to 12.2 million tons, it is easy to appreciate the economic rationale for locating factories within the producing areas to minimise costs of transportation. Nevertheless local transportation between farm and factory is an important economic activity and this generates important linkages and employment, such as lorries and drivers, which in turn create further demands including service and repair facilities.

Sugar cane not only experiences substantial weight loss but is also highly perishable, thus factories are located within the growing region. Similar weight losing and/or perishability considerations apply to rice, kenaf, fruit and vegetables, so processing factories associated with these products are also located within the region.

There is a thriving livestock rearing industry including cattle, swine, buffalo and poultry. The rearing of beef and dairy cattle has been supported by the BAAC, and in 1993 the region accounted for just over half the total number of cattle slaughtered in Thailand.

In the mid-1980s the economy of the North-East stagnated despite a national growth rate of 3.5 per cent in 1985 and 4.5 per cent in 1986. However, since 1987 the region's economic growth has averaged 6 per cent, although still under-performing the national average by approximately 2 per cent. Although unsatisfactory relative to the Central and Eastern regions' dynamic growth, 6 per cent is respectable by many other developing nations' standards and suggests that decentralisation measures have not been completely ineffective. Agriculture's share of gross regional product fell from 31.1 per cent in 1986 to 26.8 per cent in 1993 while non-agricultural production rose from 68.9 per cent to 73.2 per cent over the same period (*Far Eastern Economic Review*, 14 April 1994, p.31). Non-agricultural production is still, however, dominated by the processing of local agricultural raw materials.

The growth of Khon Kaen, designated as the regional capital of the North-East has generally kept pace with the national average. This is, at least partly, due to public sector investment in up-grading infrastructure, construction and the establishment of government administration and educational services within the area. The response by private sector investment has not been particularly encouraging, although one notable exception is the Phoenix Pulp and Paper Mill at Nam Phong, established in 1982 with Board of Investment privileges. The factory produces 70,000 tons of pulp annually and provides direct employment for over 700 people. Perhaps more significantly, it annually requires about 240,000 tons of kenaf as its raw material input which is able to bring benefits to approximately 30,000 farm households. Even so, the low price the factory was prepared to pay for kenaf caused dispute with local farmers.

A sugar factory established at Nam Phong in the late 1970s diversified its manufacturing operations in the late 1980s by producing medium density fibre board from the waste by-product, bagasse. Some other earlier attempts at manufacturing in Khon Kaen were not so successful, including a match-making factory and a canning factory, partly financed by the Industrial Finance Corporation of Thailand, since they subsequently closed down. While it is difficult to determine the exact reasons for failure it appears that, at least partly, poor entrepreneurial decision-making was involved.[5]

Until recently industries not dependent on local North-Eastern resources have been very few. In the late 1980s one or two villages were involved in gem-cutting and polishing using raw materials from Bangkok or Chantaburi, while another village produced plastic dolls (see Parnwell and Khamanarong, 1990; also the chapter by Parnwell and Suranart in this volume). However such enterprises were the exception to the rule, and the operations were small-scale, and most significantly the inputs and outputs incurred very little transport costs. The interesting feature of such enterprises is the transfer of technology into rural areas which appears to have come about by migrants returning home with skills acquired in Bangkok, and the entrepreneurial flair of one or two individuals. Whilst there may be potential for more enterprises of this nature, the scope is likely to be limited and the vast majority of cottage industries remain firmly tied to local resources, such as the production of reed mats, clay pots, sericulture and silk- and cotton-weaving.

Large industries influenced by final demand are relatively few. Fishing nets manufactured in Khon Kaen using nylon thread imported from Bangkok cater for inland fishing activities, although about a third of output is directed to Bangkok and beyond. Final demand industries are more or less restricted to personal services, repair shops for televisions, radios, motorcycles, cars and agricultural machinery, and small-scale food production such as soft noodles. Some construction materials such as bricks and cement products are also found because of their heavy transportation costs.

The labour market in the North-East is traditionally tied to the agricultural sector, and due to the predominantly rain-fed rice single-cropping system there is a pronounced seasonal demand for labour. In the off-peak seasons, when demand for labour is substantially lower, traditional economic activities such as silk-weaving and village handicrafts help to take up some of the slack. More recently, government sponsored rural works projects have increased off-farm income potential. These include construction and improvement of community buildings for health, education and welfare, village water supply including reservoirs, canals, ponds and rural transport networks. In addition, training instructors visit villages to up-grade or introduce skills which support village handicrafts and cottage industries such as textiles and basket-weaving. One notable characteristic of the North-East labour force is the circular migratory pattern which coincides with seasonal activity and which has grown significantly with the availability of cheap transportation and population pressures (see Parnwell, 1993a).

Statistics that classify over 70 per cent of the workforce in the North-East as in the agricultural sector require further elaboration. Lewis and Kapur (1990, p.1373) note that Thai farmers on average spend only 100 person days per year on farming, and pursue other non-agricultural activities, both on-farm and off-farm, including migration. However, while counted as full members of the agricultural labour force the non-farm output they produce counts as part of the non-agricultural sector's gross output, which may also distort the differentials between non-agricultural and agricultural real incomes. Nevertheless, the expansion of the agricultural product, especially into cash crops, has been a fundamental cause of economic growth in the North-East, and the rapid increase in cash crops in the region, albeit through land expansion, during the last two decades testifies to the responsiveness of local farmers to economic opportunities.

Although some supply side constraints exist in developing industrial activity in the North-East they do not generally have the same impact as the severe final demand constraints referred to earlier. Lack of skilled labour is one possible factor: when a sugar mill was first established at Nam Phong, the skilled labour input was supplied by migrants from the Central Region.

If Bangkok is contrasted with the North-East a different pattern of industrial activity is observed. Because of the influence of final demand virtually all

Thailand's resource-independent industries are located within the Bangkok metropolitan area, or in areas in close proximity to the capital city. In terms of value added in the manufacturing sector, 58.8 per cent of the total comes from Bangkok. If provinces around Bangkok are included (Samut Prakan, Nonthaburi, Pathum Thani, Samut Sakhon and Nakhon Pathom) value added increases to 76.8 per cent. In contrast, the North-East's contribution is a mere 5 per cent (*Bangkok Bank Monthly Review*, June 1990). Economics of agglomeration, including infrastructure, services, utilities and skilled labour give Bangkok a distinct advantage over provincial locations. In addition its seaport facilities make it the preferred location for both import-substituting and export-oriented industries which in many cases are heavily dependent on imported intermediate inputs and raw materials from abroad.

While the above is a rather simplified description of industrial structure in Thailand it nevertheless identifies the main components determining industrial location, namely the superior economic advantages of Bangkok associated with final demand, services and infrastructure as opposed to the dominance of resource-determined location in the North-East, influenced by considerations of weight loss and perishability, with final consumer demand being relatively unimportant. An econometric analysis on the location of provincial industries in Thailand identified final demand as a key factor: i.e. provincial income levels, and the size and density of provincial populations. It also identified inadequate infrastructure, degree of financial development and distance from Bangkok as other significant constraints (Thailand Development Research Institute, 1990).

1993 investment promotion

In April 1993 the government introduced an improved investment promotion policy which specifically aimed to promote industrial development and improve incomes in rural areas. Under the new policy the country was classified into three investment zones, with Zone 3 - which includes the North-East region - receiving the most generous incentives. Major concessions for Zone 3 include exemption of import duties on machinery, reduced import duties on raw and essential materials used in production for domestic sales for five years, and exemption of corporate income tax for eight years, followed by a further five years with 50 per cent reduction. Special privileges on a case-by-case basis include double deduction allowance of taxable income on water, electricity and transport costs for 10 years from the date of the first sales. Also, deduction is allowed from net profit of 25 per cent of the cost of installation, or construction of the project's infrastructure facilities. To encourage the decentralisation process, already-established industries which decide to relocate to provincial areas covered by Zones 2 and 3 will also be eligible for exemption of corporate income tax (BOI Announcements 1 and 2, 1993). These new measures are essentially an enhancement of existing policy as enunciated in the 1972 package. The major changes include privileges previously restricted for export promotion to be permitted for domestic production in Zone 3, and tax exemptions for firms relocating from congested areas to the outer zones.

Overall, whilst the new investment promotion policy heavily favours provincial projects, it also recognises the importance of maintaining the growth of export manufacturing industries. Additionally it recognises other key areas of national concern and attaches priority status, irrespective of zones, to projects and activities relating to infrastructure, transportation, basic industries, environment and technological development. As with previous policies, the new policy covers a wide range of objectives which, in practice, considerably dilute the potential effectiveness of the regional initiatives. The criticisms by Lohaunchit, referred to earlier, still apply.

To supplement the above fiscal measures the Bank of Thailand introduced in July 1993 a financial scheme to assist small- and medium-scale industries locating in Zone 3. In collaboration with the Industrial Finance Corporation of Thailand and commercial banks the central bank will provide low interest credit to promoted firms where total investment does not exceed 200 million baht (Bank of Thailand, 1993, p.23). As noted earlier, in the 1990s the central bank has considerably widened the range of rural industries which qualify for agricultural credit which still must comprise 20 per cent of total commercial bank lending.

It is too early yet to judge the full impact of the new decentralisation policy, although the initial response has been extremely encouraging, with application in Zone 3 totalling 801 projects in 1993 compared with 176 in 1992. Table 6.1 shows the distribution of investment applications in Zone 3 for 1993. The North-East's 159 projects comprise 20 per cent of total Zone 3 applications and draw attention to the fact that the North-East has to compete for investment not only with Bangkok but also with other regions receiving promotional privileges. Nevertheless, the 159 project applications in 1993 compare very well with 38 applications in the previous year. In the past, perhaps because of the small number, most applications have been approved by the BOI. It is also possible that potential investors, aware of more generous, forthcoming regulations, deferred their applications.

Table 6.1
Distribution of Investment Applications in Zone 3, 1993

Region	Number of Projects
Northern	185
Southern	158
Eastern	227
Northeaster	159
Central	72
Total	801

Source: Office of the Board of Investment.

In the 1990s, however, the changing political scene in the neighbouring countries of Laos, Cambodia and Vietnam, especially the opening-up of markets, is allowing economic factors increasingly to influence current and future development. Cross-border trade has grown rapidly between Thailand and Laos, and the opening of the bridge in 1994 across the Mekong river from Nong Khai to Vientiane is expected further to accelerate economic activity with the North-East region, envisaged as the gateway to Indochina. The value of border trade is estimated to have increased from US$90 million in 1988 to US$719 million in 1993 (Ministry of Foreign Affairs, 1994, p.16). Thai exports include automobiles, motorcycles, electronic appliances, footwear and dairy products. Rice exports have diminished in importance due to increasing self-sufficiency in Indochina. Imports are mainly processed woods originating from Cambodia and Vietnam which comprise 90 per cent of total imports. It seems likely that border trade will continue to grow at a fast pace, especially since it is the government's policy to encourage the growth of border areas.

The region's main focus of manufacturing growth is Nakhorn Ratchasima which tends to suggest that development within the North-East itself will be uneven. Nakhorn Ratchasima has attracted most interest from companies seeking promotional status. Already the most industrialised, its closer proximity to Bangkok and the Eastern Seaboard makes it the preferred location over outlying areas further north. The private Suranari industrial estate is also proving attractive to potential investors, most of whom are Thai (as opposed to foreign). Agro-processing is the predominant activity, although other industries, including engineering, electronics, metals and plastics exist, but tend to be small-scale. Planned public sector industrial estates in Khon Kaen, Udon Thani, Nong Khai and Ubon Ratchathani have yet to be established, but may prove vital to prevent over-concentration in Nakhorn Ratchasima.

A relocational trend in the garment industry is starting to emerge (see also the chapter by Simon in this volume). Small and medium-scale manufacturers have established factories in Northeastern towns, particularly Nakhorn Ratchasima. The availability of promotional incentives in Zone 3, especially those relating to production for the domestic market, has reinforced this trend as the Thai garment industry reacts to cheap labour competition in other Asian counties. Manufacturing operations are low-technology and labour-intensive, taking advantage of the lower wages in the North-East.[6] The system is based on sub-contracting with the small provincial factories supplying larger companies in Bangkok which control marketing (*Bangkok Bank Monthly Review*, February 1994, p.19). Apart from garments and a limited number of small-scale industries operating in Nakorn Ratchasima, other industries not directly related to the agricultural base are few and far between.

Conclusion

The initial response to the government's new regional promotional measures has been encouraging, with a significant increase of investment applications in the North-East. However, it seems unlikely that fiscal measures by themselves will be sufficient to achieve the desired objectives. Congestion, high land prices and wages in Bangkok are forcing existing firms to consider relocation and influencing new enterprises to consider locations outside of the capital city. Unfortunately for the North-East, other locations have greater attractions in terms of infrastructure, especially industrial estates, as well as closer proximity to the main areas of industrial activity and consumer demand. For these reasons Zone 2 is preferred by foreign investors including the small and medium firms linking into larger-scale industries in Bangkok and the Eastern Seaboard which underpin much of Thailand's export-led manufacturing growth. There is strong pressure on the government from enterprises in Zone 2 to grant more generous concessions, and this highlights the dilemma facing Thailand in trying to balance regional growth incentives against a highly competitive international environment where in the 1990s, most countries have significantly liberalised their foreign investment incentives.

Within the North-East similar factors which influence investors to prefer Zone 2 are at work, with Nakhorn Ratchasima situated in the lower part of the region receiving most interest. Increased cross-border trade is likely to boost economic activity in the border areas and benefit towns such as Nong Khai and Udon Thani. However until the government addresses the problem of inadequate industrial infrastructure it is unlikely to achieve its aspirations of developing metal-working and engineering industries in the region. For some time to come the North-East is destined to derive most of its economic benefits from its agricultural product and associated agro-processing industries. In view of the limited potential for industrial development it is important that the government continues to support the agricultural base in order to stimulate regional growth.

Recognising the limitations of industrial development, most policy prescriptions are directed toward agricultural development, especially with the view to improving agricultural productivity and increasing rural income levels, which are seen as one way to overcome, or ameliorate, demand deficiency that is identified as a key problem, if indeed not the most important constraint to provincial industrial development.[7] Douglass (1990) argues that the development of rural hinterlands is as important as town-centred or urban-centred investment and proposes a rural income-led regional development strategy including agrarian reform, local co-operatives, community development, decentralised planning, expansion of non-agricultural employment opportunities and selective investment in infrastructure, services and rural towns.

Lewis and Kapur (1990) also argue for an agricultural productivity-enhancing thrust in rice and diversification into non-traditional crops including fruit and vegetables. They also see the need for devolution of government functions, improved education and public works to overcome seasonal unemployment - reforestation is suggested as one possibility which would have a beneficial ecological impact. Kaothien (1991) favours the growth pole approach but recommends that it should be reformulated to place more emphasis on the tertiary sector. Grandstaff (1990) clearly identifies the low purchasing power of the rural population as a major reason for the limited scope of provincial industry, and therefore sees government support for the agricultural sector as vital. Ichikawa (1991) also argues for raising agricultural productivity and the promotion of small-scale industries. Additionally, expert opinion is virtually unanimous in calling for improved education and training in the development of human capital.

A conclusion that can be drawn is that, while the strong bias against agriculture noticeable in early development policy has largely disappeared, present policies do not sufficiently support an agricultural development strategy that would enhance rural incomes, which are seen as a necessary pre-requisite for the growth of provincial industries. Many of the policies advocated above can be found in recent development plans, although they may have been implemented inefficiently, if at all. There is also a danger of under-estimating the daunting task of up-grading large backward agricultural sectors, and the implementation and effectiveness of suggested policies may not be as easy as their proposers would have us believe. Government sponsored schemes to encourage farmers in the North-East to move into seemingly higher-valued products such as cashew nuts, silk worms and cattle-rearing have not been particularly successful, and have left a large number of farmers heavily indebted. Likewise, the provision of a Skill Training Centre in Khon Kaen in 1979 led to many of the participants seeking employment outside the North-East region. This does not mean that the government should be let off the hook, since there is a vast difference between government rhetoric in its rural development proposals as promoted in the various development plans and its actual record of implementation. With recent economic success, as measured by high national economic growth rates, the government has few excuses for what is judged by most observers as lack of commitment to rural development. The recent fiscal and monetary measures should result in some marginal improvement, but they do not represent a dramatic change from previous policies which have not been particularly effective. Increased government commitment is urgently required, along the lines suggested by Douglass and others, to improve agricultural incomes and overcome demand deficiencies. However, it should be noted that, even when implemented, many policies, such as educational development, only realise their full potential or effectiveness in the longer term. Actually to redress regional imbalances implies that incomes in these areas will necessarily have to grow at higher rates than the core urban areas. With frequent changes of government still a problem, it seems unlikely that there will be any immediate and dramatic change in the commitment to rural development, at least not of the magnitude required. At best it may be possible to halt the trend to greater inequality, although there is a danger that present policies may result in isolated pockets of development within the North-East and exacerbate inequality within the region itself. However, to conclude on a more optimistic note, the political changes in Indochina are likely to introduce into the North-East a greater number of stimulating economic factors associated with cross border trade.

Notes

1 "Measures to decentralise growth to different geographic regions are still ineffective" Government of Thailand, Sixth Plan (1987-1991), p.308.

2 Todaro describes 'trickle down' as the notion that development is purely an economic phenomenon in which rapid gains from overall growth of

GNP will automatically bring benefits, such as jobs and other economic opportunities. The main preoccupation is therefore with growth, while problems of poverty, unemployment and income distribution are perceived to be of secondary importance (Todaro, 1989, p.65).

3 Foreign aid and military expenditure played a significant part in early infrastructural development in the 1950s and 1960s (see Muscat, 1990).

4 See Tambunlertchai, 1990, p.17: this report showed, from econometric analysis, that the distance from Bangkok was negatively correlated with industrial development, with a high level of statistical significance.

5 See TDRI, 1990: this report found that provincial entrepreneurs often lacked vital information and suggested that the BOI could play an important role in disseminating business information, etc.

6 From October 1994 the minimum wage was set at 135 baht per day for Bangkok, 118 Baht for Nakhorn Ratchasima and 110 baht for the rest of Zone 3

7 See TDRI, 1990: this report found that, for small provincial firms with less than ten workers, local markets absorb about 85 per cent of total sales. As firm size increases there is a decline in the proportion of sales to local markets and a relative increase in sales to Bangkok and for export.

7 Development in Thailand's extended metropolitan region: The socio-economic and political implications of rapid change in an Ayutthaya District, central Thailand

Daniel Arghiros and Wathana Wongsekiarttirat

Introduction

In a paper reviewing the state of rural Thailand in the mid-1990s, Philip Hirsch (1994) commented that few scholars who had carried out research two or three decades ago would now recognise their original field sites, such has been the rapidity and reach of infrastructural development in the provinces. This observation applies particularly strongly to settlements in what is now called the Extended Bangkok Metropolitan Region (EBMR: see McGee and Greenberg, 1992), the eleven provinces that form corridors of development radiating from the Bangkok metropolis (see Figure 7.1). Improved road networks now give access to most settlements, replacing waterways as arteries of communication; most communities have also electricity and, increasingly, telecommunications. This chapter seeks to examine some of the changes occurring within an Ayutthaya district which, though now firmly within the sphere of influence of Bangkok, has not yet seen the establishment of the large-scale non-local industries which have proliferated elsewhere in the EBMR. The chapter takes as its focus the social, economic and political implications of change for rural dwellers.[1]

Changes in the national economy are making themselves felt in the district in a variety of ways. In keeping with broader trends in Thailand, there has been a significant shift in occupations away from agriculture and towards non-farm activities. This is explained by a range of factors which derive from local and national sources. Amongst these are the fact that rice farmers are disadvantaged by increasingly precarious water supplies, unfavourable market conditions and a lack of effective infrastructure. Land speculation and increased demand for natural resources from non-agricultural concerns also contribute to the shift away from agriculture. In this locality those who have been able to take greatest advantage of economic growth are producers of the very material from which many of the factories, shopping centres, condominiums and housing estates of new urban centres are built: bricks. In some respects the brick industry is in competition with local farmers - in particular for labour and brick-earth. The industry has developed in the last 25 years from a collection of non-mechanised

Figure 7.1
The Extended Bangkok Metropolitan Region

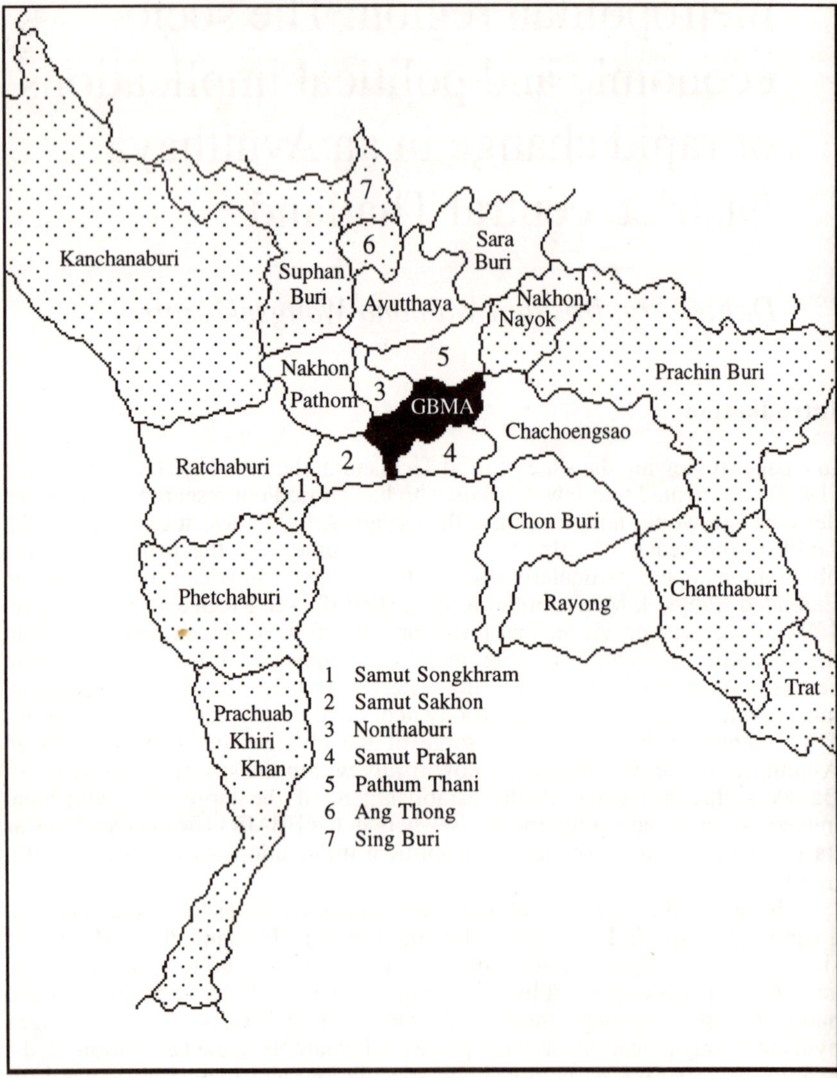

household enterprises to a mixed sector now dominated by mechanised, factory-based production.

That rural households are highly differentiated in terms of their access to productive resources is not new in Central Thailand. What is new, however, is the way in which circumstances are making these differences more permanent, such that, for example, there exists what could be called a stratum or even a class of predominantly wage labourers. As differences in the economic status of households have become more permanent, so social differences have become more pronounced. The absence of social solidarity between rich and poor is reflected in relations between local community representatives and the general population. Increasingly the new economic élite, overwhelmingly owners of brickyards, are able to insert themselves into positions of local authority, as village and sub-district headmen (*phuu yay ban* and *kamnan*). This has implications for the extent to which local state-created development institutions will represent the needs of the majority of rural residents.

The chapter begins by sketching out the socio-economic and geographical context of the study district; it examines changing patterns of local economic activity, and proceeds to explore changes in resource use that are related to recent economic expansion. It continues with an analysis of contemporary patterns of household socio-economic differentiation and touches on the ways these are played out in everyday life. Finally, the chapter explores the political implications of recent change for local 'development' institutions.

Agrarian transformation in Ayutthaya Province and Banglen District

Ayutthaya province consists of 16 districts of which Banglen is one.[2] The province is situated in the Old Delta of the Chao Phraya basin (Takaya, 1987, p.13) and the provincial town, after which the province is named, is about 70 kilometres due north of Bangkok. The province is linked to Bangkok by road, railway and river and is criss-crossed with waterways which were once the main line of transport. Like many provinces in the Central Plain, Ayutthaya's proximity to Bangkok has resulted in a high rate of out-migration (Douglass, 1984). The area constitutes a broad unforested plain and has alluvial soils well suited for rice cultivation, and, in places, for brick manufacture. Until relatively recently the mainstay of the provincial economy was rice cultivation (Amyot, 1976). Socio-economic conditions in the province have changed rapidly in the last few decades. Chulalongkorn University Social Research Institute has had a keen interest in rural Ayutthaya since 1969, and has produced, mainly under the direction of Jacques Amyot, a series of studies and surveys on specific communities in the province. A key facet of change revealed by these studies is that the primacy of agriculture as a source of livelihood for the majority of the rural population in the province is diminishing rapidly.[3] Amyot (1990, p.12) has noted that government statistics reveal that in 1990, and in contrast to all previous surveys, the proportion of farming households' income which came from off-farm activities exceeded that from agriculture: farming households derived more income from non-agricultural activities by a ratio of seven to five. Moreover, more than half of all households in the province do not operate land holdings (50.8 per cent), and many members of such households do not seek employment in the agricultural sector, giving rise to agricultural labour shortages (*ibid.*, p.13). These conclusions have also been confirmed by a survey of households originally studied in 1969 and re-examined 20 years later (Wongsekiarttirat, 1991). It was found that the size of farm holdings over this period had decreased as a result of both land sales and a reduction in land tenure. This study also found that newly-established factories were attracting younger residents who saw no future in agriculture. Moreover, none of those individuals surveyed who had sold their land in the ten years prior to the survey continued farming on a tenure basis.

To some extent, a move away from agriculture is to be expected since no excess local land is available for cultivation while population size has been increasing. However, other factors have exacerbated this trend. In recent years the productivity of rice cultivation has not increased significantly and has probably declined in some areas. Furthermore, improvements in irrigation made over the last 30 years appear to have yielded few results. In 1990, although 82 per cent of administrative villages in the province officially received irrigation for a second crop, only 12.9 per cent of villages regularly planted one (Amyot, 1990, pp.1-5). These figures indicate either that irrigation is technically flawed or that the rewards from planting a second crop are so poor as to make doing so unattractive. Additionally, rising costs of agricultural inputs, including wages, have not been off-set by stable and buoyant rice prices, and farmers cannot be sure of covering their costs.

Given the above conditions it is not surprising that many of the province's farmers are eager to give up farming. Any predisposition to sell farmland has been fuelled by land speculation and aggressive buying practices (described below). Moreover, the interest earned by capital deposited in bank savings accounts often provides a higher income than that earned from farming such that, it is probably safe to say, as Amyot (1990, p.15) has, that farmers "have lost hope in the possibility of improving their condition through agriculture" and want to escape it. From the vantage point of many year's research experience in the province, Amyot (*ibid.*, p.15) has argued that: "if anything, the situation of Ayutthaya farmers has deteriorated over the years."[4]

Farm and non-farm production in two Banglen sub-districts

In this section we look at changing patterns of economic activity in two sub-districts, Ban Thung and Ban Say, within Banglen district. The observations made above of province-wide trends are much in evidence in Banglen district. We aim to show how changing local conditions are contributing to processes of differentiation, and how political economic and environmental forces are restricting the opportunities that poorer sections of the community have for earning a livelihood outside selling their labour. Poorer farmers are under pressure to enter waged labour to supplement their meagre income, or to relinquish land, or sometimes to do both. Moreover, branches of petty commodity production and home-based piece-rate production open to small farmers and the landless alike are so unremunerative that locals opt for wage labour. Similarly, those rearing cattle are becoming polarised, with richer owners increasing the value of their herds, while poorer owners experience difficulties maintaining their own.

It would be true to say that in Banglen, agriculture is stagnating while rural industry is expanding. Deep-water paddy is highly susceptible to environmental conditions and does not lend itself to intensification. Rice cultivation is fully commercialised: capital is necessary for every stage of production. Buffalo ceased to be used for ploughing around 1970, and all households either hire or use their own tractors. Paddy is no longer threshed using animal power, but mechanical threshers with teams of labourers are hired. Rice harvests are sold outright and no portion is retained for home consumption. The short-grain variety of rice grown locally is exported mainly to India and Arab nations, thus producers are linked into and dependent on the world commodity market. Because of increased availability of local transport many farmers now market their rice directly to rice mills, cutting out middlemen and thus gaining better prices. However, they are disadvantaged by their practice of selling and not consuming part of their product: each time producers sell short-grain rice to mills and buy long-grain rice from them, they forego savings of around 11.3 per cent that would be made had they consumed their own milled rice.[5]

The conditions of agricultural production make it increasingly difficult for farmers, especially small-holders, to make a profit, or even cover costs of production. Returns are unreliable and insufficient to meet household needs consistently for all but the largest landowners. Farmers commonly said that before connection to Chainat dam and recent climatic changes, they would obtain yields of 50 to 60 *thang*.[6] Paradoxically, in this particular locality connection to the Chainat water management system made flooding more concentrated and sudden, whereas previously flooding was gradual and brought soil nutrients (Amyot, 1976, p.4). Nowadays locals consider themselves lucky if they obtain 30 *thang*. Farmers complain about increasingly unpredictable rainfall and a drastic reduction in the quality and regularity of flood water. Harvests were said to be good "before water had owners", and before the proliferation of roads which block the path of the flood water. Complaints were also often made about the unpredictability of rainfall and flooding, changes no doubt linked to the disappearance of forest cover (see Hirsch, 1987, pp.137-41). The following typical utterences reflect such concerns: "during the ploughing season the rain doesn't fall, during the harvest season it falls" and "nowadays, when the floods should recede for harvesting, instead they rise!" Many farmers express the view that no money can be made from rice farming, and that it would be better to sell one's land and make a living some other way. Farmers also deplored the rising amount of capital necessary for production and the fact that returns did not keep pace.

Another common complaint, made by large and small land-owners alike, is that harvesters could not be found at the right time and that they were commanding ever higher wages, a concern relevant to other agricultural areas (see Nipon, 1994). Several larger Ban Thung farming households hired migrant workers, often land-owners themselves, from the North-East and Lower North, a practice which is, however, not new in the province (Piker, 1983, p.27-8). These migrants hire themselves out to others in the area when their host's fields had been reaped. Because labour was generally in high demand during the harvest season, local wage labourers are not displaced by these outsiders.

Notwithstanding the poor returns to be made from rice cultivation the position of owner-operators is somewhat anomalous. Production itself brings them returns barely worth their labour, and obliges them to engage in a range of other productive or wage labour activities. Yet, at the same time, those farmers who own more than two or three *rai* are - as a result of land speculation - owners of increasingly large sums of unrealised capital.

Let us turn to consider rural dwellers' economic activities in more detail. While almost all farmers still use their land for an annual crop of 'floating rice', during the 1980s some farmers with appropriate plots and sufficient capital took to growing sweet potatoes during the dry season. For this, land needs to be near a source of irrigation and a road. Access to capital is crucial since production involves outlay on fertilizer, pesticides, shoots, irrigation hoses and pumps. Returns are substantial and can be as much as 10 times that derived from rice cultivation.

The raising of livestock is an important supplement to income for agricultural producers, as well as the landless. Recent changes in patterns of livestock-raising seem to indicate that resource-poor households occupy an ever-shrinking space and may be unable to rely on this form of petty commodity production for much longer. On the other hand resource-rich households are able to take advantage of an expanding market. For example, a combination of commercialisation and environmental changes have had a variegated impact on cattle raisers. Old limits on herd size have disappeared for capital-rich households: they are able to hire earth-moving machinery to build larger raised pens to house more than eight head of cattle during the flood season, and are able to obtain sufficient fodder by hiring others to cut it. Poorer households are still constrained by pre-existing conditions: they cannot afford to construct large pens and must use their own labour to collect fodder from flooded fields. Furthermore, the mechanisation of agriculture and climatic changes have reduced available grazing areas during the post-flood and post-harvest season. Indigenous cattle are left to graze locally while owners of expensive hybrid cattle obtain fodder from their own fields or are able to collect it from other areas using their own transport.

There are a variety of wage labour opportunities available to the landless and others whose independent economic activities do not meet their needs. These include labour in mechanised brick-yards and other local industries, seasonal agricultural work and piece-rate work. Only very few local opportunities existed in 1989/90 aside from brick-yards, but they are expanding as industry moves into the area from Bangkok. Agricultural wage labour is used mainly during the rice harvest. The recent introduction of a dry season sweet potato crop provides some work for another three months of the year. Landless labourers who do not work in the brickyards look to the harvest season as the main annual opportunity to earn money. During the dry season, work is available in the sweet potato fields and on a daily basis. Work and rest periods are often monitored closely, a recent innovation probably inspired by mechanised brick-yard work practices. Other village-based work, like emptying or digging fish ponds, is available only intermittently. Farmers who complain of labour shortages often blame local brick-yards for taking labour away from agriculture, and with good reason. Labourers benefit from the competition to a degree, in that during the harvest season many brick-yard owners increase wages by some five baht a day, obliging farmers to follow suit as the season progresses. However, brick-yard owners promptly reduce the rate after the harvest season.

Some households subsist entirely on home-based piece-work. In Ban Thung, farmers' hats (*ngop*) are produced. Market traders organise a putting-out system of production (see also Parnwell and Suranart in this volume). Households perform only specialised tasks, like stitching or attaching rims. Market traders deliver, collect and redistribute the partly finished product. This type of labour does not generate any significant surplus. Many producers commented that "you can't do it quick enough to eat." Households throughout Ban Say and in one neighbourhood of Ban Thung engage in own-account cottage industry. They produce basketry and farmers' hat headpieces respectively, purchasing bamboo poles as the primary raw material. Although these are petty commodity producers, as opposed to piece-rate producers, many made a similar complaint to the above piece-rate workers: barely enough is earned to live on. Producers complained that once they had taken account of raw materials their income rarely exceeded 20 baht a day. It is significant that many brick-yard employees formerly engaged in some form of cottage industry. Home production is most convenient for those with responsibilities like caring for children or livestock. Others combine production with fishing for home consumption and sale. Basketry and the manufacture of farmers' hat headpieces are examples of branches of petty commodity production which, because of stagnant product prices but increasing cash needs, were becoming barely viable.

What is clear from this account of livelihood strategies is that everyone is involved in the commodity economy - no section of the community lives independently of it, producing only for subsistence. However, many households do provide for some of their subsistence needs - working small kitchen gardens, fishing or catching field rats. The important point, however, is that these activities, especially where they are dependent on the environment, are precarious. Natural resource depletion - particularly of fish stocks - has meant that effectively there remain few spaces into which households can withdraw from the commodity economy.

Before proceeding to examine resource use in the district it is necessary to introduce the brick industry and its place in the local economy. The district-wide brick-making industry in Banglen is only a very recent, though rapid, development. In the early 1970s the industry was concentrated in one sub-district; it was also entirely home-based and non-mechanised. Brick production in Banglen now takes two forms, 'non-mechanised' and 'mechanised'. In non-mechanised brick-yards bricks are moulded by hand: these enterprises are often home-based, but may also be run as capitalist concerns, with piece-rate workers. Mechanised brick-yards employ between 15 and 120 workers, but the average number of employees is around 40. While some mechanised brick-yard owners had formerly been farmers, none of the 16 entrepreneurs interviewed had obtained their start-up capital from rice cultivation. Again, this is a reflection of the stagnation of the traditional agricultural sector. Locals with a surplus turn to non-farm enterprises as a means of accumulation. The number of mechanised and non-mechanised brickyards in Banglen has increased rapidly in recent years: the number of tax-registered mechanised brick-yards in the district increased from 32 to 55 in one year (1989-1990). There are about three times as many non-mechanised units. The brick industry provides employment for a significant proportion of the local population. Of 165 households surveyed in the district, more than a third (60) have at least one member employed in the industry, and almost a quarter of the work force (101 of 408 people) find employment in brick-yards.[7] The relative importance of mechanised brick-yards in terms of employment is indicated by the fact that they employed 84 per cent of these workers. Locals generally welcomed the arrival of the brick industry and workers emphasised the fact that money is earned daily contrasting this with the fact that rice cultivation yields only an uncertain income once a year. Brick-yard work is presented as preferable to cultivating rice as a tenant because it entails less risk: "It's better to hire oneself out in the brick-yards - you don't have to make any investment (*long thun*), you just use your labour." Several workers explained they had taken up wage labour because it provided them with more income than they had earned rearing ducks or making baskets. Others expressed appreciation of the fact that the industry enabled them to live and work near home rather than in Bangkok.[8]

Changing control and use of resources

As is clear from above, it is not possible to depict the local rural economy as simply an agricultural one. Nevertheless, it is still important to examine the implications of recent developments on the resources upon which agriculture depends. Growth in the Thai economy in the late-1980s and early-1990s has led to increased demand for rural-based natural resources from non-rural economic concerns, and to widespread land speculation. The expanded and new local markets for land, top-soil and sand that emerged in this period have important implications for the livelihoods of Banglen residents. These natural resources are exploited with little regard for long-term environmental and socio-economic implications. In some cases locals sell these resources in order to enhance already high incomes, in others villagers with only marginal incomes are forced by relative poverty to exploit them. In all events, however, it is probably true to say that the greatest beneficiaries are in the first instance the purchasers of these resources. With regard to land sales, buyers are able to exploit locals' lack of information regarding the future value of their land. Small-holders are also so willing to relinquish control of land, or sell top-soil and sand, because rice cultivation provides such poor remuneration when compared to the rewards offered by the new markets for these resources. This section examines these phenomena in more detail.

The natural resources of Banglen district are deployed to benefit the industrial and not the agricultural sector of the Thai economy. They are exploited to serve the needs of various branches of this sector: top-soil provides small-scale and medium-scale local enterprises with the means to produce bricks which then literally underpin the growth of urban centres; farm-land and top-soil are taken out of agricultural use to make way for factories; and sand is exploited to extend national highways.[9] In the midst of all these changes, one must not lose sight of the apparent readiness with which farmers nationally were selling their land to speculators (e.g. see the *Bangkok Post*, 20.1.1990; 5.5.1990; 25.6.1990; 30.7.1990). In the Central Plains economic growth spurred Bangkok-based speculators on to seek land, particularly near lines of transport, in the expectation that it could be sold on to manufacturing industry interests for several times the initial investment (cf. Pongsapich *et.al.*, 1993, pp.80-1). It is hard to establish the extent to which farmers have been selling up since, at least until 1990, government statistics did not quantify the actual area of land that changed hands, indicating only the number of transactions and the value of tax collected on sales. Furthermore, because statistics are compiled only by province, it is impossible to ascertain the number of sales in smaller administrative units such as districts or sub-districts. Nevertheless, province-wide statistics for Ayutthaya indicate a dramatic rise in the number of transactions and their value: tax revenue increased more than 25-fold in the period 1981-1990 and there were more than three times as many sales in 1990 as there were in pre-boom 1986 (Source: Ayutthaya Land Registration Office).

Findings from a survey of Ban Thung and Ban Say households[10] indicate the extent to which selling land was a local issue and occurrence. Just over a fifth of households which owned land in the preceding 10 years had sold some or all of it.[11] That land sales have intensified in recent years is evident from looking at when sales took place. Almost half of sales by survey households in these two sub-districts were made in 1990 itself while less than a quarter were carried out between 1980 and 1986.[12] In view of the pattern of increases in land prices this acceleration in the market is to be expected. Furthermore, a striking shift in the relative value of local land has emerged. The shift clearly reflects changing priorities in the national economy: land appropriate for industrial use is now more valuable than prime rice-growing land. Before 1987 the deep-flooding land of Ban Thung sub-district was always more expensive than Ban Say land, which was rarely submerged by seasonal flood water, while also being closer to a major road. While the former yielded excellent crops of 'floating rice', owners of the latter area were primarily dependent on rather poor rain-fed crops. This trend has subsequently been reversed as speculators seeking land to sell on to industrialists favour higher land, which requires less expenditure on land-fill to raise its level beyond floodwaters, and land that is more accessible by road.

The economic statuses and motives of people who sell land are varied, as could be expected. For some households selling is a step towards further accumulation, for others it signals their impoverishment. Some sales were voluntary, others more or less imposed. Large land-owners sold segments of their land-holdings to invest in more lucrative enterprises, for example brick manufacturing or large-scale poultry farming. Some households which sold land were not under financial pressure, but sold to either distribute the receipts among off-spring, or to make bank deposits and live off the interest. Owners may be disinclined to farm because of poor returns or because they are physically unable. As sales intensified during 1990 some land-owners found their land almost surrounded by sold plots. They often found themselves obliged to sell for fear that when surrounding plots were built on, their own land would become unworkable. They could lose access, flood water would be blocked off and field rats would breed in adjacent raised plots and focus on their harvests. Sometimes land-brokers played on such fears to force owners to accept low prices. Finally, households sold because they were in debt, commonly incurred as a result of rice cultivation, or expenditure on life-cycle ceremonies.[13] While small-holders who sell land voluntarily can modestly cash in on the land boom, those who benefit the most are villagers with large holdings. Such individuals are able to retain control over some land while obtaining sufficient capital to invest in more profitable enterprises.

Another factor in this equation is the activity of land sales brokers, about which relatively little has been written. Land sales are rarely made directly between buyer and seller. Up to four levels of brokers (*nay na*) can be involved before the final buyer is reached. According to several land brokers interviewed, most buyers were Bangkok-based speculators who purchased large tracts with a view to selling them on to companies wishing to set up factories. Local brokers are thus necessary to organise the purchase of a tract of land from a large number of owners of contiguous plots. Brokers are often local office-holders (headmen or *kamnan*) or state employees (teachers, district officials) who have the advantage of having access to local people as well as links with outsiders.

Land brokers generally work in one of two ways. They are commissioned to buy specified tracts by outsiders or they work on their own account, finding buyers for locals willing to sell. Local and outsider brokers working independently ask village landowners if they are willing to sell, offering to find them a buyer. Commissioned land-brokers, on the other hand, attempt to persuade numerous plot-owners to sell. They bargain with land-owners individually, and bargain hard since they keep the difference between the sum allowed by the buyer per *rai* (1 *rai* = 0.1 ha.) and the actual sale price. Villagers are generally in a weak position when it comes to selling: they do not know what allowance per *rai* such brokers have been allowed. One attempt by small landowners in two Banglen sub-districts to co-operate in the form of an association and bargain collectively with land sales brokers came to nothing when brokers refused to deal with anyone other than the individual land-owners themselves.

Moreover, villagers will until a late stage often be ignorant of plans, for example road development programmes, that affect the future value of their land. A vast tract of Banglen land was bought up in early 1990 by land-brokers who were reportedly acting on behalf of the then Minister of Communications: several intermediary land-brokers were said to be involved. It later emerged that the nearby Asian Highway was to be improved in that area and a feeder road would cross this land. Needless to say, the Minister would have had prior knowledge of this development. Land sales brokerage is often the focus of intense and sometimes violent conflict. Two killings related to land speculation in the district occurred during 1990: one victim was a sub-district headman, the other a teacher. Rather ironically, on at least two occasions in this period district officials asked sub-district and village headmen at their monthly meetings to advise villagers not to sell their farmland. It was common knowledge that district officials are very active land-brokers.

The expanded market for land is not the only market that is whittling away the resource base of local residents. The relatively new market for top-soil is leading land-owners to make decisions that have potentially damaging implications in the long term. Excavation of top-soil, like land sales, is not monitored or regulated by the state. During the dry season heavy machinery can often be seen digging away at the surface of rice fields throughout the district. Tipper lorries carry off the soil, destined either for construction sites, to raise foundations above flood levels, or brick-yards - and ruining local roads in the process. Some fields are dug to a depth of half a metre, others to three or four metres. Widespread demand for Banglen top-soil is only a relatively recent phenomenon: before 1987 soil did not have a cash value[14] and previously, when farmers wanted their top-soil removed to bring the land within reach of flood water, they gave it away, even if it was suitable for brick manufacture. More recently, several land-owners appeared to have sold their top-soil in order to generate income rather than to improve their land. That farmers do this is not surprising when one considers that by selling top-soil from one *rai*, dug to a depth of half a metre, an owner could make 10,000 baht, at least 20 times the average return from rice cultivation in 1990. According to farmers, land where top-soil had been removed to a depth of up to 50 centimetres needs at least five years to regain its fertility. However, land-owners often permit excavation to greater depths. In Ban Say there are several water-logged pits which are now economically useless. The owners had sold top-soil to such a depth that acidic undersoils were revealed and made the farming of local fish varieties (an alternative to rice-farming once the top-soil has been removed) impossible. The removal of soil can also cause problems for owners of neighbouring plots: one resident was said to have intentionally sold soil from a plot to such a depth (2.5 metres) that earth from neighbouring fields would gradually replenish it as a result of subsidence encouraged by rain and flood water.

The excavation of top-soil beyond a certain depth reduces the value of adjacent land and undermines the viability of local agriculture. The same is true of the excavation of sand, which, while not a resource farmers use, has similar negative effects on the local environment. Toward the end of 1990 expansion of a nearby national highway created demand for a local source of sand. Outside building materials contractors who obtained permission from the district office to excavate sand came into conflict with local farmers. The contractors tended to extract sand not just from the area for which they had obtained permission, but also from beneath adjacent fields, causing severe subsidence (see Holland, 1990 for a similar case). Several land-owners who considered their land under threat appealed to district officials to withdraw the contractors' permit but were unsuccessful. This was probably not least because the contractors had been careful to cultivate the support of district officials. They also had the co-operation of village and subdistrict leaders.

Social differentiation and status in Banglen

Agrarian differentiation has been a central theme in a number of studies,[15] which all essentially indicate that expanding capitalism is leading to more pronounced socio-economic differences in rural Thailand. While this process is well documented elsewhere, our concern here is mainly to indicate the pattern of differences, and to establish the 'symptoms' of differentiation in this particular area. Households in Ban Thung and Ban Say sub-districts are highly differentiated in terms of their control over productive resources and ability to accumulate capital. Although the broad dividing lines between village-level strata may be apparent, a cautious approach to analysing differentiation has been recommended on the grounds that because individual producers may occupy multiple positions in relation to each other "it may be premature to attempt to define exclusive categories of classes of rural producers" (Turton, 1989, p.75). As White (1989) has argued, indicators of differentiation need to be derived from a cluster of characteristics, as opposed to land ownership alone.[16] This approach has commonly given rise to three broad categories: rich, middle ranking and poor households, which, with some modifications, represents the situation in Ban Thung and Ban Say. The categorisation below highlights the most salient local indicators of differentiation: namely, land ownership and use, access to and control over resources, income sources and labour patterns. The size of operational land holdings is used to distinguish between small, medium and large petty commodity producing households. These farm sizes are based on Amyot's finding (1976, p.91) that in Ayutthaya small farmers may be said to operate less than 15 *rai* while big farmers operate more than 44 *rai*. Although not an entirely satisfactory practice, we treat the household, defined by co-residence and sharing of food, as the unit of analysis: recent literature has highlighted the fact that intra-household economic behaviour means that this model of the household as a solidary unit is something of a fiction.

Capitalist and petty capitalist households (3.6 per cent of survey households): such households own businesses or agricultural holdings which operate using predominantly wage labourers. Businesses include both mechanised and non-mechanised brick-yards. Owners may also own large tracts of land, and have a subsidiary occupation such as poultry farming, trading in agricultural inputs and commodities or money lending. They may also be land brokers (*nay na*).

Resource-rich petty commodity producing households (23 per cent of households): these households cultivate middle-sized to large-sized farms. The majority cultivate capital-intensive cash crops, such as sweet potato, alongside rice. They may also rear cattle, often the more expensive hybrid-indigenous type, and be local creditors. Typically, they will own instruments of production, such as a tractor or a thresher, which they hire out. They hire workers seasonally, and may have one or two live-in workers.

Resource-poor petty commodity producing households (17.6 per cent): these households own or control resources on a scale smaller than those of the above two categories. They do not possess expensive instruments of production, such as agricultural machinery. They operate small-holdings and may be able to finance cultivation of sweet potato. If these households are involved in credit relations, they lend money on a much reduced level, and are often borrowers from the Bank for Agriculture and Agricultural Co-operatives or from individuals. Income from the sale of agricultural commodities is often supplemented by the sale of livestock and wage labouring either in brick-yards or during the harvest season. The important distinction between these households and landless households is that they can operate without permanent recourse to wage labour. Households with fewer resources (cattle, land, etc.) are accordingly more dependent on wage labour.

Non-farming households (52.1 per cent): some of these households engage in petty commodity production (basketry, own-account peasant hat production, rearing of piglets or indigenous cattle). Others are comprised of only wage labourers. Wage labourers may sell their labour on a daily or a piece-rate basis. Most daily wage labourers work in the local brick-yards: of the 86 households in this category alone, 48 households (55.8 per cent) have one or more members who work in a brick-yard. In most cases, petty commodity production alone, in the forms and scale practised by the landless, cannot satisfy household needs.

The proportion of non-farming households derived from the field survey (52.1 per cent) corresponds closely with that given in government statistics for the district as a whole, which state that 54 per cent of households do not operate holdings.[17] Both of these figures betray a significant increase in the proportion of non-farming households as compared with three Ayutthaya villages surveyed by Amyot in 1969. At this time only 41.5 per cent of total households did not operate agricultural holdings (1976, Table 6.2).[18] With regard to tenancy, survey data indicate that more than half of farming households only cultivate their own land, while just under a third are part-tenants. Full tenants are in a minority; comprising only 14.9 per cent of households. Survey data have also shown, not surprisingly, that an inverse relationship exists between farm size and incidence of wage labouring: the larger the size of farm the less the incidence of wage labour among household members (a trend also observed by Romijn, 1987, p.227). Finally, it is worth noting the extent to which residents have diversified their livelihoods from rice-based agriculture. The extent to which this is so is reflected in the fact that 41 combinations of occupations were exhibited by 165 households.

A description of the economic differences between households can only tell us so much. They tell us nothing about social relations between households of contrasting economic status. Are these differences in economic status important in the sense of informing people's evaluation of each other, or are communities relatively socially egalitarian? It seems true to say that not only do economic differences greatly inform people's social statuses, but that as the gap between groups becomes larger, so social differences are more heavily accentuated. The distinctions generated by economic differences are so marked that in some localities they have given rise to discrete social classes. This situation mirrors, to some extent, a future envisaged by Steven Piker, who conducted research in an Ayutthaya community in the 1960s. Piker (1975, p.318) asserted that, although status distinctions were evident during his field-work, landless villagers continued to see themselves as rice farmers and did not draw class distinctions between themselves and land-owners. This, he says, was because the landless shared the lifestyle and skills of their landed neighbours, and had worked on the land of their parents. But, Piker (*ibid.*, p.319) foresaw the time when, "as memory of landownership with its distinctive way of life fades" for that and future generations, distinctions would become qualitatively different. This envisaged future represents the present situation in many parts of Banglen district. Some households have been landless for two and even three generations and have never experienced land-ownership or a farming lifestyle. Different lifestyles are a matter of everyday experience.

Evaluations of social status in Banglen are broadly based on the perceived standard of living of a household. Households are ranked by the size and quality of houses, what household members can buy and what they own: it refers to lifestyle and consumption.[19] Indigenous status classification identifies three status groups: 'the poor' (*khon jon*), 'the middling' (*ban klang*) and 'the rich' (*khon ruay*) (cf. Holland, 1990, pp.225-38). These correspond very broadly with the economic bands in which households can be placed. Those landless households without control of any means of production, and which are dependent upon daily wage labour, generally consider themselves to be poor and are so labelled by others. The poorest of such households subsist hand to mouth, giving expression to their predicament in typical phrases such as: "we look for food in the morning and eat it at dusk" (*ha chaw kin kham*) and "we work and eat day-by-day" (*tham wan kin wan*). Some resource-poor petty commodity producing households are also within this category.

The 'middling' status group encompasses those landless households with an assured income source, some resource-poor and a few resource-rich petty commodity producing households. Members of households in this category did not identify themselves as 'poor', but express their broader resource base and greater economic security as having "enough to eat, enough to use" (*pho kin pho chay*).

While most resource-rich petty commodity producing households will be spoken of as 'the rich' (*khon ruay*) by their poorer neighbours, all capitalist households will be so labelled. It should be noted that these labels are contested by the labelled: some 'rich' households will claim they are not rich, and some 'poor' households will insist they are not poor. In general, poorer villagers are acutely aware of the divide between themselves and their richer neighbours and it would be accurate to say that there was indeed very little social intercourse between the two status groups. One landless man expressed the division in the following terms: "we hardly get on together - we each go a different way. We and 'those who have' [the rich] don't get on."

Labelling of status groups is done in a context of contested moral evaluations. In terms of religious ideology, and to some degree popular perception, poverty implies a negative moral state. This is supported by official Thai Buddhism, which holds that the rich and powerful are so on account of merit (*bun*) earned from a previous life (see Hanks, 1965). The poor are so on account of a lack of merit, or of the accumulation of demerit (*bap*) from former lives. This ideology underpins the utterances of the wealthy. Moral evaluations of status groups are of course contested by subordinate groups. Basham (1989) has disputed the extent to which the "official culture", as he calls it, following Scott (1985), actually influences people's assessment of their predicament. The poor resist interpretations of their status based on 'official ideology' while the rich and powerful use it to legitimise their position. Although status differences are legitimised and explained by a Buddhist ideology, the labelled are, as Scott (1985, p.321) puts it "sceptical of a dominant ideology that rationalises their material deprivation and low status" (see also Vaddhanaphuti, 1984, pp.462-74). Religious ideology is reinforced by economic and political factors. Social status derives from the personal embodiment of power as well as lifestyle. Power or influence, in turn, can derive from wealth, especially from the possession of money. Mulder has argued that money is not only widely admired but is "the preeminent embodiment of power" (1990, p.54): it "is seemingly able to buy power, and so money is prestige" (1990, p.96). Money influences social status and the moral evaluations which accompany it.

The poor in Ban Thung express clearly the conditions underlying their position and the implications of their predicament. Some of the poor are bitter about how the local rich had accumulated capital, and perceived that their own impoverishment was linked directly to the gains made by the rich; morality and merit play no part in such explanations. As one old man, who had lost his land to a local money-lender, declared: "without a doubt, it is the poor who make money for the rich." Poorer villagers were aware that their off-spring would find it difficult to improve their fortunes. While two or three decades ago it was possible for a wage labourer to accumulate enough money to buy land on which to farm or build a house, this is no longer the case. As an old couple asked rhetorically: "how are our children going to be better off than their parents?"

New local officeholders: from farmers to entrepreneurs

Social and economic changes in this district of Ayutthaya have been rapid and far-reaching. One aspect of change that has received relatively little attention in the literature concerns local politics. Below we depict some trends which have emerged in Banglen district that have been particularly visible from the late 1980s. Firstly we show that a significant number of recently elected local office-holders are representative of an emergent socio-economic élite and explore the implications of this. Secondly, we reveal that local communities are now integrated into national- and provincial-level electoral politics and suggest that this has had socially divisive effects.

Administrative villages are represented to the state bureaucracy by elected headmen. A sub-district headman, or *kamnan* , is elected as leader of the sub-district from among village headmen by all residents eligible to vote. Sub-district and village headmen are in an anomalous position insofar as they have the twin duties of representing villagers' needs to the local bureaucracy in the district office, while simultaneously being local government servants. All headmen and the *kamnan* sit on the sub-district council, whose role it is to draw up, administer and implement five-year development plans. *Kamnan* tend effectively to dominate sub-district councils. This institution is only partially a structure for local government: members are elected and have the authority to administer and implement local development plans, but, insofar as the council is directly under the authority of the provincial government and does not have the authority to pass laws, it is simply an extension of the state. The positions of village headman and *kamnan* carry considerable prestige and yield the incumbent numerous opportunities to accumulate money by abusing the position. Currently these posts are highly sought-after in the Central Plains, and the prestige and the potential financial rewards afforded by office go some way to explaining why.

It is probably true to say that before the mid- to late-1980s most new Banglen *kamnan* and headmen were local farmers, and representative of larger land-owners. From this one should not read that such office-holders entirely identify their interests with those of residents in their communities. Nor can one assume that such representatives do no not use state funds in unofficial and illegal ways. However, one can assume that insofar as their livelihoods are tied in with farming, their economic interests are in the broadest sense bound up with the agricultural economy. Such office-holders would generally obtain office on the basis of local support. Campaigns would be won on the back of requests for support from kin and neighbours, and the giving of feasts. According to informants, vote-buying rarely played a part in such elections.[20] Vote-buying was apparently first used systematically and pervasively in the district in the successful general election campaign of General Narong Kittikachorn in 1986, who returned from exile imposed as a result of his role in the suppression of the October 1973 student-led revolt. By the early 1990s use of money was so common that it was considered unthinkable that candidates for headman and *kamnan* elections would not buy votes: candidates were perceived to have no chance of success if they did not do so. It seems likely that the practice became universal in such local elections because of prior use in general, and provincial, elections.

From the late-1980s, a new breed of office-holders emerged in Banglen district. A number of owners of mechanised, capitalist brick-yards began to launch successful bids for office as headmen and *kamnan*. By 1990, six mechanised brick-yard owners held political office, three as *kamnan* and three as headmen; half of these positions were won during the previous two years. By the end of 1993 another three mechanised brick-yard owners had obtained the office of headman, bringing the total number of such office-holders to nine. All of these individuals are members of a district-wide association of owners of mechanised brick-yards, the Brick Manufacturers' Association (BMA).[21] Campaigns were launched with the practical and moral support of co-members of the Association. These candidates did not hesitate to use their relatively superior financial resources to fund their campaigns. However, ideological strategies are also of prime importance. Candidates take pains to portray themselves as effective patrons, and morally validate their candidacy with generous sponsorship of local religious institutions. Of two brick-yard owners who obtained office in Ban Thung and Ban Say sub-districts in 1990, both were relative outsiders in the communities in which they obtained office, and their success was in the face of considerable local opposition. Moreover, the brick-yard owner who became a headman of a village of Ban Say was the first local candidate to use the practice of vote-buying in such elections and generated resentment both among his fellow candidates - one of whom stated that he simply could not afford to compete on the same basis - and among some villagers. Subsequent to his election he was seen as more concerned with his business than the duties of office. The predominance of vote-buying effectively excludes poorer members of any community from competing on an even footing.

Brick-yard owning office-holders are distinct from most other office-holders in several respects. They are noticeably wealthier and have high status within the hierarchy of the district and even provincial notables. The chairman of the District Association of *Kamnan* and Headmen, for example, is a brick-yard owner. Such is the wealth and status of such *kamnan* that two of them pay a deputy a salary, met from their own funds, to perform the daily duties of office. They thus free themselves to give more attention to the running of their businesses. These and other office-holding members of the BMA are held by district officials in high regard, and the leadership of the Association takes pains to keep good relations between the it and officialdom: the BMA contributes generously whenever the local state representatives make requests for funds for one project or another.

It is difficult to generalise about how these brick-yard owners serve in office or make use of their position. To say that brick-yard owners seek local office so that they can use the position to support their business activities, while undoubtedly accurate to some extent, is not the whole story. It is also the case that status and prestige are sought as goals in themselves (cf. Ockey, 1993, p.60). At least one of the individuals who obtained office in 1990 is widely viewed as not having acted corruptly whilst in office, despite the fact that he spent a great deal of money on his election campaign. This is less surprising when one considers that the funds obtainable by abusing office are fairly inconsequential in comparison to revenue from a mechanised brick factory. Rather than being motivated by the promise of access to government funds, bribes and so forth, such candidates seem concerned to enhance the standing of their businesses, *vis-à-vis* those with whom they do business and the district élite.

Office-holding *per se* does not give incumbents business-related opportunities to accumulate capital illegally. However, it does give the incumbent greater access to local labour, which in 1990 was in short supply. A headman or *kamnan* could by no means force villagers to work in his brick-yard, but the office-holders' brick-yard would become a first port of call for villagers seeking work. In many respects, these new brick-yard owners have become local patrons. Indeed, they often portray themselves in such terms, describing their relations with their workers in paternalistic idioms. It is important to note that, irrespective of whether a large-scale brick-yard owner is an office-holder or not, they wield considerable influence in the communities in which they operate. This is by virtue of the fact that they are wealthy, and that they are employers of large numbers of people. An example of this is the fact that in one sub-district, when the former *kamnan* was set to retire, local elders approached the young but affluent owner of the mechanised brick-yard to ask him if he intended to become the new *kamnan*. They apparently considered that they were powerless to resist a bid for the post from this man.

Insofar as office-holding brick-yard owners are wealthy and have good relations with district, and often provincial officials, they are disproportionately successful in obtaining funds to develop infrastructure in their district.[22] However, having such an individual as a *kamnan* or headman is a double-edged sword: whilst they may be successful in attracting funds, the projects they choose to support may be not address the concerns of the most needy. Projects are likely to be of the type that yield highly visible results, a feature favoured by bureaucrats. Less visible projects that may support the livelihoods of marginal and poor residents, such as improving local fish stocks, may take second place.

The comments above concerning the penetration of a new socio-economic élite into local politics have wider relevance than this district alone. The fact that the commodity produced by these entrepreneurs is bricks is almost incidental. For example, in Chachoengsao in the mid-1980s large-scale poultry farmers exercised their economic power in much the same way as contemporary Banglen brick-makers are doing (Buchongkul, 1985). Just as traditional rice cultivation has lost its pre-eminence in the Thai economy, so at the local level farmers are being pushed aside by entrepreneurs who have capitalised on increased demand for certain commodities. The danger is, perhaps, that if more positions of local office are obtained by brick-yard operators, farmers and the landless will find they have lost what was potentially a valuable institution for representing their interests.

Finally, we wish to note that national electoral politics has politicised village-level politics to an extent not evident before the 1980s. For a number of reasons parliament has acquired greater significance and influence relative to the bureaucracy. This has been reflected in greater competition for office, and a greater interest on the part of aspiring MPs in controlling rural votes. An associated change has been greater involvement of capitalist interests in national electoral politics: many of these 'new' MPs are businessmen. National politicians attempt to obtain and extend control over grass-roots votes by establishing vote-procuring networks (see Ockey, 1992; Arghiros, 1993, pp.199-202). These networks are built up by using incumbent local office-holders such as provincial councillors, *kamnan* and headmen as political clients. They may also use local business people whose business dealings give them contacts over a wide area, or they may also target large employers who have, in their eyes, 'captive voters' in the form of their employees: owners of larger brick-yards are regularly targeted by candidates in general and provincial elections. Alternatively, MPs support new candidates for these positions as and when elections arise, by donating campaign funds and resources. Obviously, when successful candidates in local elections are outsiders who are financed by MPs the likelihood that they will serve the interests of residents is diminished. If these political clients obtain office they are expected to reciprocate by mobilising the vote-procuring network which they created for their own campaign on behalf of the political patron. Several layers may be involved. An MP may use a provincial councillor as a vote broker; and the provincial councillor may then use *kamnan* and village headmen to mobilise voters at a more local level. Local office-holders are linked with national and provincial politicians in a structure of political clientelism.

When local office-holders become the political clients of higher level politicians, factionalism at the sub-district level can become endemic. This occurred over 1990 in Ban Thung sub-district, when MPs and provincial councillors demonstrated a commitment to opposing candidates in elections for a new *kamnan*. The sub-district divided in two as villagers were obliged to take sides. A few months after this primarily local political conflict, elections for provincial councillors took place. Opposing provincial councillor candidates sought the support of the existing *kamnan* and the incumbent headman whom he had defeated. These two individuals acted as vote bosses for the opposing councillors and the lines of opposition in the sub-district created some months previously were reactivated by this wider political conflict. Social relations in the sub-district were significantly affected and villagers expressed surprise that *kan muang*, politics, had entered village life. Villagers who found themselves in opposing factions ceased attending the life-cycle parties of others whom they had once considered friends.

Provincial large-scale businessmen have obtained a greater role in national politics: in this section we have seen that a similar pattern is emerging at the local level. Because of the pervasiveness of vote-buying as a campaign tool, local business-owners have an advantage over relatively poor villagers in their bids for local office. This development reflects a changing rural political economy and changing priorities in the national economy. It is difficult to predict the impact on rural areas if local businessmen obtain a greater role in local government. What does seem certain, however, is that so long as votes can be mobilised with money, such individuals are unlikely to feel compelled to represent effectively the interests of the landless and those farmers who remain.

Concluding remarks

This chapter has sketched out a number of aspects of change in a district within the Extended Bangkok Metropolitan Region. It has reviewed the ways in which local livelihood strategies are diversifying, with traditional rice cultivation playing an ever-diminishing role. Industrialisation and urbanisation has intensified demand for land and other local natural resources. However, partly because the markets and exploitation of these resources are not regulated, long term local social and environmental needs are simply not accounted for. Rural communities in areas such as this are increasingly polarised both economically and socially. While differences in access to productive resources have existed for some time, it seems that social distinctions between residents of households considered locally as rich and poor are increasingly inflexible. A new kind of local office-holder, entrepreneurs who have tapped into new economic opportunities created by industrialisation, has emerged in this environment. These entrepreneurs are bolstering their economic power with political office and status. The implications of this development for the quality of future rural political participation and representation are not encouraging.

At the time of field research large national and international businesses had not been established in the study district. Without doubt they will do so during the latter part of the 1990s as businesses increasingly take advantage of improving communications, cheaper land and so on in areas such as Banglen. When this occurs we will see even more sweeping changes than have been described in this chapter. While some of the points made here may soon need revising, we hope to have highlighted a few of the ways in which local and broader forces have interacted to generate change at the local level. The observations may well have wider relevance to other former rice-growing areas of Thailand, and indeed Pacific Asia, as they too are drawn closer into the sphere of infuence of an almost agressively industrialising economy.

Notes

1 This chapter draws on field research conducted between 1989 and 1990 and draws on findings presented in Arghiros (1993) and Wongsekiarttirat (1991).

2 Banglen is a pseudonym, used because political data are presented in this paper. Sub-district names are also pseudonyms.

3 This trend is by no means limited to Ayutthaya province: see the paper by Guy Trébuil in this volume.

4 This finding confirms those of studies conducted ten years previously, which concluded that farming in the ten-year interval between 1970 and 1980 had deteriorated: see Pongsapich (1982) and Dhiratayakinant (1982).

5 This figure is based on the following: short-grain paddy yields on average 66 per cent of its weight in milled rice. The highest price received in 1990 for short-grain rice was 4,000 baht/tonne, thus 100 kg. of short-grain (milled) rice had a value of 666 baht. The cheapest long-grain milled rice sold by the mill was 750 baht per 100 kg. Long-grain rice is preferred for aesthetic reasons (it is said to be 'tasty', *aroy*). However, one elderly farmer complained that he greatly preferred short-grain rice, saying it was more flavoursome, but that he felt ashamed to put it in monks' bowls to make merit every morning, because it was generally considered of inferior quality.

6 A volume measure of rice: 1 *thang* is equivelent to 20 litres.

7 A brief field visit in 1994 to the district indicated that a number of locals had left the relatively arduous brick-yards for the two or three new factories that had been established: work in the latter is conducted out of the sun and is less physically demanding. Migrant workers from the North-East of Thailand appear to have been used to fill the resulting gap. More research is needed to give more weight to these observations.

8 Villagers working in the putting-out gem-cutting industry in the North-East expressed similar views about the arrival of rural industry in their locality (Parnwell and Khamanarong, 1990, p.15).

9 The raised foundations of highways are constructed from layers of earth interspersed with layers of sand.

10 This survey, conducted between September and November 1990, was of every fourth household in these two sub-districts. Citation of survey results elsewhere in the chapter refer to this survey, unless otherwise specified.

11 In more detail: 17 of the 165 surveyed households (10.3 per cent) had sold land in the 10-year period before 1990. Seventy-one households (43 per cent) owned land at the time of the survey. Of these 71 households, 13 (18.3 per cent) had sold some but not all of their holdings since 1980. An additional four households (2.4 per cent) had sold all their land during the same period.

12 Similarly in another Banglen sub-district, Khayay, 64.3 per cent of sales of rice land over the period of 1970-90 took place over this same period (Wongsekirattirat, 1991, p.69).

13 In a survey undertaken by CUSRI-ORSTOM in 1991 nearly 65 per cent of land sales in their sample were considered 'distress sales', of which 80 per cent were from farmers owning small holdings. The most prevelant reasons given for land sales were loan repayment, and to meet family needs (Phélinas, 1994).

14 The going rate in 1990 for earth taken from an area of one *rai* and to a depth of half a metre was 10,000 to 12,000 baht. The price of

topsoil/land fill had risen almost proportionately with land prices: in 1988 soil was free, in 1989 4,000 to 5,000 baht, and in 1990, as mentioned, reached 10,000 to 12,000 baht.

15 For example, Chiengkul, 1983; Douglass, 1984; Chai-Anan, 1984; Turton, 1989; Rigg, 1988; Holland, 1990; Hirsch, 1990.

16 See also Holland (1990, p.84) and Rigg (1988, p.340) who notes of his field site in North-East Thailand that "the relationship between land and wealth has broken down." He found no correlation between the two sets of figures.

17 'Banglen' District Office records and 1988 Village Survey (*kho so cho song kho* , 2531).

18 This figure, arrived at by Amyot, cannot be treated as definitive, however. Even within the province there is wide variation in patterns of land holdings. For example, research in another Ayutthaya district, Sena, conducted in 1974-75, estimated that only 19 per cent of households were not rice cultivators (Tanabe, 1981, p.230). It is also close to a figure given for the nearby predominantly rice-growing province of Suphanburi in 1991, where 55 per cent of households in did not operate land-holdings (Phélinas, 1994, p.65).

19 Kerkvliet (1990, p.61) has made a similar point with regard to Philippine villagers. Essentially the distinction between class and status made here is the same as that made by Weber (1977, p.193).

20 There is evidence of sporadic vote-buying in the 1950s and 1960s (Kaufman, 1960, p.76; Piker, 1983, p.143). The point being made, however, is that prior to the 1980s vote-buying in sub-district-level elections was the exception rather than the rule.

21 Members of the Brick Manufacturers' Association (BMA) were perceived by both villagers and by themselves to belong to another social milieu or stratum: they are, as it were, outsiders. As one brickyard owner put it, villagers and BMA members "are in a different class to each other" (*yu khon la chan*).

22 The funds referred to here are from the Provincial Administrative Organisation: only a proportion of project requests submitted yearly by *kamnan* are successful.

8 Continuity, change and 'development': The case of Thai textiles

H. Leedom Lefferts Jr.

Introduction

Textiles may be the most typical product of household artisanship found in many contemporary Tai and Thai[1] villages. In North-East Thailand and among Tai in Laos, northern Vietnam, and southern China, looms are normal household furniture; in the not too distant past, looms were found in many village households in Central and North Thailand as well. This chapter focuses on the changes in weaving found in Thailand and the complex meanings of these changes. The paper examines how we might best conceptualise these changes - as continuity, 'simple' change, or as part of that peculiar process known as 'development' - and what these have meant and might now mean for the people involved, especially the women who are the producers of these textiles.

Changes in Tai weaving that have occurred over the past few hundred years are partly the result of a complex series of processes parallelling European development (cf. Kriedte, Medick and Schlumbohm, 1981). However, records and oral histories show that Thai textiles - their production and the control of that production - have been a continuing focus of Thai state activity in ways that seem not to have been part of the European experience. The concern of the Thai state for textiles continues today through state supported and private enterprise.

Meanwhile, some women produce textiles to present their skills as artisans and home makers in the context of village life. At the same time, they may be quite willing to sell some pieces, but not others. Thus, textiles may be art as well as skill; a particular piece may be sold not only as an expression of the weaver's accomplishments but also because it is the least important example in her cloth basket.

Certainly textiles, as things, present themselves not only as commodities; they connote much more. In Thai and Tai culture, textiles represent the gender of women as producers and reproducers of social and cultural systems. The gifting and wearing of textiles allocates superior-subordinate statuses and roles in village and state contexts (Gittinger and Lefferts, 1992).

In all of these cross currents of interests and purposes, Thai textiles - from their production to their uses and meanings - have certainly changed over the years. While many women today do not weave, the presentation of Theravada Buddhist monk's robes for ordination is still nominally considered a women's donation. Few men wear the male wrap-around skirt - *phaa sarong* - donning instead Euro-American style trousers and shirts; many women, especially in rural contexts, still wear *phaa sin* or skirts modelled on the *phaa sin* motif, even though few weave their own. Interestingly, as factory-produced textiles pervade mainland South-East Asian markets, locally-produced hand-woven textiles have become increasingly important as part of élite identification with nation states and as sources of pride for ethnic and expatriate wear.

Thus, clear-cut distinctions between continuity, change, and 'development' in Thai textiles may not be easy to discover. Textiles can be produced at the most local level or be the products of multi-national corporations; can be the brunt of élite policy or subject to the whims of fashion; and may possess personal meanings in terms of gender, self-hood and national identity.

A discussion of textile production and consumption, based in an historical framework and considering issues of contemporaneous meanings and political economies, may serve to highlight aspects of the general discussion concerning continuity, change and development. This chapter undertakes to consider Thai textiles as a way to explain these issues. It is not definitive; however, it may bring to light certain aspects of a little-recognised field which may prove instructive for further studies and considerations of development in the Thai context.

Continuity and change

The following are a number of factors which underlie textile use in pre-industrial Tai and Thai cultures:

Pre-industrial production

Historically, Tai textile production appears relatively advanced technologically when compared with contemporaneous production in adjacent cultures (Gittinger, 1992a). Tai textile production may have converted from a back tension loom to a stand up frame loom some time before Tai presence in the Angkor Empire, approximately 1100AD (Chou Ta-Kuan, 1987).

The complete system of textile production, prior to the intrusion of industrial processes, comprised the singlemost complex technology possessed by Tai in South-East Asia. The textile production system consists of a series of separable steps, from yarn production through to consumption of the finished product: production of raw materials - growing cotton or other fibers, raising silk worms using mulberry leaves - for yarn; yarn-processing and grading; dyestuffs production and dyeing; preparation of the warp; warping the loom; preparation of the weft; weaving; finishing the pieces; exchange, use, and, in some cases, recycling.

Women controlled this production. A single woman would be and, in many villages, remains responsible for all aspects of her own textile production and distribution except, possibly, actually building the loom.[2] Weaving's complex technology with its many separable elements thus provided a foundation for a woman's power in a household and women's power generally in many Theravada Buddhist Tai cultures. Although there is less evidence, weaving seems also to have been a major aspect of women's power in non-Theravada Buddhist Tai systems, such as the Tai Dam (Lefferts, 1993). Paying attention to textiles - their production and consumption - means paying attention to women's work, women's power, and individual women's lives.

Trade

South-East Asian Tai cultures generally, and, specifically, the Thai polity and society participated in an extensive textile trade before European intrusions. Prior to industrialisation, European merchants attempted to corner this trade as a way to gain access to the Thai economy, just as the Thai monarch attempted to maintain a monopoly on the import of these exotic pieces (cf. Gittinger, 1982: 1992b; Maxwell, 1990; Reid, 1988; Smith, 1977).

Textile trade and the exchange of information about textiles was not restricted to finished pieces imported from South Asia. Extensive trade of both whole cloth and elements of textile production with peoples in southern China is documented by early European explorers. Hallett (1890, p.87) notes

> A company of Yunnan Chinese with a caravan of twenty-six ponies camped close to our rest-house [in the Shan States, Burma]. The head-man told me that they had brought with them silk thread, straw hats, and copper pans, and had come from Nah Hseh [Yunnan Fu].

Trade between various Tai and other South-East Asian populations resulted in relationships of mutual dependency, with some peoples providing one essential part of a textile while the weaver supplied other parts. D'Orleans (1894, p.255) on 23 March 1892 observed

> Ban Loun [in the Dien Bien Phu valley, northern Vietnam] contains but 4 or 5 huts... They make an income by raising silk worms, as well as by agriculture, and they showed me some beautiful cocoons ... [The silk] is rough but it sells at Luang Prabang for 25 times its weight in silver. A superior quality is worth 5 pence for 20 grammes.

In field work conducted in 1991, I documented complex exchange arrangements by which Tai Dam process silk to sell to other Tai, such as Khon Muang and Lu, who said they did not raise silk because of Theravada Buddhist injunctions against taking life. In return, Tai Dam received cotton to use as weft with their own silk providing the warp. In another contemporary instance in northwestern Laos, Akha grow cotton that they trade to Lu women, who then weave narrow bands that are exchanged back to the Akha. Many other such arrangements have been observed in the past and continue today.

Commodification versus self-identification

Studies of South-East Asian textiles stress the role textiles play in self and group identification (Maxwell, 1990). However, evidence shows that textiles were and are fundamental to exchange; they serve as commodities as well as items of personal identification.

Thai rural women use textiles as one way to establish identity (Lefferts, 1992a). They also use them to make money. Milgram (1992) has pointed out, with reference to highland Luzon peoples, that these purposes may not be contradictory. This flexible stance helps explain the reception accorded D'Orleans (1894, p.320) when he indicated he might buy a few pieces:

> [In the afternoon of 27 March 1892, after he and his companions returned to their quarters in Luang Prabang] we were overrun by a troop of female hawkers, who settled themselves down in our quarters and spread out their wares for sale.

Hallett (1890, p.392) had a similar experience while staying overnight in a northern Thai village:

> In wandering through the village, noticing the beautifully embroidered skirts worn by the women ... I wished to purchase some. Soon the shore was thronged by people, some with new garments, and others carrying just one stripped from their person and replaced by one of a plainer nature.

On the other hand, M.Toyama, a Japanese silk expert employed by King Chulalongkorn in the early 1900s to improve the quality and quantity of silk produced by Thai weavers, remarked to a French interlocutor that he was surprised that women consistently refused to sell their finest silk yarn, but wished to conserve it for their own purposes (Governement General de l'Indo-Chine, 1903, p.587). He estimated that there were 30,000 individuals involved in silk production on the Khorat Plateau (North-East Thailand) at that time.

This silk might have been used for a fine *phaa sarong* which a mother could present to her son to wear during the period of *naak*hood (*naga*, Sanskrit: serpent) just prior to ordination as a Theravada Buddhist monk (Lefferts, 1994a), or for some other ceremonial purpose. For instance, in 1989 one elderly informant showed me silk scarves she had woven many years earlier as a young woman prior to marriage to give to her daughters and to be used to cover her coffin before cremation. These examples reinforce the point that some textiles can be quite valuable and might not be sold.[3]

Royal-commoner textiles and production

Imports indicate wealth, power to consume, and exude an exotic atmosphere; the use of imported textiles by a social category helps distinguish them from others and may, if properly displayed and dispensed, help align a number of other people to their cause. Certainly this was and is true in Thai societies. While recorded information is absent for the earliest periods, when records do become available[4] we find that citations regarding the power of imported textiles prominently figure among accounts of Thai royalty. The possession and astute use of textiles marked the Thai élite, their relations with other élites, their control over resources, and their ability to form entourages. Gittinger (1992b, pp.145-9) illustrates the use of imported textiles in 17th Century Ayutthaya to impress visiting dignitaries.

The use of cloth to cement entourage relationships seems fundamental to Thai society. A detail in a mural in the *ubossot* of Wat Suwannaram, Thonburi, Thailand, shows a subaltern of the king outside the palace walls presenting a South Asian textile to commoners. Receipt of such gifts would have been one way by which allegiance would have been gained; using such cloth signified the continuing nature of the relationship.[5]

Control of imported textiles by Thai royalty helped legitimise their exercise of authority. However, this meant that other items, including local cloth, had to be sent from Thailand into the world market. Domestically produced textiles supplied needs of the court as well as international trade. This was organised through a series of levies on outlying provinces. Terwiel (1989, p.138) notes that levies of white cloth assessed against provinces to Bangkok's north for the cremation of King Rama I in 1809 resulted in 1,970 white cotton pieces from 19 provinces. However, he also notes (*ibid.*, pp.138-9), "...in this invitation to send the cloth it was sometimes specifically written that instead of cloth, money could be sent."

Terwiel's point concerning the hold of the Bangkok monarchy over the provinces is partially reinforced by Koizumi's assessment of *suai* caravan tribute from what is now Thailand's North-East and Laos. Textiles played a vital role in the centre's control and exploitation of these seemingly peripheral parts of the realm. Koizumi (1992) notes that *suai* was part of an intricate trading network engineered at least by the times of the early kings of the Chakri dynasty, beginning with the founding of Bangkok in 1782. This system supported the exchange of indigenous cloth for foreign items. Roof tile and white cloth appear to have been the only finished items; all other material was accepted as raw material which would then be processed elsewhere (Koizumi, 1992, p.279). From 1824 to 1868, out of a total of 22 items, six related to textiles. The value of ramie, sapan wood, stick lac, cotton, and kapok was calculated by weight; white cloth was figured in monetary terms.

Bangkok had close control over its supplies and the people who supplied them. Much of the tribute arrived in the form of taxation, not purchases.

> When many monks were asked to formally chant texts dealing with impermanence over the royal corpse, a message was sent around giving details [of] how many pieces of white cloth were requested from each provincial town. This tax was not only demanded at the beginning of the nineteenth century, it persisted [until 1850]. (Terwiel, 1989, p.150)

While the evidence from *suai* records indicates that Bangkok's demands on the North-East may have been irregular, recent work indicates that the king of Chiang Mai had a massive impact on textile production in his realm. Bowie (1992) shows that, in the restricted mountain valleys of the North, the Chiang Mai king controlled people's lives to such an extent that his subalterns allocated weaving to particular women in particular villages:

> Extreme variations in costume denoted range of social classes, with élite wearing expensive garments. However, village women sometimes wore garments so ragged and patched that the host fabric would be entirely worn away, with only 'guest patches' (*cao khaek*) remaining. Other villagers told [Bowie] that, in order to save cloth in the old days, they had worn *sin kot*, or 'stunted skirts', which came only to the knees ...

> Some people were forced to beg for old clothes to wear, villagers said, and cloth was so valuable that it might be stolen. (Bowie, 1992, p.814)

In other locales I have gathered corroborating evidence concerning the political implications of textile production and consumption. Certainly, the appropriation of rural artisan production by urban élites is nothing new. However, the value of unwoven yarn should not be underestimated. Khmer weavers today, using a loom akin to the Thai, routinely remove the operating elements - warp, heddles, and beater - each night to the security of their houses. In up-country Laos where women had not resumed weaving after the devastations of war, the sets of monks robes, pillows, and other woven material that comprised part of the requisites given a young man upon ordination as a Theravada Buddhist monk could be sold from household to household. Thus households could sponsor an ordination even when their women might not have been able to produce the necessary cloth.

After charting the dynamic role of cloth in Chiang Mai's trade and the quality of life, Bowie (1992, p.819) concludes "this examination of textile production reveals a society with a complex division of labor, serious class stratification, dire poverty, a wide reaching trade network, and an unanticipated dynamism."

While information concerning North-East Thai and Lowland Lao rulers does not indicate such a firm grasp on textile production as found for Chiang Mai by Bowie, I do agree with the general principle of her analysis. The production and consumption of textiles - their political economy - was of primary interest to both individual women and their households as well as to the polities in which these women and their households lived. Textiles and items which could go into textile production formed a constant trade item and thus were of importance to local rulers. Thai textiles were subject to constant pressures for change and continuity in production, uses, and meanings prior to as well as after the massive influx of factory-produced imports and the current Euro-American concern with 'development'.

Development? Impacts of early industry on Thai textile economy

The effects of European industrialisation and increasing contact with Euro-American states were certainly felt by textile producers and their polities by the late 19th and early 20th centuries in Thailand. However, the early impacts of industrialisation on Thai textile production may not have been as serious as that documented in the replacement of Indian textiles by European goods on the world market (Gittinger, 1982). It is not clear that in Thailand these impacts led to major dislocations; on the contrary, the possibility exists that early industrial production may have led to a major textile fluorescence in Thailand. However, as the power of the Thai state became more pervasive, the impact of Bangkok on textile production, uses, and meanings became increasingly important.

Factory-produced and imported textiles

The earlier discussion of white cloth as an item of taxation and *suai* noted that replacement of cloth by cash was possible. Factory-produced textiles from the looms of England and white cloth from India (Bowie, 1992, p.818) became available in large quantities by the early-1900s. As soon as plentiful supplies of mass-produced white cloth from external sources became available, Bangkok ceased to demand domestically produced white cloth.

White cloth filled ritual as well as utilitarian functions. White cloth was used daily in royal contexts as a covering for food and for the disposal of personal items containing exceptional power. Equally importantly, white cloth was and remains the basic item for the manufacture of monks; robes in Tai and Thai Theravada Buddhism (Lefferts, 1992b; 1992c).

From the producer's view, plain cloth production without design may be among the least stimulating exercises in the Tai textile repertory. Weaving white cloth requires attention to detail in terms of loom tension, yarn quality, etc., without the presence of design elements to relieve the boredom of production. Village weavers and gift givers adopted factory-processed cloth for another reason as well: Theravada Buddhist monks prefer the relatively fast dyestuffs and smoothly finished yarn for monks' robes. Monks of the stricter Thammayut Nikaya have told me that they use cloth made of rough Thai homespun cotton for outer robes, while smoother cloth made from factory-processed yarn is desired for the inner *sabong* (cf. Taylor, 1993).

I have observed that certain elderly North-East Thai women, especially those living near Thammayut Nikaya monasteries, may weave white cotton cloth, usually with factory-processed yarn. Elsewhere I have seen younger women weaving white cloth to present to a monk at the time of entrance to the Rains Retreat, when each must have a single piece for bathing. Finally, in homes with elderly people, white cloth may be woven in preparation for shrouding the body of the deceased. However, even with these examples, it is reasonable to hypothesise that this production is much reduced from what it was prior to the advent of mass-produced factory cloth.

Factory produced textiles other than white cloth achieved distribution among Thai populations relatively rapidly. Complex factory woven fabrics, some printed in imitation of resist tie dyed *mat mii* (*ikat*) designs, were available prior to World War II in up-country areas of Thailand. James Madison Andrews, during his travels in North-East Thailand for the 2nd Rural Economic Survey (1933-34), purchased a printed *phaa sin* whose pattern imitated a *mat mii* motif.[6] This piece was probably manufactured in Shanghai, where Japanese businessmen established factories to produce cloth in imitation of specific South-East Asian designs. Today, many Thai women wear factory-produced *phaa sin* printed in Indonesian batik patterns. This and similar production has substantially replaced ordinary *phaa sin* production among most South-East Asian Thai populations.

It is not clear when the first factory-processed yarns and dyestuffs appeared among Tai groups. Hallett (1890, p.99), surveying a market in the Shan States from the British perspective, noted regretfully

> The dyes used by the people (*sic*) to within the last few years were solely vegetable; but these, and a pity 'tis so, are being displaced by German aniline dyes. The favorite colours are indigo, orange, maroon, and a reddish-brown.

Swetzoff and Wolf (1992, pp.249-51), in their chemical analysis of a sample of 17 Tai textiles (most from Thailand) which could be dated to the first four decades of the 20th century, found that natural dyes were used except when no natural dye equivalent was available. Thus, synthetic dyes initially appear not to replace basic dyes but to increase the range of colours available to the weaver. This agrees with my observations in Sam Tie, Houa Phan Province, Laos, where weavers used synthetically-dyed yarns to complement those coloured with natural dyes. It should be noted, however, that today in locales closer to markets, processed and pre-dyed yarns are the norm and women make do with a correspondingly restricted palette.

In sum, in conjunction with Thai cultural practices, market forces which had been in place prior to the explosion of factory-produced cloth and related items permitted a rapid and comprehensive replacement of both basic and even, to some extent, complex textiles and their components. It seems reasonable to hypothesise that replacement of routine household cloth production was welcomed by many rural weavers.

But this replacement did not necessarily mean that women spent less time weaving. While it is difficult to substantiate, it appears that, from the late 1800s through the early- and mid-1900s, an explosion in refined local textile production occurred in many areas of Thailand. It was at that time that women in now famous locations such as Ku Bua (Ratchaburi), Baan Mii (Lopburi), Hat Sieo (Sukhothai), Chonnabot (Khon Kaen), and elsewhere began to have the 'leisure' to weave the fine textiles for which they are known today. If this hypothesis can be substantiated, it is possible that the fancy 'antique' textiles which form the bases of important contemporary collections are also products of this period (Lefferts, 1992d).

This is not to say that this expanded production of elaborate textiles was not along 'traditional' lines: it imitated élite textiles which had always set a standard for local weavers (cf. Van Esterik, 1994). Rather I hypothesise that, for this period, many women devoted their attention to the production of traditionally defined, elaborate pieces for which they had previously had neither the time nor the resources.

Today, in many villages, textile production has become severely curtailed, as other more remunerative or more interesting tasks have become available and as the uses of elaborate textiles - to wear on formal occasions such as *wat* ceremonies and to sell to collectors - have become more restricted. In addition, production may be curtailed because of a lack of interest on the part of women; the fad of cloth production, centring on the home, has generally lessened in importance and been replaced by other more out-going activities (Lefferts, 1992d). This is especially true in terms of definitions of appropriate dress behaviour and 'development' established by the centre of Thai culture in Bangkok.

Bangkok's influences on and prescriptions for dress and production

While Bangkok as the centre influenced textile production and consumption during the industrial period, the points noted below are continuous with previous Thai constructions. That the Thai élite believed that changes in attire would produce changed international perceptions dovetails with previous behaviour. Royal and élite concern with textiles as national dress constitutes part of a 'traditional' Thai world view.

Some of the most important portions of M.R. Kukrit Pramoj's novel concerning changing Bangkok court behaviour from the reigns of Kings Rama V through VIII relate to suggested and prescribed changes in attire. These changes, transmitted from the court to people close to these centres of power and then to the Thai citizenry generally, affected both male and female dress. His remarks reflect an attitude, subsequently codified in the actions of Field Marshall Pibunsongkhram, that dress denotes modernity. M.R. Kukrit also shows that it is not just women who 'dress for development', but men are at least as much, if not, more involved.[7]

In the reign of King Rama VI (King Vajiravudh), M.R. Kukrit (1981, II, pp.12-13) notes

> [Khun Prem, a close confidante of King Rama VI] who had paid little attention to what he wore now fussed over every item - hat, shoes, jacket, panung. He'd bought stacks of new panung, silk ones and cotton ones and sought out the best materials for his jackets to wear with them. ... On the whole Ploi [Prem's wife] was amused by Khun Prem's sartorial enthusiasm, though when he pondered aloud the idea of sending his jackets by steamer to be laundered in Singapore ("they do it so much better down there, my dear") she did think he was going too far, and dealt with the situation by keeping silent while at the same time continuing to have the jackets washed and pressed at home as though he had never hinted otherwise...
>
> [When King Rama VI announced his engagement to Her Highness Phra Worakanya] [t]he young and not so young society ladies wasted no time in adopting her favourite mode of attire: waisted overblouse worn very long, almost covering the entire length of the pachongkrabane (thus making this traditional garment, when viewed from a distance at least, look very much like a European skirt); stockings and heeled shoes; and for the hair, chignon and velvet or silk headband. In such style did the young and not so young women deck themselves who did not wish to fall behind the latest fashion. (M.R. Kukrit, 1981, II, p.99)

In the novel and in 'real life' the identification of European styles with development continued, as Khun Ploi and other women adopted a more 'modern' dress code which was actually seen by many Bangkokians as beneath their station, similar to the dress of the Lao minority. M.R. Kukrit communicates this predicament when Khun Prem asks Khun Ploi to wear a *phaa sin*. Ploi responds, "'What's got into you, Khun Prem? I'm not a Lao, you know'" (M.R. Kukrit, 1981, p.141). However, soon thereafter Khun Ploi tries on a *phaa sin* and decides that she can wear it.

Field Marshall Pibunsongkhram's famous prescriptions concerning women's dress as indicators of national development firmly established the connection between women's fashion and Thailand's role as a 'modern' power. In three radio addresses in 2474 (1941), he promulgated four changes in women's dress:

i Women should wear long hair;

ii Women should stop wearing the *phaa chongkraben* and start wearing the *phaa sin*;

iii Women should stop wearing a piece of cloth to cover the upper part of their bodies (the wrap around scarf, *phaa sabay*) and should wear a shirt, *sua*;

iv Women should wear hats. Pibunsongkhram specifically linked hats with national development in the phrase, *kaan suam muak pua song serm kaan chaat*, "wearing hats promotes the nation."

Transforming dress was but one way by which Pibunsongkhram wished rapidly to develop Thailand. From adoption of the name 'Thailand' to a modified alphabet and restriction of words denoting 'self', he attempted to revise the ways Thai thought about themselves in order to bring them into agreement with the developed nations of Europe. Pibunsongkhram believed that if Thai adopted 'modern' dress, external observers would see Thai as 'up-to-date' as the observers themselves.

In partial contradiction to Pibunsongkhram's wishes, however, not all cloth produced and worn in the Thailand of those years was as modern as demanded. Rural Northeastern Thai village friends of mine described how, during World War II when cloth imports from foreign mills were embargoed, village women increased cotton production and wove large amounts of cotton cloth; their husbands travelled by railway to sell it in Central Thailand's markets.

While Pibunsongkhram was deposed and the edict on hats overturned, the changes he mandated in attire remain the standard for Thailand today. The influence of the post-World War II world system effectively dragged a willing Thailand into its embrace.

The Thai monarchy and government continues its concern for the quality and quantity of textile production as an instrument of domestic and foreign political and economic policy. King Rama V's interest in sericulture and his hiring of Japanese experts to spur silk production showed his understanding that rough Thai silk could not compete on the world market (Brown, 1980; Yoshikawa, 2525 [1982]).[8] This interest continues to the present.

Conclusion: 'development'

The period since World War II has seen a near revolution in textile production and, perhaps, the meanings associated with textiles in Thailand. A 'triple economy' of textile production has come into being, fostered by the government and large-scale capitalist ventures. In 1994 Thai textile factory production accounted for the employment of over 1 million persons and became Thailand's number one industrial export. Factory and workshop production of hand-woven textiles has also become extremely important, leading to the world-renowned reputation of Thai silk. However, underlying these large-scale enterprises, hand-loomed production by women in villages, many of whom remain unknown and unappreciated, continues to take place.

Factory production

Textile production in Thailand has been mechanised through the establishment of large factories to replace the cloth and garment factories of Europe and the

United States (a point alluded to in several other chapters in this volume). Providing access to cheap labour and preferential tax breaks, the Thai state has participated in the massive post-World War II shift of industrial processes to the 'developing' world. Since 1989 this production has further changed from an emphasis on domestic to consumption emphasising export markets, with the primary recipients becoming the United States, Japan, and the European Community. The genesis and growth of this industry could not have occurred without the benevolent oversight and encouragement of the Thai state; in this respect, the government's interest follows lines established much earlier (Pavinee, 1994a, 1994b).

None of this production stems from the women previously involved in Thai textile production, or who continue to produce textiles even as factories are established in their neighborhoods. However, textiles produced in these factories supplant weaving that might have been undertaken by young women who are now factory hands learning from their mothers and village neighbours (Mills, in press).

Factory and workshop production of 'hand woven' textiles

Through the rationalisation of cloth production which remains nominally hand-woven, Thailand has carved an enviable niche for itself. Although the smallest component of the Thai textile export market (Pavinee, 1994a; 1994b), this segment has become a leading advertisement for Thai textiles. The establishment of the industry resulted from a combination of factors: the standardisation of yarns, dyes, and processes, many of which occur under factory-like conditions, as well as the aggressive promotion of Thai 'hand-woven' textiles, all of which is associated with the pioneering efforts of Jim Thompson (Warren, 1990); and laws in 'developed' nations which permit the preferential import of 'hand-woven' textiles. While the success of this industry rests on the knowledge and expertise of village women regarding yarn and textile manufacture, the relationship is an uneasy and unequal one.

A major outcome of this 'factory' production is an increasing demand for quality raw Thai silk, out-stripping the ability of local producers to provide it. The Thai Silk Company now delegates the raising of superior silk worms to farmers throughout North-East Thailand, then gathers the cocoons and reels the silk in factories. In this way the roughness which is an essential part of Thai silk's quality is preserved at the same time as the company has access to more silk and production comes more directly under its aegis.[9] Thus, while production continues to be 'by hand', control of the operation, from yarn through finished product, is totally under a company's direction and control. This has led to the proletarianisation of rural women and men who now raise silkworms but no longer participate in the reeling and weaving of the fibre.

The growth of Thai silk production ramifies across the landscape of Thai weaving. Weavers and co-operatives now produce large numbers of similar pieces in both cotton and silk and sometimes sewn goods, such as pocket books and purses. In some locations, shops with adjacent 'factories' cater not only to individual tourists, but also to regular buyers from, for instance, Japan, who purchase bolts of *mat mii* indigo cotton cloth to be made into *kimono*. Some of the owners of these shops are involved not only with perpetuating Thai textile production but also with innovating on the expansive framework provided by this weaving. Both Thai and foreign textile experts and designers have carved sizeable niches in non-Thai markets. This is not only true of Thai workshops and their owners, but also of several in the adjacent city of Vientiane, Laos, where projects as interesting and creative as any in Thailand are tackled using the same base of Tai weaving.

In both the Thai and Lao cases, much of this evolution is under government direction, not only for export, but also for domestic markets. Her Majesty Queen Sirikit of Thailand, building on the examples of King Chulalongkorn and his predecessors, has made the encouragement and production of finished silk and cotton products a priority of the Thai élite and government. Her Majesty's SUPPORT Foundation trains weavers in traditional techniques and develops new products (SUPPORT Foundation, 2533 [1990]). Various branches of the government encourage raw material production - through sericulture laboratories and development stations - or offer instruction in dyeing and weaving complicated designs using supplementary weft and *mat mii* techniques. However, in a major change from the past, Her Majesty and the Thai élite now wear Thai textiles to identify themselves as Thai. As noted earlier, the monarchy and élite wore foreign textiles to express their modernity; now they wear Thai textiles as statements of ethnic nation-building (Anderson, 1983).

Rural production

Even with the growing industrialisation of weaving, travel through areas in Thailand where women continue to weave primarily for household consumption is still possible. However, the eventual impact of external markets, capitalist commodification, and the escape of young women to cities and factories appears overwhelming. For many women, market forces and the expansion of fragmented production have brought about a restriction in the kinds and qualities of textiles produced with an accompanying emphasis on commercial possibilities.

Textile production involves a succession of interruptible stages; this interruptibility provides a way by which the holistic process of cloth production, formerly commanded by a single woman, can become fragmented. Thai women welcomed the availability of industrial dyes and factory-processed and stronger yarns from Europe. Today, however, in many locations only synthetic dyes or pre-dyed yarn is used. During earlier field-work I became familiar with the exchange between village weavers of tie-dyed, unwoven bundles of *mat mii* weft yarn; now many bundles of such yarn are available for sale in market shops. The purchase of unfinished pillow covers is an essential way by which young girls and their mothers amass sufficient numbers of gifts for presentation at weddings. With large numbers of young women unable to weave and with an increasing tourist trade, three villages in Yasothorn Province now specialise in weaving, sewing, and finishing pillows (see also Parnwell and Suranart in this volume). Not only do men and women drive pick up trucks into villages to sell pre-dyed yarn, but within the past five years trucks arrive with yarn that is also pre-warped, for making blankets and utilitarian textiles. In such an arrangement, a weaver has only to string the warp to an appropriate set of beater and heddles, dress the loom, and commence weaving.

Consumers lack information concerning weavers who do not live in well-known locations but who do produce fine quality work with original designs. In many locations in North-East Thailand, talented weavers still produce primarily for domestic consumption. However, these independent weavers are becoming fewer since, as they grow too old to weave, they are not replaced by younger women taking over their looms. The skill necessary for weaving textiles requires hard work and apprenticeship; these skills are not easily learned and certainly are not available from a book. For instance, the quality control necessary for yarn production, even for yarn employed in weaving routine cloth, is determined by the loom and the piece; the process of weaving itself requires a comprehension of quality garnered only through experience. Many weavers find it easier to buy factory processed yarn. Except when weavers obtain extra remuneration for natural dyes, they prefer synthetic dyes to provide a broader range of colours and greater reliability in quality. The separation and incremental replacement of portions of the production process has led, for many weavers, to a 'proto-industrialisation' of weaving.

Meanings

Thai textile production and consumption seems always to have been contested: by the expectations of the individual weaver; by the household, village, and larger society; and by royalty and élite. We have seen that textile production has been a matter of royal policy - when a monarch could enforce that policy - for as long as records are available. However, production is important to individual women weavers: it permits them to express themselves, their artisanry, and the nature of their relationships with others. Such production is also a way by which women can make extra income.

Sumptuary rules governing the use of cloth are also a matter of concern, not only in Theravada Buddhist ritual by which monks, men, and women are denoted by certain kinds of cloth, but also by the Thai élite, to distinguish themselves from other classes. However, the élite now value village-produced Thai textiles as a means to show their allegiance to the monarchy and the Thai nation. At the same time, meticulously produced village textiles provide an honoured way for a mother to show her pride and affection in her son, husband, or father as he wears cloth to a religious ceremony, and for herself to show her expertise as an accomplished woman.

Consideration of the varied meanings of the production and consumption of hand-manufactured Thai textiles in the ever-emerging context of 'development' is an intricate project. Few women now produce textiles and even fewer young women are schooled in their manufacture. Many Thai women are increasingly disenfranchised from the weaving and cloth once pivotal to their lives. The merging of the concepts of commodity and identity in cloth production is central in bringing about this loss. The role of the Thai state and royalty in the drive for national wealth and distinctiveness is also formative. Finally, a capital-intensive industrial structure derived from Europe and the United States must also bear some of the responsibility for these 'developmental' changes in Thai textiles.

Notes

1 Thai refers to citizens of the Kingdom of Thailand, not all of whom speak Central Thai, the language spoken by the majority population of the Kingdom. In this chapter I often use information gathered from speakers of languages related to Thai, such as Lao, Lu, etc. These are members of the Tai language family, the largest language family in South-East Asia and southern China. I use 'Thailand' to refer to that state today and its predecessors, Siam and Ayutthaya, even though this name was not adopted until World War II.

2 Wood-working and bamboo-plaiting were usually men's activities (Lefferts, 1994b).

3 Specific categories of textiles appear to be treasured, with individual pieces handed down from generation to generation in a household. These categories usually involve textiles for funerals, garments for the *naak* and wrappers for his alms bowl, and wedding *phaa sin* (Lefferts, 1992a, 1992b).

4 A lack of recorded information hinders reconstruction of past events in Mainland South-East Asia. Much of the following focuses on the entrepots of Ayutthaya and Bangkok in order to construct inferences to understand the development of textiles in the hinterlands.

5 Production of textiles by royal women appears to differ depending on the court. In more sumptuous circles, such as in Bangkok and Luang Prabang, royal women may only have embroidered (Lefferts, 1991). However, in smaller courts, such as at Ubon Ratchathani, royal women wove outstanding pieces (Gittinger, 1992b, p.174). Finally, we have a cryptic statement by an informant that Bangkok royalty maintained domestic weaving establishments. However, no textiles from such workshops have been identified; they seem to have been disbanded at least by the time of the Thai Constitutional Revolution of 1932.

6 This item is now in the Andrews collection of the Harvard University Peabody Museum of Archaeology and Ethnology.

7 M.R. Kukrit Pramoj's novel shows an awareness of the superficiality underlying these actions. He pokes fun at Khun Prem, even as Khun Ploi eventually adopts many of the changes her husband brings home from the court.

8 But see note 9 for an account of how this 'disadvantage' has been turned to advantage.

9 It should be noted that Thai International Airways's advertisement, 'smooth as silk', is a misnomer when applied to Thai silk. Thai silk's hallmark is its roughness, a product of raising and reeling by individual women. A moderate roughness in Thai export silk is preserved by use of a warp of imported, factory-processed silk using a weft of Thai silk.

Use of foreign silk also helps in overcoming the scarcity of good quality Thai silk available on the market, which has led to illegal imports from Vietnam and Laos.

9 Rural industrialisation in Thailand: Village industries as a potential basis for rural development in the North-East

Michael J. G. Parnwell and Suranart Khamanarong

Introduction

A fundamental challenge awaits Thailand as it approaches the 21st Century: means must be found of maintaining the momentum of economic growth in the face of serious infrastructural, environmental and human resource constraints whilst *at the same time* engendering a greater spatial, social and sectoral spread of the spoils of growth. Neglecting any or all of these elements threatens intrinsically the sustainability of the economic boom.

The signs are not encouraging. In spite of optimism verging occasionally on euphoria, the same challenge has proven largely beyond Thai policy-makers since the introduction of formal planning in the early 1960s. In spite of spectacular achievements in facilitating economic growth, especially since the mid-1980s, the record in respect of distribution and dealing with the externalities of growth has been far less impressive. The level of economic concentration in and around Bangkok has intensified, but the metropolis is rapidly being choked by traffic and pollution. The industrial and service sectors have steamed ahead leaving a less buoyant and more unstable agricultural sector in their wake. Significant sections of Thailand's spatial economy have been largely by-passed by the economic boom, one consequence being that people have found it increasingly necessary to move from their home areas in search of economic opportunities elsewhere. Poverty, after declining steadily during the 1970s and early 1980s, appears once again to be on the increase in spite of - or perhaps *because of* - Thailand's so-called economic 'miracle'.

Given the above, there would appear to be scope for exploring alternative ways of promoting development in Thailand which question the effectiveness of orthodox top-down, growth-driven approaches which rely heavily on the often illusory 'trickle-down effect'. The challenge is to find a pragmatic means of combining redistribution with growth; maintaining Thailand's current economic dynamism but at the same time facilitating the development and diversification of the country's rural periphery.

The aim of this chapter is to explore one such alternative approach: rural industrialisation. On the basis of field research in the impoverished North-East, we argue that the rural industrial sector has strong and largely overlooked potential for simultaneously facilitating development *in situ* and helping to meet some of the challenges outlined above. The following discussion looks firstly at some of the principles of rural industrialisation and bottom-up planning more generally, before presenting some case studies which highlight the potential, prospects and pitfalls of rural industrialisation in North-East Thailand.

Approaches to rural development: top-down and bottom-up

Orthodox rural development planning is characterised by top-down, macro-level centralised planning strategies in which decisions taken by urban élites in central governments are imposed on peripheral rural groups and institutions. This uni-directionality of development decision-making from the top-down produces a hierarchy of 'developers' and 'developed' and consequently a large gap between 'planners' and 'people'. The 'developers' tend to have a negative attitude towards the notion of popular participation because of what may be seen as 'planning arrogance'. This is the idea that governments know best how to help the rural poor and that planning for and on their behalf is best done by urban-based experts (Holloway, 1989). As a result development is often based on conceptions about what rural people want and need without consultation with rural populations themselves. This process by-passes a considerable pool of local experience, knowledge, skills and ideas.

In this one-way flow of development initiatives, centralised government administrators assume that rural people are unable to express their needs and tend to perceive them as 'objects' of development (Farrington *et.al.*, 1993). Rural development policies thus tend to be highly paternalistic. Indeed, a mentality of dependence is often created as rural people come to perceive themselves as objects rather than agents of development and in the process become dependent upon government largesse.

Many misconceptions are held by urban-based government planners such as the idea that the rural poor are a homogeneous economic and social unit, that they face similar problems and are equally able to respond to development initiatives (Holloway, 1989). Efforts to promote development which are directed at the 'rural people', the 'rural poor' or 'farmers', as if these constitute distinct categories, fail to recognise the social, economic and geographical differences that can exist in rural areas (Oakley, 1991). As a result, both of aggregating the rural population as one enormous mass and the rigidity inherent in centralised planning and budget allocation, government policies tend to emphasise universalistic measures, lacking in flexibility and often inappropriate to local conditions and needs. Furthermore, the centralised top-down approach creates administrative overlap among government ministries and immense volumes of bureaucratic red-tape (Siedentopf, 1987). This results in inefficient structures for delivering rural development inputs and thus barriers to effective poverty alleviation.

Due to the large-scale nature of top-down development projects and minimal local input, local people frequently find it difficult to understand and hence support such indeterminate initiatives. This reduces the likelihood of long-term project success. In addition, as 'development from above' operates via existing social, economic and political systems it tends to reinforce existing power structures in rural areas as development inputs are often diverted by powerful local élites (Farrington *et.al.*, 1993; Rigg, 1991b). Hence, deep-seated and persistent development problems are maintained as the *status quo* remains unchallenged.

In short, rather than laying the foundations for self-sustaining development, top-down approaches can be seen to stifle local potential for self-reliance. The result is a widespread marginalisation of rural people from the activities of rural development as they come to accept the *status quo* and their position in a structural framework which ensures the dominance and control of the minority and the exclusion of the majority.

By the early 1970s it became clear that the top-down approach to rural development had failed to make a substantial impact upon rural poverty. Furthermore, it was evident that inequalities between urban and rural areas, economic sectors, the rich and the poor, had increased. Consequently, over the past two decades there has been widespread support for turning development around and approaching it from the 'bottom-up'.

Bottom-up development seeks to redress the imbalances of previous development strategies by emphasising empowerment and localism and by 'putting the last first' (Chambers, 1983). In contrast to 'development from above' the bottom-up approach focuses on small-scale rural development projects. Furthermore, the approach recognises that community experience and perceptions are a valuable input for the design of such projects which are consequently more closely reflective of local needs, practices and preferences. Its underlying rationale is to find individually-tailored solutions to specific problems through a participative learning process rather than a prescriptive blueprint approach (Hall, 1988). An important advantage of rural-based grassroots organisations over remote central administrative agencies is their 'shallow' hierarchical structure and their consequent accountability to the communities they serve. This factor enables them to command greater loyalty and commitment from local people.

However, bottom-up approaches suffer from a number of constraints and are therefore no panacea for the difficulties experienced by rural communities. Apthorpe and Conyers (1982, p.53) argue that the obstacles to bottom-up development include

> the difficulty of finding effective channels of communication through which individuals or groups at the local level can participate, the lack of any homogeneity of interests within such groups, the time and money required to undertake any effective form of participatory planning and, in many instances, fundamental differences between local and national interests.

A central problem is that localised grassroots initiatives eventually clash with forces they cannot control such as the broader issues of resource distribution and legal rights. Clearly, bottom-up approaches to rural development cannot succeed alone. As Annis (1987) argues, small may be beautiful, but it can also be insignificant. Only central governments have the resources and authority to create the necessary conditions for full-scale grassroots mobilisation. However, as bottom-up approaches emphasise popular participation, administrative decentralisation, and a rearrangement of the locus of power from the central political system to local communities, they are generally not easily tolerated by polities which often see them as a threat to their continued existence.

In light of the qualitative limitations of top-down over-arching state policies and structures and the quantitative limitations of bottom-up participatory approaches, there is increasing recognition that the two approaches need to be fundamentally integrated if rural development is to be both equitable and sustainable. The combination of 'small' and 'big' results in the best of both worlds: expert technical knowledge and resources on the part of government, and local participation and flexible implementation from grassroots organisations. Increased collaboration between big and small, national and local, urban and rural could result in a flexible and balanced approach to rural development which is sensitive to local circumstances.

It is this integration of small into big, and of local into national, which constitutes the essence of this chapter. It is not written from an entirely ideological or idealistic standpoint, where peripheral rural communities are viewed in isolation from the rest of the spatial economy, or where local initiatives are seen to take place within a developmental vacuum (see e.g. Friedmann and Douglass's (1978) notion of 'agropolitan development' or 'ruralisation'). Our argument follows the principle that there is development potential everywhere - although clearly more in some areas than others - but that it has often been overlooked where the prevailing orthodoxy has been centralist and top-down, and preoccupied by the 'idolatry of giantism' (Schumacher, 1973, p.65). This is consistent with the 'redistribution of growth' concept espoused by Rondinelli and Ruddle (1978), and adapted to the specific context of rural industrialisation by Anderson and Leiserson (1978). Here, economic growth remains the fundamental objective of development policy, but the relationship between urban growth and rural welfare is redefined as being mutually supportive rather than one-way, incompatible and essentially parasitic. Against such a backdrop of changing attitudes and approaches, we see considerably more scope to search out and build up local development potential.

Rural industrialisation

There has been an historical tendency to see and treat 'rural' and 'agricultural' as if they were synonymous. Thus the agricultural sector has provided the main focus of attempts to bring about rural development. This is understandable given that farming is still the principal occupation for the majority of the population in most South-East Asian countries, including Thailand (even though it may no longer provide the principal source of livelihood, much of which is now derived *ex situ*, mainly through migration). However, it is becoming increasingly clear that the potential of agriculture alone to provide the basis for the alleviation of poverty, absorption of population growth, improvement in rural living standards, satisfaction of aspirations as well as needs, and the narrowing of rural-urban income differentials is extremely limited. Accordingly, increasing attention is being paid to the rural non-farm sector as a potential *in situ* means of achieving these objectives.

Cottage industry has historically constituted an important component of the rural non-farm sector, centring in the main upon the artisanal production of utilitarian and cultural items for local use and the more specialised production of handicraft products for exchange or trade. As such there is, in many parts of the developing world, an established rural industrial sector.[1] In the main rural industry is undeveloped, by which we mean that it employs traditional means of organisation and production, and as such contributes little towards the livelihood and living standards of the producers. However, we contend that, in some cases, it has considerable development potential which could significantly improve levels of livelihood, security and opportunity in the rural sector. Rural industrialisation represents the means whereby this potential might be realised.

We should first define what we understand by 'rural industrialisation'. Rizwanul Islam (1987, p.3) sees it as involving the diversification of the rural economy through the introduction and promotion of small-scale manufacturing enterprises, whilst Parnwell (1990, p.2) has defined it as "a process involving the growth, development and modernisation of various forms of industrial production within the rural sector generally and rural villages specifically." Choe and Lo (1986, p.211) offer a wider definition which includes small-scale industry in intermediate-sized settlements away from metropolitan centres.[2] Because the principal objective of the present study is to assess the potential for fostering development in peripheral rural areas we exclude the latter definition, and also larger-scale enterprises which, although they may be located in green-field sites away from urban centres, are, to all intents and purposes, urban industries with at best only tenuous links with the rural economy.

The rural industrialisation process, where it occurs (an important caveat, as it can neither be found nor promoted universally), has potential to increase and diversify rural production and productivity, thereby expanding employment and income-earning opportunities (cf. Shand, 1983), helping to satisfy rural basic needs, and strengthening linkages with the other sectors of the economy (Romijn, 1987, p.211). However such development as occurs should be appropriate to local conditions, potential and preferences. Rural areas in the developing countries are characterised in the main by small settlements, small-scale sources of raw materials, small markets and low technological bases. To be appropriate to this setting, the scale of operation must continue to be small, whilst attention is given to extending markets, improving the delivery of raw materials, and encouraging the emergence of entrepreneurship so that rural producers do not simply become rural labourers. Schumacher (1973, p.143) envisaged the development of small-scale industrial enterprises which retained five main features, several of which are compatible with the notion of rural industrialisation:

(i) workplaces should be created in areas where people live;

(ii) workplaces should need neither large capital investment nor costly imports to operate;

(iii) production techniques should be fairly simple so demands for high skills are kept low;

(iv) production should try to use local materials and be for local use;

(v) technology should be low cost and labour-intensive in character which will allow a system of production that is affordable and geared to high employment and local needs.

In other words, he favoured decentralised small-scale enterprises, located in rural areas, under local control and employing a non-destructive use of the environment (see also Parnwell, 1994). In this paper we attempt, as much as possible, to remain faithful to this ethos but, as we shall see, some of these ideals are incompatible with the pragmatic approach we aim to adopt.

We also need to be cautious in assuming more potential than may exist in reality. There are several questions concerning the potential of the rural industrial sector that presently we can not answer with any strong conviction. For example, to what extent is it possible simultaneously to improve the productivity of rural enterprises and generate additional employment in order to absorb surplus labour and/or future rural population growth? Would improvements in productivity, which are necessary to increase income-earning potential, come about only through the rationalisation of the production process by the substitution of capital and improved technology for labour?

There are also a number of constraints which must first be overcome if the development potential of the rural industrial sector is to be realised. According to Schmitz (referring more generally to small-scale enterprises) physical factors that contribute to the underdevelopment of small industry fall into two broad categories: first, the nature of the relationship between the small and large firm sectors - small industries are exploited by large firms through various mechanisms, contributing to an unequal exchange which enhances the position of the latter and restricts that of the former; second, the development and expansion of small industries is restricted by problems of access to product markets, technology, raw materials and credit. Government policies tend to reinforce rather than ease these blockages, such as through large enterprise biases in the provision of institutional credit (Schmitz, 1982). Islam (1987, pp.11-14) further identifies the provision of infrastructure in rural areas (e.g. electricity, transportation, education) and the often conflicting demands of rural industry and agriculture as two further constraints faced by the rural industrial sector. Pye (1988, pp.14-25) points to qualitative factors such as the traditional organisation of production and prevailing attitudes towards investment and risk-taking as constraining rural industrial potential, whilst Parnwell and Suranart (1990) have highlighted incompatibilities between the design, quality and type of traditional rural industrial products and the demands of the external market.

Thus it should be clear that releasing the potential of the rural industrial sector, however desirable it may be from the perspective of equity and development, is not an easy task. A great many barriers must first be tackled, and in some cases these may prove to be insurmountable. We now turn to examine some of these within the setting provided by the Northeastern region of Thailand which, as we saw in Chapter 1, has many of the hallmarks of a peripheral and underdeveloped region. In the case studies which then follow, we shall see that there are instances which give rise to considerable optimism, and which may provide an indication of the path to be followed by other forms of rural enterprise.

Rural industrialisation in North-East Thailand

We saw in Chapter 1 that the North-East has an industrial sector of minuscule proportions, particularly when compared with the Bangkok-Central Region. Furthermore, as Table 9.1 clearly shows, such industrial activity as can be found in the region can hardly match that of the country's industrial heartland in terms of diversification and technological sophistication. More than four-fifths of industrial enterprise in the North-East consists of rice-milling, and much of the remainder is also based on the processing of agricultural and other primary produce. The picture changes slightly when we consider the distribution of industrial capital and employment, but the lasting impression is of a largely unindustrialised, and certainly underindustrialised, regional economy. With such a limited level of industrial activity to absorb locally a rapidly expanding regional labour force, fuelled by population growth and the displacement of people from agriculture, it is easy to see why such large numbers of people regularly leave the region in search of employment opportunities elsewhere.

Table 9.1
Structure of the Industrial Sector in North-East Thailand, June 1992

Type of Factory:		Number of Establishments	Total Capital Investment	Total No. of Employees
Rice Mills		36,598	6,364.0	45,479
	% of Total	81.9	17.9	27.4
Engineering		2,690	4,115.1	21,290
	% of Total	6.0	11.6	12.8
Cassava Products		2,476	5,819.9	20,451
	% of Total	5.5	10.6	12.3
Food Products		934	6,505.5	13,049
	% of Total	2.1	18.3	7.8
Non-Metallic Products		935	2,181.0	11.437
	% of Total	2.1	6.1	6.9
Wood Products		436	1,231.8	9,914
	% of Total	1.0	3.5	6.0
Textiles		260	4,057.7	32,156
	% of Total	0.6	11.4	19.4
Other		367	5,197.2	12,252
	% of Total	0.8	14.6	7.4
Total		44,696	35,552.2	166,028
	% of Total	100.0	100.0	100.0

Source: North-East Thailand Industrial Economic Centre (Khon Kaen), 1992.

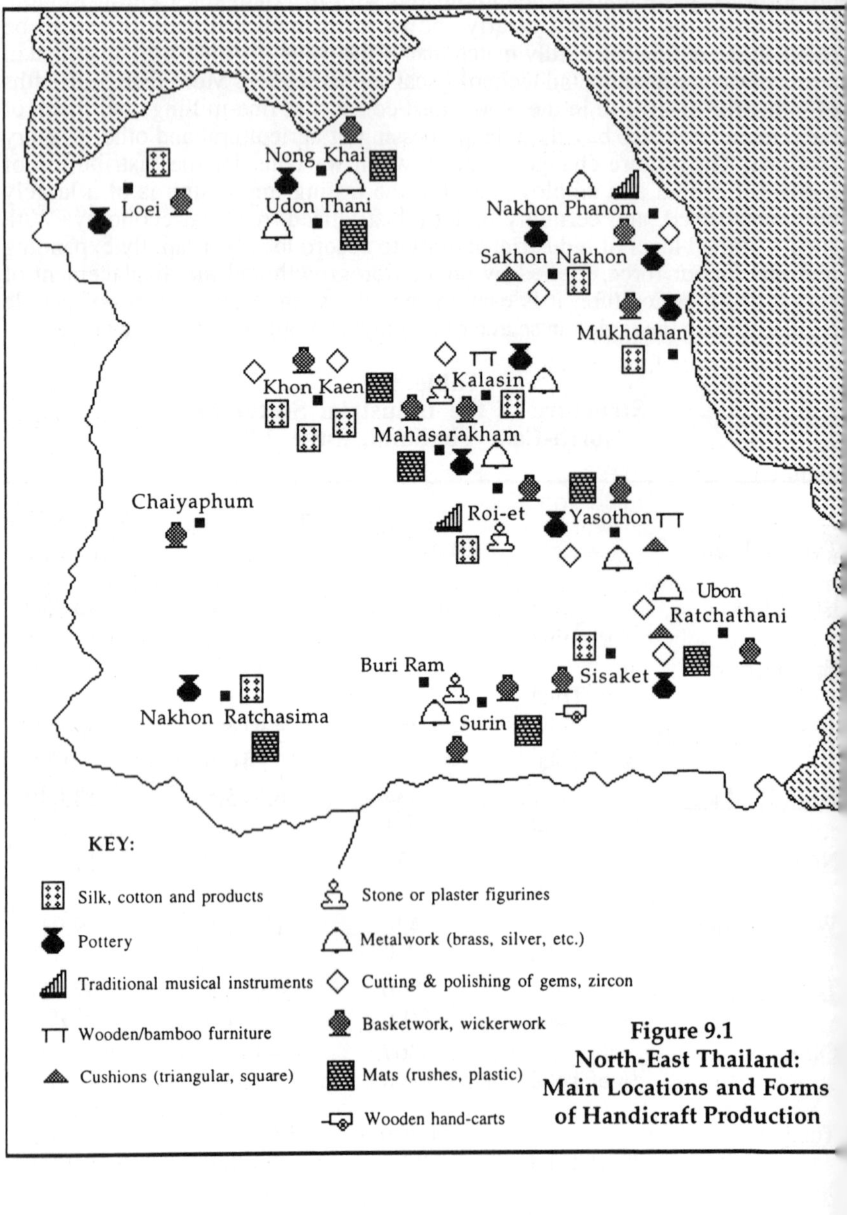

Figure 9.1
North-East Thailand: Main Locations and Forms of Handicraft Production

However, an unpublished report by the Northeastern regional branch of the Bank of Thailand expresses optimism about the future prospects of industrial growth in the region. The industries in which the Bank places its confidence, and which it suggests should be prioritised for support are:

Labour-intensive industries: these include garment manufacture, gemstone-cutting, toy-making, artificial flowers, and leather goods;

Export-led industries: food-canning, silk-making, and paper fibre;

Engineering industries: machine manufacture, electronic goods, and spare parts for vehicles;

Cottage industries: silk- and cotton-weaving, bamboo goods, mat-making, and pottery;

New products: dried bamboo shoots, pumpkin powder, straw cement, and paper re-cycling.

The Bank sees regional advantages in respect of the lower cost of land and labour (compared, for example, with the Central Region), relatively cheap raw material inputs, and reasonably good provision of industrial infrastructure in and around the regional cities, courtesy of quite heavy infrastructural investment by central government over the last three decades (see also the chapter by John Walton in this volume).

This is all well and good, but the Bank's optimism does not necessarily extend to the region's rural sector, where infrastructure is less well-developed and where disadvantages of location and accessibility would appear to outweigh any potential advantages from the availability of even lower land and labour costs. Notwithstanding this, Figure 9.1 suggests that the region already has in place a very solid foundation upon which the development and diversification of rural industries might be built. Although the Bank's thinking was somewhat urban-biased, it is clear from the diagram that a number of rural cottage industries fall into the 'high potential' groups of industries identified by the Bank of Thailand - gemstone-cutting, silk-making, mat-making, pottery, agro-processing, and so on. As our case studies will shortly reveal, some of these enterprises (such as 'diamond'-cutting, cushion-making and some forms of pottery production) already show signs of considerable dynamism and innovation in responding to the actual and potential external demand for their products.

On the other hand, many of the symbols on the map represent traditional rural cottage industries which have changed little in their structure and production methods over perhaps a century or more and which, because of the nature of the goods produced and the techniques employed, would appear to have few prospects for development and change in the longer-term. The World Bank concurs with this gloomy assessment: "[w]e can expect an almost total disappearance of [rural craft] activities in the near future" (World Bank, 1983, p.82). However, the World Bank was unable to anticipate the significant changes in the nature and sources of demand which have taken place over the last decade or so (particularly from tourism and handicraft exports, which provide a central focus of our later analysis), to which a number of enterprises have responded very positively:

> Exports are the key to the future. Domestic demand for utilitarian goods is weak in most Asian countries and sales to tourists are still negligible. The tourist market, though, will increase and should be emphasised as these goods are the same as those made for export. (IDRC, 1988, p.6)

The foregoing makes clear that the rural industrial sector is highly diverse, and contains both dynamic and stagnant, traditional and modern enterprises. This is a viewed shared by Elwood Pye, who argues that there are two distinct types of craft industries in Thailand: on the one hand, there are a number of "large factories and workshops in major metropolitan centres such as Bangkok and Chiangmai [from which] the vast majority of the country's exports come" and on the other "a large number of small, part-time artisans who are primarily farmers, but who draw on craft income to supplement agricultural earnings" (Pye, 1988, pp.68-9). As one might expect, it has mainly been the urban-centred, large-scale enterprises which have capitalised to the greater extent on the growing demand for handicraft products. The genuinely rural handicraft enterprises have been faced by a number of constraints which have (in some, but not all instances) stunted their development and restricted their potential. These constraints are outlined briefly below, and should represent the principal targets of efforts to promote rural industrialisation in the North-East.

One view (among many possible scenarios) of the requirements of rural industrialisation might be summarised as follows: a larger volume of more marketable and better quality goods must be produced more cheaply, more reliably and more efficiently. To achieve this, the supply of raw materials and finance capital must be improved, production skills enhanced, entrepreneurship developed, designs changed, new technology introduced and marketing systems extended (see also Islam, 1987). It is clearly unrealistic to expect all of these changes to take place spontaneously and independently of external involvement and support. Whilst the countryside may be considered to have a certain comparative advantage over the major metropolitan areas in terms of, for example, land and labour costs, there are also a great many constraints which impinge on rural areas relative to towns and cities. Some of the more important of these are:

(i) most rural areas are quite far-removed from the main market centres, particularly, as in the case of handicrafts, where that market is principally urban or international in nature;

(ii) the generally small size and scale of rural handicraft industries does little to underpin their efficiency and competitiveness *vis à vis* their larger and generally more sophisticated urban counterpart industries;

(iii) the predominant role of rural craft industries is as a means of supplementing agricultural earnings (Pye, 1988), and as such there may be a number of attitudinal and perceptual barriers to change which must be confronted in any effort to promote a greater efficiency and market-orientation in these industries (Romijn, 1987, p.226);

(iv) linked to (iii), because of the cyclical shift of labour between agriculture and cottage industry there may, at certain times of the year, be significant shortages in the availability of labour for handicraft production;

(v) the part-time and traditional nature of many forms of rural handicrafts production may determine that few people possess the kinds of production skills, managerial expertise and entrepreneurship which may be essential pre-requisites for the modernisation and development of the industry; and finally

(vi) there may also be quite severe local capital formation constraints which may similarly restrict the capacity for technological change in rural industrial production.

Thus, before rural areas can expect to capitalise on the growing demand for traditional craft products, a number of quite fundamental changes must be instigated. In essence, there are six key areas where such changes must be concentrated:

(i) training and education, in order to up-grade production skills, develop entrepreneurship and, perhaps also, overcome attitudinal barriers to change;

(ii) design and market orientation, in order to ensure that rural handicraft products are not only more directly targeted at the booming tourism and export market but also that they are of a style, quality and price which will guarantee that they will capitalise on this external demand;

(iii) input delivery systems will have to be improved in order to ensure that producers can keep abreast of a potentially rapid increase in demand for their products;

(iv) there may be a need to introduce entirely different production techniques in order to increase levels of productivity;

(v) there must be adequate provision of finance capital in order to support such changes as may be deemed necessary in the process of handicrafts production; and finally,

(vi) there is perhaps a strong case for strengthening linkages between rural and urban areas in support of rural industrialisation, such as through sub-contracting and putting-out arrangements, as a way of combining the comparative production advantages of both villages and towns.

Rather than dealing with these elements separately, as has happened on several occasions with disappointing results (see, for instance, the discussion below of pottery manufacture in Ban Mor, Mahasarakham province), there is a need for a co-ordinated and integrated approach wherein all constraints are tackled simultaneously. The following short case studies of rural industries in North-East Thailand help to illustrate both the difficulties which exist for the transformation of rural handicrafts production, and the achievements of some enterprises which, in turn, underpin the considerable vein of optimism (or should we say lack of defeatism?) which runs throughout this chapter.

Case studies of rural industrialisation in North-East Thailand

The following discussion attempts to provide insight into both the constraints and potential of the rural industrial sector in North-East Thailand by means of a number of short and selective case studies. These case studies are based on extensive field-research by the authors in several of the region's provinces during the early part of the 1990s. For the sake of analysis these industries are placed into four broad categories. The first, which we simply call 'traditional industries', helps to highlight some of the difficulties faced as archetypal cottage industries attempt to come to terms with a changing economic world. The second category consists of three instances where tourism has provided a powerful impulse for the modification and modernisation of industrial production, to which the featured enterprises have generally responded in a very progressive manner. The third category, which goes under the general description of 'imported industries', consists of enterprises which have been introduced to rural parts of the North-East, and which therefore do not share the traditional roots of the other industries under consideration. This category is used to illustrate the potential which exists for rural areas to, in essence, 'take advantage of their own underdevelopment' by providing a locus for industrial enterprises which might more typically be described as 'urban', or which incorporate a certain urban-rural division of labour. The final, related group of industries is categorised according to the prevailing process of production which engenders a rural-urban division of labour through the sub-contracting or 'putting-out' system.

Traditional Industries

Such long-established industries are arguably more important for the way of life that they mould than as the epitome of capitalist. Most still employ age-old technologies, and have found it hard to come to terms with a changing world which has seen increased competition from external sources that are able to produce larger volumes of better quality and more durable products, more cheaply and more efficiently. Such competition has highlighted these traditional industries' inherent weaknesses which, in turn, have made it difficult for them to respond to changing economic conditions. The pertinent question here is not so much <u>how</u> as <u>whether</u> they ought to change: or should they instead be allowed peacefully to pass away, a relic of a by-gone era?

<u>Pottery</u>

The village under study, Ban Mor (Tambon Kwao, Amphur Muang, Mahasarakham Province), consists of approximately 120 households, three-quarters of which are engaged in the production of pots, stoves and other pottery products using clay from a nearby *nong* (lake). The products of their enterprise, made by hand using quite rudimentary methods, have traditionally been used within the village and by people in nearby villages, where they were originally exchanged for other products. More recently, cash has been the sole medium of exchange. The market, and thus the producers' income-earning potential, is restricted by several inter-related factors, including limited local demand and/or purchasing power, the poor quality and utilitarian nature of the product, and also a lack of ability/inclination to penetrate a wider market by means of transportation, itinerant trading or promotion (in fairness, there is little that is worthwhile promoting). Some middlemen purchase items for sale further afield, but only very rarely. Furthermore, traditional earthenware products have very rapidly been superseded by urban-produced plastic and aluminium items over the last couple of decades (Buasri, 1990, p.35). Now, the unfashionable pottery items are mainly purchased by those who are unable to afford these more durable, but also more expensive, substitutes.

The villagers are generally poor, although some have alternative sources of income from outside the village (mostly through migration to regional urban centres and, particularly, Bangkok). Most of the producers do not possess agricultural land, and thus rely on the industry as their principal source of income. There is thus a strong case for the development of the pottery industry as a means of improving producers' livelihoods *in situ*. However, it would appear that such potential is extremely limited. First, the industry faces pressing raw material constraints, with villagers finding it increasingly difficult to obtain good quality clay from the nearby *nong*, or from others in the vicinity, partly because the lakes are drying up through over-use for irrigation and because conditions in the region are gradually becoming more arid. Second, there would be a need fundamentally to change the methods of manufacture in order to increase the quality and volume of production. It is difficult to see where the necessary spark, and requisite investment, will come from. Even the attentions of a well-meaning non-governmental organisation came to nothing. Recognising shortcomings in the methods of production, the NGO introduced a diesel-powered potters wheel to the village. Whilst the villagers were thus able to produce many more pots and stoves, for the reasons outlined above they were unable to sell them. They were thus not able to generate the additional income with which to purchase fuel to operate the wheel, which, at the time of our field-work, was already unused and gathering rust in a corner of someone's yard. This emphasises the folly of external intervention which isolates just one aspect from a complex of economic/production processes. A similar situation appertained in relation to efforts by the government's industrial promotion agency to introduce a large furnace in order improve quality control and to allow more pots to be fired at a time. The furnace also required more fuel (when traditional sources such as straw are in increasingly short supply) and new fuel sources (charcoal and wood) which are expensive and which could not be financed from the continuing low prices for the industry's products.

Third, because the market for the village's bulky, poor quality products is very limited, there is a need to change the nature and up-grade the quality of the product in order to penetrate a different, and wider, market. Evidence from elsewhere in the region shows that it is possible to transform the pottery industry in this way. Producers in Ban Dan Kwean, Nakhon Ratchasima Province, have successfully changed the style and shape of the products they manufacture, shifting from utilitarian items like those produced in Ban Mor to modern ceramics and earthenware plant pots, both of which have an assured urban market. Producers in this village have received assistance from Khorat Technical College in respect of improving production techniques and designs. The College has also helped to promote the village's products in order to expand the market. Entrepreneurs have emerged from within this village, and now play an important role in the industry's organisation and the marketing of its products. This illustration highlights the industry's potential, but in general the producers of Ban Mor are unlikely to capitalise on it. None of the villagers possesses the skills, information and contacts to make the industry's modernisation a meaningful proposition.

Mat-making

A similar situation appertained in the case of Ban Hua Sai, Nong Khai province, which has formed part of a tradition of mat-weaving in the North-East which Udom Buasri (1990, p.64) has traced back more 100 years. People prefer mats to chairs, not least in the temple where they are culturally obliged to sit with their heads at a level lower than those of the monks. The raw material, freshwater reeds (genus *Cyperus*), are locally abundant in natural lakes and water courses. Producers in Ban Hua Sai initially produced mats for household use, but now the enterprise in becoming increasingly commercialised, driven partly by rapidly rising cash needs within the village. Most of their mats are sold via merchants who come from the provinces of Udon Thani, Kalasin and Roi-et to purchase the mats, which are then sold throughout the North-East and elsewhere in Thailand. The middlemen have tended to benefit more than the producers, but the arrangement is seen as preferable because of the producers' lack of marketing experience, and because the associated travel and transport costs would eat into already slim margins of profit.

Although the mat-weavers of Ban Hua Sai have managed to capitalise on the market potential for their products to a greater extent than the potters of Ban Mor, they face a number of similar constraints which restrict the industry's potential for further expansion. For instance, the reeds are becoming increasingly scarce, especially during the dry season, which is when the villagers have most time available for mat-making. Sometimes they must travel as far afield as Mahasarakham and Khon Kaen in order to find their raw materials, which also adds to the cost of production. Income is also a problem because of the low-value product that they produce, and because of the margins which the middlemen command. It is difficult to envisage how mat-making can be turned into a high value-added enterprise as occurred with the manufacture of ceramic tiles in Ban Dan Kwean. The industry is also facing competition from substitute products, such as linoleum and floor-tiles. Accordingly, the number of producers is decreasing, and thus the future of the industry, and its potential as an *in situ* source of rural development, would appear to be limited.

Industries related to tourism

We have chosen tourism as the backdrop for our assessment of some of North East Thailand's more dynamic rural industries for several reasons. First tourism has been one of the country's most successful economic sectors over at least the last decade. Second, in contrast to some of the other forms of economic activity which were discussed in Chapter 1, tourism has perhaps the highest potential to spread the benefits of development to peripheral areas. Indeed, it is the Thai periphery that a large majority of tourists come to the country to enjoy (see Hitchcock, King and Parnwell, 1993). Because tourism also plays a very important role in generating demand for Thai handicraft products, it also has some bearing on the development and diversification of the rural industrial sector. Third, an analysis of the role of tourism in the development of Thailand's periphery is also relevant to the theme of other chapters in this volume (see Dearden, Williamson and Hirsch, and Toyota; also Lefferts, and Walton).

Cushion-making

The manufacture of traditional triangular cushions, *morn sam lian*, in Ban/Tambon Sri Than (Amphur Paa Tiw, Yasothon Province) represents a classic illustration of a cottage industry which has managed successfully to adapt to changing market conditions by quite fundamentally transforming its system of production. As such it provides a model example which other industries in the North-East might learn from.

The sub-district (a collection of six villages) has been involved in the production of cushions for more than thirty years. Originally, the cushions were produced for use by the villagers themselves and people from nearby villages, either for ornamentation of the house on special occasions, or for the comfort of respected guests, or for donation to monks of the village temple (*wat*) during special religious festivals (Gittinger and Lefferts, 1992, p.115). Most of the manufacturing is done by women. Men are more typically involved in agricultural work, although they do occasionally help by transporting raw materials and finished products. Traditionally, one person would undertake all parts of the production process - weaving, shaping, sewing, stuffing, finishing, and so on - but now there is a clear division of labour, which provides the clearest illustration of how the industry has changed in recent years. Individual producers now specialise on one of the above tasks, and other areas of specialisation - such as preparing the raw materials (kapok and straw), recycling, transporting, marketing, etc - which have been introduced as the industry has expanded. There is also an emerging division of labour among villages in the vicinity, with Ban Po Sri, Ban Po Sai and Ban Pa Tong specialising in weaving and shaping, and Ban Krajai and Ban Sri Than subsequently stuffing and sewing the cushions. Tambon Sri Than has become one of the principal production centres for these cushions in North-East Thailand, and the market for the product now extends throughout Thailand and also internationally. Some 60 per cent of the Tambon's more than 1,000 households are engaged in the industry.

The expansion and transformation of the industry can be linked to two principal factors. Firstly, the expanding market for the Tambon's produce was facilitated by a government promotion agency which a number of years ago was instrumental in encouraging the villagers of Ban Sri Than to sell their cushions in Bangkok. The government's policy was one of putting rural producers in touch with the market, and in particular with wholesalers in Bangkok. The government built up a central market (*or tor kor* in Thai) as a central meeting point in Bangkok. Through this, Bangkok traders came to be aware of the cushions produced in Ban Sri Than, and thus the market extended beyond the North-East, where it had previously been concentrated. The triangular cushions, as a striking manifestation of Thai material culture, became a popular souvenir for tourists. The Bangkok-based traders also had connections with the international market, and through them a global trading link was established.

As we saw earlier in the case of Ban Mor, simply changing one element of the economic process whilst allowing the others to remain unchanged is a recipe for disaster. In the present case, expanding the market for this traditional Thai handicraft would clearly not have been enough to underpin its modernisation and development. There was a parallel need for the volume of production to be increased, quality to be improved and regulated, and for the nature of the product to vary, at least to a limited extent, in accordance with the nature of the external demand. Such parallel transformations were accomplished by the second important agent of change, the village entrepreneur. Tambon Sri Than has four major and three minor entrepreneurs who are also very important players in the industry's development. They act as intermediaries between the villagers and wholesalers in Bangkok and elsewhere, and are influential in introducing fresh designs on the basis of market intelligence they pick up in Bangkok. They arrange transportation to the market, and regulate the supply of raw materials. They also played a crucial role in introducing the division of labour which has allowed levels of production to expand rapidly (from 20-30 cushions per day in the mid-1980s to around 200-500 today). They are also very wealthy, and politically powerful. Although they have clearly derived the lion's share of the economic benefits which the industry's transformation has brought, they have also undeniably brought financial benefits to the producers, as well as other benefits such as the development of potentially marketable skills.

Producers' earnings were around 60-80 baht per day in the early 1990s which, whilst not a huge amount by local and regional standards, has none the less enabled many households to improve the quality of their dwellings and enjoy a generally better standard of living. However, the recent developments have not been without a number of difficulties which, in turn, reiterate points made in the earlier discussion about the constraints which face the rural industrial sector. One problem which we have already identified with other forms of production was a growing scarcity of raw materials as the volume of production increased. In particular, the kapok which is used to stuff the cushions became very scarce, and thus increasingly expensive, because producers had hitherto used a few local kapok trees, and had not thought to plant more in anticipation of increasing demand. Such a serious constraint may well have represented an insurmountable barrier for some rural industries, but in the case of Tambon Sri Than was quite easily overcome. On response was to substitute straw (locally abundant after the rice harvest) for kapok. The other even more innovative reaction was for a small number of households to specialise in the recycling of kapok, travelling regularly to Bangkok and other urban centres and acquiring spent kapok from discarded mattresses and cushions.

This case study of a successful rural enterprise highlights the potential which exists within the rural sector for *in situ* development and diversification. It is true that the success of Tambon Sri Than was, to some extent, a response to a serendipitous set of circumstances, but the crucial point is that the villagers responded positively to external market stimuli, and in the process have built an excellent foundation upon which to capitalise on Thailand's most dynamic economic sectors, tourism and handicraft exports. It is significant that levels of out-migration (particularly to Bangkok) from the study communities are presently very low, whereas in neighbouring districts and provinces they are very high. Indeed, there was even some evidence from our field research that some young women were returning from Bangkok because of the employment and income-earning opportunities that the cushion-making industry provided. However, given the industry's recent dynamism and prominence, it is interesting to note that very few producers have dedicated themselves full-time to the industry. Most continued to engage in various forms of agricultural activity, especially rice-cultivation, and the vast majority described themselves as 'farmers' rather than 'industrial workers', even though they often spent more of their time, and certainly derived more of their income from cushion-making. There is an interesting cultural and attitudinal angle which we do not have space to examine at this juncture.

Ban Chiang pottery
In contrast to the earlier case study of pottery-making in Ban Mor, the example of Ban Chiang (Amphur Nong Han, Udon Thani province) shows what can be achieved with the economic stimulus provided by tourism. An ancient burial site was discovered in the vicinity of the village in 1970 by members of the School of Archaeology of Pennsylvania State University (Sangvichien, 1990, p.16). It contained skeletons and pottery dating back some 4,000 years and was important in signifying a locus of civilisation which pre-dated several earlier discoveries on mainland South-East Asia. The discovery drew academicians to the area and, later, domestic and international tourists. A museum was established adjoining the burial site.

The influx of souvenir-hungry tourists created a market opportunity for local villagers, who came to specialise in the manufacture of pseudo-Ban Chiang pots of various shapes and sizes. Initially lacking the requisite skills, the villagers were given advice and training by the Community Development Department. This included the shaping and painting of pots to match the diagnostic Ban Chiang styles, and also the incorporation of rice husks with the clay in order to give the pots the feel and appearance of 4,000-year-old 'authenticity'. In this particular instance, the low quality of the pottery and lack of quality control are a distinct advantage! Those with a serious interest in archaeology and Thai pottery are very unlikely to buy the pots.

Over time, a division of labour has developed involving other villages in the vicinity. Ban Kam Or and Ban Mor Din produce the pots, which are then painted in Ban Pulu and retailed in Ban Chiang. Visitors seldom if ever stop off in villages other than Ban Chiang even though they all lie within a radius of 1-2 kilometres.

Brassware manufacture
The final case study in this sub-section, the manufacture of brassware items in Ban Pa Ao, Ubon Ratchathani province, contrasts quite sharply with the foregoing. Here we have an industry which, were it not for tourism, would probably not have survived, at least in its present form. Villagers still produce brassware in the time-honoured manner, using production techniques which have been passed down through the generations and which are very primitive when viewed against the more sophisticated methods which are found in more modern urban foundries and establishments. The regional museum in Udon

Thani shows evidence of very similar technology being employed 300-400 years ago. Faced with stiff competition from the latter, the Ban Pa Ao enterprises appear to survive because of their primitive technology, rather than in spite of it. Busloads of tourists regularly visit the village to observe the manufacture of brassware using clay moulds, the 'lost wax method' (thin strands of beeswax are wound around clay moulds, rudimentary patterns are applied by hand using simple wooden and plastic wheels, and then molten bronze is added to the moulds. The pattern is imprinted on the bronze, before the heat discharges the wax), and a charcoal furnace which uses hand-operated bellows. At the end of the 'show', they are encouraged to purchase some of the villagers' wares. The finished product - betel containers, buffalo bells, etc. - are of a very poor and variable quality, but somehow this does not appear to matter. The tourists are interested in observing the perpetuation of their stereotype of the traditional and primitive, and it is on this basis that the industry survives: should it attempt to change, the products would lose their rustic charm and would become fully exposed to competition from elsewhere.

Most of the requisite materials - clay, charcoal, bamboo - can be found locally whereas the blocks of brass and the wax is purchased in Ubor Ratchathani. In spite of the tourist market, the industry is in gradual decline poor sales are encouraging many producers to look for jobs elsewhere. It seem that the industry can only survive by clinging to a traditional hand-made niche ir the market. In some senses, therefore, the industry has become fossilised. It is difficult to imagine how the industry could undergo the same kinds of transformation which have been recommended for other forms of rural industry which are discussed in this chapter.

'Imported' industries

We next examine briefly some forms of rural enterprise which have no strong foundations within the region but which have, instead, been recently introduced principally to take advantage of apparent cost advantages of a peripheral rural location. If such advantages can be shown to exist, we argue that they might provide the justification for public and private sector institutions looking more closely at the region's potential for the promotion of other forms of enterprise as part of a wider rural industrialisation strategy.

'Diamond' – and gemstone-cutting

The cutting and polishing of gemstones and artificial 'diamonds' (zirconium) i essentially an 'urban' industry which has been imported into the North-East since the early 1980s (Thammawat, 1991, p.5). There was no established tradition of gemstone-cutting in the study villages. The principal sites are Ba Non Fan Rua in Khon Kaen province and Ban Sang Ming in Ubon Ratchathan province. The techniques were brought back to these villages by returnin migrants with previous experience of work in stone-cutting enterprises i Chanthaburi province and Bangkok.

In Ban Sang Ming there were 20 'diamond'-cutting workshops at the tim of our field-work in the early 1990s (later field visits have shown that th number of workshops has expanded considerably, as has the number of village in the North-East engaged in the industry). Two of these enterprises belong t the returned-migrants who brought the industry to the village, and who now act as the industry's main entrepreneurs. The owners of the other workshops originally obtained their skills and experience by working in the enterprises of these entrepreneurs. Most of the cutters and polishers are local villagers, though some come from nearby villages and from other parts of the region. Each workshop has between five and fifty young workers who are employed on a piece-rate basis. The raw materials - zirconium and uncut gemstones - are brought to the village by motor car from Bangkok, and the cutting equipment (various saws, grinding tables, etc.) also come from the capital city. The market for the finished products is mainly within the cosmetic jewellery industry, again based in Bangkok.

A similar situation appertains in Ban Non Fan Rua, and the nearby villages of Ban Ba Yao and Ban Non Sathorn. The industry expanded here after the area benefited from the government's rural electrification programme. Although communications infrastructure is very poor, and their location somewhat isolated, it does not appear to have affected the industry's dynamism. Production is buoyant and trade, via merchants in Tambon Nong Kae, eight kilometres away, is brisk. The traders also provide the machines and raw materials. It appears that the unique character of the industry, and especially its products - light, high unit value and easily transported - has had an important bearing upon its locational flexibility, counteracting any negative locational forces associated with the North-East's peripherality and underdevelopment.

There is a gender division of labour, with the young men engaged in the more dangerous task of cutting strips of zirconium into small pieces using an open band-saw, and the women mostly engaged in the more precise and dextrous task of angle-grinding and polishing the stones. Working conditions are generally rather poor, with the constant risk of injury from machines added to the considerable strain on eyesight which results from undertaking intricate tasks in a poorly lit and ventilated environment. For this reason most of the workers are aged less than 25 years: damage to eyesight is usually so significant by this age that few can continue to work in the industry. The long working hours (often up to twelve hours a day) also require the stamina of youth.

There is considerable evidence that the 'diamond' industry has had a significant impact on patterns of migration in the study area. In addition to providing a focus for migrants from elsewhere in the North-East, the industry has reduced levels of out-migration from the study villages (by providing non-farm income-earning opportunities which did not previously exist), and has also encouraged the return-migration of villagers who were previously working in Bangkok and elsewhere. The young workers expressed a preference for working in the North-East and close to their rural homes and, although they could expect to earn more in Bangkok, the much lower cost of living in the rural North-East considerably narrowed differentials in spending power. In addition to providing full-time permanent work, the industry also provides more flexible seasonal employment, thus allowing workers to combine their occupation with the shifting demands of the agricultural cycle. The industry also provides a much-needed employment outlet for young women: the majority (two-thirds) of workers are female.

Some 55 per cent of workers had previous experience of non-agricultural employment prior to joining the gemstone industry, and 38 per cent had previous experience of migration. Eighteen per cent had returned from migratior because they preferred to work in their home village. One respondent explained:

> I worked as a construction worker in Bangkok for about six months. Three years ago my friend told me that this job provided a fairly good income so I returned and tried the work. I found that it was true. So, since then I have not needed to migrate elsewhere. Although the earnings are a bit less than in Bangkok, I love to work here if there is a job available because it is my home.

Some 47 per cent said that they would have no option by to migrate to Bangkok were it not for the gemstone industry. Furthermore, 86 per cent of gemstone cutters believe that migration has been curtailed by the industry's development.

In spite of the industry's considerable success, its development has not been without difficulties. These resultant problems give further evidence of some o the difficulties associated with rural industrialisation. One of the most significan problems is that, in some senses, the industry has been too successful. Becaus of the profit, employment and income-earning opportunities it provides, larg numbers of people have attempted to jump on this particular bandwagon Accordingly, the industry has spread like wildfire throughout the central part o the North-East, leading to the overproduction of 'diamonds' which has seen profit margins and piece-rates plummet. It has now reached the stage where a number of entrepreneurs and workers are questioning their continued involvement in the industry: for many it is no longer the attractive enterprise i once was. As one respondent explained:

> In the past when the number of workshops was limited, the income obtained from gemstone-cutting was very good. Each cutter could earn an average of 4,000 baht per month, and entrepreneurs 15-20,000 baht per month. Presently, the income has been reduced to only 1-2,000 and 10,000 baht respectively because there are so many workshops and thus the middlemen can reduce their purchasing price. I have been to sell my products in Bangkok 2-3 times because the price was higher than in the local market, but unfortunately the Bangkok buyers wanted only the beautiful [high quality] pieces so I could sell only half of what I had. also do not know many buyers in Bangkok, so I prefer to sell in Nong Kae District [the local market] even though the price there is lower. I can sell all and need not pay for travelling to sell in Bangkok.

The lack of regulation of the industry has clearly contributed to its downfall which is unfortunate considering how valuable the industry has been t Northeasterners and that, without over-production, the industry could have continued to exist in its earlier form. Lack of regulation is manifested in anothe form: it is clear from our field observations that entrepreneurs are taking advantage of their employees by investing very little in providing an adequate working environment. Conditions are very bad by urban standards, and yet the prospects of factory inspectors descending on the villagers are very slight.

Industries using the sub-contracting system

We finally consider other forms of enterprise which evince an emerging urban-rural division of labour that, we argue, represents one potential means of overcoming some of the locational problems faced by the rural industrial sector. The 'putting-out' or sub-contracting system allows enterprises simultaneously to take advantage of the cost benefits of the rural setting and the scale benefits of urban industry. Urban firms can minimise overhead costs, such as for accommodation, transportation and other forms of welfare for employees, and can enjoy greater flexibility with regard to working conditions, working hours, and so on. Investment requirements are also reduced by taking advantage, in the main, of rural labour employing hand-produced methods. Firms also pay piece rates rather than regular salaries, and thus the worker and not the employer carries most of the attendant risk of market fluctuations. It is also a flexible system which allows production to be scaled up and down according to market and other conditions.

Benefits also accrue to rural villages, however, thereby fulfilling some of the criteria which were introduced earlier in this chapter. It is a flexible system which allows people (especially women with child-care responsibilities) to work from home. It may provide a supplementary source of income where earnings from the farm are inadequate or irregular. For many, the putting out system may represent their only realistic means of earning a cash income, given the limited opportunities which may exist within the village, and their limited opportunity of obtaining urban employment, due to circumstances, qualifications and so on.

The fish net industry

The villages of Ban Savati and Ban Kok Lam (Tambon Ban Tum, Muang District, Khon Kaen province) have contracts with two factories in Khon Kaen town which produce fishing nets for the domestic and international markets. In these factories the nets are manufactured by machine, but they have to be finished by hand. It is this part of the production process which is undertaken by villagers in their homes. The firms provide the villagers with training, the tools and materials they require to undertake this work, and also arrange delivery of inputs and collection of finished products. The villagers are paid 1-2 baht for each net they finish. This allows villagers to earn between 100-150 baht per day or 2,000-3,000 baht per month, depending upon their level of commitment to this work and the range of other responsibilities they have. This income compares quite favourably with many other forms of non-farm work in the area. Altogether, there are some 1,000 villagers in Ban Savati and nearby who are engaged in this form of work.

The industry has expanded rapidly, and with it the number of sub-contractors and villages involved. The putting-out arrangement was originally introduced by villagers who had previously worked at the fishing net factory in Khon Kaen town. With the growing numbers involved the factories have introduced small offices in each of the study villages in order to facilitate the extension of the arrangement. The villagers are reasonably satisfied with the incomes that they are earning, and the factories are content with the present arrangement. An interview with one of the factory's entrepreneurs in November 1992 revealed considerable optimism about the business's future:

> My factory has 2,000 permanent employees and 2,000 sub-contracted villagers. I need to find another 1-2,000 sub-contracted workers because the business is expanding quickly, and permanent employees are becoming increasingly difficult to find. I believe that my sub-contracting system enables rural people to have more income, and I would encourage the government to make more use of this sub-contracting system in its rural development strategy.

Most of those engaged in the industry are young women, the majority of whom are unmarried. Many might otherwise have been expected to migrate to find work in Bangkok were it not for the work provided by the fishing net factory. In this sense, the industry should be seen as very advantageous in respect of the *in situ* opportunities it has created. Even though they work from home, most respondents considered the sub-contracting work to be their main occupation. Before the industry most had worked as farmers and, because their land-holdings were small and the land infertile, most were very poor. Their earnings from finishing fishing nets are lower than the (salaried) workers in the fishing net factories, but they have the advantage of no transportation costs, lower living costs and a much more flexible working environment.

The silk industry

A further illustration of the sub-contracting system is provided by the silk industry in Nakhon Ratchasima (Khorat) province. The silk industry is a widely-established industry in the North-East. In 1977 there was a thriving silk-weaving industry in Paktongchai District, some 19 kilometres from the urban centre of Khorat. About half of the production from the district was sent to outlets and showrooms in Bangkok, and the remainder exported to the United States, Europe and Australia. The production method was very labour-intensive, and there were 500 permanent employees and another 800 villagers who were sub-contracted to the industry. All weaving was done by hand, with traditional looms. A large land area is needed for a factory containing up to 500 weaving looms, which may help to explain the industry's location in Nakhon Ratchasima province rather than the hinterland of Bangkok, where land costs are extremely high. However, the silk enterprises are experiencing increasing problems in finding sufficient women from Khorat town to work in their urban factories, and thus the population of nearby villages is being drawn into the industry through a sub-contracting arrangement.

The sub-contracting system involves the factory providing the villagers with the raw materials and tools, which the villagers take back to their rural homes. There are also a number of silk 'factories' in the town itself where upwards of 100 women weave under the same roof, but also using the frame loom which their rural counterparts have traditionally employed for generations. Expansion of the industry has been constrained by the need to preserve the hand-made character of the product, thus preventing the introduction of machines and other mass-production methods. Expansion thus took the form of increasing the number of looms in operation, as well as introducing a division of labour (in a similar way to that observed in the other major producing centre in the North-East, Chon Na Bot district in Khon Kaen province). A further problem was that of quality control - a problem which is particularly common in the putting-out system. However, the factory was able more effectively to control quality through a contract system - providing training to help improve product quality, but also rejecting material which did not meet its quality control standards. The enterprise would also seldom take silk woven by producers operating outside the putting-out system.

The success of the industry encouraged other firms to enter the market, also employing the putting-out system. Thus there were several villages in the district of Paktongchai which were using the sub-contracting system. Producers could earn between 40-80 baht per day - not a high income by other industrial standards, but a useful supplement to otherwise depressed rural incomes. Because of lower living costs in the village, sub-contracted workers are often able to save a greater proportion of their earnings than their urban counterparts. Wages were paid on a piece-rate basis of 10 baht per metre woven. One producer in Ban Naa Care, Tambon Mueng Pak, made the following observation:

> In 1977 this wage rate was quite acceptable, but now [1990], because the factory still pays the same rate while the cost of living has increased, many sub-contracted villagers are starting to leave the industry because the wage rate is no longer attractive. They can find better-paid employment elsewhere.

This raises some important issues about the fickleness or fragility of rural industries. It would appear that the industry was exploiting the villagers' lack of alternative sources of supplementary income, and was maintaining profit margins by keeping piece-rates at low levels. A substantial increase (or any increase) in the costs of production - which are mostly made up of labour costs - could have threatened the industry's hard-won dynamism and success. However, as piece rates become less competitive (or as wage expectations become higher) and as alternative employment opportunities become available in what is one of the North-East's more dynamic provinces, people may be expected to leave the industry in growing numbers. To off-set this trend by raising wage rates would risk undermining the presently precarious competitive position of this particular rural enterprise in the periphery of Thailand.

Another problem is a shortage of raw materials, particularly silk. As with the cushion-making industry discussed earlier, the silk industry has expanded so rapidly in recent years that it has outstripped the supply of raw silk, which is also mostly produced in villages in the North-East. To overcome the problem, buying stations have been established by the silk enterprises in many parts of the region, and some 20-30 per cent of the yarn is now imported from Japan (this stronger yarn is mainly used as weft, with the Thai silk forming the warp).

Some former sub-contractees have themselves become entrepreneurs in their home villages, and have introduced small workshops which employ between five and twenty local villagers. They also sub-contract work out to fellow villagers who weave in their own homes. They either sell the produce to the factories in Khorat or to wholesalers in Bangkok. One such entrepreneur in Ban Na Kae explained her history:

> I worked as a sub-contractor in a silk-weaving factory for 5 years, but I thought that the wage was very low so I tried to become an entrepreneur. My business has just started, but the income is better than in the past, even though the work is harder. Many others have attempted

> to make this transition from sub-contractee to entrepreneur, to escape the low wages, but entrepreneurship requires capital which only a few of us can afford.

Generally, those expressing a desire to make the transition were those who had worked in the industry for some time (more than 5 years), and had thus developed the expertise and contacts, and had been able to save sufficient capital to facilitate the transition. As with the gemstone industry, there is a limit to how many women can establish themselves as entrepreneurs in this business, however dynamic it may be at present. It is here that the government may have an important role to play by simultaneously facilitating and regulating the industry's expansion.

Conclusion

This chapter has outlined the potential for confronting uneven development in Thailand by building development initiatives from the bottom or grassroots upwards. We have shown that there is a lot more potential than may generally be assumed by those who take a conventional, detached and largely myopic view of economic development in the Kingdom.

The important point about the foregoing discussion is that it is presented as a pragmatic means of dealing with development differentials in Thailand. We do not advocate an entirely idealistic strategy which sees the balance of power shift radically from centre to periphery, or from the city to the countryside. Rather, we present a strategy which would allow rural producers to swim more effectively and advantageously <u>with</u> the tide of economic development, rather than against it, which has typified their struggle hitherto. Thus Thailand could extend its competitive advantage (a growing necessity as other low-cost Asian producers move confidently into the arena) by drawing the rural sector more centrally into the industrialisation process. At the same time considerable potential benefits would accrue to the rural sector, one further advantage of which could be an alleviation of the imperatives for out-migration. This in turn would have the dual benefits of easing some of the tremendous social, environmental and welfare pressures on the metropolitan region, and at the same time stemming the haemorrhage of human resources from the rural periphery.

Rural industrialisation is not a panacea for the ailment of uneven development, however. Our case studies have drawn attention to the considerable, and on occasions insurmountable, difficulties which face such a bottom-up strategy. There are very good reasons why the pattern of industrialisation in Thailand is so heavily biased in favour of Bangkok, as the discussion in Chapter 1 clearly shows. Equally, there are a great many disadvantages associated with a peripheral and rural location. We should also be aware that the 'industrialisation of the countryside' carries the attendant risk of spreading more widely some of the problems which have come to characterise industrialisation in the urban setting, not least among them environmental and resource pressures (see Parnwell, 1994). As we have seen, it is considerably harder to regulate change in the dispersed rural setting than in the city. None the less, our case studies have also shown that a great deal of progress has recently been made in a number of forms of rural industrial enterprise. Provided the pace and characteristics of rural industrialisation can be matched to the needs, potential and limitations of the rural setting, there is no obvious reason why the lessons learned from the 'success stories' could or should not be applied to other forms of rural industrial enterprise.

Just as there are many populists who share E.F. Schumacher's (1973) notion that "small is beautiful", so there are a great many pragmatists who would probably concur with Wilfred Beckerman's (1995) view that "small is stupid", even though, in this politically correct world, they may only express the view in public that "small is insignificant". The latter may indeed be so, but only because the diminutive is so easily overlooked. It is our hope that this chapter will have made a contribution, however modest, to building up the stature of the rural industrial sector in Thailand, and that, in the process, we may have helped to challenge the view, expressed in the concluding chapter, that uneven development may represent the Kingdom's inevitable and irrevocable destiny.

Notes

1 Indeed, some 30 to 50 per cent of the rural labour force in developing countries is engaged, either primarily or secondarily, in some form of rural non-farm activity (see e.g. Shand, 1986; Chuta and Sethuraman, 1984; Chuta and Liedholm, 1979; Mukhopadhay and Lim, 1985a and 1985b; and Islam, 1987).

2 This comes closer to the definition of rural industry which is used in Thailand, although this has more to do with the vernacular translation of 'rural' - *chonnabot*, meaning literally 'countryside', is generally taken to indicate 'up-country', i.e. away from Bangkok (see Parnwell and Suranart, 1990).

10 Tourism development and social differentiation in Koh Samui

Peter Williamson and Philip Hirsch

Introduction

Tourism in Thailand has been hailed as a 'ticket to development', the country's largest earner of foreign exchange, one of the largest employers of labour outside agriculture and a stimulus to local economic development. Alternatively, tourism has been criticised as a harbinger of environmental and cultural degradation, a vehicle for domination of local economies by international and urban interests, an agent of actual and metaphoric prostitution of Thai bodies and values to things foreign. As such, much of the popular imagery of tourism falls broadly within either the modernisationist or dependency approaches to development.[1]

While there are clearly bases for truth in all of the above notions of tourism development, they provide little by way of insight into local process. In particular, local social, economic and political transformation in the context of rapid tourism development has received only minor attention to date (e.g. Cohen 1982a: 1983a; Wahnschafft, 1985; Meyer, 1988; Dearden, 1991). Despite the considerable work done on social differentiation in the context of agrarian change (e.g. Turton, 1989; Ganjanapan, 1989; Hirsch, 1990), little attention has been given to similar transformations in other rural contexts in Thailand.

In this account of the transformation of Koh Samui in the context of recent and rapid tourism development, the basic question addressed is that of who has benefited (and, by the same token, who has lost out)? The question is approached in two steps. First, attention is given to the extent to which local entrepreneurs have taken advantage of opportunities, and the resultant reshaping of political and economic power on the island. Second, the complexity of the emerging social formation is illustrated, in an attempt to put paid to simplistic assumptions about tourism development that emanate from the perspectives outlined above.

The island of Koh Samui (see Figure 10.1) lies in the Gulf of Thailand, 600 km. south of Bangkok, and is a district of Surat Thani province. The island is 28 km. from the mainland (between closest points); its people have historically

Figure 10.1
The Island of Koh Samui

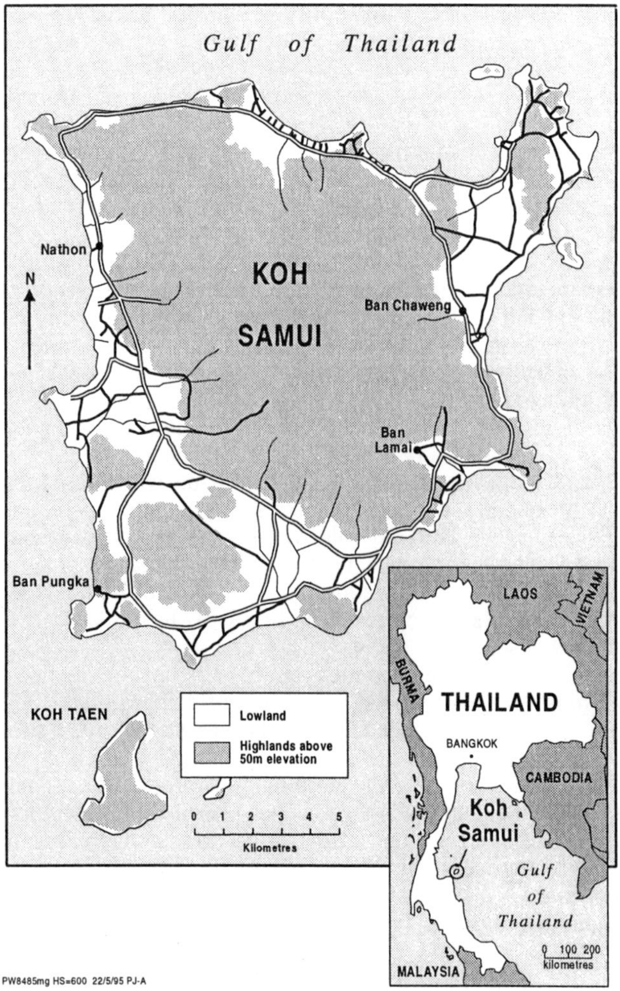

PW8485mg HS=600 22/5/95 PJ-A

enjoyed a high degree of political autonomy from the mainland, but there has long been extensive trade between the islanders and others.

Before tourism development in Koh Samui the island was a major producer of coconuts and partly-processed coconut products for export to the Thai mainland and other countries. Over 95 per cent of the island's agricultural land was used for coconut production, and most of the island's approximately 30,000 inhabitants were engaged in coconut production and related industries. Roughly ten per cent of the population was engaged in fishing and some rice was grown; both rice and fish were for local consumption. As coconuts are a non-staple commodity, there were many merchants on the island and the local economy was much more monetised than other comparable districts in Thailand which may have produced mainly rice or fish. Thus, there was already an established merchant class on the island and significant use of waged and piece-rate labour. The merchant class were mostly Sino-Thai, the descendants of the more successful of the many Chinese immigrants to Samui in the late nineteenth century. Many traded in coconut products, acting as middlemen between the Thai growers and the mainland buyers or the owners of processing factories on the island and the mainland. Wealthy Chinese merchants frequently married into the more influential Thai families on the island, from whom many village heads and *kamnan* (sub-district heads) were drawn. Many such families were major land-owners, and these marriages united political and economic power giving rise to a local Sino-Thai élite.

Land was crucial to Samui's main economic activity of coconut production, and because of the availability of paid labour the island's wealthy were able to acquire and work large land-holdings. The merchants were often money-lenders too and, not infrequently, the land of debtors was ceded to merchants in lieu of debts. Easily accessible land suitable for coconut production was in limited supply, unlike many other parts of Thailand where the land frontier was not yet reached. There was, as a result, a continuous out-flow of islanders to the nearby mainland provinces where land could be acquired cheaply or forest land could still be claimed and settled.

Since the mid-1980s the coconut economy has been in decline for various reasons, the most significant being a fall in world copra prices. Other factors include declining yields because of drought and aging of trees, substitution of palm oil for coconut oil in various foods, the smuggling of cheap palm oil into Thailand from Malaysia, and the coming into production of new coconut plantations, on the mainland, which are better-placed with respect to the market. Consequently, Samui's high rate of out-migration has increased further. The growth of a local tourism industry was potentially a timely boost to a troubled island economy.

Land, labour and capital in bungalow development

Overview of bungalow development

Tourism development in Koh Samui effectively began with the arrival of low-budget travellers in the early 1970s. Accounts of Samui's white beaches lined with coconut palms, its relaxed atmosphere and cheap accommodation, spread by word of mouth and budget travel guides such as the Lonely Planet series. Samui became a stop on the hippy trail from Kathmandu to Bali. Access to Samui from the mainland was by a slow, overnight ferry and this, together with the simplicity of the accommodation, ensured that the tourists were mostly young low-budget travellers with plenty of time.

Prior to this time the island had only a few small hotels which catered almost exclusively for domestic visitors. It was not until the late 1970s that tourism development gradually became a notable part of Koh Samui's economy. By 1984 there were 81 bungalow enterprises on the island, and 13 of these were owned by outsiders (Justice and Peace Commission, 1984). By 1989 the number had risen to 225 enterprises with one-third owned by outsiders. Figure 10.2 shows the growth of bungalow resorts on the island and demonstrates well the rapid growth in the number of outside-owned establishments. However, it also shows that local ownership has continued to increase in absolute terms, even though it has lost out relatively.[2]

Tourism development in Samui has involved a number of phases of investment. Early investment, up until about 1984, was on a small scale and locally-owned. Resorts were established on family-owned land and run as small family enterprises. In general, the families continued to engage in other economic activities and the resorts did not displace the coconut plantations along the beaches.

While this form of investment continued through the 1980s, a new phase of tourism development began around 1984 with the Tourism Authority of Thailand designating Koh Samui as a tourist destination and outside investors establishing the first up-market resorts on the island. The Thai government also drew up a master plan for the tourism development of Samui (Tourism Authority of Thailand, 1985). State authorities began to require formal approval for resort development which had to follow set guidelines. The state also set about the improvement of infrastructure to facilitate the movement of tourists to and from the island, and their movement on the island.

Some of the new resorts were joint ventures with local people, and some were on land leased by islanders to outsiders, but many were fully-owned by mainland investors. The latter were generally more capital-intensive and introduced more formal labour relations between employers and workers. For the most part, they did not rely on unpaid family labour.

In about 1987, a third phase of investment began with the building of international standard corporate-owned resort hotels on the island. By this time most of the available beach-front land on the more popular beaches had been used up or sold off to outsiders. There was some consolidation of existing resorts and many entrepreneurs introduced changes in an attempt to shift into higher-priced accommodation and attract more free-spending tourists. At the same time, mainland companies were establishing an air service to Bangkok and planning a hydrofoil service linking Samui with Bangkok and other resorts and ports on the Gulf of Thailand.

Changing control over factors of production

The role of local entrepreneurs and associated shifts in local configurations of power are illustrated through examination of the changing control over land,

Figure 10.2
Numbers of Presently Existing Bungalows and Hotels Established by Given Year

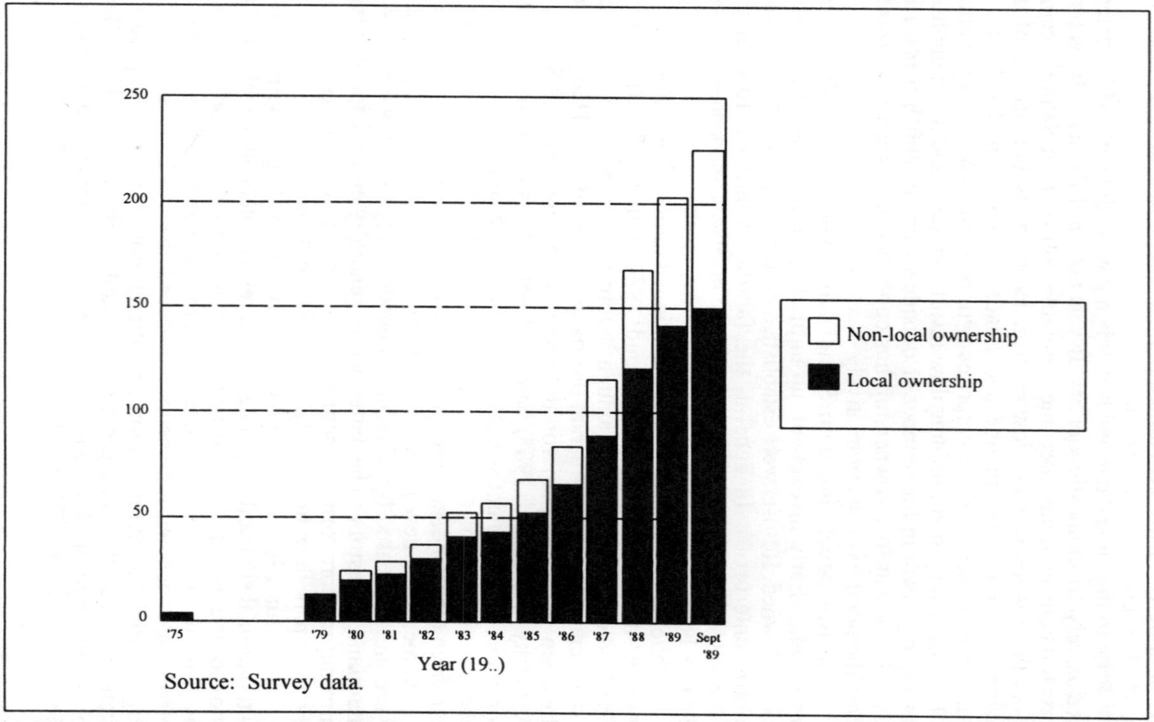

labour and capital as inputs into the productive process. Although this approach to differentiation has been applied mainly in studies of agrarian change, it is also relevant in the context of other rural economic processes, including tourism.

Land

The term land is used here to mean natural resources such as water and soil, as well as land in its usual more limited spatial sense. The ownership of land in Samui has historically been very unequal. With change from predominantly agricultural land use to wider use of land in resort development, there has been a changing conception about land, land-ownership, its use and its value. Traditionally, land was valued primarily for its productive potential. Land that was not agriculturally productive, including sandier areas along the beach, was of little value. Other uses, such as for the beaching or repairing of fishing boats, for housing, or for passage between two places, were quite compatible with coconut production, allowing multiple uses and users.

The Sino-Thai placed greater emphasis than ethnic Thai on legal land title. They also accumulated land for its own sake, even though at the time there was little practical use for unproductive beach-front land. For example, one bungalow owner of Chinese descent said that his parents had been of the view that buying land was bound to be in their long-term interest, although they had no idea that tourists would ever come to Koh Samui.

As tourists started arriving on the island in increasing numbers, land prices along the beaches began to rise. Prices rose from about 5,000 to 10,000 baht per *rai* in the 1970s, and to over four million baht per *rai* in the late 1980s on the more popular beaches. The boom in land prices prompted many islanders to sell and generated many 'instant millionaires' on the island. The buyers were almost always outsiders, as even the rich on the island tended to be large land-owners with comparatively little in capital assets. The island's village heads and *kamnan* were in a position to influence land sales and, especially, to act as agents or middlemen for villagers wishing to sell to outsiders. Sometimes they would buy land when they knew that they had a buyer waiting and willing to pay a higher price. The island's traders, who had established contacts with mainland traders and business people, were also in a strong position to act as agents for outside buyers.

The Sino-Thai traders tended to own land along the beaches for a number of reasons. Being the least productive, it was usually the first land sold by indebted farmers or ceded to creditors. Second, the traders tended to favour beach-front land because of its cheapness and proximity to the sea, thereby making easier the loading and unloading of boats, especially those vessels which carried coconuts from the island to the mainland.

Another land-based resource has become crucial in the tourist economy: water. Tourism development has greatly increased the demand for water (cf. Meyer, 1988, pp.366-7) and there is now a general shortage. Samui's supply is mostly taken from ground-water, but this resource is gradually being depleted and declining in quality as seawater seeps in to replace water pumped out and not replaced through rainfall. Sale of fresh water is thus lucrative for those with access to the resource.

Hotel and bungalow owners have adopted a range of strategies for ensuring supply. The Imperial Hotel group, which has three resorts on the island, has water trucks which they fill from private wells, the owners of which receive substantial payments. The company has also acquired land along streams with plans to build a private reservoir. One of the managers referred to water supply as a 'political problem' and mentioned donations to temples in order maintain goodwill and ensure supply.[3]

Other owners have bought land specifically for the water that lies beneath it, and some spoke of private pipelines to bring water to the resorts. Such strategies are only open to the wealthier resort owners and are impractical for small-scale resorts. Many resort owners must simply accept the declining quality and security of water supply, and some resorts have at times been forced to close because of lack of water. Water has even been brought by truck via the ferry from the mainland. Officials from the Thailand Institute of Technological Research said in personal discussions that the water problem was now a major impediment to the island's development.

Other land problems are also emerging. Excavation of sand for road and resort construction is causing erosion on hillsides. Untreated effluent and inadequate garbage disposal procedures, scuba-diving, souvenir-hunting, and the anchoring of pleasure boats on coral reefs, have all had a detrimental impact (Parnwell, 1993c, p.290). These changes, along with flagrant breaches of the planning controls, are jeopardising Samui's reputation for beautiful beaches and a peaceful atmosphere.

Labour

The first bungalow resorts on the island used mainly unpaid family labour; in fact, the early services to tourists were basically an extension of family hospitality to visitors to the island. With the expansion of the family resorts and also the investment in resorts by outsiders, local villagers were given waged employment. More recently, there has been a general trend in Koh Samui away from employing local workers towards employment of workers from the Thai mainland.

The tourist boom created a greater demand for labour, and outside workers migrated to the island to take advantage of the new opportunities. The trend towards employing outside workers, however, was not simply in response to a shortage of local workers, and has occurred largely at the expense of local people's opportunities to find work in the tourist industry. Figure 10.3 shows a breakdown of the origin of waged workers at Samui's bungalow enterprises for local and non-local ownership.

There is a notable difference in the use of outside labour by different kinds of establishment. Locally-owned resorts are more likely to employ local workers, but even so there is a growing tendency to use non-local workers. Less than one-third of labour in locally-owned enterprises is accounted for by non-wage family labour. Moreover, more than half of the labour employed in these enterprises comes from outside Samui. This is an indication of the extent to which local enterprises are engaged in capitalist production relations, more often than not drawing on a national pool of labour.

In general, there is a policy of discrimination against local workers in the bungalow resorts. One-third of all resort managers acknowledged that they had a policy of not employing local workers. They cited reasons such as the unreliability of local workers, their laziness and dishonesty, and their tendency

Figure 10.3
Wage and Non-Wage Labour in Bungalows and Hotels

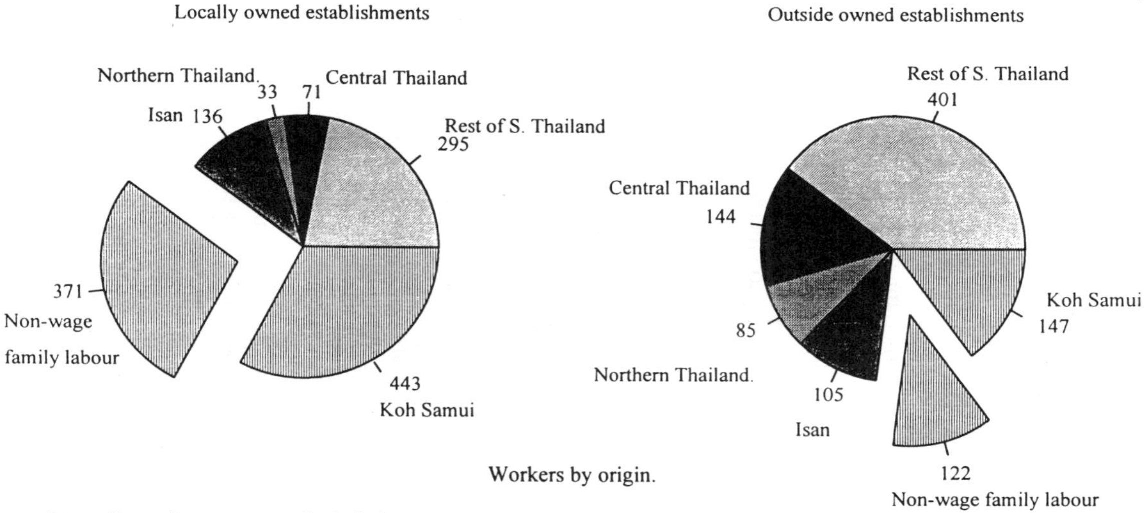

Note: Owner/ managers not included.
Imperial Hotels not included.

Source: Survey data.

to request time off work to attend to social and domestic obligations. The most obvious reason, however, is that outside labour is cheaper. Migrant workers, one manager said, are also less likely to walk out over minor disagreements and are more willing to work long hours without time off. The shift by local entrepreneurs towards the employment of outsiders was gradual with relatives or other villagers being replaced with outsiders as the opportunities arose.

Figure 10.3 also shows that significant numbers of local people are employed by outside-owned establishments, but there is a surprising twist to this. In contrast to the smaller resorts, the large Imperial hotels on Koh Samui have a policy of employing local workers, who account for about half of the chain's staff on the island. Locals employed are concentrated in the more menial jobs, but managers claim that if workers are happy to stay with the corporation and accept transfers to other Imperial hotels in Thailand, they will receive training and be able to move into more skilled and better-paid jobs. However, the corporation is imposing on its workers a very different employment relationship to that with which local people were previously familiar. Managers claimed that the Imperial had a special relationship with Samui, having invested in the island early and thereby shown confidence in its economic future. They were keen to maintain this special relationship and emphasised that working closely with those in positions of influence was crucial to successful business ventures on Koh Samui.

Capital

Over the period of Samui's tourism development there have been many changes in the sources of capital available to developers. The most common source used to be loans from usurers. These usually covered only short-term needs and were at high rates of interest. A small bank on the island, established by local Chinese, could meet some commercial needs. Investment in tourism, however, was mostly limited to those with immediate access to suitable beach-front land and access to enough capital to establish low-cost bungalows next to the beach.

The Bank of Agriculture and Agricultural Co-operatives (BAAC) was the first source of institutionalised credit available on the island, and continues to be the most widely used in Koh Samui; in practice, loans are difficult to obtain for those with small or no land-holdings, and the loan amounts are not sufficient for those wanting to start a bungalow business. Although BAAC loans, strictly speaking, are available only for agriculture, loans are commonly taken out under a pretext of agricultural use and then used for other purposes.[4] The most common source of finance for resort development is now the commercial banks which have established branches on the island. Bank loans are only given to those able to provide security; land is the most common security offered and this has enabled land-rich local people to enter the tourist industry as entrepreneurs.

The Board of Investment has recently given low-cost finance to investors who have plans to build hotels exceeding a certain minimum standard and size, well in excess of the average resort in Samui. In practice, such state support for hotel development is only available for large projects and is mostly given to the corporate sector. Such a policy is at odds with the aims spelt out in the planning document (Tourism Authority of Thailand, 1985), to set aside Koh Samui for low-intensity development and maintain its environmental qualities.

While early investment was entirely from local sources, outside capital has played an increasingly important role in Samui's recent development. International hotel corporations are notably absent in Samui, except the part share in a resort by the French resort group ACCOR, and it is domestic hotel chains which are making their presence felt. But even these are finding great difficulty in buying suitable land at acceptable prices, since the island is already lined with small-scale resorts. Ironically, foreign investment is mostly made by people who would probably be marginal even in their own countries (cf. Williamson, 1992); investors tend to be owner-managers of bars and restaurants.

Table 10.1 shows that outside investment tends to be in the more capital-intensive enterprises. A measure of capital intensity is given by the approximate maximum nightly room takings in each enterprise. Figures are given for the island as a whole, as well as for the two beaches of Chaweng and Lamai, which are discussed below.

Table 10.1
Scale of Enterprises Showing Distribution and per centage of Enterprises which are Locally-Owned

	Samui		Lamai		Chaweng	
Scale factor	No.	% Local	No.	% Local	No.	% Local
<2500	92	77.1	27	96.3	20	75.0
2500-10,000	82	69.5	19	84.2	22	50.0
10,000-120,000	45	42.2	9	77.7	22	45.5
>120,000	2	0.0	--	-----	1	0.0

Note: The scale factor for each enterprise was calculated by averaging the minimum and maximum high season room rate and multiplying this by the number of rooms. It is, therefore, an estimate of the maximum nightly room takings in baht. While this is not the best measure of the scale of an enterprise, it is the best estimate that can be made without figures showing actual capital invested or annual turn-over.

Source: Survey data.

Outside ownership of resorts, however, is not as straightforward as might appear, since many resorts are built on leased land, some of which is still owned by local people. Table 10.2 shows that outside enterprise owners are twice as likely to be tenants as are local owners, but the data do not show the origin of the land-owner.

Table 10.2
Enterprise and Land Ownership

	Ownership of land			
	Enterprise		Other	
	No.	%	No.	%
Ownership of enterprise				
Local	111	74	39	26
Non-island	36	48	39	52

Source : Survey data.

In summary, there is a trend towards outside control and greater concentration of control of factors of production. Land, especially that along the beaches, but increasingly other land away from the beaches, has been bought up by outside investors and speculators. Although foreign ownership of land is illegal, foreigners are buying land under various schemes using Thai nationals as fronts for their investments. Land sales have generated large profits for Samui's larger land-owners, but the enormous rise in the land prices has also made land less accessible to most local people.

The high land values have enabled Samui's wealthy to use their land holdings as security for loans to establish themselves in the tourist industry. Thus land ownership has been a crucial factor in islanders' ability to raise capital for tourism development. But for the near landless there is little benefit from rising land prices unless they wish to sell and leave the island. Thus, higher land prices in effect encourage out-migration of the poorer islanders.

Water resources are also increasingly falling into private hands for, although water itself is not privately owned, there is no limit on individual consumption and the means of accessing and transporting water are in private hands. Thus, water as a resource is becoming accessible in commercial quantities only to those with access to these means.

Labour, too, is now drawn mostly from outside the island, as the tourist industry shifts towards more compliant workers who are willing to put up with harsher conditions. This process is marginalising the island's workers who, while migrant workers are streaming onto the island to find jobs in tourism, are leaving Samui in numbers greater than ever before.

While access to capital has always been limited, the capital intensification in resort development is shutting out opportunities for Samui's families to engage in small-scale tourist enterprises. There is a trend away from island sources of capital towards sources controlled from Bangkok, that is, the major Thai banks and the Thai state. While the interest rates offered are better than those offered previously, the sums required to establish businesses are many times greater than in the past and, in practice, the opportunities for ordinary villagers to start tourist enterprises are more limited.

Social and economic transformation of Lamai and Chaweng

Socio-economic changes need to be examined, not just in terms of the outsiders taking control, but also in terms of local transformation of social relations. Two contrasting communities, Ban Lamai, in which tourist enterprises are predominantly locally-owned, and Ban Chaweng, in which nearly half the enterprises are owned by outside entrepreneurs, are discussed below.

Ban Lamai

Ban Lamai lies on the island's east coast and is the second most intensively developed beach area. Lamai is characterised by a high level of local ownership in the tourist industry; of the 57 bungalow resorts in Lamai, 49 are locally owned. The owners are mostly drawn from the village's more privileged families, most of whom had substantial land-holdings. Most bungalow owners are related to one another, and some families own more than one resort. Three cases are useful by way of illustration.

'Daeng', 62, is a former school teacher and respected elder in Lamai and all over the island. His sister is married to the past *kamnan*, who was the first person to open bungalows in Lamai. His wife's sister is also married to a *kamnan* and bungalow owner in Chaweng Beach. In 1983, he decided to open bungalows himself, and they were built on land he had bought years before tourism development began in Koh Samui. His son ran the business which was very successful and the standard of accommodation was later up-graded to attract tourists who would spend more. Daeng decided to open a second set of bungalows; this time on inherited land. The second resort was also successful, and so a third was opened; his four children now manage the resorts and he has retired to a large, modern house, which replaced his old house in the village.

Daeng has made some large land sales, the proceeds of which he put into developing bungalows, and the children are now expanding the business into areas such as travel agencies and tour operations.

'Sompong' is from a respected although not prominent family in the village. He is related to many of the resort owners. One, his maternal uncle, is a former village head. The family was fortunate to own, amongst many small plots of land on which coconuts and rice are grown, two plots adjacent to the beach. One beach-front plot they sold, and on the other they built a resort with ten bungalows, but two were lost in a flood. Sompong runs the resort with his sister, while his father does much of the maintenance. His parents, however, consider themselves coconut farmers and still do some work in the plantations. The family hires workers from the mainland to help in the plantations, and two others who work in the resort.

The enterprise makes a small profit but is also indebted to a commercial bank, and during the low season when occupancy rates drop very low, the resort barely brings in any money. Sompong's parents were able to give most of their children tertiary education, and all but one of his brothers and sisters have left the island to find work on the mainland.

'Lek' is the village head and owns a village store. The store has recently expanded greatly and now stocks a wide range of goods for tourists, migrant workers and villagers. He used to be a coconut dealer and still owns a small mill in which coconuts are processed. His land is used for growing durian, which are very much more profitable than coconuts. Lek's latest venture is a bakery which he said was doing well in gaining contracts to supply bread to the bungalows. Two of his children work in the store and bakery, while the third, who is studying commerce at a university in Bangkok, intends to return to Samui upon graduation and work in a family business. Although Lek is not directly involved in the tourist industry, his businesses serve the industry and he has a vested interest in the industry's expansion.

The three cases discussed above are a cross section of the village élite, who are benefiting from Lamai's tourism development. However, there are also differences between the bungalow owners, some of whom, such as Sompong, are struggling to maintain the viability of their small businesses while others, such as Daeng, seem to be establishing substantial enterprises.

The majority of the villagers, however, were never large land-owners or involved in commerce, and at best they can participate in Samui's tourist industry as wage labourers or as informal producers and sellers of foods for sale to the tourists. The latter can be seen selling fresh fruit, sweets or cooked foods along the beach or from trolleys which they wheel along the dusty roads parallel to the beach. But their livelihood is under threat from the numerous restaurants which have opened, many of which are run by *farang* (Europeans, Americans and Australians), from the bungalow owners who keep them away from guests by refusing them access to the areas, and from the many village stores, such as that of Lek, which are now offering goods for sale to tourists.

Chaweng

While Ban Lamai shows a high level of local participation in the tourist industry, especially in the ownership of resorts and tourist businesses, the case of Ban Chaweng stands in distinct contrast. Chaweng Beach is the most developed on the island, with 65 resorts, only 36 of which are locally owned. In general, the prices in Chaweng are considerably higher, reflecting the capital intensity of resort development along the beach.

'Noi' is in her late twenties and owns a resort in Chaweng. She is from a southern province, where her father owns hotels. After graduating from a Bangkok university, Noi worked with her father before buying land in Koh Samui. The land was bought cheaply from a Chaweng villager, and on this land she established her resort. The resort is one of the more expensive on the island, and she says with pride that she has built up the business herself. Noi's brother also owns a resort in Chaweng, and they hope to expand further.

The largest and most expensive enterprise in Chaweng is the Imperial Samui Hotel, owned by the Bangkok-based Imperial Hotel group, which is now the largest in Thailand. The Imperial group pioneered corporate investment in Koh Samui. The group's strategy for securing supply of water has been discussed, as has its policy of employing a large per centage of local workers in its hotels. The corporation also appears to have a policy of creating enclaves around its hotels so as to keep out low-budget bungalows and, presumably, low-budget tourists. Around its Chaweng hotel the corporation is buying land, including adjacent low-budget bungalows. These have been closed down and the company claims that it will eventually expand the hotel onto the newly-acquired land.

While Ban Lamai, despite the differentiation taking place within, retains its village focus and a sense of community, Ban Chaweng has all but disappeared. There is no longer a discernible village centre, for this has given way to three strips of development parallel to the beach. Along the beach is a line of bungalow resorts and newer resort complexes following a more contained 'hotel' pattern. Behind these runs a service road, and on the inland side of the road is a line of restaurants, bars, shops, banks and travel agencies, discotheques, and cheap accommodation for migrant workers. Further back is low-lying swampy land, once rice fields, but now being filled in to accommodate large bar/restaurant complexes and other services for tourists. The island's main ring road runs parallel to the beach further inland, and the remnants of Ban Chaweng are relocated in ribbon development along this road, together with shops and other services oriented more to the needs of villagers and migrant workers.

The cases above are a cross-section of resort owners in Samui, but the vast majority of people in the industry are employees, drawn mostly from the mainland. A typical example is 'Chit', a twenty-five year old from a village in Central Thailand. He has worked in hotels in Bangkok and Pattaya, and speaks English with confidence. He enjoys mixing with young tourists. Chit has been in Samui a little over a year and whilst he enjoys it, he is not sure how long he will stay. He says that the pay is quite good, but the island is expensive and he never saves any money.

'Sompong' is from Ban Pungka, a small village in Samui. His family are coconut farmers and also grow vegetables, but most of his siblings have left Samui to settle on unclaimed forest land in Chumpon on the mainland where they grow coffee. After leaving school at sixteen, Sompong was employed in a bungalow resort in his village, but left after a year to join his sister in Chumpon. The family now divides its time between Chumpon and Samui, with most energy and capital being spent on the coffee farm. Sompong later returned to Samui and a friend of his father helped him get a gardening job at the Imperial Samui in Chaweng. He lives behind the hotel in workers' accommodation, and considers himself lucky to have been employed.

New threads in the island's social fabric are the tourists themselves. In peak season, there are many thousands on the island at any one time. Some stay for months, living in the cheaper bungalows or even renting houses. Bars and restaurants owned by *farang* investors are a feature of both Chaweng and Lamai. *Farang* have an advantage in the provision of these services because of their knowledge of the languages and culture of the tourists. Such establishments also tend not to employ local workers, in part because of the stigma attached to working in bars which are places of prostitution. Nevertheless, restaurant and bar development serves the interests of local land-owners who build bars for rent to *farang* operators, and of local entrepreneurs whose interests are in general associated with the growth and intensification of tourism development in Koh Samui. Both the *farang* entrepreneurs and the mainland investors tend to employ strategies of forming friendships with locals of power and influence, such as village heads and police (Williamson, 1992).

In general, the new *farang*-run establishments also form part of a new space where only tourists and Thais with money and the cultural capital to feel comfortable in such places are able to go. Much of Samui's business is done in the bungalows and other tourist establishments from which most locals are effectively excluded.

There are many more ways in which Samui's people have engaged with the island's tourist industry. There are a few people who, with little land or capital, have become wealthy through tourism. One made money selling bottled water to bungalows. Some street vendors have greatly increased their incomes by selling food to the late-night revellers in the bars of Chaweng and Lamai. But such examples are the exceptions, and most islanders still have little to do with the industry.

The coconut farmers, once the back-bone of Samui's economy, are now marginal to it. Many, like Sompong's family, spend most of their time and energy, and their capital, trying to establish new farms on the mainland.[5] Some eventually sell what land they own in Samui and cut their ties with the island. Others maintain their links through parents and grandparents who are too old or otherwise unwilling to move. Many of the island's out-migrants complain of high prices (for food, transport and services) on the island; others lament their lack of English language skills which would help them secure work in the bungalow resorts. Some simply say that Samui has changed, that it is no longer as friendly and that people there only think about money. One said that he is a farmer and Samui is no longer a place for farmers.

Samui's emerging social formation

The discussion demonstrates that the social formation emerging out of Samui's tourism development is more complex than is implied by approaches to tourism development which emphasise outside forces (and usually local dependency) or approaches which emphasise tourism as an agent of development or modernisation. The first point to be made is that the social context in which intensive tourism development has taken place continues to shape the emerging social formation. Secondly, other trends such as the decline in agricultural commodity prices also continue to shape tourism development in Samui; the island now has an economy divided into two distinct sectors (agriculture and tourism) which, although they are interrelated in some ways, respond to different outside forces.

It has been useful to examine ownership and employment within the tourist industry along the lines of outsiders and insiders. Cohen (1983a) did this for Samui early in its tourism development. However, the distinction is now blurring and it is significant that people's interests in the industry are by no means divided along these lines.

The distinction between insiders and outsiders simplifies the dynamics of investment in tourism, of migration onto and off the island, and overlooks the significance of emerging classes whose interests and composition may not be definable in such terms. To speak of local ownership in a resort refers to the origin of the nominal owners, but these should not imply that the owners' interests are aligned or coincide with others of the same origin. Locally-born owners of bungalows certainly have an interest in the intensification of tourism development. This must necessarily come from outside investment as the industry absorbs far more capital than can be invested by local people. However, Figure 10.2 shows that, while outside ownership has increased, there has been a steady increase in the number of locally-owned enterprises. Furthermore, as Table 10.2 shows, many outside owners are tenants and therefore do not have full control of their enterprises. A further point is that while it is clear that outside ownership is most prevalent in the large-scale enterprises, in both Chaweng and Lamai there is evidently a group of medium-scale enterprises in local hands, indicating the existence of an indigenous capitalist class.

Large land-owners have been actively encouraging land speculation and sales to outsiders, driving up their own land values. They are, in many cases, able to act as agents for either outside buyers or local sellers through their leadership positions within the village or their outside contacts made through commerce and trade.

It was frequently stated by villagers that in the past there was little in terms of lifestyle and consumption that distinguished people in the village. While there were certainly rich and poor, landlords and tenants, they usually lived alongside each other, met each other in the course of their day-to-day activities, and at village functions. They ate the same food and everybody knew each other.

Conspicuous consumption is now a part of Samui's culture. Some such consumers are those who have sold land and are living on the proceeds, but most are the new entrepreneurial class. Luxury cars, lavish entertaining in air-conditioned restaurants, and heavy betting on the island's renowned buffalo fights, are increasingly seen. New houses, of concrete rather than the traditional timber, are a notable feature of the landscape. Most notable are the resorts which line the beaches. The owners have gradually moved their meals, their children, and their socialising, to within the boundaries of these places. There has been a transformation of social relations which parallels the economic transformations which have taken place.

Conclusion

Many local people are identifiable losers in tourism development, their positions within the Samui economy made worse by through inflation of food and land prices, by being displaced by resort development, or by decreasing access to public resources such as beach space, fishing places, water, forests and the food they produce. As noted above, some have surrendered their places within Samui altogether.

Generalisations about outside agents in Samui's development are misleading. As much as outsiders include investors from Thailand's metropolitan capitalist élite, wielding power through large companies entering into Samui's tourist industry, they also include mainland seasonal migrants who come to work in Samui's bungalows under conditions of long hours, having to pay high prices to local landlords for very poor accommodation. The conditions of the hundreds of prostitutes are most precarious and dangerous. Outside entrepreneurs are themselves a diverse group which includes *farang* entrepreneurs, some of whom made investments of as little as a few thousand dollars to establish bars, and whose social, legal and economic marginality places them in a precarious position (Williamson, 1992).

The material presented belies the common assumptions made in the tourist literature, being the tendency to characterise locals as dispossessed wage labourers, and thus losers, and the winners as outside investors in the form of large companies. Samui's economy and society is increasingly differentiated, but along lines that tend increasingly to blur distinctions between outsider and local. The material also shows that tourism development is more complex than suggested by either the modernisationist or dependency views.

Tourism development is characterised by all the complexities of development or change in other industries, such as agriculture (to which we have already alluded). Clearly there are both winners and losers in tourism development, and individuals may, themselves, both win and lose. The benefits of increased employment opportunities must be weighed against the cost of loss of amenity, inflation of food prices, and the loss of communal values and a new attitude on the part of the rich towards their obligations within the village community.

Tourism in Koh Samui is playing an important part in terms of transforming social relations from those more characteristic of pre-capitalist Thailand towards those identifiably capitalist. Tourism development should thus be seen in terms of capitalist development in Thailand. Its uneven distribution of costs and benefits is a reflection of the inequalities prevalent throughout Thailand and its capitalist development within the world economy.

Notes

1 The dependency approach is most explicitly spelt out by Turner and Ash (1975); such views are also popularly held and currently espoused in publications such as *Contours* (the newsletter of the Ecumenical Coalition on Third World Tourism). Tzong-biau and Pye (1983) exemplifies the modernisationist approach.

2 The term 'locally-owned' refers to parcels of land or enterprises which are owned, or predominantly owned, by people born in Koh Samui, or who have grown up there. Early in Samui's development, the distinction between local (or island) and outside (or mainland) ownership was easily made, but the distinction is increasingly unclear as some islanders enter into partnerships with mainlanders. Furthermore, some outside entrepreneurs are taking up residence in Koh Samui to conduct business, and sometimes marrying locals.

3 In at least two villages people expressed disquiet about the leasing of temple land to resort developers. In a third, villagers were reluctant to criticise their abbot as he was powerful and seen sometimes to use his influence for the benefit of the village.

4 This was claimed by BAAC officials and confirmed by others who admitted that they were using BAAC loans for purchases of fishing boats and motor-cycles, and for general living expenses.

5 They are not always successful, facing insecurity of land tenure, violence from gangs and local strongmen, and the vagaries of coffee and rubber prices.

11 Trekking in northern Thailand: Impact distribution and evolution over time

Philip Dearden

> [Trekkers] ...go in and sort of take over the village. ...They smoke opium, drink and have sex on the front porch. This is polluting the culture and now the tribes are getting into the wheeling and dealing themselves (Gorton, 1988).

> The people ... from the varied hilltribes of northern Thailand are attracting more and more attention from overseas. It is not because the area is well known as a source of the opium poppy, but rather because the diverse lives that these people live-out show an increasingly materialistic world that riches and possessions that money buys are not the source of happiness.
>
> Happiness is a state of mind, something that is beyond price and these people, poor though they may be in material things, live a life that can honesty [sic] be called 'HAPPY' (*Trekking in Northern Thailand* brochure, 1990, Orchid Group).

Introduction

Tourism in Thailand is a multi-million dollar business. Overseas visitors brought in over US$4 billion in foreign exchange in 1990 and the Seventh National Economic and Social Development Plan predicts that the numbers of tourists will rise 25 per cent between 1992 and 1996 (*Bangkok Post Economic Review*, Dec. 31 1991). These bald facts, however, tell only part of the tale. They tell little of how the income is distributed within Thai society and the impacts that this may have, and they only reveal one dimension - the financial benefits. There are also financial costs associated with the enterprise. Furthermore, the contents of the impacts are not restricted solely to matters financial - they also include other social, cultural and environmental values.

The above is also true of specific sub-components of the industry, be it the entertainment provided at Pattaya, or the focus of this discussion - trekking in the highlands in the North. In all cases it is instructive to try to asess the nature of the impacts of the activity and how these are distributed amongst the participants. This is especially significant, however, in cases such as trekking where the information base is quite limited and the activity quite distinct from others which might provide analogous situations elsewhere. It is also important when dealing with potentially fragile situations, in both the environmental and cultural contexts, where systems may have high sensitivity and low resilience.

The focus of this paper is to explore two questions relating to trekking amongst the hill-tribes on North Thailand. The first is to assess the impacts of trekking and how they are distributed amongst the players in the activity. There are several ways of doing this. One is to conduct in-depth longtitudinal studies of one or several villages to assess how they change over time as a result of trekking (see the chapter by Toyota in this volume). This approach necessitates caution with regard to separating the effects of trekking from the myriad of other changes that are occuring in the highlands, and the basis for generalising from the particular villages studied to a wider population (see Michaud, 1993; Dearden, 1995a). The other approach is to study a broad spectrum of villages that have differing degrees of exposure to trekking, and try to assess through this 'space for time' substitution approach the varying effects that might be ascribed to trekking. This approach, which is the one used here, must also be used with caution in terms of the ability to separate the impacts of trekking from other changes. Both approaches, if undertaken with rigour, yield valuable information, and should not be looked at as competing but rather complementary ways of trying to understand a very complicated phenomenon (for this reason both approaches are incorporated in this volume).

The second question addressed by this chapter concerns how the impacts and their distribution change as the industry grows. Are there, for example, stages of growth which seem to maximise the benefits to a certain party, such as the hill-tribes, while minimising the adverse effects? Before addressing these questions a brief background to the activity is required. This synthesis is the result of a decade of enquiry into the topic by the author and associates, and also uses the observations of other researchers where relevant. As such, sources range from empirical surveys of trekkers through to interviews with guides and hill-tribe peoples, and participant observation.

Trekking in northern Thailand

Trekking as an organised, commercial activity amongst the hill-tribes in the North started over two decades ago. From these early beginnings the industry has mushroomed to embrace over 100,000 trekkers per year with a median trek length of three nights each, giving some 300,000 trekker-nights per year in the highlands (see Dearden and Harron (1992a) for a further discussion on various sources of trekker statistics). Most treks still originate in Chiang Mai, but important smaller centres include Chiang Rai, Mae Hong Son and Pai in particular (Figure 11.1). Trekking companies advertise and organise the treks from these centres, although the trips now penetrate practically every area in the highlands. The most popular areas are those that provide the potential for trekkers to see a variety of different hill-tribes, preferably still engaged in a

Figure 11.1
Northern Thailand, Showing Main Areas for Trekking

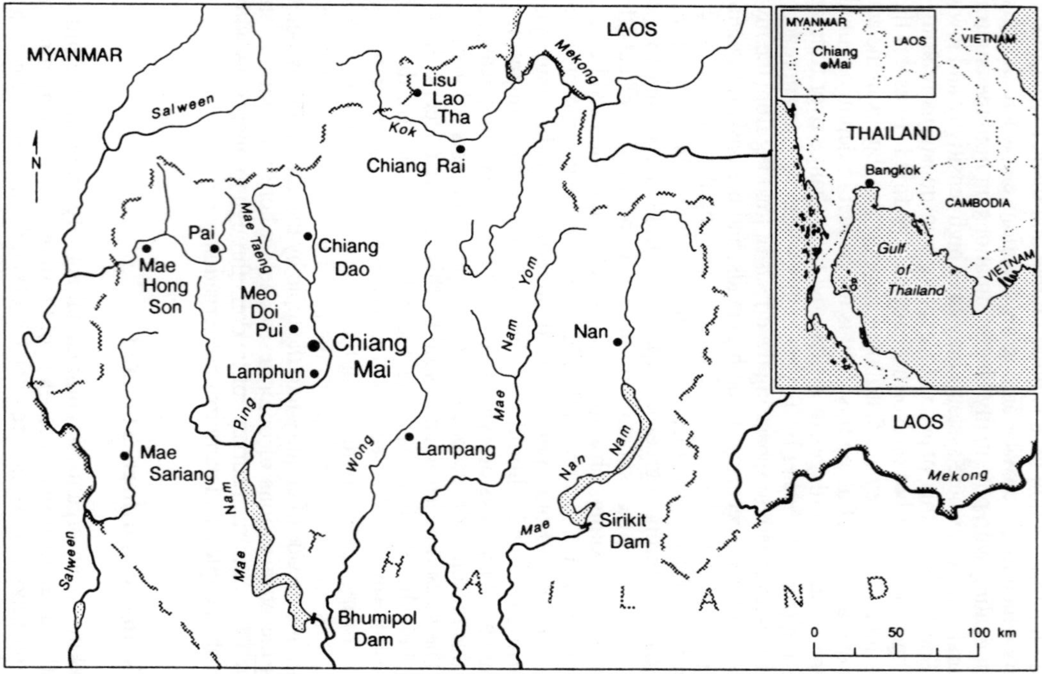

relatively 'authentic' way of life (e.g. see Cohen, 1989a), that are relatively accessible and that provide opportunity for the trekkers to ride elephants and rafts, now a standard part of most treks. The Mae Taeng is the most popular area.

Trekkers are generally young, well-educated westerners on an extended tour of the region. Dearden and Harron (1992b) found from surveys of the trekking population that 58 per cent had university and college degrees and a further 24 per cent had attended college. About a third could be classified as professionals (e.g. doctors, lawyers, managers and programmers), while 17 per cent were teachers and 14 per cent still students. Mean age was 28 years. Total trip length showed a wide range from two weeks to five years, with a mean length of six months. Trekking is the main motivation to come to Chiang Mai for 60 per cent of the trekkers. The remainder make the decision to go trekking after reaching the North. Given the number of trekkers, and the importance of trekking as a motivation to come to the North, then it is obviously of some interest to understand the nature of the activity and its sustainability within the context of the tourist industry in the North.

Assessing impacts

Three main groups can be identified as players in the activity: the trekking companies, the trekkers and the hill-tribes. Each group can potentially be exposed to impacts under three headings: economic, environmental and socio-cultural (Figure 11.2). Within each category, a particular effect may have both positive and negative impacts. For example, increasing interaction between hill-tribe people and others involved in the activity, such as guides and trekkers, may have not only negative impacts in terms of cultural change, but there may also be some positive aspects to the interaction in terms of satiating the curiosity of the hill-tribes about outsiders. In general, the relative strengths of these positive and negative aspects are difficult to compare, especially by outsiders. Only in the case of financial transactions is this comparison relatively straightforward. In the 'economic' column of Figure 11.2, only the dominant impact is shown. Hence, although there are negative as well as positive financial aspects of trekking for both the companies and the hill-tribes, these are cancelled out by the profits that can be made. Furthermore, the positive impact of today may have a longer term negative impact, and *vice versa*. Some attempt will be made in the second part of the chapter to come to terms with these changes, but the perspective will still be relatively short-term; longer-term, inter-generational impacts are extremely hard to identify.

One thing should be immediately apparent from the rather crude summary presented in Figure 11.2: the hill-tribe cells are all full. This contrasts with the cells of the other two parties, which are half full in the case of the trekkers and with only one entry for the trekking companies. Unfortunately, the party most affected, the hill-tribes, have virtually no say in the organisation and direction of the activity. They are passive partners at best; the exploited class at worst.

Attention will now turn to summarising the contents of each cell, using the particular theme rather than party involved as the organisational tool.

Figure 11.2
Summary Matrix of Positive (+) and Negative (-) Impacts Associated with Trekking in Northern Thailand

	Economic	Socio-cultural	Environmental
Hilltribes	+	+ –	+ –
Trekking Companies	+		
Trekkers		+	

Positive (+) and Negative (-) impacts

Economic impacts

Few reliable statistics are available to assess the economic impacts of the activity. On the basis of a questionnaire survey of trekkers, participant observation, and interviews with trekking companies, guides and hill-tribe representatives, Dearden (1991) suggested some initial figures (Table 11.1), and much of the following is based on this source.

Two of the parties can be dismissed fairly rapidly. The economic costs to the trekkers vary depending upon the length of the trip. A survey of 208 trekkers during the period of summer 1989 and winter 1990 revealed a median trip length of three nights at an average cost of 1,375 baht (US$55). Surveys of trekker satisfaction revealed 97 per cent of trekkers assessing the trek as 'enjoyable' or 'very enjoyable', with 99 per cent saying that they would recommend a trek to their friends. Such an endorsement suggests that the negative economic impact of trekking on the trekkers is out-weighed by the positive socio-cultural impacts of the experience on the trekkers.

The second party is the trekking companies, which in this case also includes their employees, such as the trekking guides. The companies, on the basis of 100,000 trekkers per year at 1,375 baht per trek would gross 137.5 million baht (about US$5,500,000). They do, however, sustain substantial costs related to provision of transport to and from the trekking region, costs associated with elephant riding and raft construction, food and accommodation costs on the trek, wages for guides and other employees, and other miscellaneous costs that may vary considerably, such as subsidies to certain villages for providing items such as blankets. Due to the uncertainties and variability between these costs no attempt will be made to derive a net figure. However, given the number of trekking companies in Chiang Mai alone (some 200), it can be assumed that there is a comfortable profit to be made in the industry.

The only real incentive for the hill-tribes to be involved in the activity relates to the economic benefits that might accrue. Meyer (1987) reported that the headman's family at one trekking village, Lisu Lao Tha, in the early 1980s was making 3,500 baht (US$140) per month and other families up to 1,500 baht (US$60) per month. Seewuthiwong (1989) also provides a few statistics regarding income from opium and porterage in another village. Dearden (1991) suggests that the total amount generated (Table 11.1) is just over 53 million baht (US$2.12 million), a substantial amount, especially in a poverty-stricken region such as the highlands. However, a word of caution is in order. First, these are gross amounts and do not take into account the costs of providing the goods or services being purchased. In the case of some items this could be a substantial proportion, such as the 6.7 million baht (US$268,000) raised by food and drink sales. Most of this food and drink would be purchased in lowland Thai villages and re-sold at a profit. Beer and candy bars are favourite items. The profit charged is not large, and a bottle of beer that has been bought in a lowland market and carried on someone's back to the village may still be cheaper than the customer would pay in a bar or restaurant in Chiang Mai.

Secondly, we know little of how the income is distributed within the highlands. Accommodation income will tend to stay in the villages where the trekkers have slept, often in the hands of the headman, his relatives or whoever has provided the accommodation (e.g. see Cohen, 1979; Meyer, 1987;

Seewuthiwong, 1989; Kesmanee and Charoensri 1994). Rafting income is more complicated due to the wide variety of circumstances. On the most popular rafting river, the Mae Taeng, rafts are used just once, then abandoned or sold for a minimal amount for their bamboo logs. This means that new logs are usually cut and rafts built for each party. Ten years ago, bamboo supply was adequate right next to the river, now logs may have to be transported quite a distance and guides may have problems ensuring that rafts are available. This makes the price of rafts quite variable depending upon the laws of supply and demand. Nonetheless, rafts are still usually constructed by highland people, in this case local Karen villagers, although lowland Thais may also be involved in some locations.

Table 11.1
Estimated Annual Income of Hill-tribes from Trekking

	Participants (n)	Average Cost (baht)[a]	Total (baht)
Income Category:			
Accommodations	300,000	30	9,000,000
Handicrafts	44,000	71	3,120,000
Transportation			
Elephant riding	96,000	400	19,200,000
Rafting	20,000[b]	600	12,000,000
Miscellaneous services			
Food-drink sale	72,000	94	6,770,000
Opium sale	40,000	69	2,760,000
Posing	5,000	29	145,000
Marijuana sale	5,000	14	70,000
Other	5,000	44	220,000

Notes: [a] Per trekker; 25 baht = US$1.00.
[b] Number of rafts with an average of 4.5 trekkers in each.

Source: Dearden, 1991.

Elephant riding is now a standard part of most treks and 96 per cent of th trekkers interviewed had this experience. Traditionally the elephants wer owned and operated by their Karen mahout. There is increasing evidence th lowland Thais are now managing to consolidate the business, such that on owner may have a dozen or more elephants that are used in trekking. Little known of how the elephant riding income is distributed.

From the foregoing it is obvious that considerable economic benefits a being generated by the activity. There is a much lesser degree of certaint regarding the distribution of these benefits, although it seems safe to sugge that most of the profits are being captured by the trekking companies. The profits to many villages involved in the activity, especially those that do not provide transportation services, may be minimal in terms of the overall amount being generated. To hill-tribe people under constant threat of food deficiencies (Dearden, 1995a), any amount of additional income will be welcome.

Socio-cultural impacts

Given the scale of the activity described above it is to be expected that there will be social and cultural ramifications for the parties involved. The impacts upon the trekkers and companies seem relatively straight-forward. The economic costs incurred by the trekkers are off-set by the value of the experience. The latter is composed of various life-enriching experiences that range from the cultural values of having opportunity to observe a society very different from their own at relatively close quarters, through to the more ephemeral values associated with the recreational aspects of the trek, such as rafting and elephant riding.

Maneepresart *et.al.* (1975, p.9) in an early study on the impacts of trekking found that nearly half of the trekkers interviewed had an "almost academic interest in their [hill-tribe] culture and traditions" and "few admitted to visiting purely for adventure or fun." By the latter part of the 1980s this emphasis for trekkers overall seemed to have changed to one that placed higher values on the recreational aspects of the trip. Dearden and Harron (1994) suggest that this reflects changes in the type of tourist now trekking and a shift from primary ethnic tourism to a broader purview of cultural tourism as defined by Wood (1980). In such tourism, the ethnic people are no longer the prime focus of interest, but constitute just one item of interest within a broader landscape.

Meyer (1987, p.436) suggested that what might normally be considered negative aspects of a vacation can be seen in a different light while trekking: "For some tourists, the occasional robbing and even killing of tourists that are reported in the newspapers of Thailand and the victim's home countries may just add the necessary thrill and risk to their experience..." However, notwithstanding the specific nature of the benefits accrued, they must be substantial in order to promote the high rates of satisfaction reported earlier and the continued growth of the industry.

There may also be some small socio-cultural beneficial aspects of trekking that accrue to the trekking companies and their personnel involved in the activity. In general, lowland Thais have little appreciation of the highlands and their inhabitants. Conflicts occur over a wide range of issues. Trekking is one way in which greater knowledge and hence understanding of the highland way of life may be spread. This is most direct with the trekking guides who lead the trips. There has been an increasing tendency amongst the companies to select guides for their English language-speaking abilities rather than the more traditional skills as route-finders and hill-tribe liaison, as the treks have become more routinised (e.g. see Cohen, 1982a; Dearden and Harron, 1994). These guides may have little familiarity with highland life and yet on occasion have been witnessed to play a very important role in bringing news to the villages and also in the reciprocal movement of highland news to the lowlands. Whether on balance this contributes to the generally negative stereotyping that the lowland

Thais have of the hill-tribes, or does, in fact, add to a greater understanding is open to question.

This theme of greater awareness may also have beneficial socio-cultural impacts for the hill-tribes. The world in which they live is, both metaphorically and literally, shrinking as the pressures of the outside world draw in (e.g. see Cooper, 1984; Tan-Kim-Yong *et.al.*, 1988; McKinnon and Vienne, 1989). These forces - commercial penetration, lowland settlers, missionaries, resource extraction, military and government missions, video halls, development projects and so on - are the very same forces that are in effect throughout the world. In short, they cannot be resisted, even if it were deemed desirable so to do. One way in which traditional societies can be eased into being able to understand and deal with these changes is through greater knowledge. Trekking aids in this process by exposing the hill-tribes to increasing contact with the lowlanders, especially through the trekking companies and their guides, and also the trekkers.

One far-reaching example of this is given in the *Bangkok Post*, "From hillside to roadside" (February 13 1990). The article discusses the recent and very noticeable appearance of Hmong people on the main thoroughfares of Bangkok to sell 'hill-tribe' wares of varying degrees of authenticity. The Hmong interviewed attribute the seasonal move not only to deteriorating conditions in the hills but also the realisation of the potential for selling handicrafts as increased numbers of trekkers visited their home villages. This move appears to be a logical one for a peoples who have traditionally moved to take advantage of economic opportunities (e.g. see Geddes, 1976). Parnwell (1995, personal communication) has suggested that the Hmong are often manipulated by lowlanders in terms of handicraft sales. How widespread such manipulation may be is open to question, although other researchers (e.g. Cohen, 1995 personal communication, and Howard, 1995, personal communication) have found little evidence of this among the Hmong.

The continued migration of the Hmong to seek better economic opportunities may be a difficult 'benefit' for many to appreciate. In downtown Bangkok, the Hmong do not particularly look to be beneficiaries as they join the hordes of other poor street vendors trying to hawk their wares amidst the noise and pollution. If, however, any store is put in the notion that a main component of development assistance is to promote self-determination (e.g. see Goulet, 1992), then this situation must be viewed through the eyes of the Hmong who have made that decision. Perhaps the street vendors of today become the parents of the doctors, professors and lawyers of tomorrow.

Beside this rather extreme example, interviews with hill-tribe villagers and printed interviews in newspapers and magazines reveal a pronounced human trait, curiosity, on the part of the hill-tribes about visitors. "We like strange faces", Akha Leebai u-sue is quoted as saying in an article in *Time* (December 29 1986, p.8), and Seewuthiwong (1989) provides something of an insider's account of trekkers in an Akha village that reflects similar interest. Unfortunately, the window on the outside world that the trekkers provide for the hill-tribes is not very large, as emphasised by the earlier socio-economic profile statistics of trekkers: a very atypical stereotype of outsiders may be the result.

Nor should it be thought that this interest is focused solely on *farangs*. A report in the *Bangkok Post* (June 25 1988, p.27), interviewing villagers in Akha Ban Pakha Sukjai, 20 minutes from the rather more famous settlement of Doi Mae Salong, revealed the following: "Having tourists coming into our village broadens our horizons because they bring with them the world outside. We love to watch them, especially the Thai tourists, because we want to be able to speak Thai and to be Thai." As is shown in the next section, this interest may well be ephemeral, but as villages first become involved in trekking the hill-tribes may be as curious about the trekkers as the trekkers are about them.

These are some of the potentially positive socio-cultural impacts of trekking that may accrue to the hill-tribes, but there are also negative impacts. Many observers have commented on the latter (e.g. Judd, 1988; Durst, 1987; Mirante, 1990; see also Mika Toyota's chapter in this volume), and they have been given prominent newspaper coverage with headlines such as "Tourism: a cash crop that can hurt the hilltribes" (*Bangkok Post* February 14 1988), "Feeding time at the human zoo" (*The Nation*, March 26 1992, p.2), and "Travellers give Thailand's hill tribes a new addiction - money" (*Bangkok Post*, January 14 1988, p.6). Even from these headlines it can be seen that one of the main concerns is that of the additional cash flow into the villages as a result of the activity and the impact that this might have on the villagers.

The effects of this additional supply of money in the village are not to be unexpected in such poor societies. Many villagers may not be able to get access to this supply through more normal means of trade and interaction, and begging may result. This seems to be especially the case in Akha villages. The latter may also be especially aggressive in selling handicrafts to visitors, but more subtle manoeuvres may be seen in many different tribal villages as described by Cohen (1979, p.15): "Some inhabitants have learned to play the role of 'professional natives', and to extract a benefit from the tourist: thus one old man sits motionless in his home, smoking a pipe, while tourists take pictures; but he comes very much alive when they are about to leave and asks for his remuneration." He goes on to suggest that tourism is having "an impact on traditional values; in particular it engendered a preoccupation with the making of money and the evaluation of everything in monetary terms." (*ibid.*, p.20).

The above statements have a ring of truth. It is important, however, to place them within the context of the overall commercialisation of the subsistence economies that is occurring, and also within the context of the similar kinds of changes that tourism produces in other locations, be it London, Hawaii, the Amazon or even lowland villages in Northern Thailand (e.g. see Boonchote and Dearden, 1994). Begging occurs on a regular basis on the tourist streets of Victoria, Canada. Perhaps the main difference in these situations is that in the highlands, visitors go to the villages to see something different (as alluded to in the quote with which this chapter opens), not to see people that suffer from their own addiction, materialism and money. They wish to believe in the 'noble savage' image that is portrayed by many of the trekking companies (e.g. see Cohen, 1989a). However, this seems quite hypocritical in light of the critical poverty of many of the hill-tribes. As Seewuthiwong (1989, p.423) intones, "there is nothing romantic about life in an Akha village."

Besides these concerns over the 'polluting' effect of the monetary income on individual values, there are more indirect effects relating to broader values in highland societies. The distributional one has already been mentioned above. Philip Hirsch (1990), in his study of incorporation of subsistence village societies into a wider cash economy in western Thailand, reports increasing social differentiation and conflict. The richer, more adaptable strata of society are given opportunity to capture more resources for personal gain to sell to a wider market. Hithertofore, such abilities have been constrained by the lack of such a market, amongst other things. Durrenberger (1983) has discussed the dynamics of the balance between redistributive and reciprocal economic systems in the Highlands in some more detail (also see Geddes, 1976; Cooper, 1984; Radley, 1986, for insight into wealth differences amongst the Hmong), and Dearden (1995b) has discussed some of the implications of this increasing differentiation.

Interviews and personal observation in the highland villages support the hypothesis that most if not all of the additional income generated by trekking is captured by one or two families in each village. Meyer (1987, p.433) supports this view and found that trekking represents, "important supplementary incomes for the relatively wealthy families," and "reinforces the traditional social and economic divisions." Whether this acts merely to reinforce these traditions or to accentuate them enough to generate conflict is difficult to say, although one case study Lisu village in the Mae Taeng (Dearden and Harron, 1992) did experience conflict between the headman and his family and other families in the village over distribution of trekking income. On the other hand, in some opium growing villages, Crooker (1988) suggests that already 20 per cent of the households receive 85 per cent of the aggregate income. Further research is needed to provide more insight into this question.

There are similar examples of the more indirect effects of increasing monetarisation in other spheres. Dearden and Harron (1994) have discussed the importance of trekkers in promoting the development of retail sales in some villages. Initially this might start with a few handicrafts, but can soon spread to offering a wide variety of consumer items, such as beer, soft drinks and chocolate that trekkers might buy. From such innocuous beginnings retail stores can become established in the villages that, in turn, may develop their own market amongst the villagers now exposed to such consumer temptations on a daily basis. Many studies (e.g. Hinton, 1975; Thai-Australia World Bank Land Development Project, 1985) have indicated that a high proportion of villagers is already in substantial debt. The last pressure they need is for more consumption with few opportunities for increased income. There may also be further reaching implications. Tangwisutijit (1990, p.4), for example, suggests that

> ...changing social attitudes brought about by materialism have induced girls to be prostitutes. Parents have become desirous of big houses fully equipped with facilities like what people in the big cities have. Thus the only way to make quick money is to sell their daughter to prostitution.

At the moment there are few reliable studies to ascertain how widespread such motivations may be.

Another commonly reported effect of tourism on more traditional societies is the cheapening of traditional customs and handicrafts as the people try to adapt them to tourist demands (e.g. Smith, 1977; de Kadt, 1979; Lea, 1988). Thus one observer comments in the *Bangkok Post* (July 6 1986) "...with *farang* coming through every day, a lot of villages probably dance every night. When New Year rolls around, what's the point if there is no money in it?" The effect on handicrafts is more complicated (Cohen, 1979; 1988b). On the one hand, tourist interest can be beneficial in supporting the continued production of handicrafts that might otherwise no longer be produced. On the other hand, the handicrafts made for the tourist market are often but sad reminders of the splendour of the original products.

A less ambiguous effect that might fall under the 'influence on traditional practices' category is opium-smoking (e.g. see Geddes, 1970; Grandstaff, 1979; Toyota in this volume). As can be seen from Table 11.1, opium-smoking produces quite a significant amount of income for the tribes. But there are negative impacts. These relate mainly to the increased addiction resulting from nightly displays of opium-smoking to interested trekkers. In effect, the addicts are getting positive feedback, not only in terms of money but also in terms of being the centre of attention, for undertaking a debilitating activity on a regular basis. Some (e.g. see Thepthong, 1988) have suggested that trekking is a main motivation for once-cured addicts to return to smoking.

The negative socio-cultural impacts associated with trekking for the hill-tribes are obviously substantial. A main challenge, however, is to try to differentiate the effects of trekking from those brought on by other causes. Trekking does contribute to increased monetarisation of the societies and perhaps to differentiation and conflict too, but how significant trekking is in comparison to other forces promoting change in the highlands remains an elusive and probably unanswerable question. The main difficulty is in establishing controls to distinguish the relative importance of all these factors. Studies such as those of Michaud (1993) that have attempted to generalise about the impacts of trekking based upon research in one village that has also been the focus of a long-standing international development project, are particularly troubled by such methodological problems.

Environmental effects

Relatively little attention has been directed toward the environmental effects of trekking. Figure 11.2 suggests that the hill-tribes are, once again, the group most affected. The two primary impacts are the deforestation resulting from bamboo-cutting for raft construction, and the disposal of human waste. Faecal contamination is a major problem in the highlands with coliform counts of many water supplies well in excess of international standards (Dearden, 1992). The problem can only be exacerbated with the addition of another 300,000 person-nights in the area as a result of trekking.

Over 70 per cent of the trekkers themselves feel that they have some impact upon the environment according to the survey data discused earlier. The main concern raised by the trekkers is the amount of garbage created (37.2 per cent of respondents), followed by bamboo deforestation (13.9 per cent), 'Thai problem' (13.9 per cent), trail erosion (12.5 per cent) and lack of toilets (7.2 per cent). 'Thai problem' is a reflection that the respondents thought the environmental effects of trekking to be no different from environmental problems in the rest of Thailand. This was a point of view especially related to the ubiquitous manner of garbage disposal: dump it anywhere as soon as possible. Thus trekkers would become very disturbed at the sight of trekking guides in particular dumping garbage, such as plastic water bottles *en route*. Indeed some respondents thought that trekking might have a beneficial influence upon the environment overall due to the consciousness-raising effects of the trekkers on the guides, and to a lesser extent on the hill-tribes, regarding garbage disposal. This suggestion is noted as a small positive impact in Figure 11.2.

There may also be additional indirect positive environmental impacts. If trekking does provide an alternative to agriculture for economic support, then this may not only reduce the need of the people to over-exploit their environment, but also deprive them of the time so to do. Elliott (1995) suggests that this is the case with a Hmong village, Meo Doi Pui, in Doi Suthep National Park. Although not a trekking village, sales of handicrafts are a main source of income to tourists who drive to the village. Over time, this has resulted in the abandonment of some agricultural land in the Park by the Hmong to concentrate on the tourism industry.

Changes in impacts over time

The impacts outlined above are not static in nature nor do they necessarily have a linear relationship with the numbers of trekkers visiting the village. The purpose of this section is to explore some of the implications of this observation with special reference to the impacts experienced first by the hill-tribes and then by the trekking companies and trekkers. The changes experienced by a tourism area over time have been conceptualised by Butler (1980) as being akin to the product life-cycle. This idea has been used as an organisational framework for many studies since (e.g. Keller, 1987; Martin and Uysal, 1990) and was adapted by Dearden (1988) to discuss the evolution of trekking villages over time as visitation increased (Figure 11.3). The model can be used to envision the passage of an individual village, region or entire area over time or as a snapshot in time of various villages or regions in varying states of evolution with regard to the development of the trekking industry.

Dearden (1988) suggested five different stages of evolution for the interaction of villages with trekking. It should be pointed out that villages do not necessarily move along this progression, but may stay at any given level depending upon a wide number of endogenous and exogenous factors. The first category is those not visited by trekkers and need not be of further concern here other than to point out that there is no comprehensive understanding regarding what proportion of villages in the highlands are in this category.

The second category includes those villages that can be categorised as explorer villages (Figure 11.3). These villages would experience only very occasional visitation, usually on an *ad hoc* basis by a guide with considerable experience and hill-tribe liaison skills, perhaps a highlander or a past member of the Thai Border Patrol. Infrastructure for trekkers would be minimal; hospitality may still be provided free of charge as was the historical tradition. There may be some minor costs associated with this hospitality; few economic benefits would be gained (Figure 11.4a).

Figure 11.3
Hypothetical Life Cycle Relationship Between Numbers of Trekkers Over Time, Showing Suggested Village Stages

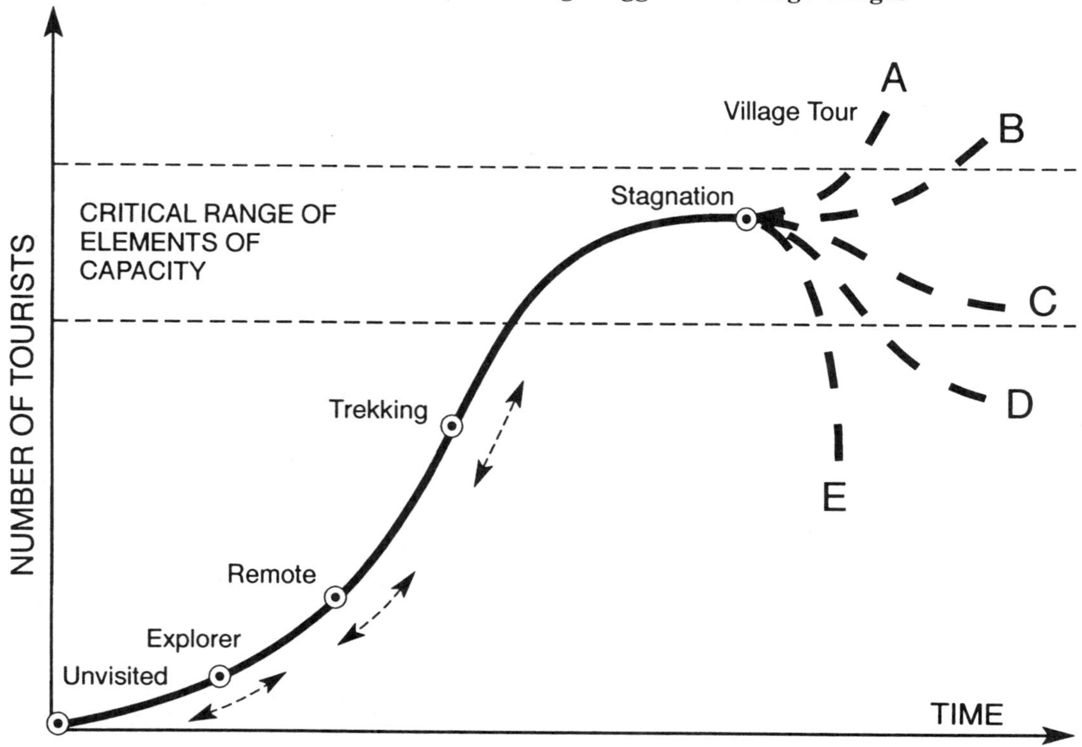

Figures 11.4a,b,c
Trekking Village Life Cycle, Showing Hypothesised Relationship of (a) Economic Benefit:Cost Ratio, (b) Social Impacts, and (c) Environmental Impacts for Hill-tribes from the Rising Number of Tourists Over Time

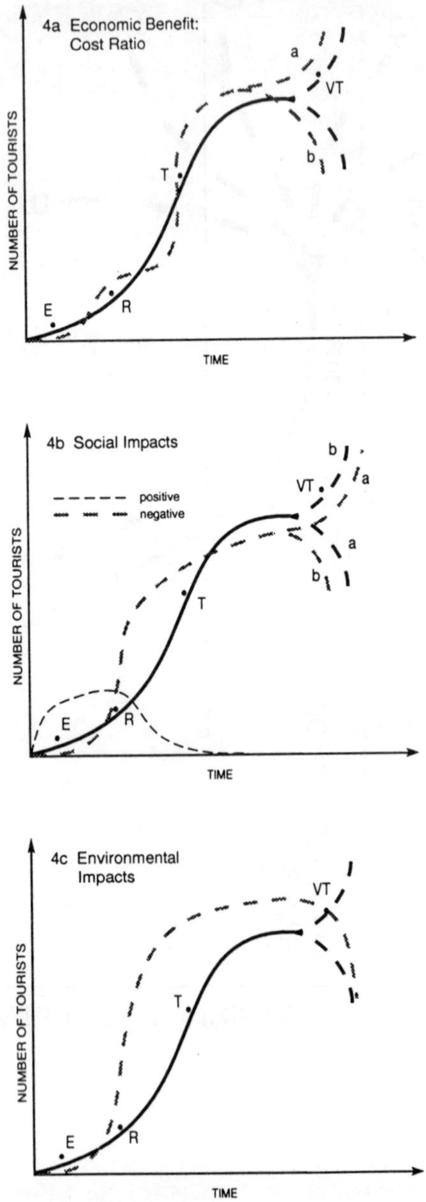

The socio-cultural impacts at this stage are also minimal (Figure 11.4b). The positive impacts of trekker visitation might rise quite quickly as highlanders gain their first views of outsiders and satiate the curiosity discussed previously. Negative social impacts associated with this intermittent visitation would be few, as would environmental impacts (Figure 11.4c).

If the village is relatively accessible and still retains an air of what the trekkers might consider authenticity, then it may develop into the next stage, a remote village. This would entail fairly regular but relatively infrequent visits, perhaps once or maybe twice a month. At this stage, the transaction becomes not one of traditional hospitality, but one of monetary exchange, with the guide paying for hospitality services received in the village. The amount received is a function largely of the number of trekkers for accommodation. The other categories of income-generation, suggested in Table 11.1, would be largely absent in this kind of village, although there may be opportunity to buy opium from local addicts. Few facilities would be provided for trekkers; guides would supply blankets (Figure 11.4a).

In terms of social impacts it may be anticipated that positive aspects may still continue to rise for a while, albeit more slowly, as the diversity of visitors increases (Figure 11.4b). In explorer villages the villagers might be quite shy and even hide from the trekkers; by this next stage most are used to the sight of outsiders and may even like to have their photographs taken. Inevitably, however, there are associated negative impacts with the additional numbers and the beginnings of some of the influences described earlier begin to rise. Opium might be smoked as a demonstration; authentic items of dress and handicrafts might be sold at minimal prices to be replaced, if at all, by much cheaper or western items. Overall though, negative social impacts are relatively minor and perhaps still out-weighed by the positive aspects of the increased exposure to the outside world. Environmental impacts (Figure 11.4c) continue to accumulate, but are also still relatively minor.

By the next stage, the trekking village, the nature of these relationships can change dramatically. Trekkers come in increasing numbers as the village becomes a regular part of one or several routine treks. Trekkers may be in the village virtually every night, and on some occasions several trekking groups may be in the same village at the same time. As the economic return generated by many of the items in Table 11.1 is a reflection of the number of trekkers, the amount of income that can be generated at this stage obviously rises considerably. The increasing numbers also give greater opportunity to market various items ranging from beer and chocolate through to handicrafts.

There are economic costs involved, however, especially with the provision of infrastructure. Special sleeping quarters will have to be constructed by now, sometimes one or two additional huts. Blankets, plates and cutlery will also be provided. Guides may be provided with free opium as an inducement to visit the village on a regular basis and encourage consumption of opium. A small retail store might be constructed. Once these investments have been made, a regular income should result until some threshold is reached that might negatively influence visitation levels.

This threshold level might well be reached by dint of some of the socio-cultural changes that are now taking place in the village as a result of trekking. By now the novelty of having outsiders in the village has worn off. There are few, if any, social benefits at this stage. The villagers become prey to be stalked by the cameras of the trekkers; the trekkers become the prey for the money-hungry villagers. Charges may be made for taking photographs. Begging may be endemic, or at least, sales techniques extremely aggressive. Dances and songs may be performed at a price. Opium may be demonstrated every night. Tacky souvenirs may be offered for sale. Traditional dress may have been sold and more modern dress, as worn by northern Thais and even the trekkers themselves, become predominant. Negative social impacts soar rapidly (Figure 11.4b).

Environmental effects also become more noticeable at this stage. The village may experience a shortage of building materials as bamboo is cut down more quickly than it can grow in order to build rafts. Water pollution increases through insanitary practices and the lack of absorptive capacity of the rivers compared to the amount of waste. Garbage accumulates along the trails and around the villages; trails erode (Figure 11.4c).

Ultimately these kinds of changes start to limit visitation. Trekkers are not interested in visiting villages that appear to be acculturated nor suffering from environmental pollution. New villages are found, and the process of evolution is repeated. Some villages may surmount this drop in visitation by developing a new market and becoming part of the 'hill-tribe village tour' undertaken, not on foot for several days, but by road, usually for a short, daily visit. The focus is often on shopping and there will be several retailers offering a wide variety of goods, most not related to the village. Meo Doi Pui, close to Chiang Mai, is the classic example of this type of village (e.g. see Maneeprasert *et.al.*, 1975; Cohen, 1979).

Villages that make this transition successfully may be able to develop a very viable tourism-dependent cash economy ('a' in Figure 11.4a). However, the distribution of these benefits may not be restricted to the village, as outside interests, noting the success, may start to establish retail outlets. This increased leakage may, in fact, set in earlier, in successful trekking villages. Elephants, for example, might be owned externally, and profits flow to outside owners. Villages that are not able to generate a new market after exhausting the trekking market may well find a rapid reduction in income from trekking commensurate with the drop in visitor numbers ('b' in Figure 11.4a). The infrastructure will still require servicing, however, so the cumulative benefit:cost ratio may well fall more quickly than the actual numbers of trekkers, as costs remain constant against declining incomes.

The likely effects upon socio-cultural values depend upon which path is taken. If the village does develop into a hill-tribe tour village then it is likely that overall negative impacts per visitor will fall ('a' in Figure 11.4b). These visitors are more interested in the merchandise than poking their heads into every house. They do not, as a rule, stay in the villages overnight, so the potential for some of the social interactions discussed earlier (e.g. opium demonstrations) is more limited. Most of the negative social impacts related to visitors have already been absorbed in the painful evolutionary process.

However if, on the other hand, transition is not made and the village income falls substantially then negative social impacts may rise considerably ('b' in Figure 11.4b). By this stage villagers will be used to the income provided through trekking, and will not be adjusted either mentally or physically to gain

Figure 11.5 a,b
Rising Number of Trekkers Over Time and Hypothesised Relationship to (a) Trekking Company Benefits and (b) Trekker Benefits

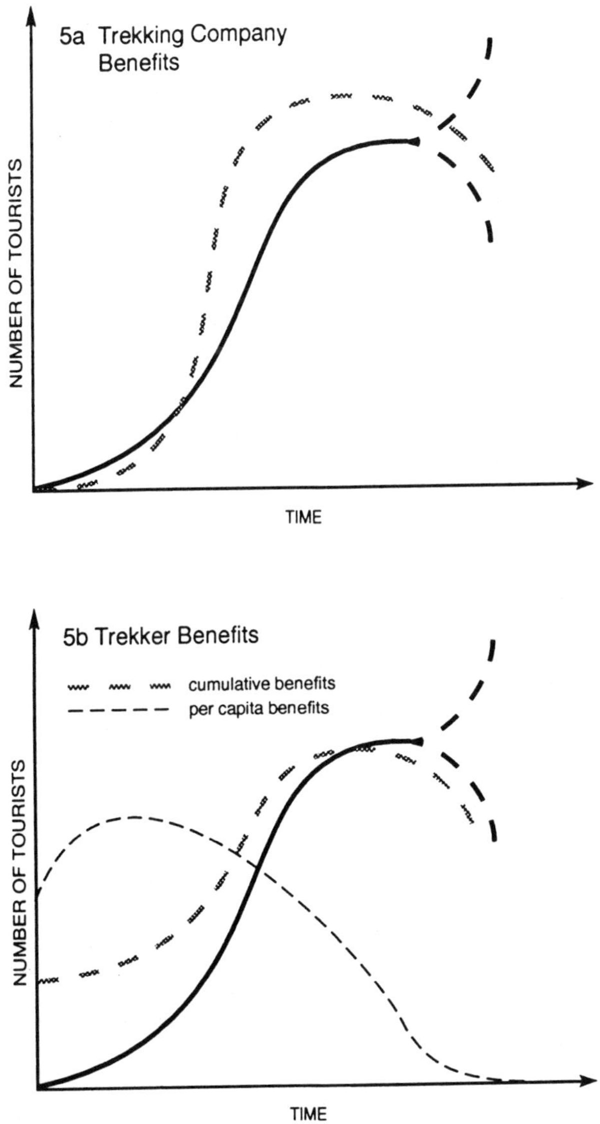

access to alternative forms of income, even if they are available. They will have absorbed all the negative social impacts, but now be bereft of the economic benefits and further socio-cultural adjustment costs may ensue.

The cumulative environmental impacts per trekker are likely to decrease no matter which final path is taken from the summit of the trekking evolution (Figure 11.4c). Day visitors to a highland village are unlikely to be involved with rafting. Garbage is more concentrated and collection easier to control. Toilet facilities are usually provided should they be required. If the village does not develop in this direction then the environmental impacts simply fall with the numbers of trekkers.

It is also worth briefly considering similar curves for the trekking companies and trekkers to suggest how their benefits might change over time. For the companies it is likely that their economic benefit:cost ratio (Figure 11.5a) is going to be initially reduced with low numbers of trekkers as certain costs may remain high (e.g. provision of transport, financial guarantees to elephant owners) irrespective of numbers. Once these costs are covered then economic benefits (profits) should rise more or less according to numbers. There may be some economies of scale achieved as the numbers grow. Unlike the hill-tribes, however, there are few additional services sold by the companies in addition to the basic cost of the trek. Hence there is not really the opportunity to sell more additional services as numbers rise.

The comparative curves for the trekker benefits are quite interesting. Two may be suggested, one showing cumulative trekker benefits, the other per capita benefits (Figure 11.5b). The overall benefits curve shows a total but disproportionate rise in benefits over time. The rationale behind this is that the per capita benefits will be relatively higher when there are fewer trekkers. Survey results indicate that trekkers do not mind, and in fact may enjoy, encountering other groups on their treks. There is however, a limit to this and as numbers increase there is a strong relationship between number of groups seen and effect on enjoyment (Dearden and Harron, 1994). Ultimately, this question of social carrying capacity may be one of the critical factors that causes visitation rates to fall. Per capita benefits decrease over time with increasing numbers and the cumulative satisfaction curve declines until it finally becomes lower than the numbers trekking and the numbers trekking falls to reflect this loss in benefits.

Discussion

From the foregoing it can be seen that determining the distribution of impacts from trekking is not easy. Overall it would certainly seem that the trekking companies have the optimal situation; they maximise their economic gain and incur no significant socio-cultural or environmental costs. The trekkers also have a relatively easy equation in that, as pointed out earlier, the economic costs sustained must be surpassed by the socio-cultural benefits that accrue from trekking, or they would not report such high satisfaction levels, nor would the industry continue to expand at such a rate. Individual trekkers anticipate that the experience will be worthwhile before they go; surveys on return indicate that 99 per cent feel that their decision was correct and that they would help further development of the activity by recommending it to their friends.

A far more complicated situation exists for the hill-tribes. While overall the economic benefits exceed the economic costs of being involved, there are also substantial negative impacts related to socio-cultural and environmental values that they must sustain. The difficulty is that many of these impacts are difficult to ascribe to trekking alone, and even when they can be, how do these compare in any meaningful sense against the dollars being generated? Perhaps it is only the hill-tribes themselves who can take responsibility for such a judgement call.

Some insight can be given into the importance of relative negative and positive impacts by comparing how they might change over time as a village or villages became increasingly exposed to larger numbers of trekkers. The results of this kind of examination are summarised in Figures 11.4a, b and c. Are there certain stages in growth which seem to optimise positive impacts relative to negative impacts for the hill-tribes?

In the explorer stage positive social impacts rise rapidly while social and environmental negative impacts are relatively minor. Unfortunately, economic returns are probably negative. This, however, changes as the remote stage is reached. Economic benefits are relatively high compared to costs, and social benefits are at a maximum. Environmental impacts are starting to rise, but are still not excessive. As the village evolves into a trekking village increasing costs are encountered initially, before additional trekker numbers start to bring in more profits. Social benefits start to fall rapidly and negative social impacts rise to reach their maximum per trekker on the entire evolutionary scale. Environmental impacts also rise sharply. The future direction depends upon whether the village starts to experience declining trekker numbers or not and whether it is able to generate a new market clientele, the day-visit market, in response. If it is, then economic returns can be quite favourable. Negative social impacts per capita also fall over time as do environmental impacts.

The foregoing would suggest that there are certain stages in the evolution of villages that are more preferable than others in terms of the relative positive and negative impacts for the hill-tribes. One of these relatively favoured positions is in the remote stage, another would be in the mature trekking stage before reductions in trekker numbers occur. There are also relative per capita advantages in the development of the village tour market. Perhaps the least desirable stage is in the early trekker stage. Here there may be significant economic costs related to returns and social and environmental impacts per capita are maximised.

For the trekking companies it seems to be in their interests to maximise the numbers of trekkers up to, but not exceeding, the carrying capacity thresholds that would cause numbers to fall. This threshold is likely responding to several factors, some of which can be controlled by the companies, others over which they have very little influence. Social carrying capacity thresholds are the most easy to address for the companies - simply voluntarily limit the trekker numbers. Other factors, such as the changes in perceived authenticity of the hill-tribes, may be more difficult to manipulate (although see Cohen, 1989a; and Dearden and Harron, 1994). A mature trekking village is probably the ideal stage for the companies.

The optimal stage of development for the trekkers would depend upon a value judgement of whether to maximise enjoyment on a per capita or aggregated basis. As long as benefits are higher than numbers it could be argued that this will maximise overall benefits to society and the maximum numbers of trekkers up to this point should be accommodated.

The foregoing is a reflection of mainstream trekking as it has evolved over the last two decades. There are, however, important variations that help provide a perspective on how impacts might be distributed. One of the most noteworthy is a trekking company, P Travel Service, run by Pipat Chaisurin in Chiang Mai. Kuhn Pipat is an experienced guide, a past-President of the Chiang Mai Guides' Association, with an extensive background in the highlands and rural development. Over a decade ago he started to become distressed about the imbalance between costs and benefits to the hill-tribes and initiated a project 'Rural Development Through Tourism'. Instead of hiding trekkers from the reality of the hill-tribes - the poverty and the forces of change - he tries on his treks to promote understanding of this reality. Trekkers actually meet the villagers rather than just gawk at them; they also get opportunity to help the villagers through contributions of time, money or expertise. Ten per cent of the profits of each trekking trip go toward funding the project. This is spent on establishing schools, funding scholarships, building water and toilet systems, developing sustainable agricultural practices and providing opportunities for further educational training for the hill-tribe villages involved.

Other initiatives are also under way that specifically try to maximise the economic and employment benefits to the hill-tribes while minimising social and cultural impacts. One such avenue is through ecotourism, which removes the hilltibes from becoming the tourist attraction but retains their services, such as by guiding and making use of their traditional ecological knowledge to help understand ecosystems. One proposal is planning to construct, in conjunction with the local Karen village, a small scientific and accommodation facility to assist in biodiversity conservation of Doi Inthanon National Park (Dearden, 1995d). It is hoped that this kind of initiative will also lead to more cordial relationships between government agencies, such as the Royal Forestry Department, and hill-tribe communities as they move toward co-management strategies.

Conclusion

Many authors have criticised trekking (e.g. Durst, 1987; Judd, 1988; Mirante, 1991; Michaud, 1993) for its cultural impact upon the hill-tribes in return for relatively few benefits. This is certainly the most obvious reaction. In order to get beyond this reflex response, often built upon western myths of the splendid isolation of the noble savage, it is necessary to examine in some more detail the role of trekking in the rapidly changing cultural and environmental fabric of the North, and the distribution of impacts.

This chapter has focused upon this latter aspect and tried to assess how impacts are distributed between the participants and how these might change over time. The hill-tribes certainly sustain most of the negative impacts, but there are also positive aspects. It is difficult to compare the two since most of the negative impacts are socio-cultural and most of the benefits economic. However, the industry is not structured to maximise benefits to the hill-tribes, nor are any significant efforts made to minimise negative impacts. Examples do exist of how tourism can help increase the flow of benefits to the hill-tribes. These should be supported and emulated to help enlist trekking as a positive force for change in the highlands.

12 The effects of tourism development on an Akha community: A Chiang Rai village case study

Mika Toyota

Introduction

In this chapter I intend to examine the effects of Thailand's rapid economic development on peripheral areas - in this case the upper North. The study examines the social and cultural impact of trekking tourism and thus, whilst it adopts a rather different, more focused approach, can be seen as complementary to that of Dearden which was presented in the previous chapter. My chapter is concerned with changes which have taken place in one study community over a period of eight years, and which the writier has been able to observe first-hand during the course of several field visits since 1988.

No society, it appears, can claim total separation from the influence of the all-pervasive political and economic system of today's world. By the same measure, no matter how hard escapist tourists may seek an 'unspoiled world', more or less any society, however peripheral, is already internalised within a wider social framework. Indeed, tourism can be seen as one of the social phenomena which accelerates the incorporation of peripheral and minority groups into the wider socio-economic system. Minority groups in peripheral areas, such as the hilltribes of northern Thailand, tend, as we have seen in Dearden's chapter, to be regarded in outsiders' clichéd perspectives as 'exotic', 'noble savages'. These images are used in tourism promotion by tour agencies, and they develop and manipulate these images for their own sake in order to attract tourists. In this process, due to an unequal political and economic relationship between the minority group and the majority population, minority peoples themselves have little direct power to project their own society and culture to the outside world, nor to control the pace and pattern of the outside, seemingly all-pervasive power.

The hilltribes of the 'Golden Triangle' in the North of Thailand attract both anthropologists and tourists from overseas due to their colourful costumes and unique cultures. At the same time, from the viewpoint of central government, these societies in peripheral areas are often regarded, conventionally, as 'backward' societies or 'problem areas' in terms of national integration

Therefore, either negative images or romanticised images tend to be attached by outsiders to minority groups living at the periphery.

The aim of this chapter, however, is not to criticise the differentiation between the image projected by outsiders and the one produced by native people themselves; nor is it simply to point out the unequal power relationship which runs parallel to this. It should be noted that, if we only look at the people of the host society as 'victims' of this exploitative system, or of strong penetration from the modernised world, it might constrain our ability to view them as anything other than a passive target. In other words, we may overlook the important fact that they can not simply be lumped together in the same fixed category of 'poor exploited people'.

Much of the macro-level debate on the effects of tourism has focused on whether its effects are beneficial or negative. However, this kind of normative cost-benefit framework, which assesses whether effects are 'good' or 'bad', is too simplistic if we are to analyse the dynamic process of socio-cultural change in the host society which arises as a consequence of tourism. Through my observations of an Akha community, I have come to realise that culture is not passive, but that each villager has their own set of choices, and that different people have a different degree of ability to absorb or adapt to change, and are affected in different ways in the process. Villagers are therefore not just passive recipients of outside influences, but actively respond to new opportunities and constraints.

There has been little longitudinal micro-level research on tourism based on the collection of primary data across a series of field visits to one particular community in order to obtain insight into the implications of the impact of tourism development, especially in relation to the dynamic process of socio-cultural change within the host community. It is thus hoped that the present empirical study will contribute a useful counterpoint to the large number of macro-level studies which have been made of tourism.

Background

The highlanders, referred to by Thais as *chao khao*, constitute about one per cent of the country's total population, and they mostly reside in the hilly and mountainous areas of northern, northeastern and northwestern Thailand. The six main groups which have some touristic interest are the Karen, Meo (Hmong), Lahu, Yao, Akha and Lisu. Most of the montagnard peoples originally lived in the southern part of China and reached what is now Thailand in their southward migration. The Akha are spread widely through southern China, Burma, Laos, Vietnam as well as Thailand. At present the total Akha population is in the region of 1.7 million, with approximately 40,000 residing within Thailand. The first Akha village in Thailand was established around the turn of the present century.

The Akha language belongs to the Tibetan-Burmese group. There is no writing system. They call themselves Akha, whereas the Thais call them 'E-khaw' - an appellation for which the Akha have no great liking. The Akha are famous for their patrilineal name system. As part of their tradition, they memorise the names of their ancestors right back to the beginning of their history. In this way they can recognise themselves as part of a great historical chain of the Akha people

The staple food of the Akha is rice. They used to practice the swidden method of cultivation, but now this is prohibited by the central government. Like other hilltribe villages around this area, the crops they cultivate do not provide subsistence for the whole year, due to the shallow soils of the mountain area which are rapidly depleted by agriculture and have been seriously affected by deforestation. Thus there is a strong need for additional cash income in order to purchase rice to feed the family. For example, three families operate small shop-houses, selling myriad goods for daily use which they purchase in the lowlands. There are two televisions in the village, although there is no electricity system (they can watch for a few hours a day using their own generators). Some families have sent sons or daughters to the lowland area in order to seek either education or work. Through migration and other forms of connection with the 'outside world', the penetration of socio-cultural influences from lowland Thailand and further afield is clearly apparent in the study area.

Such a sketched profile is important to the present discussion because it emphasises that the effects of tourism can not be isolated from other factors which have contributed towards change in the way of life of the highlanders in a broader social, economic and cultural context. Nevertheless, for the purposes of this chapter it is necessary to limit the discussion to issues relating specifically to tourism.

Since the location of the study village is not too far from downtown Chiang Rai, it has become an important trekking destination, with groups of tourists visiting quite frequently since the beginning of the 1980s. The villagers have become accustomed to seeing tourists in the village during the last ten years: indeed, there was at one stage a sleeping hut for tourists to stay in the village; since it was demolished the number of visiting trekkers has decreased.

The impact of trekking tourism

The socio-economic effects of opium-smoking

Smoking opium in the hilltribe village has developed as a 'thrilling adventure' for the attraction of tourists since the 1970s. Today it is said that fifteen per cent of trekkers are involved in drug consumption in the tribal villages. In some cases, trekkers have been persuaded to try drugs by their guides (*The Nation*, 9 August 1991). The implications of 'opium tours' will be drawn out in this section.

Since the 'golden triangle' area, where many hilltribes reside, used to be known as an important opium cultivation area, trekkers are often persuaded to accept the explanations of the jungle guides such as:

> Originally the Akha people had a custom of smoking opium; opium used to be a medicine to cure their illness. It is treated something like coffee or tea, so when a guest comes into their house, the headman would offer opium to the guest as a sign of hospitality, in a manner similar to the way that we offer tea to a guest. They are poor because they smoke opium.

Following this explanation, some guides encourage trekkers to try the 'authentic' experience of Akha culture by smoking opium.

It is important to clarify whether smoking opium is as much a part of Akha culture as the jungle guides have suggested and trekkers have come to accept. In order to ascertain whether there is indeed an underlying custom, I asked the villagers why only the older people smoke opium and not the younger ones. The villagers' reply was that "...if young people smoke opium they cannot get married; none of the young women want to marry a man who smokes opium." It is clear that smoking opium is not recognised as favourable behaviour among the villagers. According to the villagers, smoking opium is considered the habit of a retired old man who is beyond the age of 50. They continued: "when people reach to this age, aches and pain associated with old age are relieved by smoking opium, so they smoke opium to make themselves feel better. Therefore old men smoking opium is accepted, although, for the young men it is considered a shameful thing to do". von Geusau (1988, p.227) pointed out that opium is not mentioned in ritual texts or songs, which means that their ancestors were not familiar with it, and thus were not able to define rules either for its growing or its consumption. When I asked some young women why many men start smoking after they get married, they explained, "no hope... no future... they become lazy." This suggests that they start smoking opium because of growing poverty and their rather depressing prospects for the future. Thus it suggests a prevalent response to economic stress rather than being an integral part of traditional culture.

Akha people used to cultivate rice as their main crop, using slash-and-burn methods. This requires a period of about twelve to fourteen years of fallow for these fields to recover fertility sufficiently for them to be planted again. Thus even small communities of highlanders require very large amounts of land to produce sufficient rice to feed their inhabitants year by year (Keyes, 1987, p.10). Consequently, all Akha people, as well as other highlanders in Thailand, are faced with problems of resource scarcity, due to change in their immediate environment, and an increasing population. Akha people have an urgent recognition that alternative modes of livelihood must be sought which will enable them to purchase rice from the lowlands to feed the family, and to purchase additional goods such as a TV, motorbikes and tin roofs that subsequently improve their standard of living. Therefore, while the demands of expenditure have rapidly increased as their lifestyle has changed, the economic opportunities available to the Akha are rather limited. In this regard, the offering of opium to tourists is one option which villagers have been able to take. When I first visited the village in 1988, many villagers had just started in this business, many seeing it as a way of making 'easy money'. Thus, from the villagers' view point, offering opium to tourists provided an economic opportunity for the villagers, rather than constituting a part of their traditional custom or culture, as the jungle guides often explained. It should also be noted that it was the jungle guides who initiated this business and not the villagers themselves. The discrepancy between the perceptions of outsiders and those of insiders in explaining the phenomenon of opium-smoking is appropriate to the context of the tourist-guide-host encounter which will be discussed in further detail in the next section.

The consequences of the opium business had become more apparent four years later (1992). Contrary to expectations of becoming richer, many villagers had found themselves appreciably poorer. Several factors contributed to this outcome. Firstly, the economic contribution of the business was not as good as people had expected. The operators - that is, the jungle guides - obtained most of the money paid by trekkers, whilst the villagers received very little. Secondly, the villagers were so busy looking after the trekkers they were unable to spend enough time in the fields looking after the cash crops that sustained their economic subsistence. Thirdly, by demonstrating opium-smoking for the benefit of the trekkers, several villagers including the younger generation had become addicted to opium themselves. Since the village is not involved in the cultivation of opium poppies, the villagers have to buy opium from outsiders for their own consumption. Most of the opium for sale in Thailand is grown in Burma. This increased consumption of opium could not, however, be financed from the trifling returns from tourism.

In addition there was a gender dimension to the problems associated with opium-smoking. Several women commented that they deplored the situation which often arose when their husbands needed opium, in that, the men would lose all sense of rationality and would use all the household's money, saved for the purpose of purchasing rice, to buy opium. A woman said

> In the past, men and women would help each other. While women were doing the housework the men would go hunting, and although men and women would leave the village and come back one by one, they both go to work in the fields. But now women are obliged to work very hard; they have to do everything, cultivating rice fields, carrying water, cooking, raising children, etc.

Another woman said

> When there is not enough money, my husband beats me, because he needs money for opium. It is a very, very sad situation. Previously, husband and wife used to complement one another. But now a husband beats his wife. Women are very sad.

In Akha society, there used to be a sexual division of domains, but it was balanced and complementary (Hanks, 1988). Kammerer (1988) observed that the Akha gender system shifts with changes in context, for example depending on which social ritual is occurring, so as to give prominence to men at certain times and prominence to women at others. From my observations, as a consequence of the opium business, women who have opium-addicted husbands are most heavily affected by the tourism business.

In the case of the study village, the peak period of tourism was the late 1980s. However, as the way of life has been changed through the influence of lowland Thais, as in many other tribal villages after 1990, it is no longer considered as an attractive destination from the perspective of the jungle guides. Previously, it was mainly its socio-cultural aspect that intrigued groups of trekkers, such as handicrafts, dancing, singing, etc. Selling handicrafts to the trekkers used to provide a good income for the villagers. However, as such cultural scenes have gradually disappeared, due to the reduced interest and opportunity of the younger generation to learn Akha culture from their elders, the type of tourists visiting the village has changed accordingly. The heroin habit had been introduced to this village by another jungle guide (1991), partly as a result of bringing heroin addicted tourists (including Thais) to the village as a 'safe place to consume the drug'. In 1992, among the villagers aged 15 and over (from a total population of about 270), only 14 men did not smoke opium, while only 8 women did smoke opium. In 1992-4, some villagers had shifted from smoking opium to both smoking and injecting heroin, which has further contributed a devastating effect on the health of the villagers. In 1994, three heroin addicted people were already known among the village population. Visitors to the village now are mainly local Thais or individual foreigners who come to smoke opium or heroin, and who show no real interest in Akha culture.

As a basis for comparison, I would now like to take as an example a family which does not rely on the business of offering opium to the trekkers. In spite of the fact that all his friends of the same generation have become opium addicted after marriage, my 36-year-old respondent (whom I shall call 'Lek') was alone in not relying on the drug. He explained the reason in this way.

> Everyone knows how bad opium is, but when people become hopeless they can not help but start smoking opium. But as for me, I know more than anyone how bad it is. When I was a child, my family used to be the poorest in the village because my father was addicted to opium. I had no blanket to sleep on in my childhood. I suffered a lot in my childhood because of poverty. Thus since I was a child, I kept telling myself that I would not let my children have the same experience that I had. Therefore my determination in refusing the temptation of smoking opium is so strong. I was confident in myself that even when my friends started smoking it, I would not.

He has since been wisely accumulating money, little by little, to build up his economic security.

Since Lek was diligent enough to learn to read and write Thai by himself, he was able to make contact with local Thais and to engage in some small-scale business, while the others could not. Most of the other villagers aged over 30 years did not have the opportunity to go to school to learn Thai as there used to be no village school system. As a result, Lek did not get involved in the new tourist business, unlike the others, whose only other available option is to be the cheapest source of labour in Thai society.

During the seven years (1988-1995) that I have been able to observe this family, Lek has rebuilt his house into a more solid structure, and has purchased a motorcycle, which allows easier access to the lowlands. Moreover he has been able to send all four of his children (one son, three daughters) to the lowlands for education. Since most of the hilltribe villagers have only a limited level of education - usually up to the age of eleven is the maximum - in order to get a higher education they have to go down to stay in the lowlands. This entails the large expense of living costs for accommodation and food. Lek said "I have tried to give the younger generation better prospects. I wanted to prove that there is a way to enjoy a better life without relying on opium. I want to be a model for them." He further showed his concern for the problem of opium smoking in the village by stating that, "the rumour of smoking opium among the

Akha people which has been spread by trekkers and jungle guides makes our people lose face."

It is clear from his statement that even before tourism affected the Akha village, opium addicts existed and this habit resulted in poverty due to lack of effective manpower. At present, the number of addicts has greatly increased compared to the past, and it has spread out to both the older and younger generations with depressing prospects of the future, as they are placed in the most disadvantaged position in Thai society.

Furthermore, although Akha society is often regarded as a consistently 'egalitarian' society, there was an economic differentiation as well as social stratification among villagers as a consequence of their degree of ability and commitment to work. The point I want to emphasise is that each person has their own set of choices and coping strategies according to their own degree of ability and opportunity, and so different people are being affected in different ways in any process of social change. This can be found in the present and the past, and will be in the future. Thus we should not look at them as simply lumped together and placed in the same fixed category of 'poor exploited people', otherwise we overlook the dynamic and various responses of the villagers to social changes caused by tourism development.

The socio-political impact of the tourist-guide-host encounter

The host-guest relationship has been the focus of attention of anthropologists and sociologists, as they consider it a form of acculturation. However, within the context of trekking tourism, guides take on a crucial role as cultural brokers who not only mediate between the two different cultures of the hosts and guests, but also, by way of their explanation or interpretation, of the hosts' culture. It is a jungle guide who directly constructs and exposes the image of hilltribe people to the trekkers. Thus it is essential to realise the importance of the role of guides in order to demonstrate the mechanism of the image-production system in the tourist setting. Attention should also be paid to the power differentials among these three actors - hosts, guides and guests.

In previous work on the subject, some people have looked at the commercialised relationship between hosts and guests. They point out the fact that, as an effect of tourism, social exchange between hosts and guests has been replaced by economic exchange and the profit motive whereby their hospitality has become commercialised. However, the question I want to ask in this section is not whether this host-guest relationship is commercialised, or to assess whether the explanation of guides is 'right' or 'wrong', as there is no fixed 'authentic' culture to be determined firmly. Since culture is a product of interpretation, rather than a self-contained entity, its interpretation varies and depends upon whose perspective it is viewed from. In this sense the tourism setting can be understood as a crossroads of different interpretations. This mechanism is what I intend to examine in this section, concerning the image of Akha women in particular.

Besides selling handicrafts, another limited option for Akha women to profit from tourism is to offer massages to trekkers. This skill stems from the Akha practice of occasionally massaging family members after a hard day's labour. This is done between husband and wife, and by children to the elderly. It i similar to *shiatsu*, Japanese acupressure. By massaging trekkers, they can get twice as much income compared to working in the fields - work such as cutting and drying a type of grass used for Thai broom fibres, cultivating ginger or collecting mushrooms from the forest. The Akha consider massaging trekkers simply as a means of earning additional money for their survival. On the other hand, the jungle guides explain it in this way: "In Akha society, women are traditionally obedient to men, they treat men well with their devoted efforts, and while men are doing nothing women work hard." Trekkers who are looking for 'authentic' experiences are happy and willing to accept the explanation made by guides as a 'correct' interpretation of the Akha's 'traditional' culture. They prefer not to see, or are incapable of seeing, the actual motivation of the villagers, which would risk deflating their image of the 'noble savage' - unspoilt, genuine, human beings.

Many of the jungle guides - who were mostly born and grew up locally in the northern region, and are usually below 35 years of age - are not interested in, or are unable to answer intelligently, the tourists' questions concerning the hilltribe's culture. Many are often poorly qualified for their job: about 60 per cent of them had never received formal training to be tour guides (Putsatee, 1992). Most entered this business because of the expansion of trekking tourism and the demand for jungle guides, even though many are largely ignorant of the culture and way of life of the highlanders. In the early 1980s there were around twenty or more jungle companies in existence around Chiang Mai (Cohen, 1989a, p.37), but by 1992 it was estimated that there were more than 200. Most choose this occupation simply because they are familiar with the region: "They have widely varying prior experience of the jungle: while some served with the BPP [Border Patrol Police] or Thai army in the region" (Cohen, 1982a, p.242). Thus with few exceptions, the northern Thai dialect is used to communicate between the trekking guides and tribal people, as trekking guides usually cannot speak the hilltribe languages. Most acquired their knowledge about tribal people primarily from personal experience and conversations, and it is highly influenced by the ethnic images which are widely held among local Thais. Hence, this image-generating operation conducted by the jungle guides could be quite harmful to the Akha people. Concerning the gender dimension of image representation, the jungle guide's explanations often exaggerate and beautify the image of Akha women as an 'ideal' female for men's conveniences. One of these images is based on a song written by Charan Manopet, a popular Thai singer:

Up in the sky there are clouds, surrounding the mountain high.

The well-known girl lives in the land that is blind.
The venue, 'Galalarzer.' Boys murmur her name.
Other girls come up to this girl, who is 'Mida.'

The girl is waiting for innocent guys.
She herself has no desire.
Teaches them all about the flesh.
And then, sacrifice.

A beautiful and lone widow she is.
All that is harmed, is chosen to be Mida.
The boys who have never been taught.
Never come to the venue.

She does it whether she likes it or not. She acts as though she were blind.
One by one she embraces, sacrificing her body.
As she becomes older and withered,
A new one takes her place.

This is a story in a glazed land, given the name 'E-khaw'.

Due to this song, it is widely believed among Thais that there is a women called 'Mida' selected in each Akha village to teach teenage boys about sex, and who is always ready to sacrifice herself for a man. This image of 'Mida' represents Akha women in the perspective of guides, and his explanation sometimes goes further, suggesting that, according to a guide, "Akha women are ready to sacrifice themselves for men." This kind of perception sometimes leads some guides to justify Akha women becoming prostitutes. Since being a jungle guide is a marginal occupation, and income being low (Cohen, 1982a), getting a kick-back from offering tribal women to the trekkers as prostitutes is an option for earning additional revenue for jungle guides (Putsatee, 1992, p.16). As a result, they construct the explanation which is convenient for their own sake. According to Akha people, however, the word *mida* simply means 'unmarried young women', and nothing else. Accordingly, in Akha language, for example, I will be called *mida jebu* (a Japanese unmarried young woman), which does not imply a kind of 'comfort woman' at all.

This kind of disinformation projected and propagated by jungle guides about Akha people is harmful to their culture, especially when an unequal political and economic power relationship exists between minority groups in peripheral areas and the majority population. Trekking tourism has not been initiated by highlanders themselves, nor do the villagers have much say in its organisation, or in the direction or regulation of its development. It is operated by outsiders, mainly local Thai entrepreneurs based in Chiang Mai. Thus, while the outsiders have the power to initiate, produce and expose the image of minority groups, the minority people themselves seldom have the opportunity to get involved with the process of representing themselves, and to portray their own interpretation of their culture to the outside world. It should be noted that the present system of image production by the tourist industry is conducted under socio-political circumstances whereby there is an unequal power relationship between hosts, guides and guests. In a broader context, the projected image of 'primitive' people can be found as a world-wide phenomenon.

Talking with villagers, some are very much aware of the conflicts between their political interests and those of the Thai people. This is especially so in relation to land. Highlanders mostly reside in the hilly and mountainous areas of northern, northeastern and northwestern Thailand which have long been geographically, economically and politically peripheral from the central Thai government. During the 1960s, however, those areas lying close to the borders of the nation state became pivotal in terms of national security, in particular in preventing a communist 'invasion' of Thailand. Since the 1970s, population pressures both in the highlands and lowlands have increased. While the highlanders are pressing downward towards the river valleys, the Thais are pushing upwards from the overcrowded lowlands into the uplands. Thus competition between highlanders and lowlanders has become more intensive, and the widely practised slash-and-burn method of cultivation has increasingly been criticised by the Thais. From the Thai government's point of view, the Akha as well as other highlanders are immigrants with no historical or legal claim to the land. The land where Akha people reside is considered a 'national park' which is owned by the government. Since only Thai citizens can gain title to land by law, the cultivation of this land by highlanders who seldom have Thai citizenship is considered to be an illegal action. Thus highlanders in Thailand are in a very vulnerable position in this regard. At the end of the 1980s the price of land increased rapidly in Chiang Rai as a result of a land boom caused by the development of its tourist industry, the building of the multi-million baht Chiang Rai airport, and government plans to make Chiang Rai province another tourist destination. This has prompted local Thai speculators to obtain land from hilltribe peoples. Moreover, infrastructural development has helped to ease access to the remote parts of the country for both Thais and travellers who are able to encroach into the peripheral areas of Thailand more easily.

In the 1990s, with increasing awareness of the natural resource crisis and the world-wide environmental movement, the Thai government has fortified the natural resource management policy, which sometimes deprives highlanders of their residential land under the name of resettlement projects. Thus, highlanders are highly aware that some co-operation with the Thais is indispensable for their survival in the future.

The headman of the village said:

> When tourists come to the village, some of them are genuinely interested in our way of life, and they try to be friends with the villagers and ask many questions about our culture through the tour guides. Although I do not understand the language, I can sense that the explanation they offer is wrong, and I really want to correct the information, and to explain about Akha culture myself. But unfortunately I can not speak the language and can do nothing about it. I am very much frustrated when this happens.

When I showed him a post card of an Akha village explaining that they are sold to tourists because there are many people who are interested in Akha life and culture, the headman said:

> Thais are using us to make money [and then continued] they bring tourists to let them smoke opium, making money, and when they get back they say that Akha people are bad people because they smoke opium; in this way Akha people lose face. They look down on us. [He complained that] some guides come to my house, without ever asking me, and start cooking as if it were their house, dealing with the tourists as if they own everything. I believe that as I get to know more about what is happening in the world, I can not stop getting angry. [And then his irritation goes further] The Thai government does not treat us well, I mean not only the Akha, but also other mountain people.

From his statements, it is obvious that he is aware of the unequal power relationship between guides and themselves, and is highly discontented with this situation. He also showed his awareness that this unequal relationship exists not only between the jungle guides and the Akha but also in the more broader context between the Thais and highlanders. His frustration strengthens when economic interest is added. He said that:

> As for opium, we first thought we can earn money in this way, and we invested a lot of effort in treating the tourists. But as a result, most of the money goes to the guides and little money comes to us. The same thing happens with the selling of handicrafts, with the guides taking half the money that the tourists pay.

To summarise, we have observed in this section a differentiation in the interpretation of culture among hosts, guides and guests due to their respective motivations and interests. It is important to realise that this image-production system in the tourism setting is operating under unequal socio-political circumstances for the hosts. When a misleading image is projected by outsiders, especially about women, it could be damaging the cultural pride of minority groups in peripheral areas. Along with infrastructural development in mountain areas, trekking tourism has also intensified the relationship between the local Thais and the highlanders. From my observations, tourism seems to have been partly responsible for reinforcing political tension between the Akha and the Thais, or perhaps more widely between the highlanders and the Thais in general.

Over a longer time-span, it may well be that, as a response to the effects of tourism, the highland people may share a common interest in improving their situation, and this may lead to a greater sense of solidarity amongst them: i.e. a new common cross-cultural identity as highlanders may emerge when 'culture and tourism' is perhaps increasingly emphasised in the scheme of a tourism promotion strategy. At present, however, the Thai government has not yet considered the highlanders as a diverse cultural attraction, rather regarding them as illegal migrants, and problematic people.

According to the Tourism Authority of Thailand in Chiang Mai, tourism is the region's greatest source of revenue, earning 15 billion Baht in 1994 and receiving 2.1 million tourists, 30 per cent of whom were foreigners, and 70 per cent Thais. Nevertheless trekking tourism, receiving between 150-300,000 trekkers each year (Putsatee, 1992; Dearden in this volume), is not fully recognised as an attractive resource for 'cultural' and 'ethnic' tourism in the framework of national tourism development in the north. Rather, attention has been paid to regulating and training jungle guides in order to maintain the safety of the trekkers. A Tourism Business and Guide Act was promulgated in 1992 for the purpose of controlling the quality of the guides, including jungle guides. Under this law "the guides have to have accredited professional status before they can practice their occupation" (Putsatee, 1992, p.48). The Tourism Authority of Thailand has only recently (October 1992) started organising a training course and official certificates for jungle guides, in co-operation with the Teacher College in Chiang Mai. However, it is very difficult for hilltribe peoples to attend this course as participants are required to be able to speak English and to have secondary level education to the age of 15. Furthermore this 90-hour course costs 3,500 baht, a huge sum to most highlanders. The average daily labourer's wage for highlanders is approximately 80 baht. Thus, in order to ease some of the problems associated with the tourist-guide-host relationship, the hilltribe people themselves should be encouraged to become trekking tour guides, rather than being prevented from so-doing by a lack of government-provided education.

Cultural effects on ethnic identity and 'tradition'

As far as the cultural effects of tourism are concerned, a great deal of literature has sought to answer normative questions, asking whether cultures are spoiled, broken down, demeaned, preserved, or strengthened. The normative approach tends to look at 'tradition' as 'unspoilt', 'unchangeable', 'primitive', 'self-sufficient', based upon a romanticised view (Wood, 1980, p.564). In this approach tourism is often assessed with the common assumption of whether it has positive or negative effects on 'traditional' culture. Some studies credited tourism with preserving heritage, while others accused it of the 'commoditisation of culture'. It was evaluated whether it is beneficial or disadvantageous for the host society; however, there is an emerging consensus that this kind of normative cost-benefit framework to argue whether the effects are 'good' or 'bad' is too simplistic, not least as a basis for the analysis of socio-cultural change emanating from the tourist-host encounter (Wood, 1993, p.49).

It should be realised that an over-reliance on this approach tends to shut off the precise components of cultural change in the host society. Note that if we only look at the people of the host society as a passive target of the strong penetration from the wider world, it might constrain our ability to see the fact that villagers are not just passive recipients of outside influences, but respond to new opportunities and constraints. When outside influences come in, causing a reactive movement to adjust to the change, this is an active response of local participants in the host society. Culture is not passive. People continuously develop their culture in order to incorporate change.

Cultural process has recently been understood as "internally differentiated, active and changing" (Wood, 1980, p.565). Or, in Marcus and Fischer's (1986) words, "any culture in this world is a historical product of adaption, resistance and compromise. Cultural situation is continuously changing". Thus, the aim of this section is not to assess whether tourism has positive or negative effects on the 'traditional' culture in the host society, as culture is not a fixed entity handed down from generation to generation. Rather it aims to to demonstrate the mechanism in which 'traditional' culture and ethnic identity exist based on the perspective that they are products of interpretation constructed in the present, to which each individual attributes their own meaning. Therefore, cultural changes which are perceived by outsiders, such as the declining prevalence of 'traditional' costume, dance, ceremony and so on, might not necessarily imply a sign of weakening ethnic identity in their own perception.

It is widely believed in the tourist guidebooks and advertisements that the Akha used to live a life of self-sufficient plenty, in complete isolation, conservatively preserving their own 'tradition'. They are considered to be 'innocent' people who are far away from civilisation and commercialisation.

Furthermore, tourism has been criticised for introducing consumerism, eroding their traditional values and spoiling their 'innocence'.

However, the Akha in fact have a long history of contact with other societies. An old Akha proverb shows the Akha way of hospitality: "even when a dog comes to your house, you treat him with food, so why not human beings?" From the view of the Thai nation state, they lie at the edge of the national boundary, and are living in a peripheral mountainous area where access by central government is difficult. Yet it does not necessarily mean that they live in an 'isolated' or 'remote' area: the region has long been an important cultural cross-roads between southern China, Burma, Laos and Thailand. Thus, it is unlikely that Akha people are 'untouched' by the outside world.

According to von Geusau (1988, p.227), the Akha have been involved in market systems and have practised a type of mixed economy for hundreds of years: "They seem to have been involved not only in local markets, but equally in mercantilist and colonial market systems both in China and in Burma." We should realise that the Akha people are not 'isolated' people living in a 'remote' area enjoying an 'innocent' life, but rather that they have a long historical experience of contact with the outside world. They must have experience in adapting to, resisting or compromising with influence from outside.

A Christian missionary, Elaine Lewis, described in 1957 why the Akha people are more difficult to convert to Christianity than the other hill tribes, the reason being that the Akha way of life is "more highly developed" than that of other groups of highlanders (cited in Kammerer, 1990, p.279). This gives a basis to believe that the Akha are more conservative than other ethnic groups of northern Thailand. In her point of view, Akhazang, the Akha way of life, based on the experiences and knowledge of their ancestors, including beliefs etiquette, and daily activities of village life, seems to constrain them from undergoing rapid change.

With reference to contact with outsiders, a 52 year-old man, whom I shall call 'Dam', said: "when people come from outside the village, it is good that we can learn something from them, because I like to know what is happening in the outside world. People from outside are always important to us." He continued "when outsiders bring something new to us, we know what we need and what we do not need for our life." As I noted down his comments, he pointed at my paper and said, "writing is good, it is what we can learn from the outside, it is easy to remember, but for the Akha, we can not write things down, and so we forget."

When Dam was emphasising the importance of education, educating the next generation to write, I asked him a question: "if your son goes to school and starts learning from the outside and does not want to continue the Akha way of life any more, what would you think?" He replied quietly, "he can choose his own life. After I die I will not know." Then he added, "but if he learns writing he can write down the Akha way of life, which will remain forever." He is aware that the situation is changing, and that adaptation is required to meet the needs of change. His attitude shows that cultural strategies of adaptability are not passive. As a whole, however vulnerable a situation one may be in, there is always a choice they can take. Dam is a skilled basket-weaver and commented "a lot of Akha skills are dying and nobody wants to learn any more." He was also anxious over village solidarity, adding "there appear to be no rules in this village any more." However, he has no intention of forcing the next generation to follow the same way of life as his generation, and seems ready to let the next generation define its own interpretation of the Akha way of life. von Geusau (1983, p.276) also mentioned a flexibility of Akhazang as it advises "to take the middle road in order to move forward in history; to compromise to make something acceptable in order to survive; to remain flexible so that you can adapt to majorities and other outside pressures." Thus, contrary to the stereotypical stubborn image of the Akha from outsiders, especially from the missionaries, Akhazang seems in fact not to be a constraint, but more a tool-kit to judge their strategy of action. Therefore, Akhazang is not simply an inheritance passed down from generation to generation, but it is what people acquire in each generation.

Lek, to whom I referred in the first section, has successfully established personal economic stability without selling opium to trekkers; has built himself a solid house, which is not in the 'traditional' Akha style; and always wears a red baseball cap, which has no relation to Akha costume. However, from the interview, it is obvious that he firmly believes in and hopes for Akha cultural survival and he is proud of being Akha. His appearance, when riding around on his motorcycle with a red baseball cap on his head, is far from that of the stereotyped 'traditional' image of the Akha. Although outsiders tend to see the changing 'traditional' custom as a sign of deprivation of culture, it seems that the changing 'traditional' lifestyle does not necessarily relate to degradation of ethnic identity in his own perception.

On the other hand, some young Akha who stay in the lowlands for a while do not want to learn anything from the old generation in the village. They pretend to be Thai, by imitating the Thai way of life and refusing to speak the Akha language, as they feel ashamed of being Akha. These consequences vary as a result of whether and how they have acquired their own ethnic identity, the criterion of which determines what they need or what they do not need from the outside world.

To sum up, it should be recognised that, since ethnic identity is a product of adaptation, resistance and compromise, it may be renewed, modified and remade in each generation. It is important to perceive this process from the local point of view in order to examine the dynamic process of the construction of ethnic identity. Moreover, regarding the case presented in the previous section, the headman of the village seemed to have acquired the identity not just of being Akha, but also of being a hilltribe person. The category *chao khao* is a term created for the sake of the Thai government to lump the highlanders - the minority groups of the mountainous area - all together, to be contrasted with the majority Thai lowlanders. It was a category created by the perception of the Thai government.

Highlanders themselves, each of them having significant cultural differences from one another, do not have any common identity among themselves. However, as circumstances have changed due to the political boundary of the nation state, the state of identity also changes to adapt to the new situation. The perception of identity change operates not only at the individual level of interpretation, but also within the sphere of categories. Thus tourism encourages the fluidity of the state of identity.

Conclusion

This empirical case study sought to achieve several objectives. In the first section, where we assessed the socio-economic effects of opium-smoking, I examined the changes which had taken place over eight years following its introduction as a tourism business. I also identified the various coping strategies of different groups of people within the community, showing how different people are affected or involved to different degrees, using gender, age and socio-economic power as the basis for this differentiation. In the second section, which examined the socio-political impact of the tourist-guide-host encounter, I demonstrated the mechanism of representation of culture in the tourist setting, through which the image of the host society is projected by outsiders. Particular reference was made to the gender dimensions of this situation. In the third section, where cultural effects on ethnic identity and 'tradition' were examined, we highlighted the various coping strategies which had been adopted by the host society. Neither ethnic identity nor 'tradition' is a fixed entity, inherent from generation to generation, but rather they are products of interpretation, symbolically constructed in the present. In this sense, it is crucial that the native's point of view is brought in to the interpretation of ethnic identity.

Changes which outsiders who hope to preserve 'unspoiled society' see in negative terms - such as the declining prevalence of costume, dance, ceremony, and so on - might not necessarily imply a sign of weakening ethnic identity from the perception of the society itself. On the basis of this argument, the question as to what extent tourism threatens traditional culture, which is asked by those who wish to examine the effects of tourism on the host society, ceases to be appropriate. This is because there is no bounded, unchanging core of ideas and customs which we can identify as real ethnic identity or real traditional culture for us to measure and assess. In this sense, the tourism industry can be understood as a cross-roads producing representation of culture from both outsiders and native people. However, the problem is that, at present, outsiders tend to dominate the projection and representation of native culture, while the native host community in the periphery is seldom in a position of self representation. Such is the unevenness of the development process in Thailand.

13 Farmer differentiation in southern and central Thai agrarian systems: Who benefits from agricultural growth?

Guy Trébuil

The contradictory process of 'development/elimination' in Thai agriculture

Agricultural development is considered here as gradual changes occurring in agricultural production processes that are assumed to be socially beneficial by satisfying changing needs. In the case of the Thai rural sector, such changes are rapid and, in some areas, even brutal. A knowledge of the evolution of these production processes and farmers' needs, their transformations in time as well as space, is of paramount importance for any critical appraisal of the current agrarian situation. It is also a pre-requisite for the formulation of courses of action aimed at modifying existing production structures and ameliorating undesirable changes taking places in a given area.

The general context of the Thai agriculture

For more than a century, the growth of the Thai agricultural sector has been remarkable (Trébuil, 1990, pp.203-6). Before 1960, it was based on an increase in the export volumes of a handful of basic commodities (rice in the central plain, rubber in the south, teak in the northern region, etc.). Between 1850 and 1950, the volume of Thai rice exports jumped from 50,000 to 1.5 million tons. This was achieved without any significant increase in the paddy yield (from 1.1 to 1.2 tons/hectare), but the cultivated area per inhabitant almost doubled during this period (from 0.16 to 0.3 ha./person), in spite of steady population growth. After 1960 and until the late-1980s, the expansion of the cultivated area was still partly responsible for further impressive increases in rice exports which peaked at around 6 million tons in 1989, representing some 40 per cent of the volume of world rice trade in that year. It was also the case for a wide range of increasingly diversified industrial cash crops that have been planted on a large scale during the last few decades on undulating land above the rice fields, and also replacing the forest along very dynamic pioneer frontiers (Trébuil, 1994; 1995). During the 1970s, for example, the area planted to cassava and sugar cane increased by 20 and 15 per cent respectively on an annual basis. Today, Thailand is the leading world exporter of cassava and lies in second place for the export of cane sugar.

The general evolution of Thai agriculture over the last thirty-five years has also been characterised by a more or less rapid and complete introduction of the techniques and means of production belonging to the contemporary 'second' or 'green' agricultural revolution (motorisation, mechanisation, use of chemicals, breeding and irrigation, regional specialisation). In the paddy fields, the new production techniques have helped the average national paddy yield to increase modestly to some 2 tons/ha., although this still represents one of the lowest national averages in Asia. In the south, the traditional jungle rubber small-holder plantations have been gradually replanted to high-yielding clones, leading the country recently to the status of the world's leading exporter of natural rubber, even with a relatively low yield compared to plantations in neighbouring Malaysia. Because the new inputs and means of production are costly, they have been used to increase both soil and labour productivity only on production units that could afford to secure them (Mazoyer, 1988;Baert and Bergez, 1987).

The acquisition of the new farming technology has contributed to a contradictory process of 'development/elimination' or 'development/crisis' among Thai farmers (Mazoyer, 1988): improvement occurs for some but at a cost to others. Some ten years ago, in the four study areas which provide the basis for discussion in this chapter, 70-85 per cent of the labour force was employed in agriculture; the current range is now estimated at 45-60 per cent. At the national level the share of the agricultural labour force in the total workforce has also decrease by one to two per cent annually during the last fifteen years.

This contemporary agricultural revolution has led to the marginalisation and elimination of a growing number of resource-poor farmers. In line with the previous experience of rapid industrialisation in South Korea, Japan and Taiwan, the rural labour force has been consistently drained through an exodus from the agricultural sector and an incorporation (or partial incorporation) into the expanding industrial and services sectors. Because of the growing unification of the world economy and the parallel erosion of several of Thailand key comparative advantages (soil and water resources, wage levels, etc.), this process of labour absorption could be much more difficult to repeat in the future (Handley, 1993b).

Following rapid improvements in the means of communication and exchange across the country, the pace of transformation of production processes is occurring more and more rapidly in areas where farmers are able to capitalise on its undoubted benefits. However, the majority of agricultural production units are still not able to adopt the whole package of means of production associated with the second agricultural revolution. These farmers are tending to adopt only a part of the package - typically the more accessible and less costly or less risky elements - or none at all.

The agro-industrial boom around Bangkok which occurred in the the late 1980s and early-1990s drained the young (especially female) labour force to the newly-established factories. The syphoning-off of rural labour has had significant consequences for the agricultural sector. In the rice fields, wet seeding has had to replace the more labour-intensive practice of transplanting for the establishment of the rice crop, while at harvest contractors' mini-combine harvesters have replaced the sickle and the axial flow thresher in just three four years. During the same period, in the more disadvantaged rain-fed lowland rice areas of the northeastern region, direct seeding of rice has expanded significantly and the mechanical thresher has tended to replace threshing by hand. Across the country, less competitive farmers are being pushed to the margin, mainly because of the declining trend in commodity prices which has resulted from the reduced production costs within the most efficient production units. Such a trend will continue as long as the latter producers are able further to improve their productivity. The situation can also be aggravated by the national agricultural policies of Thailand's major competitors. Because differences in labour productivity among Thai farmers in a given area are still relatively limited (see below), this trend of decreasing prices due to foreign competition constitutes the main threat to Thai producers, especially the resource-poor ones.

The relevance of the global concept of 'agrarian system'

The global concept of Agrarian System (AS) can be used to characterise such key trends and changes in production processes at the regional level and in the long run.[1] At the cross-roads between agro-ecology and agro-economy, the concept's main variables are the cultivated ecosystem, and the instruments and means which are used to produce, maintain and exploit it, creating a specific mode of exploitation of the environment (its geographical limits corresponding to the agrarian system's boundaries). Other essential inter-related variables that have also to be taken into account to explain key transformations of agrarian systems are the division of labour between various economic sectors, the relations of production, ownership and exchanges of products, and also the dominant political and cultural conditions and institutions (Mazoyer, 1985; Trébuil, 1988; 1989; Trébuil and Dufumier, 1992). The application of the concept of AS leads to an understanding of the origins, extent, conditions and consequences of such important historical transformations and geographical adaptations of agricultural production processes, and especially their economic and social implications: what kind of evolution of labour productivity takes place? What degree of social differentiation occurs among various farmer categories? What are the respective levels of sustainability of their existing farming systems?

This global concept has been recently used in Thailand (i) to propose pertinent diagnoses on the current state and on-going evolution of agriculture in the country's geographical regions; and (ii) to formulate adapted orientations for the future development of agriculture, especially for the less-favoured groups of farmers.

Original characteristics of the four study areas

For the last ten years, a similar approach to understanding regional agricultural changes has been used at the following four complementary sites in southern and central Thailand (see Figure 13.1), representing a complete toposequence from the sea-shores of the south to the mountainous highlands along the border with Burma:

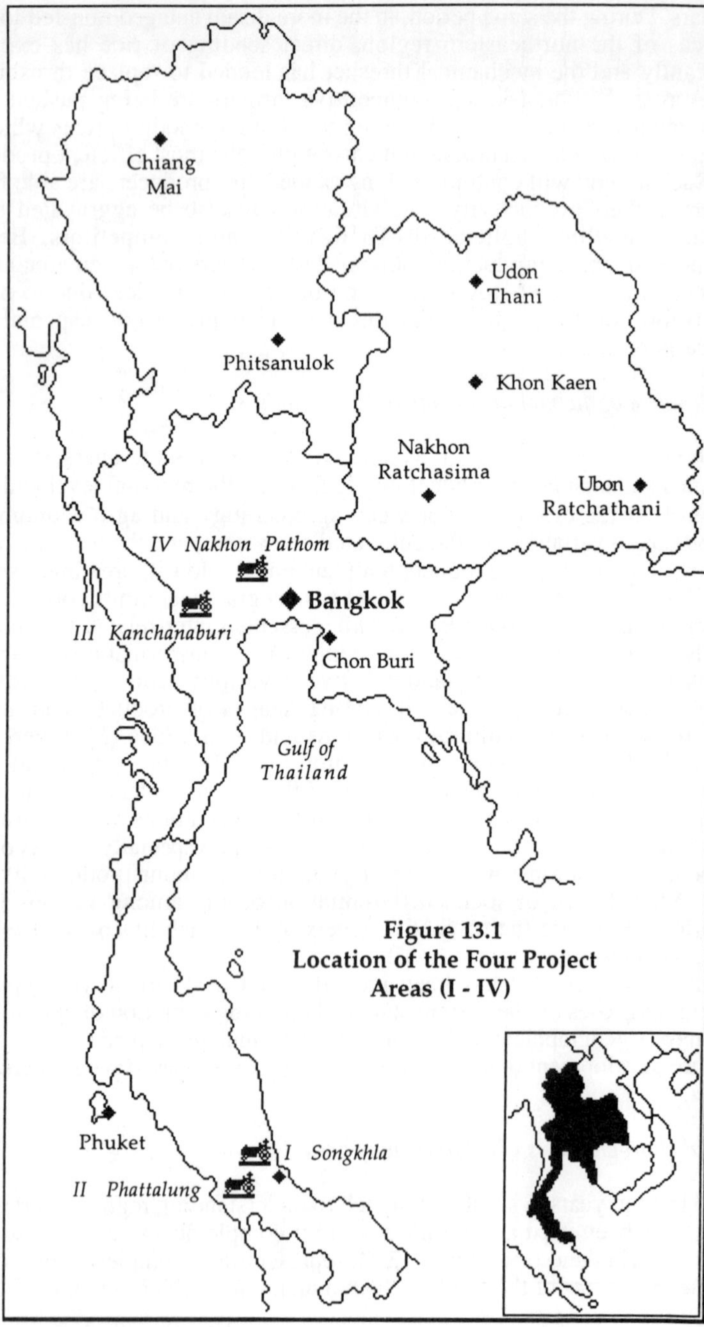

Figure 13.1
Location of the Four Project Areas (I - IV)

Table 13.1
Characteristics of the Four Complementary Study Areas in Thailand

District: Province:	Sating Phra Songkhla	Khao Chaison Phattalung	Kamphaengsaen Nakhon Pathom	Saiyok Kanchanaburi
Period	1982-1985	1985-1989	1989-1991	Since 1991
Agroecosystem:	Rain-fed lowland, alluvial plain. Rice-sugar palm	Partly irrigated alluvial plain. Rice in+off - rubber	Irrigated alluvium fan. Sugar cane-rice in+off - vegetables	Pioneer front, mixed forest. Annual + tree cash crops
Bio-Physical Constraints:	Soil (heavy clay) - water drainage	Water control in rice	Loamy (crusting) soil structure	Pests and diseases
Integration into the Market Economy	Low to medium	medium to high	very high	low to medium
Characteristics of the Target Group of Resource-Poor Farmers				
Indicator:				
Land/Labour	<0.8 ha.	<1.5 ha.	<0.8 ha.	<1.0 ha.
Frequency (%)	80	60	60	55
Management Criteria:	Optimize family labour productivity in palm sugar	Optimize net margin in rain-fed lowland rice low to medium	Maximize net income per land unit in vegetables	Optimize net margin of maize-cotton relay crop
Sustainability:	Very low	Low to medium	very low (debts)	Low (land tenure)

(i) *Sathing Phra district, Songkhla province, Southern Region:* a coastal area of rain-fed lowland paddies where rice cultivation is closely associated with palm sugar production on the smallest farms (Crozat, 1986; Trébuil and Boonchoo, 1988; Trébuil, 1988; Trébuil *et.al.*, 1983). This area displays a very complex and original traditional agricultural system, well-adapted to the local soil and climatic constraints, but which is now in crisis due to the recent connection of the area with major regional urban and industrial areas;

(ii) *Khao Chaison district, Phatthalung province, Southern Region:* a partially irrigated (diversion dam) rice-growing alluvial plain adjacent to small-holder rubber and fruit plantations on higher ground (Baert and Bergez, 1987; Moreau, 1988). Inequalities in access to irrigation water in the paddies and to well-drained land for rubber plantation are the dominant factors which explain differentiation among the local farmers;

(iii) *Kamphaengsaen district, Nakhon Pathom province, Central Region:* a low terrace irrigated area where sugar cane, irrigated rice and vegetable production dominate in a wide variety of very commercialised farming systems (Naritoom, 1990). The research was carried out here during the peak of the agro-industrial boom allowing the direct observation of its effects on the sustainability of the different types of farming system;

(iv) *Saiyok district, Kanchanaburi province, Western Region:* an upland cultivated frontier where pioneer annual cash crops (maize-cotton relay cropping system, sugar cane and cassava, etc.) under rain-fed conditions are being gradually replaced by perennial plantations (Ngernprasertsri *et.al.*, 1992), associated to vegetable production and livestock-rearing. Here the DORAS project addressed the issue of the degradation of natural resources: dynamics of deforestation along the pioneer front, ecological balance between insect pests and predators of annual cash crops threatened by ill-conceived pesticide applications (Trébuil *et.al.*, 1994).

Table 13.1 displays several of the original characteristics of these four agrarian systems. It can be seen that these selected areas are at different stages in their integration into the global market economy. The comparative analysis is very useful in predicting the evolution and extent of farmer differentiation in the less advanced areas.

Key tools and outputs for holistic diagnosis on regional agrarian systems

Efficient interventions in agriculture must be based on relevant scientific knowledge of the conditions and modalities for promoting agricultural development in a given agrarian system. This is of particular importance when the objective is to support the less-favoured farming systems facing elimination within an increasingly differentiated Thai peasantry. A preliminary diagnostic analysis prior to any intervention is essential (Trébuil and Dufumier, 1992). The main objective of such a diagnosis is to identify and prioritise factors and conditions (ecosystem, availability of means of production, social relations) which are determining the choice and evolution of the various types of farming systems in the area. It also leads to an understanding of how these key factors and conditions are actually involved in the transformations of local agriculture. Subsequently, its conclusions can explain how key limiting factors can be improved to steer the local agricultural development process in a way more suitable to the common good.

Based on the theory of the "evolution and differentiation of agrarian systems" (Mazoyer, 1985), a methodology for Development-Oriented Research on Agrarian Systems (DORAS), has been tested and gradually refined (Trébuil, 1988b; Trébuil *et.al.*, 1990). Figure 13.2 displays the articulation between the four iterative phases of this approach to on-farm research and development. The integrated set of key tools used in the systemic analysis of farmer circumstances is briefly introduced below.

Agro-ecological zonation

First, the target area is divided into relatively homogeneous zones presenting a similar dominating mode of exploitation of the ecosystem and related key questions for agricultural development. The objective of such a zonation is to assess both agro-ecological and socio-economic potentialities and constraints which influence the choice and the evolution of the various kinds of farming systems. The most important result of this zonation is to be able to identify, characterise and locate the main technical systems used by farmers in artificialising and exploiting various agro-ecosystems. Their origins have also to be understood.

Historical analysis of farmer differentiation

To discern and understand the significance of the most important transformations and regional adaptations of agricultural production processes as well as their existing conditions and consequences the following steps are used:

(i) to distinguish and characterise the main changes in the state of the agricultural production processes in the given area over time through informal interviews;

(ii) to identify the origin and follow up the development of any 'new agricultural order', while monitoring the recession of the ancient organisation of agriculture it is replacing;

(iii) to determine the existing conditions for such a change, particularly the economic, political and socio-cultural conditions at that time which permit, accelerate or slow down such a change; and

(iv) on the other hand, to discern the obstacles and restraining factors which forbid or hamper the change towards the new agricultural order (Trébuil, 1989).

In both cases - expansion of a pre-existing AS or establishment of a new one - the concept assumes that an improvement in the process of production presupposes previous changes in the relations of production and exchanges, as well as in the institutions and ideas that are dominating and regulating the old agrarian system and which could hamper the gradual development of the new one.

The final output in a given area is an evolutionary series of agricultural transitions-transformations, of AS having increased capacities for agricultural

Figure 13.2
Articulation Between the Four Phases of the DORAS Approach

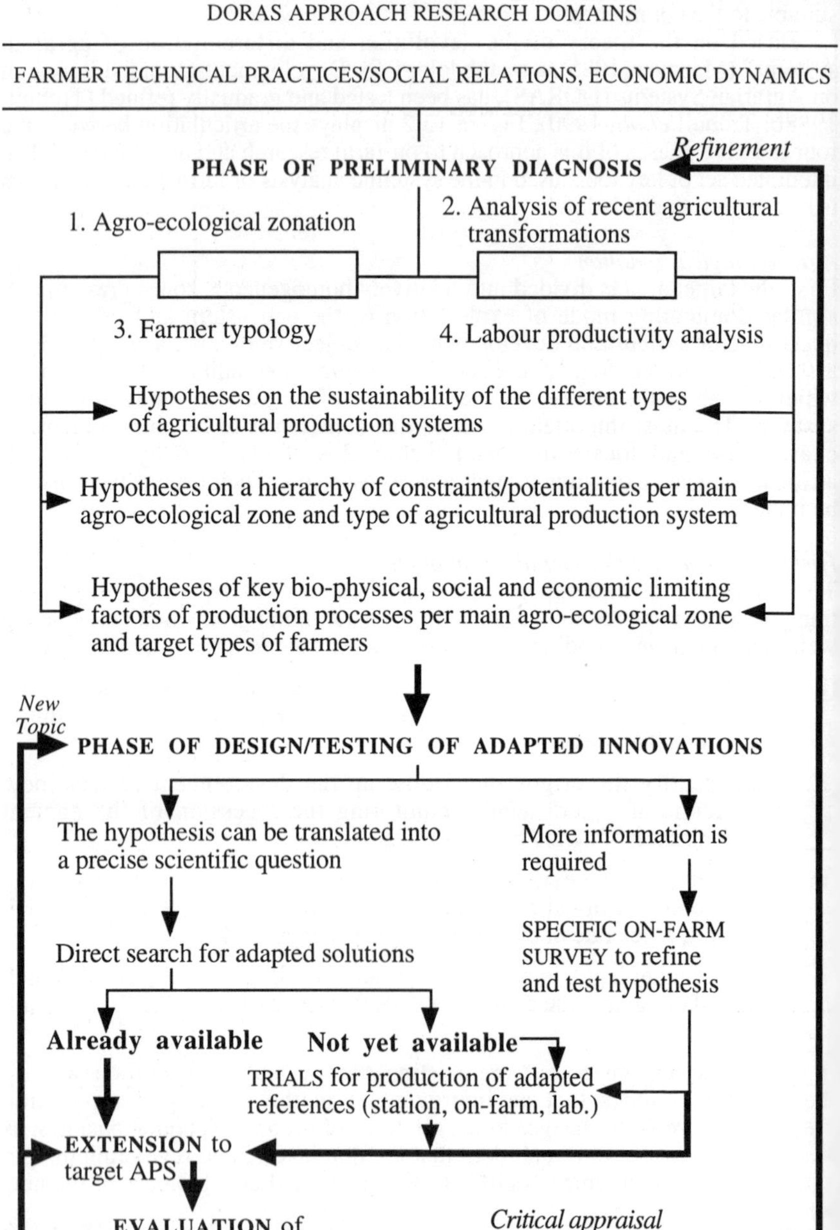

Figure 13.3
Sequence of Agrarian Systems for the Kamphaengsaen Area, Nakhon Pathom Province, Central Thailand

AS Variable Components	A.S. 1	A.S. 2	A.S. 3	A.S. 4
Ecological Events	Dense forest ecosystem still dominant in upland areas; Lowland swamps converted into rain-fed dry-seeded paddies.	Gradual expansion of cultivated area; complete in lowland paddies, bamboo forest-shrub replace dense forest in upland zone.	Deforestation is completed in upland areas; Beginning of irrigation; Annual flood until 1974.	Irrigation system completed; No annual flood; Control of salinity, pests & diseases is more crucial.
Means of Production	Local varieties, manual tools+draught animals (in paddies)	Local varieties, manual tools+draught animals (in paddies)	Introd. of heavy machinery in sugar cane (tractor, truck); Light machinery in paddies + vegetable (hand tractor, thresher, pump, sprayer); First artesian well dug.	No mechanization of sugar cane harvest yet (in 1990); Irrigation is available.
Techniques Applied	Very close crop-livestock association at all APS levels; Dry seeded paddy production dominates in lowlands (1-2t/ha.; Slash and burn cultivation of tobacco, chillies, eggplant, etc. in upland zone.		Recommended varieties + industrial inputs (fertilizer + pesticides) available; Motorization of land preparation + harvest work; 3 year cycle for sugar cane.	Pre-germinated sowings replace transplanting in paddies.
Production	Lowland rice (1 crop/yr); Tobacco-chillies-local tobacco; Forest products; Livestock	Lowland rice (1 crop/yr): local; More tobacco, chillies, eggplant; Less forest products; Livestock.	Sugar cane area=60% of total (cotton); Lowland paddies (1 or 2 crops = 20%); Domestic market vegetables (onion, green leaves)+fruits=10%.	Sugar cane still v. important but decreasing; Rice = stable; Increase in labour-intensive vegetable systems (baby corn, asparagus); Dairy farming is introduced.
Demographic Pressures	<50-80 inhab/sq.km.	80-130 inhab/sq.km.	150-200 inhab/sq.km.	250-350 inhab/sq.km.
Marketing Conditions	Barter exchange at village level; High degree of self-sufficiency.	First road to Suphan Buri, Nakhon Pathom: opening to market economy.	More roads, easy access to provincial+Bangkok markets; Many large sugar mills located in the area.	Improvement of communication networks in world economy - boom in agro-processing for exports (proximity to harbour, airport).
Farm Supplies (inputs, equipment)	Production of tools at the village level by craftsmen; Manuring for paddy and vegetable production.		Dominance of the 'Quota Headman' system in sugar cane; Same with middlemen in vegetable production.	Same as before + more 'contract' farming through brokers, companies.
Rural Credit Patterns	No institutions (low level of monetarization of exchanges).	At village level (monetarization of the village economy).	Through 'Quota Headman' and middlemen mainly.	Same as before for those with no access to BAAC and commercial banks.
Land Tenure Patterns	Individual colonization according to family labour by migrants (s + w areas).	Paddy land is more and more scarce.	Nor Sor 3 land titles given; New migrants rent land for cash; Land market is set up.	More rental system; Sales of land to clear debts occurs; Land speculation is rife.
Labour Market	Family labour exclusively, no hired labour yet.		Hired labour widely used for planting + harvesting sugar cane; Local hired labour at vegetable harvest.	Labour is lacking on large sugar cane and vegetable-based APS; Wages are increasing rapidly.
State Intervention	Access to land difficult for ethnic Chinese - slash and burn in upland areas and specialization in market products (chillies, tobacco) for accumulation of savings and capital.		Attribution of land titles; Beginning of irrigation works; Creation of BAAC.	Protection of domestic sugar price after it plunges; Local + foreign investment incentives.
Farmer Income, Productivity	Family self-sufficiency, low level of monetarization.	Still high level of self-subsistency on rice-based Thai-Lao AS; Cash income dominant on Chinese cash crops, vegetable-based APS.	Cumulative indebtedness is building up on many farms dependent on 'Quota Headmen'.	Indebtedness is important; Value-added/rai: asparagus 15X sugar cane; value added/worker: sugar cane B15,000, asparagus B50,000.
Farm Differentiation	Very low	Cash crop-based (Chinese); Rice-based (Thai-Lao).	Already important: 0 rai = new migrant; 400 rai = Quota Headman.	Increasing: 0 rai - debted 1-2X annual Y; 1,000 rai, productive capital of millions of baht.

production. Figure 13.3 displays such a series of AS for the Kamphaengsaen area, west of the Central Plain. By recapitulating the history of agricultural practices and related changes in social relations in the target area, one can understand the mechanisms of differentiated accumulation of fixed capital among farmers which are at the origin of spatial specialisations and farming systems differences in their levels of economic sustainability or ability to continue.

Construction of a farmer typology

Because in the past various categories of farmers could not accumulate the same levels of production means, they are not producing in the same economic and social conditions. In a given ecological zone, different categories of farmers can better meet their goals by using different techniques and managing different types of farming systems. It is then very important to identify these main types of farmers, by considering their goals, strategies, means of production and the social relations in which they are operating. This is the role of the farmer typology, a central tool for the diagnostic analysis of agrarian realities (Trébuil and Boonchoo, 1988; Trébuil, 1992). Today, different types of farmers do not necessarily believe that their best interests lie in optimising, or maximising, the same kind of economic ratios in order to improve their standard of living. Thus, the farmer typology needs to determine the different management criteria which are considered by the various types of farmers when implementing their respective production systems and assessing the suitability of possible technical innovations to their specific situations. Some examples of management criteria which are found when analysing farmers' strategies in Thai villages are as follows: maximisation of the annual (but sometimes even monthly or daily) cash income per unit of family labour or land; priority given to the production of a certain amount of user value over cash income generation; and maximisation of family labour productivity or rate of profit on invested capital. Figure 13.4 shows such a farmer typology prepared for the Kamphaengsaen area in Nakhon Pathom province, an area opened to the market economy for a long time and where intra-regional inequalities are already very extensive.

Differences in labour productivity among farmer categories

Studies on labour productivity in Thai agriculture are rare or provide only a rough picture at the provincial or regional level (Siamwalla, 1987b). They do not look at the already quite important differentiation that exists among farmers' systems, between areas as well as among producers in a given region. However, the analysis of such differentiation is essential if one is interested in an understanding of the dynamics of local agriculture: what is the extent of the process of 'development/elimination' among farms? What is the relative position of the various farmers' systems in terms of labour productivity in comparison with other employment opportunities? What is their respective capacity to resist increasing local or foreign competition and to continue in the future?

During a limited number of detailed on-farm surveys, a computation for each main cropping or animal-rearing system was carried out as part of the analysis of the farming system functioning in order to appraise its annual gross product, variable or fixed costs and the subsequent economic performance assessed by the produced value-added (= gross product - variable costs - fixed

Figure 13.4

Typology of Agricultural Production Systems in the Kamphaengsaen Area

Key Characteristics/Types	A1	A2	B	C	D
Cultivated area/family worker:	<0.8 ha.		0.8-2.0 ha.	>2.0 ha.	>4.0 ha.
Hired labour/total labour:	<10%	10-25%	<35%	15-40%	>60%
Labour productivity on value-added (x1,000 baht/worker/year):	5-20	20-100	5-50	10-30	>50
Production = (% cultivated area)					
Sugar cane:	20-75	0-55	0-95	75-95	>80
Vegetables:	+/++	+++	+/+++	+	+
Economic management criterion:	Maximum net income per land unit		Maximization of family productivity	Maximization of rate of profit	
Frequency (%):	60		36	3	1
Ability to continue:	Very low if not vegetable based		Yes if intensification	Yes if mechanisation and sugar cane price protection	

Figure 13.5
Evolution of Labour Productivity According to Farmers' Productive Resources Among 10 Agricultural Production Systems in the Sathing Phra Area Between the 1982-83 and 1987-88 Crop Years

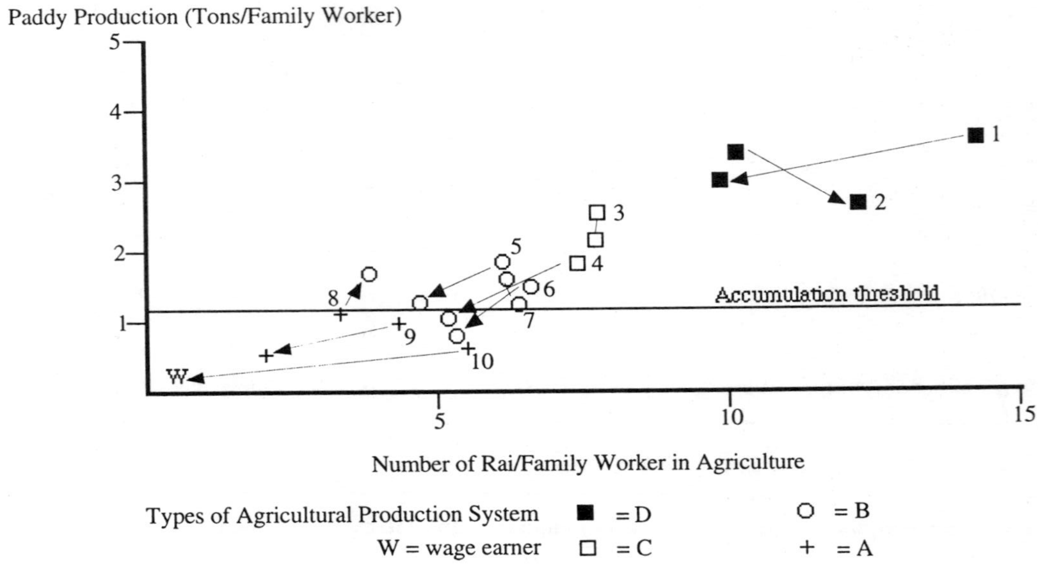

costs) per hectare and per year. The labour productivity for each technical system (differing mainly according to their levels of mechanisation: manual tools, draft animals, light mechanisation with a hand-tractor, or heavy mechanisation with a four-wheeled tractor, thresher or ginner) can then be assessed through the added value per labour unit ratio, as well as the farmer's family income (= labour productivity - hired labour - all social relations-related costs such as taxes, rental cost of land, loan interests, etc. which represent the distribution of the added value produced on the farms among the rural society).

On completion of this task, it becomes possible to compare and group the different types of farming system according to their evolution, availability of means of production and economic results. Figure 13.5 shows the key output that can be prepared at this stage in the case of the southern Sathing Phra area. Each farmer's system is plotted on a graph showing its level of labour productivity as a function of the availability of means of production. In Thailand, past case studies have demonstrated that the cultivated area per economically-active family member is a relevant criterion for the assessment of such a discriminating variable (Trébuil, 1988; Trébuil and Boonchoo, 1988; Baert and Bergez, 1987; Naritoom, 1990). The economic sustainability of each main type of farming system is then assessed through a comparative analysis between the dynamics of labour productivity (added value/worker/year) among the various farm types and several relevant 'accumulation thresholds', such as the regional wage levels of on-farm or alternative off-farm jobs, or even subsistence levels when no such alternative jobs are available. The group of less-favoured farming systems facing elimination because of their lack of competitiveness can thus be identified: they are located under the threshold line. Figure 13.5 shows the results of the same kind of study carried out in the Sathing Phra area at a five-year interval and visualises the process of elimination of the less productive farmers.

Appraisal of the frequency of each type of farmer

This last step of the diagnosis is also used to verify to what extent the results of the previous detailed case studies, which are carried out on a limited number of diverse farming systems, can be extrapolated to the whole local farming community. This is done through a rapid sample survey in order to record only a very limited number of key pertinent characteristics which are easy to identify. At the four study sites, it was found that between 60 and 80 per cent of the total number of farming systems, having less than 0.8 to 2.0 hectares of cultivated land per family worker (see Table 13.1 and Figure 13.6), could face elimination due to their very low level of economic results (Trébuil, 1989; Naritoom, 1990).

The current extent, conditions and mechanisms of farmer differentiation in Thai villages

Extent of farmer differentiation

In Thai villages, farmer differentiation measured in terms of access to productive resources is already very important (Table 13.2). Figure 13.6 shows that for the three most recent regional studies, differences in labour productivity among farmers are also extensive. Such extensive ranges of labour productivity between the least and most efficient producers (about 1:20) can be compared to the more limited range (1:4) recorded ten years ago in the more marginal Sathing Phra area. At that time, the gap in rice labour productivity with a modernised Taiwanese producer was about 1 to 10, and had already reached 1:100 between a Sathing Phra paddy grower and the average Californian producer! The process of 'development/elimination' or 'modernisation/elimination' among Thai farmers seems now to be well-established in the country and its effects can be magnified by the policies of key foreign competitors (like the USA and Vietnam in the case of the rice market during recent years).

Table 13.2
Extent of Farmer Differentiation at Four Locations in Central and Southern Thailand

Location	Sathing Phra	Khao Chaison	Kamphaeng-saen	Saiyok
Year	1982-83	1986-87	1989-90	1990-91
Farm size (ha.)	0.9-7.5	0.8-6.0	0.5-15.0	1.0-18.5
Land/labour (ha./unit)	0.5-1.2	0.8-5.6	0.25-11.7	2.3-20.8
% hired labour	0-34	0-95	0-57	0-85
Productive capital (US$)	400-12,000	n.a.	200-46,000	40-64,000
% resource-poor farms	80	60	60	60
Entrepreneurial farms (%)	5	10*	4	2

Notes: n/a data not available
* this is likely to be an over-estimate

Conditions and mechanisms of increased differentiation

This level of differentiation can largely be attributed to the modalities of farm mechanisation and motorisation in Thai villages (Trébuil, 1990). Incomplete light motorisation is still predominating and most of the time concerns only land preparation, water-pumping, threshing and transportation practices. So the ratio of size of cultivated area per worker is still limited by crop implantation weeding or harvesting operations, which are still often done manually. Moreover, farmers who do not possess any instrument for land tillage

Figure 13.6
Sustainability of Farms in the Patthalung (a), Kamphaengsaen (b) and Saiyok (c) Areas: Labour Productivity as a Function of Land/Labour Resources

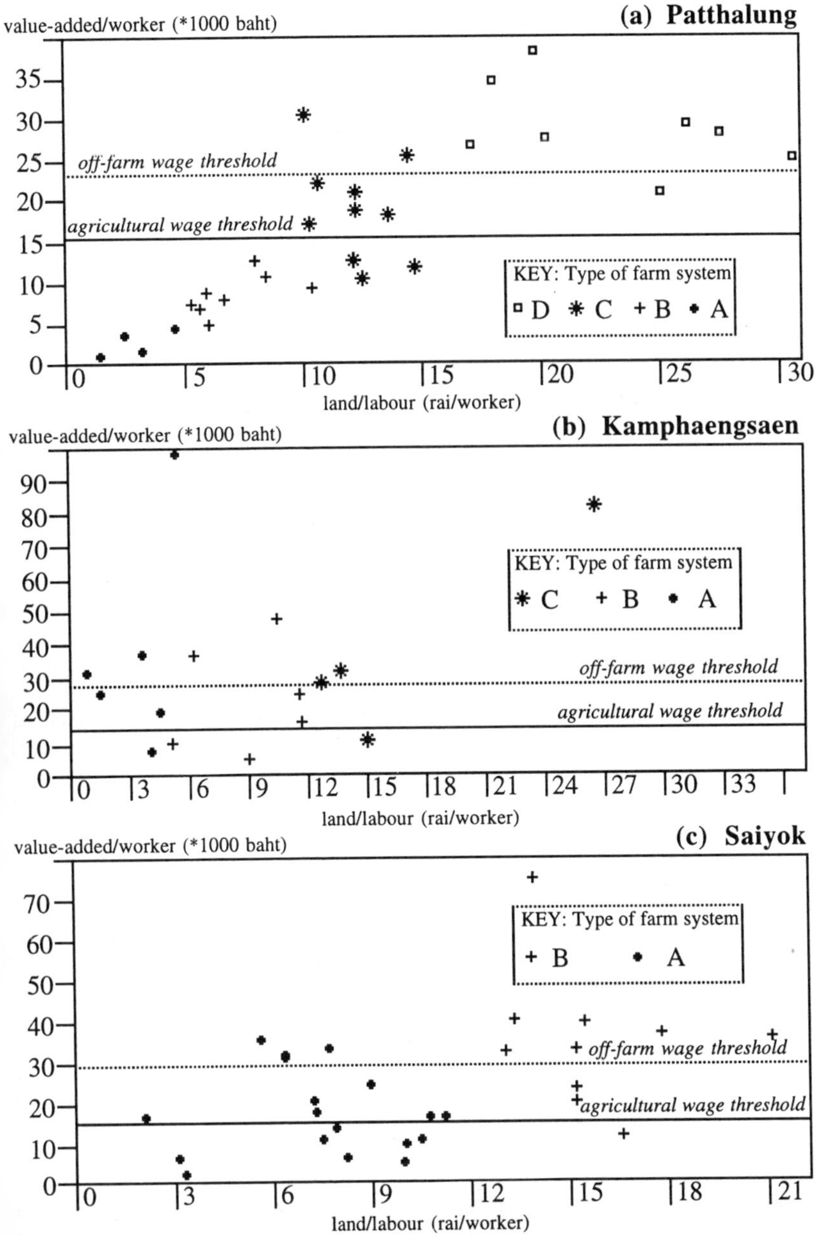

threshing or shelling are able to hire the equipment from local contractors or motorised entrepreneurial farms generally owned by Sino-Thai village traders (their frequency is indicated in Table 13.2). Apart from other complementary functions (such as input procurement, marketing of cash crops, provision of seasonal credit and social security), these village middlemen play a determining role in introducing, testing, adapting and disseminating the technical innovations of the 'green' revolution among the local farms which can afford them (Trébuil, 1990).

Until recently, differences in labour productivity between areas and farms resulted more from differences in the availability of irrigation water and its control, or of 'living' capital (herds, plantations), than from farm equipment. But, as can be seen in the example presented in Figure 13.4, the existing differences in access to productive resources are already sufficient to generate far more important inequalities now that, for example, improvements in low labour rice crop implantation techniques (direct seeding of pre-germinated seeds) and hiring of small local-made combine harvesters are widespread in the central plain and is now being introduced beyond its boundaries. Compared to previous techniques, the adoption of these two innovations can raise the land/labour ratio from 2 to 8 hectares and increase the level of labour productivity more than ten-fold (in terms of value added/worker/year from US$750 to more than US$8,000: Trébuil, 1990). The rapidly rising costs of wages and farm labourers no longer slow down the development of such more complex moto-mechanisation equipment, as can be seen with the rapid expansion of the use of small combine harvesters in the paddy fields of the central plain and beyond.

Such development, associated with the use of more inputs from research and industry (recommmended varieties, fertilizers, pesticides, etc.), could occur more rapidly in areas where tenant farming and share-cropping are widespread and could give way to the creation of larger farms after the elimination of the small tenants and share-croppers. In such a case, by allowing a very significant increase in the ration of cultivated area per worker, the productivity of agricultural labour on such large farms could make a significant jump forward and accelerate the elimination of other less efficient production units, destabilising the existing social structures in the Thai countryside. Another related key question is to know for how long the less-favoured farmers living in the most difficult and less-developed areas could resist such competition and avoid an increase in unemployment and rural exodus. This will depend, on the one hand, upon the rapidity of the development and dissemination of the more advanced production processes both abroad and within the country, and, on the other hand, upon the kind of agricultural policy and rural development strategy which is implemented in Thailand. Key questions for the development of these less-favoured production units are: through what kind of technical, economic, social and political measures can farms which are in a state of stagnation or crisis be saved if necessary (i.e. if farmers are interested to stay on these farms or, at a macro-level, if the growth of the other economic sectors is slowing down and makes it difficult for them to absorb the labour force quitting agriculture)? How can a cumulative process of increase in their productive resources and economic results be re-started? These questions are now essential ones as the equity issue has officially becoming a major concern in a very rapidly-changing Thai society. Relevant and operational answers to these questions can only be found through a fresher and more decentralised look at the agricultural policy issues that will allow the optimal and sustainable utilisation of the diversity of human and natural resources available in the Thai countryside.

A fresh look at agricultural policy issues: an inventory of differentiated regional situations and the decentralisation of planning

For the policy-maker or project manager, the key question at the end of a diagnostic phase of enquiry at the national or sub-regional level is how to make sure that the different types of producers can achieve their respective goals, and then to conceive and plan adapted state interventions in both the technical and economic fields. The problem is that, under certain economic and social conditions, the farmers do not see their interest lying solely in choosing the most suitable techniques to maximise the production of value added for the common good. It is therefore up to the state to implement the necessary modifications to prevailing conditions in order to ensure that farmers, while working according to their own objectives, can also adopt production systems and cultivation practices which meet the needs of the whole society (i.e. optimum production of value-added at the regional level, optimum use of infrastructure, no degradation of natural resources, and so on).

From standard recipes to diverse recommendations

For the past fifteen years, the national agricultural research and extension agencies have focused their attention on the production and dissemination among farmers of standard green revolution 'technical packages'. Because of the cost of their adoption, in so-doing they have fuelled the general process of 'development/elimination' among farmers. At the same time, the agro-industrial boom supported by private sector investment is also reinforcing this mechanism. Following several years of promotion of Farming Systems Research and Extension (FSRE) projects across the country, the importance of regional diagnostic studies and the production of targeted and diversified innovations, designed and tested in close partnership with farmers, is now widely recognised. Unfortunately, the very limited resources available to the research and extension agencies limits their ability to promote a more balanced form of agricultural development. Meanwhile, a powerful private sector, with access to large sums of both domestic and foreign investment capital, a refined grid of contacts from the small village to the factories, ports and airports, and encouraged by successive governemts, is firmly in the driving seat. Because of their multiple roles and activities (input procurement and linkages with markets, trialing the introduction of new technologies, procurement of seasonal credit, 'social security' agents, etc.), the very entrepreunarial village middlemen, mostly Sino-Thai *taokae*, have been the key agents commanding rural transformation nation-wide for the past decades (Trébuil, 1990).

The key role of the regional diagnostic study

To intervene efficiently in agrarian realities in an adapted, co-ordinated and coherent way requires a clear and pertinent knowledge of the target agricultural system and its on-going transformations. In order to obtain such a picture, the following requirements must be met:

(a) It is necessary to know not only the inherited initial state of an agrarian system and be able to characterise precisely the cultivated ecosystem, means of production and mode of exploitation-maintenance of the environment, but also the framework of relations of ownership and exchange as well as the socio-cultural conditions in which it functions;

(b) It is important to know and characterise the new components and changes that have occurred at all these levels because of the adoption of new means and practices and their economic and social implications. It is also fundamental to be able to discern the incomplete, contradictory and possibly negative aspects of these on-going transformations at each of these levels;

(c) In order to get a pertinent judgment of these transformations and to draw up a diagnosis, not only for the present situation but also a prospective one, it is generally necessary to extend the observed trends into the relatively long term, in order to elucidate more clearly the deficiencies and contradictions of the on-going evolution, as well as to evaluate the redress to be operated;

(d) Having characterised in terms of agrarian systems an initial past situation, a present transitory state and a future non-desirable picture, it is recommended to formulate in the same terms the gradual and accessible objectives that will be pursued by the activities and development policies to be implemented;

(e) Regarding these means and policies, they suppose that the conditions and mechanisms which are leading to a non-desirable evolution (for example the wide-scale degradation of soil and water resources) have been perfectly identified and explained. They suppose also that the means to be implemented in order to reach the target objective have been identified, explained and evaluated (adaptation, cost, etc.).

This cannot be achieved without a sharp knowledge of the regional agricultural situation and its recent evolution. Such a diagnostic analysis allows the conception of new conditions to be created so as to steer the evolution of the production systems in a more desirable direction. For example, how can policy-makers and practitioners make sure that a maximum number of farms can remain above a minimum accumulation threshold (Figure 13.5) in order to slow down the rural exodus toward already grotesquelly over-crowed cities?

The answer for the Sathing Phra area was through the improvement of the palm sugar production process, showing that 'minor' crops can locally have a major function! Fuel-saving stoves designed with farmers improved the quality of the final product, the working conditions of mainly female family workers in charge of sap-processing, and doubled the family labour productivity (Trébui and Singrat, 1990). Figure 13.7 shows that this adapted rice-palm sugar system allows the survival of most of the farms in the area by providing a level of productivity and net income higher than that which could be expected from alternative opportunities such as wage-earning in agriculture or the construction sector. Some four hundred families of sugar palm tappers (one-third of the target group of 1,200 households) adopted the new pan-evaporator during the 1986-1990 period only. But even for these production units, the maintenance of the tightly-knit rain-fed lowland rice-sugar palm agro-ecosystem is not yet certain as the young generation is reluctant to continue this tedious cottage industry which is seen as an obstacle to the satisfaction of their new social needs.

The conclusions of the preliminary diagnoses are used to propose not only technical but also socio-economic innovations tailored to the specific capabilities and interests of the majority of less-favoured farmers, in order to direct the local agricultural development process towards the common good. When completed, the diagnosis results help in formulating adapted interventions to improve the sustainability of such less-favoured farmers. In the Kamphaengsaen area, with a value-added of up to 50,000 baht per *rai* (312,500 baht per hectare) as early as the first year (nearly twice that of the best existing cropping system), the introduction of the very labour-intensive production of green asparagus for exports (a crop which can only be harvested manually) was found to be an attractive solution for a majority of very small farmers who had generally become indebted after many years of low-yielding sugar cane cultivation (Figure 13.4). But to gain enough bargaining power against the marketing companies, their organisation into a well-structured producer group was necessary to benefit from this exceptional agronomic potential (Naritoom *et.al.*, 1991).

From a technical point of view, alternative production systems which are fitting farmers' goals and management criteria have to be designed and tested through extensive interaction with the producers concerned. From a socio-economic point of view, the past transformation of agriculture in the area and the current farmer typology point to the conditions to be created and means to be implemented, so as to ensure that a majority of farmers will see their interest lying in the modification of their production systems in a way more consistent with the common good. In the case of the rice-palm sugar system in the south, the initial diagnosis showed that any new palm-sap processing technology must be designed to be adopted at the household level as sugar producers were very reluctant to mix their sap productions an evaporate them on larger co-operative stoves. Confirming the pertinence of the diagnostic phase, a prototype of such a stove, which was more efficient in saving scarce firewood than the smaller one our project designed and extended, was constructed in the area by an NGO based on an introduced normative conception: it has never been used by the farmers! In the case of the Kanchanaburi pioneer frontier, the diagnostic phase showed that local farmers had found a way gradually to move from a system of economic and social dependence on the village middlemen based on annual cash crop production (maize, cotton, sugar cane or cassava) to a more sustainable farming system incorporating plantation crops (cultivated trees replacing the initial mixed deciduous forest), vegetables and sometimes livestock production. It was then found that a policy encouraging more farmers to join this trend could be more effective than efforts strictly to prohibit land clearings in an area

Figure 13.7
Dynamics of Labour Productivity in Sathing Phra Agrarian Systems

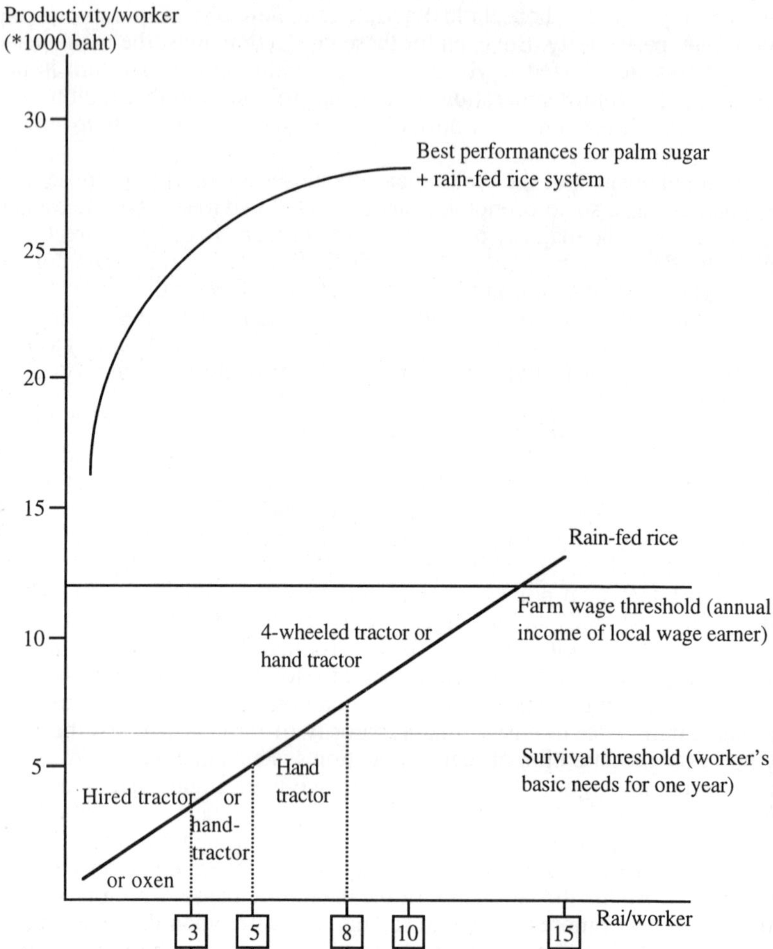

Type of farmer	A	B	C	D
Frequency	60%	20%	15%	5%

receiving a regular flow of new migrants. The role of such diagnostic analysis to define precisely the conditions to be created so that these different interests could converge (firewood saving at the community level and household independence in the production process in the case of the above-mentioned small-scale palm sugar production in the south) is of special importance to guarantee the active participation of a large majority of economic agents towards the improvement of the sustainability of small farmers' production systems.

Actions at all levels of the agrarian system are required

To intervene in such a way in the on-going transformations of agrarian systems in the interests of 'agricultural development', one has to consider actions at different levels:

(a) *At the plot or herd level:* propositions and actions aimed at the improvement of the technical operations of production, itineraries of techniques, cropping or animal-raising systems. The identification of economic sustainability thresholds, at the plot and farm-holding levels, is again of primary importance in order to design viable, but also productive enough alternative systems for the currently less-favoured ones: what to produce, at what level of productivity, and for what level of social needs in order to be able to compete with off-farm opportunities? The role of such new systems is to allow rural people to continue to farm if they see their interest in so-doing. Concerning the example of the introduction of green asparagus in the Kamphaengsaen area, its rapid adoption was due to the fact that, as the initial diagnosis predicted, a majority of small farms was looking for ways to maximise their net income per land unit (Trébuil *et.al.*, 1990);

(b) *At the farm-holding level:* propositions and actions aimed at the improvement of the management of the whole system, which is a combination of its various sub-systems (see the example of the rice-palm sugar association in the Sathing Phra area, or mixed farming in Kanchanaburi province);

(c) Propositions and actions aimed at improvement of the *means of production* (tools, machinery, breeds and varieties, etc.) which also implies the design and testing of the corresponding practices, itineraries and systems (refer back to points a and b);

(d) These new technical means, however, are always costly and their adoption by the production units which do not have them supposes the availability of outside *resources for financing* them: grants, seasonal credit, etc.;

(e) Meanwhile, the cumulative and self-sustained development of a group of farms which are stagnating or in crisis requires the creation of a sufficient and permanent *capacity for self-payment.* Such a capacity cannot completely result from the short-term effects of the actions mentioned in points a and b, and later c and d. The creation of this non-existing, or insufficient, capacity for self-payment usually requires the implementation of a new taxation and pricing policy. Such a policy,

Figure 13.8
Dynamics of Farm Land Used in Tha Sao, Saiyok District, Kanchanaburi Province: Changes Between Current and Future Combinations of Production

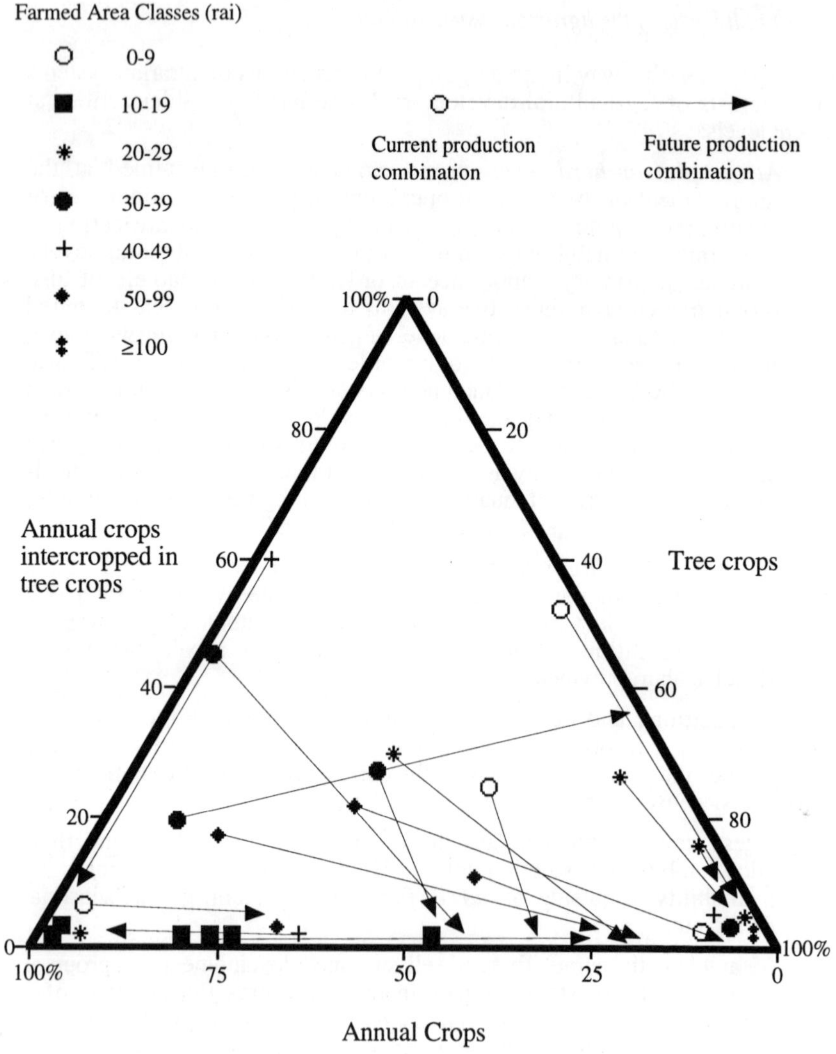

combined with the improvement of marketing conditions, constitutes very often a pre-requisite for the development of these marginal farms;

(f) Finally, stretching and improving the *capacity for production* of the agricultural land cultivated by the farms in crisis frequently constitutes another preliminary measure for their development: land reform and land development schemes ('farm structures' and land development policies). In the Sathing Phra area again, an agronomic survey showed that only better water drainage in the rain-fed lowland paddies during the peak of the wet season could significantly help a majority of the farmers with less than one hectare of land per worker to raise their levels of farm equipment, productive capital and labour productivity in rice. However, past actions have aimed at providing supplementary irrigation, with canals further impeding drainage (Crozat, 1986). Along the cultivated frontier in the Saiyok area of Kanchanaburi, Figure 13.8 shows that a significant number of Mon ethnic farmers (located in the left angle of the triangle) are kept out of the pervasive process of replacement of a first generation of annual cash crops by perennial plantations generally associated with vegetable-growing or livestock-rearing. Only improvements in their formal access to land could make them join this more favourable stream, in terms of community interest in preserving the local natural resources, including here the pest/predator biological balance in the agro-ecosystem, and limit the risk of further deforestation in the area (Trébuil and Dufumier, 1992).

Conclusion

In the present state of Thai agriculture, characterised by an increasingly rapid intra- and inter-regional differentiation among farmers, regional in-depth studies characterising the local conditions of the process of 'development/elimination' or 'modernisation/crisis' among farmers are of paramount importance to improve the current course of local agricultural development. They could lead to a renovation of agricultural policy by looking at decentralised, innovative and diversified ways to initiate a cumulative process of increasing the means of production and economic returns for the majority of farmers in difficulty. By strengthening their capacity for production, such a policy would boost the growth of a rural domestic market by adding an important solvent demand from these farmers. Such a solution to an eventual agrarian crisis that could arise if more and more poor farmers have to leave agriculture and flood the urban (and rural) labour market in the near future, appears also to be a good one for the national economy, which could become less dependent on the outside world in the process. The setting up of Regional Offices for Agricultural Research and Development in the Ministry of Agriculture and Co-operatives could be a way to implement such an innovative approach to regional rural development. But to be effective, such a public agency should receive more government financial support than at present. It is particularly difficult to conceive a better inter-regional distribution of national wealth without voluntary transfers decided by the government for the benefit of poverty-stricken areas to counter-balance the dominant process of 'development/elimination' among farmers - a process that is gradually increasing the pre-existing natural inequalities between regions.

Beyond providing a theoretical framework for such studies, the application of the global concept of Agrarian System also offers the possibility to generate an agricultural development science of its own. It could be used at the newly-established regional universities to articulate an understanding of the current rapid changes occurring in the regional economies with the transformation of local farming systems.

Notes

1 Agrarian system is an historically constituted and durable mode of exploitation of the environment; a technical system adapted to the bioclimatic conditions of a given area and which complies with its social conditions and needs at that moment (Mazoyer, 1985).

14 Who benefits from agricultural extension? 'Training and visit' and the role of rural people's organisations in the upper north of Thailand

Chris Garforth and Paiboon Suthsupa

Agricultural extension in Thailand

Agricultural extension agencies provide advice, information and other support services to farmers to enable them to improve their farming and farm incomes. In developing countries, they are key actors in rural development policy: where a majority of the population relies directly on agriculture for their livelihood, there can be no national economic or social development without development of the agricultural sector. This remains the case for Thailand, despite recent rapid growth in manufacturing employment and output.

Extension agencies are found in the public, commercial and voluntary sectors. Public sector organisations work towards national policy goals, which may include ensuring a supply of basic staple food at a price the urban population can afford, or an increased contribution by agriculture to foreign exchange earnings. There is a continuing debate over equity objectives in public sector extension, reflecting ambiguity over extension priorities (Röling, 1988, pp.93-107): some criticise government extension services for concentrating their efforts (whether by intention or by default) on more affluent, larger-scale farmers with relatively good access to resources; while others argue that this is a legitimate way to achieve national economic and food security objectives.

Commercial entities such as tobacco and cotton companies are guided by profit considerations and will seek to achieve high quality standards in the crops reaching their processing plants, and an assured level of production to meet plant and market capacity. The voluntary sector, comprising a large number of non-government development organisations (NGDOs) ranging widely in size, scope and ideology, has the welfare of the farm family at the centre of its concern. Agencies in all three sectors seek to achieve their objectives by influencing the farming decisions and practices of large numbers of rural households. The extension methods they use range from individual farm visits to demonstrations, other group-focused activities and the mass media (Garforth, 1995). A major (though not exclusive) preoccupation is with making available to farmers information and technology derived from agricultural research.

In Thailand, the most significant publicly-funded extension services are those of the Ministry of Agriculture and Co-operatives (MOAC). Of its nine major departments, the Department of Agricultural Extension (DAE) offers a nation-wide service dealing mainly with arable crops. It operates through a cadre of front-line extension workers, the *kaset tambon*, who are supported by supervisory and specialist technical staff at *amphoe* and *changwat* level. The Departments of Livestock, Fisheries, Land Development and Co-operatives Promotion provide services in respect of animal husbandry, fish raising, land development and the organisation and management of co-operatives respectively, with their front-line staff based at *amphoe* level. The Tobacco Monopoly operates extension services for tobacco growers while the Rubber Replanting Aid Fund provides extension support for rubber growers under replanting schemes. Sugar factories offer extension services to farmers growing sugar cane under contract.

There are other government departments whose work with rural households also draws them into offering agricultural advice and services. These include the Community Development Department of the Ministry of the Interior, the Ministry of Defence (which assists former military personnel to establish agricultural enterprises in border areas), the Royal Forest Department (which works with hill-tribe communities as part of its efforts towards forest and watershed conservation in upland areas) and the Royal Irrigation Department. Efforts are made to co-ordinate these, or at least share information, through *changwat*-level committees.

Problems with extension pre-1980

During the 1970s, as government policy sought to boost agricultural production and exports as key elements in economic growth, a number of weaknesses became apparent in the operation of MOAC extension services. Extension's impact on farmers' practices and resource management, and therefore on yields, overall production and the standards of living of rural households, was limited. This was seen as a major constraint to economic and rural development. Among the various weaknesses identified, three in particular were targeted by subsequent reforms.

Inadequate and ineffective contact between farmers and extension agents

A critical variable in extension work is the amount of productive time spend by extension officers in direct contact with rural producers. In the Thai context extension officers at *amphoe* and *tambon* level carried the main task of face-to face communication with farmers, which they did mainly through responding to requests from individual farmers and by visiting them in their homes or on their farms. It was not possible for them to serve the whole rural population directly in this way because each extension officer had an average of 4,400 farm families in his or her area of operation. One consequence was the tendency to concentrate their attention on a few influential farmers who had relatively good access to resources. Moreover, the small-scale nature of farming (average land holding per rural household was less than 5 hectares) meant that time spent in contact with an individual producer inevitably gave a limited return because, unless there was a significant transfer of information and advice from the individual to others who were not in direct contact with the extension officer, only a small area or output could be influenced directly by the extension officer's advice. The effective use of extension officers' time was further eroded by a heavy load of administrative and other non-extension duties: as in many other countries, field-level extension staff were seen as convenient instruments for a wide variety of tasks from collecting survey data to securing repayment of bank loans.

Weak linkage between extension and research

Extension and research agencies need to keep in close contact with each other. If they do not, researchers may remain ignorant of farmers' needs while extension officers, although in contact with the farmers, may not have the necessary knowledge, without the researchers' assistance, to offer appropriate advice. Over-departmentalisation of the Thai government bureaucracy left extension and research institutionally and professionally separate, with researchers tending to concentrate on their own theoretical concerns rather than on problems of practical relevance to farmers.

Insufficient training

Most front-line extension officers were graduates from the agricultural vocational schools where they spent only three years in general education. The curriculum did not cover agricultural subjects to any adequate depth. Consequently extension staff had insufficient basic knowledge of agriculture either to advise farmers or even to keep abreast of latest research developments. In addition many were from urban backgrounds and lacked the practical experience which is needed to gain the confidence of farmers.

Two responses to these short-comings were a major investment in upgrading the quantity and quality of extension work, particularly in the crops sector through the DAE, and an increasing focus on working with and through local farmers' (and other) organisations. The remainder of this chapter considers how far these two initiatives have succeeded in spreading the benefits of agricultural extension more widely.

The National Agricultural Extension Project

In common with many countries in Asia, Thailand introduced the Training and Visit (T&V) system of agricultural extension within the DAE in the late 1970s, initially on a pilot basis in selected *changwat* and later, under the National Agricultural Extension Project (NAEP), throughout the country. Promoted by the World Bank through its lending activities in the agricultural sector, T&V was intended to increase the flow of relevant advice and information to farmers by a programme of regular training for *kaset tambon* and a closely-monitored schedule of visits to selected 'contact farmers' who were expected to pass on advice and information to other farmers in their community (Benor, Harrison and Baxter, 1984). NAEP involved a reorganisation of the structure and functions of the extension system and an increase in the number and capability of extension personnel in order to expand the volume and quality of extension activities. More than 8,000 college and university graduates have been recruited into the service since 1977, 70 per cent of them as *kaset tambon*. The ratio of extension officers to farm families has risen to 1:1000.

Under NAEP, the *kaset tambon* in each *amphoe* are trained at a fortnightly training session. Topical issues (known as 'impact points') and relevant recommendations provide the focus for these sessions. Other staff, such as training officers, and subject-matter specialists at *changwat* and *amphoe* level (see below), are given training at annual refresher courses, monthly workshops and occasional seminars, to enhance their technical knowledge and practical skills in analysing farmers' needs and problems. Staff development, through higher education and special skills training, is important to enable the extension service system to cope with changing social, economic and technological circumstances. With NAEP funding, many staff have undergone advanced courses in domestic and overseas institutions.

In order to establish a closer linkage between agricultural research institutions and the extension service, researchers and extension personnel participate in monthly extension workshops. These are an opportunity for the participants to review the current situation in farmers' fields and their reactions to previous advice, and then to identify appropriate impact points for the next rounds of fortnightly training sessions. Subject matter specialists in various disciplines have been appointed, whose job description includes conducting adaptive research, liaising with research institutes and training extension staff as well as giving technical back-up to field level officers.

In the field, each *kaset tambon* is responsible for about 10 villages and is expected to visit some 100 contact farmers on a regular fortnightly schedule. Those selected as contact farmers are supposed to be innovative, respected by neighbouring farmers and willing to disseminate new ideas and technology to other farmers.

T&V has had a major impact on the organisation and management of agricultural extension in Thailand. In terms of the weaknesses identified in the previous section, the amount of contact between extension agents and farmers has increased, functions have been clarified and streamlined, competencies improved through training, and links with research strengthened. However while recognising these benefits, commentators on T&V have criticised the system on three main grounds (Hulme, 1991), all of which can be applied to the Thai experience: limited socio-economic impact, a rigid and authoritarian approach to management, and non-sustainability.

The T&V system in Thailand does not address structural causes of rural poverty and inequity, which are rooted in access to land and to political and economic power. Indeed, in some respects it reinforces them when, for example, village headmen (*phu yai ban*) are selected as contact farmers. As Turton (1987) observes, the rural élite use their privileged position of access to government programmes and services to extend their influence over the rural population. This is probably one of the reasons for the weak flow of information from contact to other farmers (Suthasupa, 1983; Damrongkiattisak, 1984) as high-status farmers either deliberately, or through lack of effort and opportunity, fail to act as a link between extension services and 'non-contact' farmers. The phenomenon of the "communication effects gap" (Shingi and Mody, 1976) also highlights the potential effects of increasing the availability of technical information and the means of disseminating it within communities where the distribution of productive resources and of political power is inherently skewed. By treating production and rural livelihoods entirely as technical issues, to be improved by speeding up the flow of technical information and advice to rural households, the system almost guarantees that those with more land, more capital and more influence will be the main beneficiaries.

The hierarchical and bureaucratic structures of the DAE do not in practice facilitate the two-way flow of information that is supposed to be at the heart of T&V. Relevant technologies or 'messages' are identified by regional committees dominated by research scientists and then passed on to farmers through the programme of in-service training and regular visits to contact farmers. Impact points tend to be repetitive and insufficiently tailored to specific local circumstances or farming systems. In response to this inflexibility, efforts have been made in recent years to adjust the extension approach to take more account of the variability in farming systems and to enable *kaset tambon* to respond more effectively to the needs and priorities expressed by their farmer clients.

Doubts have been cast on the sustainability of the system now that the full costs have to be met from the government's own resources (in addition to the burden of paying back the World Bank loan from which most of the costs of the NAEP were met). Recurrent costs of the system are high, with much of the extension budget taken up by salaries and little to spare for operational costs. The number of visits to contact farmers has had to be restricted, training sessions and other events often fail to happen because of shortage of funds, and extension staff mobility has been curtailed.

These observations are by no means unique to Thailand. The need for greater flexibility, local responsibility and financial sustainability is now generally acknowledged (World Bank, 1990; FAO, 1990). It is in this context, as well as in response to the shortcomings of the contact farmer approach, that the potential for a greater role in agricultural extension for rural people's organisations has attracted interest.

Extension and Rural People's Organisations

The active involvement of members of rural communities in decision-making is widely recognised as a pre-requisite for achieving development that meets local needs with a measure of equity. An institutional structure is needed within communities to allow this to happen and, where existing structures do not adequately serve the purpose, it is seen as a legitimate concern of development intervention to promote the formation of local organisations (Cernea, 1991). Consequently extension agencies in the government, voluntary and commercial sectors have frequently expressed interest in working with and through local organisations of rural people (Garforth, 1990). Models have ranged from representative committees of farmers who assist field-level extension workers in planning local extension programmes and activities, to groups of farmers who come together to engage in a joint activity for which they can secure external resources (Curtis, 1991). The reasons for this interest fall broadly into five headings.

Efficiency

By meeting farmers in groups, it is assumed that an extension worker can contact and influence more farmers than by contacting them individually. For extension agencies that are trying to reduce staffing levels, or to increase the impact of extension without recruiting more staff, this is an attractive argument (Garforth, 1982; Swanson, 1994). It leaves open, however, questions of quality of contact and of the access to groups of those who have previously had little contact with extension.

Effectiveness

Interaction among farmers in a group (whether permanent or temporary) can speed up learning, acceptance, attitude change and adoption of new ideas. Similarly, problem identification, diagnosis and screening of possible solutions will benefit from the exchange of several points of view in a group setting where consensus can be reached (Hayward, 1990; Chambers *et.al.*, 1989). Where actions to improve agricultural production or the management of natural resources need to be taken collectively rather than simply on individual farms (for example in rodent control, watershed conservation and community forestry), this is more likely to happen when there is a local organisation which can make decisions, organise action and mobilise local resources (Martin and Yoder, 1987; Tippenawar, 1990).

Equity

Rural people's access to extension services varies considerably. For many reasons, rural women have relatively poor access, even in areas where a high proportion of women farm in their own right and most agricultural work is done by women. Under T&V, women and resource-poor households are not well represented among contact farmers. By encouraging the formation of homogenous groups of various categories of client (Sen, 1992), or by working with existing groups with different memberships, it is argued that extension workers can serve a wider spectrum of clients more equitably and target extension support to disadvantaged categories of rural people (Uphoff, 1984; Röling, 1988).

Demand orientation

Farmer organisations can provide a structure for ensuring extension becomes demand-driven (responding to the needs and problems and potential of farmers as articulated by them within their groups) rather than supply-driven (delivering pre-determined 'messages' or technology). These can be formally elected farmers' committees which meet with an extension worker to plan extension programmes, or less formal groups which the extension worker consults to find out local needs and priorities.

Those who see poverty and disadvantage as an inevitable consequence of a lack of economic, social and political power argue that through their own groups and organisations, disadvantaged rural people can find a voice and economic influence to confront the structures and processes that sustain their disadvantaged position. This reasoning has been an important element in the motivation and methodology of NGDOs working in rural development and poverty alleviation in Thailand and elsewhere (Oakley et.al., 1990; Turton, 1987).

Thailand has a rich history of rural people's organisations (RPOs) in the agricultural sector. Some pre-date the emergence of the modern Thai state, such as the *muang fai* irrigation associations which, for centuries, have created and managed stream diversion irrigation systems (Surarerks, 1986). These have developed procedures, rules and sanctions to ensure that water is delivered to all members' fields and that the physical structures (weirs and canals) are maintained. Similar associations are still being formed (with support and encouragement from government agencies) as small-scale irrigation schemes are developed through local initiative, independently from the major schemes for which the Royal Irrigation Department is responsible (Box 14.1).

Box 14.1
Chaisombat Irrigation Association

The *tambon* council of Wiangchai *tambon*, *amphoe* Wiangchai, *changwat* Chiang Rai, arranged the building of a dam in 1963 on the Mae Ta Sai by the farmers of the *tambon*, replacing a temporary structure built the previous year which was destroyed by monsoon rains. Over the next 13 years, a network of secondary canals and subsidiary dams, fed by the 30 kilometre main canal, was developed using local labour. Eventually, 1,821 families in 20 villages had land totalling 19,798 *rai* (3,130 hectares) served by the system. The money for this was raised locally. In 1982, the Royal Irrigation Department (RID) stepped in to fund the building of a new dam. Four years later, the Department provided funds for the lining of part of the main canal to reduce water loss and improve efficiency of water distribution. Members still provide a large part of the labour for these new structures and improvements.

The Chaisomabat Irrigation Association was formed by the farmers served by the system in 1963. By 1982, the Association was divided into 42 local water-users groups, one representative from each of which sits on the executive committee of the Association. Members pay an annual fee for each *rai* of land connected to the system. A condition of continued membership is contribution of labour for annual maintenance and repair, and non-attendance at regular groups meetings attracts a fine. The Association is regarded by MOAC and RID as a successful example of farmers' self-help, which government is able to support with technical advice and with financial contributions towards the further development and improvement of the system.

Others are more recent creations, including agricultural co-operatives based on European models which were introduced early in the twentieth century to stimulate savings and the collective purchase of inputs among rural producers. Although nominally independent of government, the co-operatives have in practice been heavily dependent on government support. After a series of legislative changes, there are now primary co-operatives in each *amphoe*, federated at *changwat* and national levels, with *tambon*-level sub-groups providing an internal structure for the election of officers and the day-to-day running of society business. Commodity-specific farmers groups have been established, with varying degrees of formality and legal recognition, to serve particular local interests. Examples range from cattle-owners' groups set up at the instigation of the Department of Livestock as a vehicle for distributing improved breeding stock or of developing improved pasture, and the housewives' groups established by the DAE as a means of bringing extension support to rural women, to spontaneous groups formed to deal with a specific issue (Box 14.2). Village savings societies have enabled even the poorest families to build up sufficient capital and to gain access to loans for investment in agricultural activities (Box 14.3). More rare have been politically-active farmers' movements whose goal has been to represent rural producers within the political process or to campaign on specific aspects of government policy of concern to farmers. The fate of the Farmers Federation of Thailand, which collapsed after its leadership was purged by government in the late 1970s (Grace, 1981), has done little to encourage further attempts to build political pressure groups among rural producers.

Box 14.2
Mao Tao Klang Farmers Group

The group began when Song Muang Nga, a 55-year-old rice farmer, asked a number of relatives and neighbours in 1971 if they would join him in selling their rice together. The immediate stimulus was the low rice price. With 30 farmers taking part in the scheme, Song negotiated a price for the bulk sale 15 per cent higher than was being paid to individual producers. Some of the profits were used to build a rice silo so that paddy could be stored until prices went up later in the season, and also to buy up rice from other farmers. After five years the group shared out the accumulated funds.

Song then initiated a more formal group in 1975, with 60 farmer contributing 1,050 baht each. He asked the Community Developmen Department for advice on legal and procedural matters, and the group bega offering loans to members. Later in 1975, the group was formally registere with the *kaset amphoe*. There are now over 100 members and the group's mai activities are giving loans to members and bulk purchase of agricultural input for resale to members at reasonable prices.

Song is aware of the value of close liaison with the *kaset tambon* and *kase amphoe*. He persuaded the group to help finance the building of the *kase tambon* office, on land which Song donated. Although he is no longe chairman, he is still a powerful moral force within the group.

Box 14.3
Mao Tao Klang Savings for Production Group

The group had its origins in a savings group which was set up in 1977 in a neighbouring village, after initial suggestions from an officer of the Community Development Department. Two people from Mae Tao Klang joined, and then left in 1980, dissatisfied with the way the group was being run. They suggested to a village council meeting that a savings group be set up in Mae Tao Klang. The Community Development Department was asked to give advice and the group was formed. At first 60 households joined. By 1988 membership had grown to 260 - 70 per cent of the households in the village. The group runs its own affairs, only asking for outside help if they have a problem they cannot resolve or feel they need professional advice. Members bring their savings each month. These are deposited in a bank in Mae Sod. A sub-committee scrutinises and decides on members' applications for loans, which are only given for agricultural purposes. In the 12 months May 1987 to April 1988, 600,000 baht was loaned, representing a year's savings of almost 200 baht average per month for the 260 member households.

Meanwhile, the group in the neighbouring village has declined to a point where it no longer functions. Members insisted on withdrawing their savings because they were dissatisfied with the leadership and management of the group.

Within this variety of organisations and experience, elements of all five sets of arguments in favour of working with RPOs can be found in the expressed policies of extension agencies. Indeed, for over 25 years, it has been Thai government policy to promote RPOs in the interests of agricultural development. The Second National Development Plan (1967-1971) had as a specific objective the promotion of "agricultural institutions, such as farmers associations, cooperatives, people's irrigation associations, and young farmers' associations, so that these institutions can represent the farmers and express their interests" (quoted in Johnson, 1969). More recently, since the rise and fall of the Farmers Federation of Thailand in the 1970s, rural institutions have been seen more as an efficient means of maintaining contact with and providing services for the large number of small-scale farming enterprises in Thailand. The main priorities for the MOAC have been the efficient diffusion of agricultural information and technology, the distribution of inputs, mobilisation of local resources and administration of farm credit. In the past few years, partly as a response to the high recurrent cost of the T&V system, field-level extension officers have been encouraged to work as much as possible through organised groups of clients. By the mid-1980s, Chirapanda (1986) estimated that from a national total of 4.5 million farm families, 2.6 million people were members of RPOs which were active in the agricultural sector.

In order to find out whether the anticipated benefits of working with RPOs are being realised, the Universities of Reading and Chiang Mai conducted research into the interaction between extension agencies and RPOs in the Upper North of Thailand, between 1988 and 1992. The main aim was to identify lessons which might help RPOs or extension agencies increase their impact on agricultural development. In this context, agricultural development was seen in terms of equity and security of livelihoods as much as agricultural production and innovation.

Previous research on RPOs in Thailand has been specific to a village or part of an *amphoe* (e.g. Judd, 1977: 1987; Moerman, 1968), specific to a particular type of organisation (e.g. Surarerks, 1986), case studies of single organisations (e.g. Saiprasert *et.al.*, 1985) or concerned with a specific client group (e.g. Turton's (1987) study of organisations for poor farmers). The Reading-Chiang Mai study was concerned with the contribution of RPOs in general and so encompassed all local-level organisations of rural people which were engaged in activities relevant to agricultural development. This is a very broad category, including savings associations promoted by the Community Development Department of the Ministry of the Interior, which mobilise local resources for investment in private income-earning activities, and ex-soldiers' associations which help retired service personnel establish new agricultural enterprises, as well as farmers' associations and the local branches of agricultural co-operatives.

The study[1] began with a series of interviews with the *kaset changwat* (provincial agricultural officers) in the nine *changwat* of the Upper North, on the role and activities of RPOs in their area and their views on the effectiveness of RPOs as instruments of agricultural development. These were followed by a postal questionnaire to all *amphoe*-level officers of MOAC departments, asking for basic information on each RPO in their *amphoe*. Officers reported almos 6,500 RPOs and provided data on 4,968. The final stage of the first phase o the study was the collection of detailed information on RPOs in a sample of 28 (out of 94) *amphoe*. This was done by a team of research assistants, with th help of key informants at village, *tambon* and *amphoe* levels.

During discussions at *changwat* and *amphoe* level, a basic distinctio emerged between RPOs which were formally registered with a governmen department (just over half) and supported by extension staff, those which wer linked to commercial companies or to NGDOs, and independent groups whic had emerged without any initiative from an outside agency. Of the registere RPOs, by far the largest category (42 per cent) were housewives' groups followed by young farmers or '4H'[2] groups (19 per cent). Only 15 per cent o the registered RPOs were described as farmers' groups - despite the view o *kaset amphoe* and *kaset changwat* that the main purpose of working with RPO is to speed up the transfer of agricultural technology to farmers. Among th unregistered RPOs was a lower proportion of housewives and 4H groups an more enterprise-specific farmers' groups.

The more detailed collection of data in sample *amphoe* brought to light man more RPOs than had been recorded in *amphoe*-level questionnaires: more tha one in three of the 2,877 had not been identified at the earlier stage. The exter of government involvement with RPOs - including unregistered ones - was clear: government staff were instrumental in the formation of 78 per cent. Outside support had been received by 83 per cent, with advice and training mentioned much more frequently than material inputs and finance. Some RPOs seemed to have no real existence apart from their relationship with the agency which supported them, meeting only when called together by an extension officer.

The main objectives of RPOs were seen as the improvement of members' incomes and giving them better access to scientific and technical knowledge. Credit disbursement, management of a group or community facility, welfare and social activities were also mentioned frequently. The activities reported for RPOs reflect these objectives, with training and practice in agriculture the most common.

In the second phase of the research, case studies explored processes of formation and subsequent development of RPOs in more detail, to identify factors which influence the sustainability of RPOs, analyse the links between RPOs and extension agencies and assess the effects of membership on households' access to agricultural resources (including advice, information and training). These studies revealed an even larger number and variety of RPOs than had emerged in the *tambon*-level data collection. In *amphoe* Mae Sod, for example, which had been described by the Tak *kaset changwat* as having a relatively low and unsuccessful level of RPO activity, a total of 95 separate organisations was identified in ten villages with a population of 2,636 households. Of these RPOs, 38 had a direct relevance to agricultural development - a ratio of one RPO for every 69 households (Garforth *et.al.*, 1993).

Despite this plethora of RPOs, their membership did not cover all farming households. Some RPOs are in principle open to all households in the community (housewives and 4H groups, for example), though not all choose to join or to take part in group activities. Others are restrictive in membership by the very nature of their activities or membership criteria. Some farmers' associations, for example, set a minimum farm size or the possession of specified farm equipment as membership criteria. Co-operatives and paddy farmers' groups in Payao were inaccessible or unattractive to most farmers partly because of the requirement to buy shares or pay membership fees and partly because the *tambon*-level of organisation was perceived as too remote. In Tak, members of RPOs tend to come from households of greater wealth and income than non-members. Generally, RPOs which are organised around a productive activity or enterprise have memberships which do not reflect the composition of the communities in which they are found.

Membership patterns may also reflect ethnic differences. In a village in *amphoe* Mae Sod, *changwat* Tak, a group of 22 bamboo shoot growers (a new enterprise in the village) had formed an association and were receiving advice and inputs from the *kaset amphoe*. Although a majority of households in the village were of hilltribe origin, 20 of the group members were ethnic Thai.[3]

Restricted membership of individual RPOs does not necessarily mean that a policy of working through RPOs will discriminate against certain categories of rural household. It is the overall pattern of membership across all RPO types that is important. To some extent, the variety of RPOs does cater for a wide cross-section of rural households. While resource poor households tend not to be members of agricultural co-operatives; for example, they do join savings groups through which they can gain access to small amounts of capital to invest in agricultural activities. However, the fact remains that households whose members belong to RPOs enjoy on average a higher material standard of living than those without RPO members. While some might attribute this to the effect of membership on household income, the case study evidence suggests that it is households with relatively high levels of wealth and income which are more likely to become RPO members in the first place.

Official membership lists may mask the pattern of involvement in RPO activity. Recently formed livestock groups in *changwat* Tak, for example, consisted of a list of livestock owners drawn up by the *phu yai ban* and submitted to the livestock extension officer without consulting those whose names were on the list; and in Payao, some village housewives groups had all households listed as members, through payment of a subscription, although poorer households tended not to take part in the groups' activities.

Evidence from the case studies supports the efficiency argument fo working with RPOs. In *amphoe* Mae Sod, RPOs clearly provided a structure for efficient communication between key individuals and extension agencies and between RPO leaders and members. Many farm households had more access to information, advice and training than they would if they had not been members of RPOs. On the other hand, members tended to be those who already had better access to sources of agricultural expertise external to their village members were more likely to derive benefits from agricultural radio and television broadcasts than non-members; while non-members did not make up for their relative lack of access to advice from extension agents by making more use of media sources (Garforth *et.al.*, 1993).

Box 14.4
Ban Kued Sam Tha Fishery Group

The first move towards the formation of the fishery group came from th amphoe fisheries officer who came to meet the *phu yai ban* and the villag council. He then came to a meeting of the whole village and told them about th department's programme of supporting communal fish ponds for the raising c fish. Those who attended that meeting were considered to be members of th group, with the *phu yai ban* as chairman. Later, when construction of the pon began, others joined. The group has not yet found a way of resolving conflic over the practice of stealing water from the pond and although a system c maintaining and protecting the pond by group members has been set up, it is n working satisfactorily yet.

Political factors within the community, and in particular the role of the *ph yai ban*, are crucial to the successful establishment and long-term impact RPOs. A rice farmers group in *changwat* Nan, for example, was in danger collapsing because local political pressure had forced the committee to advan fertilizer on credit to non-members who then refused to pay back the advance he nature of Thai rural communities and the authority structure within them ake the support, and preferably the active involvement, of the *phu yai ban* vital 3ox 14.4). Some extension officers go to the extreme of assuming that the *phu ai ban* or his/her spouse must be the leader of each RPO formed in the village. his may work against the involvement of a wide cross-section of households. Payao, poorer farmers preferred to belong to RPOs where the leadership was ss tied to formal village structures. In the Bank for Agriculture and gricultural Co-operatives (BAAC) credit groups, for example, leadership otated among the members with external supervision of loans carried out by AAC loan officers. Under pressure to reduce costs, however, the Bank has ore recently reduced the number of loan officers and given responsibility for an supervision to formal village and *tambon* leaders.

In every RPO which was regarded by its members and extension officers as eing successful, there was a key individual whose vision, enthusiasm and ommitment to the RPO had been conveyed to others and which continued to istain the organisation. In some cases, this was the *phu yai ban* or a local xtension officer. In most cases, however, it was not. Indeed, with frequent aff transfers, reliance on the personality of the extension officer makes the PO liable to collapse when that person leaves the area (a frequent problem for H groups); while the *phu yai ban* has to represent so many interest groups that s or her whole-hearted commitment to a single RPO may be compromised.

Differences emerged between extension officers and RPO members in their erception of success and failure, reflecting different views of the benefits and irpose of RPO formation. This was particularly the case with housewives' oups: MOAC staff saw these as failures if there was no sustained productive tivity and little evident impact on household incomes, while members saw iccess in terms of group unity, caring for one another and the ability to share ew experiences and new knowledge with each other (Goldey, 1990). Internal oup dynamics and the quality of relationships within the RPO were seen by embers as more important indicators and explanations of the success or failure RPOs than the nature and degree of support provided by outside agencies.

For many RPOs, particularly those formed around an agricultural enterprise productive activity, access to credit was one of the main factors which ought members together. For some farmers' associations and the BAAC oups, this involved access to external sources of credit while for savings oups the emphasis was on mobilising members' savings for lending within e group. Successful credit organisations have gone on to provide other rvices to members. In *amphoe* Samoeng, *changwat* Chiang Mai, credit unions small-scale farmers which formed with the encouragement of an integrated iral development project in the area have branched out into the organisation of aining and other activities.

External credit has proved a mixed blessing, with many farmers' groups iling because members have defaulted on loans from banks or the MOAC, or ecause inputs supplied by the group to members on credit were never paid for. *changwat* Nan, for example, extension officers claimed that of the several addy farmers' groups registered with the MOAC, none could any longer be garded as functioning. They had been set up with encouragement from the IOAC to be a channel for the provision of technical and business advice and of iputs. From the members' point of view, the provision of inputs on favourable terms was by far the most important reason for joining. Conversely, fear of becoming indebted was the most common reason given for not becoming members of farmers' group. The high level of defaulting on input loans can be explained partly by farmers' attitudes towards hand-outs from government agencies.

Conclusions: who benefits?

Of the five sets of arguments for working with and through RPOs reviewed above, three are supported by the evidence of the Reading-Chiang Mai study. Efforts by the MOAC to improve the efficiency, effectiveness and demand-orientation of its extension services has benefited from the existence of RPOs, and from the ministry's policy of encouraging their formation. In view of the current pressures facing the T&V system in Thailand, this is an encouraging finding. Field staff are able to spend a higher proportion of their time in productive extension activity; and communication with RPO leaders seems to be more efficient in terms of linking extension officers with communication networks within rural communities than relying on T&V's individual contact farmers. RPOs provide a forum where training is conducted, and where the local identification of extension priorities takes place. Where extension staff have productive resources to make available under specific projects, such as crop protection equipment, distributing them to RPOs has made them accessible to relatively large numbers of farmers.

It is also clear that members of rural communities in northern Thailand perceive benefits from forming or joining RPOs. Households use RPOs to help them respond to external changes in their environments by enhancing access to productive resources, to income and market opportunities and to the benefits of common property. The nature and extent of this access varies with the resource base of the community, the socio-economic strata of households and the degree of security of access which RPOs can assure.

MOAC policy, however, has also reinforced patterns of exclusion from extension services. This is perhaps not surprising, since equity has not been a specific objective in the MOAC's efforts to promote the formation of RPOs. No particular attempts have been made to target extension support towards resource-poor households. By contrast, the Community Development Department has been relatively successful in encouraging poorer households to participate in the formation of Savings for Production groups. The activities and benefits of these groups are attractive to those who do not find institutional credit or co-operative society membership a viable option; and Community Development field staff have specific training in facilitating and supporting group development.

A policy of promoting and working through RPOs does seem to offer the potential of greater efficiency and effectiveness in the provision of agricultural advice, training and information. This may, however, be at the expense of equity. Where equity is a policy objective, it will be important either to suppo the formation of groups and organisations specifically for resource-poor client (or at least ones which do not discriminate against them in their membershi criteria, structures and procedures), or to retain some proportion of extension activity which continues outside the RPO focus.

There was little evidence of empowerment through RPOs which were closely linked to government or NGDO agencies; nor was this an express objective in promoting RPO formation, even among NGDOs active in the area. However the case of the Mao Tao Klang farmers group (Box 14.2) demonstrates how collective action by farmers can enhance their economic power *vis à vis* the middlemen who buy the output of their farms.

One should not ignore the learning opportunities represented by the experience of RPOs. This was seen clearly in *changwat* Payao, in reactions to the limitations of formally registered housewives groups. Poorer households saw these as exclusive and expensive to participate in, and too cumbersome in their structures and procedures. In one neighbourhood, women from poorer households who were disenchanted with the housewives' group formed a local savings group. The members lived in close proximity to one another and the group required only small amounts of their time because they were not trading, cultivating or attending training sessions as a group. More important were the fact that they trusted each other because they had all shared in this learning experience, and the fact that they had formed the group themselves which had created a strong sense of ownership and self-confidence.

RPOs in northern Thailand are more likely to have emerged and survived when there has been:

(i) a problem or opportunity, whose solution or exploitation could be more effectively realised through collective action;

(ii) a respected individual who took the initiative and then continued to sustain the process of RPO formation;

(iii) a supportive political environment within the village;

(iv) a general commitment in the village to the well-being of the community as a whole, or, within a particular set of households, for the well-being of that set.

The scope for agencies to create these conditions where they do not exist is obviously limited - which is another reason for being cautious about policies which exclude contacts other than with or through RPOs. Households in villages with weak or disputed leadership, for example, will suffer if extension agents are discouraged from working with individuals. At the same time, where RPO formation is an important plank in an agency's policy, agents must take some initiative to increase the rate of formation. Through informal discussions, or a more formal problem census, agents can stimulate the articulation of problems and the recognition of unexploited potential. With the assistance of the *phu yai ban* and others, they can identify individuals who could take the initiative in forming RPOs. The agents would then need to work closely with those individuals to give them the support and encouragement they need, as well as any technical or material inputs which might be appropriate. They can also spend time gaining the confidence of local leaders so that political support for RPO initiatives will be forthcoming - and avoid losing support by making promises or commitments which cannot be met. Where members of new RPOs have little experience of running the affairs of a group, particularly where money is involved, agencies should be prepared to work with them for an extended period, adjusting the level and nature of support to the increasing self-confidence and expertise of the RPO's members and committee (Box 14.5).

In turn, extension agents require training in these process skills, to complement their technical knowledge and their expertise in more directive extension methodology. Training is needed in group approaches to extension, in strategies for fostering sustainable and independent RPOs, and in interpersonal communication skills. Where such training is not available, it is not surprising if a large number of RPOs formed at the instigation of extension agents falter in their early stages, either because the members see no real reason for their existence, or because those nominated or identified as leaders of an RPO have no real commitment to its future.

Box 14.5
Ban Pa Lan Credit Union Group

Ban Pa Lan is a village in *tambon* Samoeng Neu-ah, *amphoe* Samoeng, *changwat* Chiang Mai. An integrated rural development project was begun in the *amphoe* in 1975 by the Friedrich Naumann Foundation (FNF) in co-operation with Thai government agencies. A major element in the design and implementation of the project was that it should stimulate the ability of the families and communities of the *amphoe* to take the initiative in their own development. In keeping with this principle, the project encouraged the formation of credit unions, following the pattern established by the Credit Union League of Thailand (CULT).

The Ban Pa Lan group was set up in 1977 after discussions between a FNF project 'motivator' and people in the village, with 19 members and an initial capital from members' savings of 3,000 baht. Ten years later, membership had grown to 87 and the revolving fund from which loans are financed stood at approximately 200,000 baht. New legislation meant that the group became part of a *tambon*-level federation in 1981 which was formally registered as a credit union co-operative. The group opened a store in 1982 but closed in 1986 because some members who had taken goods on credit did not pay back. Initially, a member needed two guarantors in order to be given a loan from the group's fund. However, because of a lack of responsibility among some members, the group now insists on collateral for all loans. Money is not intended for long-term investments and loans are to be repaid in full within eight months, in order to maximise the rate at which funds can be recycled as further loans.

Although the group manages its own affairs, it relies on government officials for financial advice and auditing of the accounts. The early years of the group saw a phased withdrawal of support from the FNF: the motivator visited the group at every monthly meeting for the first five years, reducing this to every second month and then to twice a year by 1984.

With the future of publicly-funded extension under threat in many countries (Rivera and Gustafson, 1991) and T&V systems facing budgetary pressures extension agencies in Thailand need to become more cost-effective. At the same time, if they are to contribute to the wider social and economic development goals of the country, they need to take account of the equity implications of their activities. Working with existing RPOs, and encouraging the formation of new ones particularly among disadvantaged rural households, can make a significant contribution. It will require, however, a change in emphasis in the training of extension officers and a willingness to fit extension support and advice to the needs and circumstances of RPO memberships.

Notes

1 A full account of the methodology and findings of the first phase of the study is given in Garforth and Munro (1994), and the final report of the study can be found in Garforth (1994).

2 These are clubs for young people (in Thailand, the maximum age is 21 years) the model for which originated in the USA. The four 'H's are the head, health, hands and heart of the individual members which provide the resources as well as the purpose of the club.

3 Most members of this group formerly made their living partly by collecting wild bamboo shoots from the surrounding forest. As supplies of wild shoots were becoming increasingly scarce, one of them had begun to experiment with the cultivation of young bamboo plants brought from the forest to his farm. It was his approach to the *kaset amphoe* for advice that led to the formation of the association.

Conclusion: Future paths toward development in Thailand

Michael J. G. Parnwell

This volume has highlighted a number of areas where 'uneven development' is manifest in contemporary Thailand. Whether we look at the spatial economy or political economy, the pattern or industrialisation or the process of rural transformation, Thailand has come to epitomise uneven development.

In the main, the contributors to this volume have steered clear of making value judgements of the material they have presented (refer Chapter 1, pp.2-3: Lummis, 1992). Up to a point this is to be commended. With the possible exception of the Thai contributors, whose inside perspective on domestic development carries some weight and justification, none of us can claim the moral high ground from which to judge what we observe occurring in Thailand today. The manifestations and degree of inequality may be different, but our own mostly Western societies have no lack of familiarity with the phenomenon and process of uneven development. Additionally, there is no universally accepted blueprint for the 'ideal' society, were such a thing achievable, and of the best way of proceeding towards such a society. We should also not underplay the positive aspects of Thailand's recent economic transformation. In the face of strong global competition, Thailand has achieved much in recent years, socially as well as economically, and although the spoils of growth may not have been evenly distributed, the vast majority of Thais have seen a quantitative, and to some extent also a qualitative improvement in their living conditions.[1] Moreover, by encouraging the rapid expansion of the economy, the means have increasingly become available to the Thai authorities for redistributive investment; what is presently lacking is the strong political will to give redistribution the required priority to tackle uneven development effectively and fundamentally.

In the above paragraph, the phrase 'up to a point' is used advisedly, however. In value terms there is a sharp distinction to be drawn between uneven development as an environmental, geographical and sequential inevitability, and uneven development as a political, economic and social destiny. Thus, for instance, exploitation, discrimination, greed, corruption, and the abuse of power take us beyond a notional humanitarian threshold into a world where people are disadvantaged because they are disadvantaged, and where hopelessness and despair regularly define people's lives. In assessing possible development futures for Thailand we need to keep this distinction in mind. Whilst the technocrats might be relied upon to chip away at the superficial manifestations of uneven development, the more fundamental socially- and politically-defined barriers to an equal and just society may prove much harder to surmount.

This latter point is made particularly clear in the assessment by Daniel Arghiros and Wathana Wongsekiarttirat (Chapter 7) of changes taking place in the dynamic hinterland areas surrounding the Bangkok Metropolitan Region. In this instance, the expansion of the market for bricks, gravel and sand, and the proximity of Ayutthaya to Bangkok, has created a strong stimulus for business development in the study area. Powerful entrepreneurs have emerged as a consequence, and have used their economic status to alter fundamentally the structure and process of local politics which, in turn, has helped them to consolidate their economic position. The new-found prosperity has brought short-term benefits to many in the local community, but the weakness of the poor and politically powerless appears to have been magnified as others have capitalised on the opportunities provided by the market place and ballot box. Land and top-soil have been sold, often reluctantly, for short-term gain which, in many cases, is traded-off against longer-term economic vulnerability. Intra-community inequality has widened considerably, with the weaker echelon having less opportunity now to influence development decision-making through a corrupted political process, and fewer chances to exert themselves in the economic sphere. Whereas a superficial view of the study community might thus emphasise its outstanding economic achievements over the last decade, a deeper assessment would highlight the disenfranchisement and disempowerment of its disadvantaged stratum.

A similar set of circumstances can be identified in the chapters which deal with rapid tourism development in Thailand. Peter Williamson and Phil Hirsch (Chapter 10) have shown how Koh Samui has derived considerable (mostly economic) benefits from its dramatic development as a tourism destination since the early 1980s. However, some islanders, and many from outside the island, have been in a much stronger position than others to capitalise on the industry's rapid expansion. Meanwhile, the externalities associated with tourism development, including the degradation of the landscape and physical environment, pressures on natural resources, and myriad negative socio-cultural effects, have been experienced directly by the island's population, and especially those who lack the means to avoid or escape them. Powerful entrepreneurs have bought up the land with a voracious appetite, in the process marginalising and weakening the position and longer-term prospects of many islanders. Local people who may initially have been somewhat ambivalent about the arrival of tourism now have little say in the pattern and process of its future development.

The same is true of the hill-tribes of northern Thailand, who Philip Dearden (Chapter 11) and Mika Toyota (Chapter 12) have depicted as largely passive actors in an inexorable process of development taking place predominantly at the hands of outside agents and for the principal benefit of the external (and especially the international) community. It is doubtful whether the economic gains from trekking tourism adequately compensate for the mostly unquantifiable social, cultural and environmental costs which the hill-tribe communities have endured as a consequence of trekking tourism. Mika Toyota's illustration of opium addiction being perpetuated, or even promoted, by the niche market which guide-brokers have encouraged, provides a salutary illustration of a disequilibrium in the distribution of costs and benefits, to which the communities' initial and continuing weakness, peripherality and marginalisation is both a contributor and consequence. The fickleness of the tourism industry is also highlighted by Toyota's chapter, bringing into question the desirability of this particular form of 'development' for the communities concerned.

Chris Dixon (Chapter 2) and Peter Bell's (Chapter 3) analyses are no less pessimistic, highlighting as they do the problems and contradictions associated with Thailand's rapid and relentless incorporation into the global economic system. Whilst the scale of their enquiry may be much wider than that discussed above, a similar set of constraints is evident. Chris Dixon has shown how international agencies have exerted a very powerful influence over the direction and process of Thailand's recent economic transformation, including the introduction of various austerity and restructuring measures. Whilst these have undoubtedly contributed to a more efficient and streamlined economic system, they have at the same time squeezed a number of important economic and social cushions - subsidisation, over-'manning', a limited taxation burden - from the poor and disadvantaged. Thus, it might be suggested that structural adjustment and the attendant globalisation of the Thai economy, rather than being important developmental forces in Thailand, have in fact been among the principal forces behind the inequitable development which has taken place since at least the onset of the economic boom.

Bell likewise comments on the way in which the feverish globalisation of the Thai economy has increasingly compromised the degree of autonomy which is enjoyed in development decision-making: dancing to an international tune, while necessarily turning a largely deaf ear to a range of domestic diapasons. There is an air of anxiety in Thailand, lest the Kingdom should fall off the thundering NIC bandwagon. The pervading philosophy appears to be encapsulated by the following aphorism: "if there's one thing worse than being exploited by a transnational corporation, it is not being exploited by one." FDI-fetishism and EOI-idolism nonetheless create a tension with the needs of labour and domestic development - hence Bell's term 'maldevelopment'.

Trébuil also shows (Chapter 13) how the promotion of economic efficiency in the agricultural sector has yielded 'winners' and 'losers'. Those advantaged by being advantaged - by virtue of land-ownership, access to capital/collateral, knowledge, education, advice and labour - have capitalised significantly on the 'second green revolution'. But many - perhaps up to one-third of the agricultural workforce in Trébuil's cross-section of study communities - have been disadvantaged by agricultural modernisation, resulting in their economic and social marginalisation within their home areas, and/or their displacement from the land which, in many cases, leads to their out-migration to the urban sector (where this is a feasible option - see below).

Returning to the earlier point, it is neither possible nor desirable to state categorically whether the processes described above, and elsewhere in this volume, are 'good' or 'bad'. It depends very much upon the criteria which are used to inform one's judgement. For example, if we look at Trébuil's illustration from a purely economistic perspective, the fact that there appears to have been so much 'slack' in previously 'inefficient' agricultural systems would seem to justify the 'weeding-out' process which the green revolution has quite ruthlessly effected. However, a humanistic perspective would adopt an entirely different perspective, focusing on those who have been marginalised and displaced in the process. As citizens of the same country, is not their fate of as much concern as those who are advantaged as much by serendipity and historical circumstances as through their own endeavour?

In looking towards Thailand's development future, it is worthwhile pondering briefly some possible implications of the *laissez faire* approach which continues to dominate the mainstream of development practice in Thailand, irrespective of policy statements and political rhetoric to the contrary. Because of constraints of space, I will focus on just one scenario. Several chapters in this volume have touched tangentially on the phenomenon of migration. As I have discussed elsewhere (Parnwell, 1993a), there is a close link between uneven development and migration, each as a contributory factor to the other. The prevailing pattern of population movement in Thailand - from countryside to city, agricultural sector to industry and services, periphery to economic heartland (TDRI, 1990b) - mirrors very closely the pattern of development and economic dynamism in the Kingdom. The economic boom has done nothing to slow the pace or alter the pattern of migration, such has been the degree to which activity has concentrated in and around Greater Bangkok (see Chapter 1). People continue to flock to the cities, and to the Extended Bangkok Metropolitan Region in particular, drawn by the prospect (however illusory) of employment and other opportunities. In comparison, their home communities offer little in the way of incentive or means to keep them 'down on the farm'.

Without strong government intervention to manipulate the spatial pattern of economic growth, we can expect substantial flows of people to continue moving towards the metropolitan region in future. The implications of this with regard to uneven development are significant. Bangkok-centred economic dynamism will continue to create opportunities for migrants from up-country, and also to project an image which the young and impressionable will find hard to resist. Meanwhile rural and peripheral areas, starved of investment and support, will have little with which to withstand such attractions, and will thus continue to be selectively drained of the key to their longer-term development potential - people - whilst the urban heartland will continue to enjoy the plentiful labour resources which hitherto have underpinned its globally and regionally competitive position. We are thus faced with a cumulative process which matches John Connell's claim (1981, p.254) that "[m]igration proceeds out of inequality and further establishes this inequality". It also appears that this process will continue unabated irrespective of the externalities associated with over-urbanisation (congestion, pollution, diseconomies, anomie, pressure on utilities, shortages of housing, etc.): economic and social needs and preferences seem always to supersede concerns about the quality of life and the living environment. Thus, regardless of the theoretical notion of diseconomies of concentration, it is difficult to see where the practical limit to the size of Bangkok or the level of economic concentration in Thailand lies. As such, limits will have to be defined in other-than-economic terms, such as by environmental sustainability, quality of life and the dangers of social and political instability.

It is such factors that have underpinned a gradually building challenge to the *status quo* in Thailand, and which give grounds for a modicum of optimism for the future. The forces of change are nicely summarised by Sanitsuda Ekachai (1994, p.130), in her book *Seeds of Hope: Local Initiatives in Thailand*:

> Thailand's dramatic economic transformation in recent years, seen primarily in the development of Bangkok's goods and services and the expansion of the business and industrial sectors, has generally not brought about an improved quality of life to the rural and urban poor. These communities, bypassed by the new wealth and opportunities, have instead experienced economic hardship and burgeoning social problems. One of the positive consequences of this increasing disparity of wealth has been to force a reaction from these forgotten people... The impetus is strong when the communities have lost, or are in danger of losing what they once had, when the loss threatens their moral dignity or economic survival.

The latter sentiment is echoed by Sopon Pornchokchai (1995, p.169):

> ...the poor who live under oppressive socio-economic conditions will fight for themselves. Labourers will fight for a sufficient income; slum dwellers will fight for the survival of their houses. In general, it can be said that the poor will fight whenever they face unbearable conditions.

Thus the disadvantaged are increasingly coming to realise that, through collective action and their own innovation, they can begin to confront uneven development and social inequality: "through grassroots initiatives, individuals who possess vision and courage have attempted to develop their communities and together fashion their own future" (Ekachai, 1994, p.xii). Thailand's recent history is dappled with instances of popular protest, on a national and local scale, and of effective actions which increasingly challenge the prevailing development orthodoxy. From the Thai student protests against military dictatorship in the 1970s, through to recent pro-democracy movements and myriad grassroots initiatives, the tide is slowly turning in favour of the underprivileged in Thai society: disadvantage is no longer synonymous with despair.

At the forefront of these recent changes has been a rapidly growing corpus of Thai non-governmental organisations (NGOs), for whom popular democracy and fundamental human rights have provided the principal rallying-point (NGO Support Project, 1995, p.5). They have thus set themselves to challenge or confront the deeper, more fundamental aspects of both the phenomenon and process of uneven development. Not only have development NGOs and advocacy groups come collectively to represent a formidable force to challenge public as well as private sector actions, they have also succeeded in raising people's awareness of injustice, exploitation, discrimination and the abuse of power. This is important, as awareness is the first step along the road towards change. Over the last decade or so issues such as commercial logging plantation forestry, squatter eviction, power-generation schemes, shrimp farming, and child prostitution have been thrust to the forefront of the policy agenda by the populist movement (see Ekachai, 1994, for further illustrations). In many instances government has been pressured into amending some of its policies - the shelving of the Nam Choan dam project is often cited as a *cause célèbre* - and into taking greater responsibility towards balancing the current trend in development (Srisuwan Kuanacharn: in NGO Support Project, 1995, p.75). Thai NGOs have even been consulted in the process of drawing up the current 7th and forthcoming 8th National Economic and Social Development Plans, and in the Kingdom's submission to the 1992 Earth Summit in Rio.[2]

It is in the field of environment (which is just as centrally relevant to the context of uneven development as social and economic matters) that the most far-reaching changes have been effected, as Kirsten Ewers (1994, p.11) has shown:

> Prior to the 1980s there was almost nothing on environment in the [Thai] newspapers or on TV... During the 1980s more emphasis on the larger social and political context gained influence as middle and upper class Thai asked for environmental protection and clean cities. Environmental disasters such as the large landslides in November 1988 in the southern part of Thailand which killed many people suddenly made an impact. The government banned logging, cancelled concessions and the year 1989 was declared Year of Environment. The creation of an environmental conservation awareness gained momentum... This was fuelled by the controversy in the 1980s over the planned Nam Choan dam... [T]he national and international focus and debate ... became very sharp. Strong public protests caused ... the Nam Choan dam project [to be] shelved in 1988... This was unexpected and shows how strong the environmental movement, national and international, was...

However, we should avoid getting too carried away by the ebullience created by a number of successful local and national challenges to the *status quo*. Ewers' own research (1994, pp.13-14) shows clearly how some people have been adversely affected by well-intentioned efforts to improve conditions and prospects for others. The establishment of wildlife sanctuaries in the threatened forests along the Thai-Burmese border involved the establishment of 'buffer zones' into which people would be allowed to settle provided that they, in effect, acted as stewards of the ecosystem. Land-starved Thais from the lowlands migrated into the area, and were provided with a package of development services in exchange for compliance with certain management dictates. Whilst this programme succeeded both in strengthening conservation management and in bringing stability and improvement to lives of the immigrant farmers, the programme had a considerably, detrimental impact on the Pwo Karen who had traditionally made their homes in the area. These peripheral and marginal people face eviction from an area they have farmed for several generations, principally because their slash-and-burn farming practices are seen to be in conflict with the needs of conservation, however environmentally benign they may be in reality.

We should also not be drawn into believing that grassroots actions will inevitably turn the tide against iniquitous and inherently unsustainable practices. There is still a formidable range of barriers to the introduction of what might be seen, from the viewpoint of uneven development, as 'appropriate' approaches. One brief illustration, concerning illegal salt-mining in the North-East of Thailand, must suffice at this juncture (see *Far Eastern Economic Review*, 7.6 90). It shows how powerful actors from the business and political arenas (the same thing in this and many other instances) played an active role in supporting the illegal, environmentally damaging and socially devastating activity of extracting salt from the rock strata which underlie much of the North-East, and especially Mahasarakham where this particular episode unfolded. One consequence of this activity was the severe pollution of the fields of a reputed 300,000 farmers in the vicinity, many of whom suffered a significant decline in their already precarious livelihoods as a result. On the other hand, government ministers and other businesspeople stood to gain considerable financial advantage from salt extraction and the industrial activities associated with it, to which the then-Chatichai administration was apparently willing to turn a blind eye. Illustrative of prevailing power differentials was the way that the grassroots reaction was dealt with. Farmers, together with students and other supporters, protested this illegal activity and its environmental consequences but, rather than bring the full force of the law down on those who had transgressed the 1967 Mineral Resources Act and a ban imposed by Prime Minister Prem Tinsulanonda in 1980 (and, ironically, reaffirmed by Prime Minister Chatichai Choonhavan in 1989), a paramilitary police force from Mahasarakham was brought in to break up the demonstration. As a result some forty protesting farmers and students were arrested, and several were also injured in the violent scuffles which ensued. This illustrates where the real seat of power still lies in Thailand, and the difficulties that grassroots actions have faced in confronting the *status quo*.

Corruption of the political process is another case in point, to which reference has been made earlier in this chapter. The abuse of power and influence may create substantial economic benefits for those involved, but the cost has to be paid somewhere. Phongpaichit and Piriyarangsan (1974, p.174) show where the disproportionate burden lies in this regard: "many lower-echelon groups are growing increasingly aware that they are the ones who bear the cost of corruption." They go on (*ibid*., pp.160-61) to illustrate some of the circumstances which support this conviction:

> [C]orruption has a moral cost as a result of the way in which it puts wealth in the pockets of ... bureaucrats, politicians and businessmen. Many also perceive that corruption has a high social cost, which occurs in several forms. First, official corruption has caused damage to the environment and public safety. Vast areas of the country's forests have been destroyed. Officials have allowed factories to release industrial waste into rivers, the sea and the air, resulting in pollution, environmental deterioration, and health risks. Second, the commission fees on government construction projects ... cause the government each year extra expenditure to the tune of thousands of million Baht. Third, corruption enables some businessmen to have special privileges, giving rise to situations of unfair competition. Costs [are] passed on to consumers. Finally, corruption causes the public administration system to deteriorate. The public lose faith in it.

They also claim (1994, p.133) that people have become inured to the fact that powerful people exploit their position of authority and influence. If society at large has become accustomed or even resigned to this situation, then the prospects of popular opinion wresting the *status quo* from the tight grip of Thailand's élite minority would appear to be quite limited, and with it the prospects for greater distributive justice in the development process.

Where, then, are the signs of hope for the future? We round off this concluding discussion with the words of some important Thai commentators who outline their visions for the future and the paths to be followed. Ajaan Sulak Sivaraksa (in Ekachai, 1994, p.x) suggests that we have to look backwards to go forwards:

> [A]ncient wisdom ... teaches us how to live and what to value. It is sad that decision-makers promoting 'development' have no frame of reference from which to understand this wisdom and have done so much to undermine and discourage its use. Indeed, the development process itself destroys the confidence and self-respect of the people, both the downtrodden and the elite alike. The whole society is grasping for material success at any expense. Economic growth is the new state religion.

Sanitsuda Ekachai (1994, p.xi) has a more straightforward vision which seems to espouse the Buddhist principle of moderation:

> [W]e can live more simply, consume less, and share more, not as acts of charity, but because the lifestyles and social structures we have created and supported have been the cause of pain for many. We need to change both our lifestyles and social structures, not only to serve those people in the lower social strata, but also to create a better quality of life for ourselves [in the middle- and upper-classes].

Professor Sippanondha Ketudat (1990, p.111), a former Minister of Education in Thailand, adopts a similar line of reasoning. His 'middle path' to development deals with

> ...Thailand's achieving <u>both</u> modernisation <u>and</u> development. The first can be achieved without any close harmonisation of new techno-economic mechanisms with our overall system of values and ethics. The second cannot. That is, in my lexicon, <u>true</u> 'development' implies that a new situation be realised which, both overall and in its major individual features, is <u>congruent</u> with the way our people conceive and define the good life. I grant that every modernising nation finds it necessary in some cases to compromise some of its values in various ways in order to build infrastructure and achieve growth. My possidiction in the case of Thailand, however, is that these compromises will be relatively minor, temporary, and subject to later adjustment so as to achieve harmony with value and ethical standards that are basic to the culture at that point in time. Our national population is, of course, overwhelmingly Buddhist... Our political culture has thus been deeply influenced by Buddhist standards. The standards we use in evaluating our progress toward true development will thus tend to be consistent with Buddhist standards. [original emphasis]

Finally, Robert Textor *et.al.* (1980, pp.95-6) also advocate a culturally grounded approach to future development in Thailand, where religion plays an important guiding role. They consider three competing directions for Thailand's development future, based upon extensive interviews with some of Thailand's leading scholars:

> The 'democratic capitalist' pathway is doubtless the one that various influential outside interests would prefer to see Thailand follow. It would probably succeed in producing considerable economic growth, but might sorely exacerbate existing inequities. The 'authoritarian socialist' pathway is doubtless the preference of another, quite different, group of outside interests. This approach would probably result in substantial gains in equity, but its capacity to produce adequate economic growth would seem questionable; moreover, this approach would seem to be clearly 'un-Thai' in its denial of personal autonomy and freedom. The 'democratic mixed' pathway is probably closest to being optimal in its growth-equity-freedom trade-offs, and, in any case, would seem to come closer, overall, to the 'middle way' (*madchimma patipathaa*) of Buddhism.

The authors were quite foresightful, not so much in mapping out the optimal direction for future development in Thailand but in identifying the consequences of following other pathways. The economic boom which got under way soon after the publication of their research has followed very closely the first pathway they identified, 'democratic capitalism' (although there may be serious doubts about the adjective used). True to form, and as we have seen in this volume, outside interests have played an important role in promoting this pathway, and with it the resultant trade-off between economic growth and social inequality.

There is no doubt that the Middle Path represents an attractive ideal for future development in Thailand which not only accommodates the need for continued economic growth but which also espouses a form of development which is in tune with the wider needs of society and the limits of the natural environment. It is also rational that religion, which ostensibly provides the fabric of society, should be advanced as a platform for future development efforts. But Thai Buddhism itself has in recent years been tainted by a number of scandals involving the alleged sexual misdemeanours of rogue monks, rumours of growing avarice and commercialism in certain prestigious temples, and the emergence of new largely urban Buddhist movements which are doing more the adapt the religion to the modern reality than *vice versa* (Sathaanand, 1990; Taylor, 1990). Thus it is difficult to envisage how these distinguished commentators' idealised visions can be turned into reality. There is a very strong sense that they may be 'preaching to the converted': like-minded people will listen to the message and act accordingly; otherwise, it will fall on largely deaf ears. Worse still, some of the key actors on the stage of uneven and unsustainable development have hypocritically commandeered these principles as a public relations camouflage for their very un-Buddhist actions.

In such circumstances, it is difficult to be too optimistic about the prospects for a rapid and fundamental challenge to iniquitous development in Thailand. The most realistic scenario is that the economy will continue to grow apace, and that more and more of the Kingdom's citizens will be drawn along in its wake

Average levels of livelihood will continue to improve, but this will mask a considerable degree of variation between groups and areas. Bangkok's petty commodity traders may gain some benefit from an expanding economy, but not as much, for example, as those who speculate on the stock market. Young rural women who migrate towards Bangkok's burgeoning factories will enjoy an improvement of sorts in their livelihood, if not also their life-style, but to a lesser extent than those who are driving Thailand's industrialisation. Meanwhile, those who lack mobility - be it economic, social or spatial - will continue to be by-passed by the boom and the benefits it potentially bestows. Others will be pushed further towards the country's margins - both literally and figuratively - by 'virtue' of their weak and vulnerable position.

The populist movement, none the less, does provide some grounds for future optimism. The dawning realisation that progress does not have to be compromised by fairness (or, indeed, that the two may be synonymous) will gradually penetrate a wider public consciousness and will contribute to more innovative and enlightened development policies, measures and mechanisms. It is important, however, that such changes also occur on an international scale. Thailand's integration within the world economic and political system determines that no degree of domestic change will be successful in changing the *status quo* unless the global context within which it occurs is conducive to its effectiveness and sustainability.

Notes

1. Philip Hirsch (1994) and Jonathan Rigg (1995) both comment on the rapid pace of change, in up-country areas as well as Bangkok.

2. In reality, only a limited cross-section of NGOs which are acceptable to the government has been consulted. These included NGOs which have been established by former military personnel and politicians, and NGOs which have come to recognise that they can operate more effectively in tandem with government. More radical NGOs which remain diametrically opposed to government are much less likely to be drawn into the process of policy formulation.

References

Abonyi, G. and Bunyaraks Ninsananda, 1989, *Thailand: Development Planning in Turbulent Times*, North York: University of Toronto-York University Joint Centre for Asia Pacific Studies.

Adulavididhaya, Kamphol and Tongroj Onchan, 1985, "Migration and Agricultural Development of Thailand: Past and Future", in: P.M. Hauser, D.B. Suits and Naohiro Ogawa, eds, *Urbanization and Migration in ASEAN Development*, Tokyo: National Institute for Research Advancement, pp.427-54.

Agarwal, B., 1985, "Women and Technological Change in Agriculture: The Asian and African Experience", in: I. Ahmed, ed., *Technology and Rural Women: Conceptual and Empirical Issues*, London: George Allen and Unwin.

Ajanant, Juanjai, 1983, *Export Promotion in Processed Foods and Textiles*, Bangkok: NESDB.

Ajanant, Juanjai, 1986, *Trade and Industrialization of Thailand*, Bangkok: Social Science Association of Thailand.

Akira, Suehior, 1989, *Capital Accumulation in Thailand, 1855-1985*, Tokyo: Centre for East Asian Cultural Studies.

Akrasanee, Narongchai, 1980, *Comparative Advantage of Textile and Cement Industries in Thailand*, Bangkok: Industrial Finance Corporation of Thailand.

Akrasanee, Narongchai *et.al.*, 1987, *ASEAN Co-operation in Second Phase Import-Substitution*, Kuala Lumpur: APDC.

Akrasanee, Narongchai, 1991, *Thailand's Export Led Growth: Retrospect and Prospects,* Bangkok: Thailand Development Research Institute, Policy Study No. 3.

Akrasanee, Narongchai and Atchana Wattananukit, 1990, "Changing Structure and Rising Dynamism in the Thai Economy", *Southeast Asian Affairs*, pp.360-80.

Allal, M. and E. Chuta, 1982, *Cottage Industries and Handicraft: Some Guidelines for Employment Promotion*, Geneva: International Labour Office.

Amsden, Alice H., 1989, *Asia's Next Giant: South Korea and Late Industrialization*, Oxford: Oxford University Press.
Amyot, J., 1976, *Village Ayutthaya: Social and Economic Conditions of a Rural Population in Central Thailand*, Bangkok: Chulalongkorn University Social Research Institute.
Amyot, J., 1990, *National Rural Development Committee 1988 Village Survey: Pilot Analysis - Ayutthaya Province*, Seminar on "Social and Economic Change in Ayutthaya", Chulalongkorn University Social Research Institute, Bangkok.
Anderson, Benedict O'G., 1983, *Imagined Communities*, London: Verso.
Anderson, D. and M.W. Lierserson, 1978, *Rural Enterprise and Non-Farm Employment*, Washington: World Bank.
Anderson, K.L. and B. London, 1985, "Modernization, Elites, and the Distribution of Educational Resources in Thailand", *Social Forces*, 63, 3, pp.775-94.
Anderson, K.L. and B. London, 1986, "Elites and Development: High Status Occupational Groups and Government Expenditures in Thailand", *Journal of Political and Military Sociology*, 14, 2, pp.235-48.
Angel, S., 1988, "'Where Have all the People Gone?' Urbanization and Counter-urbanization in Thailand", *Journal of the Siam Society*, 76, pp.245-59.
Annis, S., 1987, "Can Small-Scale Development be a Large-scale Policy? The Case of Latin America", *World Development*, 15, supplement, pp.129-34.
Apibunyopas, Preeyanuch, 1993, "TNCs and Impacts on Industrialisation in Thailand", *Regional Development Dialogue*, 14, 4, pp.94-117.
Apthorpe, R. and D. Conyers, 1982, "Decentralization, Recentralization and Popular Participation in Developing Countries: Towards a Framework for Analysis", *Development and Peace*, 3, 2, pp.47-59.
Arbhabhirama, Anat, Dhira Phantumvanit, J. Elkington and Phaitoon Ingkasuwan, 1988, *Thailand: Natural Resources Profile*, Singapore: Oxford University Press.
Arghiros, D., 1993, "Rural Transformation and Local Politics in a Central Thai District", Unpublished Ph.D. Thesis, University of Hull, England.
Ariff M. and H. Hill, 1985, *Export-Oriented Industrialization: The ASEAN Experience*, Sydney: Allen and Unwin.
Armstrong, W. and T.G. McGee, 1985, *Theatres of Accumulation: Studies in Asian and Latin American Urbanization*. London: Methuen.
Arndt, H.W., 1983, "The 'Trickle-Down' Myth", *Economic Development and Cultural Change*, 32, 1, pp.1-10.
Arnold, F. and Suwanlee Piampiti, 1984, "Female Migration in Thailand", in J. Fawcett, Siew-Ean Khoo and P.C. Smith, eds, *Women in the Cities of Asia: Migration and Urban Adaptation*, Boulder: Westview, pp.143-64.
Ashakul, Teera, n.d., *Migration: Trends and Determinants*, Bangkok: TRDI.
Asian Development Bank, 1994, *Asian Development Outlook 1994*, Manila: ADB.
Asian Cultural Forum on Development, 1990, *Promotion and Transfer of Appropriate Technology Among Asian NGOs*, Bangkok: Asian Cultural Forum on Development.

Askew, Marc, 1994, *Interpreting Bangkok: The Urban Question in Thai Studies*, Bangkok: Chulalongkorn University Press.

Atkinson, A. and C.P. Vorratnchaiphan, 1994, "Urban Environmental Management in a Changing Development Context: The Case of Thailand", *Third World Planning Review*, 16, 2, pp.147-69.

Ayal, E.B., 1992, "Thailand Development: The Role of Bangkok", *Pacific Affairs*, 65, 3, pp.353-67.

Baert, V. and V. Bergez, 1987, "Un système agraire du sud-Thaïlande: Patthalung", unpublished DAA thesis, INA Paris-Grignon, France.

Bailes J. and N. Tabtieng, 1993, "Developing Management Practices in Thailand", Bangkok, Chulalongkorn University, Cusri-Orstom seminar.

Bain, Anthony, 1993, "Battle of Beliefs", *Bangkok Post*, 23 November 1993.

Bangkok Bank Monthly Review, various issues.

Bangkok Post, various issues.

Bangkok Post, Mid-Year and Year End Review, various years 1989-1994.

Bank of Thailand, 1993, *Bank of Thailand Annual Economic Report*, Bangkok: Bank of Thailand.

Banpasirichote, Chantana and Amara Pongsapich, 1992, *Child Workers in Hazardous Work in Thailand*, Bangkok: Chulalongkorn University, Social Research Institute.

Basham, R., 1989, "'False Consciousness' and the Problem of Merit and Power in Thailand", *Mankind*, 19, 2, pp.126-37.

Belassa, Bela, 1981, *The Newly Industrializing Countries in the World Economy*, New York: Pergamon.

Bell, Peter F., 1978, "Cycles of Class Struggle in Thailand", in: A. Turton, T. Fast and M. Caldwell, eds, *Thailand: Roots of Conflict*, Nottingham: Spokesman, pp.51-79.

Bell, Peter F., 1982, "Western Conceptions of Thai Society: The Politics of American Scholarship", *Journal of Contemporary Asia*. 12, 2, pp.61-74.

Bell, Peter F., 1990a, "The Thai State, the Development of Capitalism and the Rural Areas in Thailand", in: Ananya Bhuchongkul, ed., *State and Village in Thai Studies*, Bangkok: Thai Khadi Research Institute, Thammasat University (in Thai).

Bell, Peter F., 1990b, *Essays on the Political Economy of Thailand, 1960-1985*, Bangkok: Faculty of Economics, Chualalongkorn University (in Thai).

Bell, Peter F., 1991, "The Impact of the United States on the Development of the Social Sciences in Thailand", *Studies in Third World Societies*, 45, pp.95-116.

Bell, P.F., 1992, "Gender and Economic Development in Thailand", in: Penny van Esterik and John van Esterik, eds, *Gender and Development in Southeast Asia*, Toronto: Canadian Council for Southeast Asian Studies, XX, II, pp.61-81.

Benor, D., J.Q. Harrison and M. Baxter, 1984, *Agricultural Extension: The Training and Visit System*, Washington: World Bank.

Bhruksari, W., 1989, "Government Policy: Highland Ethnic Minorities", in: J. McKinnon and B. Vienne, eds, *Hill Tribes Today: Problems in Change*, Bangkok: White Lotus-ORSTOM, pp.5-32.

Bhongmakapat, Teerana, 1990, "Income Distribution in a Rapidly Growing Economy: The Case of Thailand", *Singapore Economic Review*, 35, 1, pp.161-79.

Biggs T., *et.al.*, 1990, *Rural Industry and Employment Study*, Synthesis Report, Bangkok: TDRI.

Boadway, Robin, *et.al.*, 1992, "Required Returns on Investment by Small and Large Firms in Thailand", Paper Presented at the Year-End Conference, Bangkok: TDRI.

Boonchote, T. and P. Dearden, 1994, "Tourism Growth and Impacts at Ban Sob Ruak, the Golden Triangle Village, Thailand", *Mahidol Journal of Ecology*, 21, pp.62-67.

Booth, A., 1993, "Progress and Poverty in South East Asia", Paper presented to the British Pacific Rim Research Group, Liverpool John Moores University.

Bowie, Katherine A., 1992, "Unraveling the Myth of the Subsistence Economy: Textile Production in Nineteenth-Century Northern Thailand", *Journal of Asian Studies*, 51, 4, pp.797-823.

Boyes, J. and S. Piraban, 1992, *A Life Apart: Viewed from the Hills*, 2nd edition, Bangkok: Silkworm Books.

Brandt Commission, 1980, *North-South: A Programme for Survival*, Report of the Independent Commission in International Development Issues, London: Pan.

Britton, S., 1982, "The Political Economy of Tourism in the Third World", *Annals of Tourism Research*, 9, 3, pp.331-58.

Brookfield, Harold and Yvonne Byron, eds, 1993, *South-East Asia's Environmental Future: The Search for Sustainability*, Kuala Lumpur: Oxford University Press/The United Nations University Press.

Brown, D., 1994, "Internal Colonialism and Ethnic Rebellion in Thailand", in: D. Brown, *The State and Ethnic Politics in Southeast Asia*, London: Routledge, pp.158-205.

Brown, Ian, 1988, *The Elite and the Economy in Siam, c.1890-1920*, Singapore: Oxford University Press.

Brown, Ian, 1980, "Government Initiative and Peasant Response in the Siamese Silk Industry, 1901-1913", *Journal of the Siam Society*, 68, 2, pp.34-47.

Brummelhuis, Han ten and J.H. Kemp, 1984, *Strategies and Structures in Thai Society*, Amsterdam.

Brummit William E. *et.al.*, 1992, "Exports, Structural Change and Thailand's Rapid Growth", Papers Presented at the Year-End Conference, Bangkok: TDRI.

Buasri, Udom, 1990, *Tourism Development in North-East Thailand*, Thailand: Khon Kaen University (in Thai).

Buchongkul, Ananya, 1985, "From Chaonaa to Khonngaan: The Growing Divide in a Central Thai Village", Unpublished Ph.D. Thesis, University of London.

Buckley, M.J., 1982, "Planning and Budgeting in Thailand: The Plight of Rural Farmers", *The South East Asian Economic Review*, 3, 1.

Bunbongkarn, Suchit, 1987, "Political Institutions and Processes, in: Xuto Somsakdi, ed., *Government and Politics of Thailand*, Oxford University Press, pp.41-74.
Bunjongjit, Naruemol and Xavier Oudin, 1992, *Small Scale Industries and Institutional Framework in Thailand*, Technical Paper 81, Paris: OECD.
Bunnag, Jane, 1973, *Buddhist Monk, Buddhist Layman: A Study of Urban Monastic Organization in Central Thailand*, Cambridge: Cambridge University Press.
Business Review, "Learning from Akha", *Business Review*, April 1987, pp.40-49.
Butler, R.W., 1980, "The Concept of a Tourism Area Cycle of Evolution: Implications for Management of Resources", *The Canadian Geographer*, 24, pp.5-12.
Caldwell, J. A., 1974, *American Economic Aid to Thailand*, Lexington: Lexington Books.
Castells, M., 1991, "Guest Editor's Introduction", *Regional Development Dialogue*, 12, pp.iii-vi.
Cernea, M., ed., 1991, *Putting People First: Sociological Variables in Rural Development*, Second edition, Oxford and New York: Oxford University Press.
Chai-Anan Samudavanija, 1987, "Political History", in: Xuto Somsakdi, ed., *Government and Politics of Thailand*, Oxford University Press, pp.1-40.
Chai-Anan Samudavanija, 1987, "The Bureaucracy", in: Xuto Somsakdi, ed., *Government and Politics of Thailand*, Oxford University Press, pp.75-109.
Chai-Anan Samudavanija, 1989, "The Role of the Military in National Development", in: Prasith-rathsint, S., ed., 1989, *Thailand's National Development: Social and Economic Background*, Thai University Research Association, pp.149-65.
Chai-Anan Samudavanija, 1990a, "The Military and Modern Thai Political System", in: Pinit Ratanakul and U. Kyaw Than, eds, *Development, Modernization, and Tradition in Southeast Asia: Lessons from Thailand*, Bangkok: Mahidol University.
Chai-Anan Samudavanija, 1990b, "Economic Policy-Making in a Liberal Technocratic Polity", in: John W. Langford and K. Lorne Brownsey, eds, *Economic Policy-Making in the Asia-Pacific Region*, Canada: The Institute of Research on Public Policy.
Chai-Anan Samudavanija and Suchit Bunbongkarn, 1985, "Thailand", in: H. Crouch and Zakaria Haji Ahmad, eds, *Military-Civilian Relations in Southeast Asia*, Singapore: Oxford University Press.
Chai-Anan Samudavanija and Sukhumbhand Paribatra, 1993, "Thailand: Liberalization Without Democracy", in: J.W. Morley, ed., *Driven by Growth: Political Change in the Asia-Pacific Region*, Armonk, N.Y.: M.E. Sharpe.
Chaiworaporn, Anchalee, 1994, "Blocking the Winds of Change", *The Nation*, 28 March 1994.
Chamarik, Sanah, 1993, *Democracy and Development: A Cultural Perspective*, Bangkok: Local Development Institute.
Chambers, R., 1983, *Rural Development: Putting the Last First*, London Longman.

Chambers, R., A. Pacey and L.A. Thrupp, eds, 1989, *Farmer First: Farmer Innovation and Agricultural Research*, London: Intermediate Technology Publications.

Chanawongse, Krasae, 1991, *Rural Development Management: Principles, Propositions and Challenges*, Khon Kaen University: Research and Development Institute.

Chanawongse, Krasae, 1992, "Future Challenges in Thailand", *International Journal on World Peace*, 1992, 9, 3.

Chanjaraen, Chanyaporn, 1994, "Prostitution as a Family Trade", *Bangkok Post* , 30 May 1994.

Charoenloet, Chira, 1971, *The Evolution of Thailand's Economy*, Bangkok: Thai Watana Panich.

Charoenlert, Voravidh, 1990, *Thailand in the Process of Becoming a NIC: Myth or Reality?* Working Paper, Faculty of Economics, Chulalongkorn University, Bangkok.

Charoenloet, Voravidh, 1991, "Thailand in the Process of Becoming a NIC: Myth or Reality?", *Journal of Contemporary Asia*, 21, 1, pp.31-41.

Charoenlert, Voravidh, 1994, "Informal Sector: The Economy of the Poor?" in: Amara Pongsapich *et.al.*, eds, 1994, *Entrepreneurship and Socio-economic Transformation in Thailand and Southeast Asia*, Chulalongkorn University Social Research Institute, Bangkok.

Charoensin-o-larn, Chairat, 1988, *Understanding Postwar Reformism in Thailand: A Reinterpretation of Rural Development*, Bangkok: Duang Kamol.

Chaturabhawd, P., 1980, *People of the Hills*, Bangkok: Editions Duang Kamol.

Cheema, G.S., ed., 1981, *Institutional Dimensions of Regional Development*, Singapore: Maruzen Asia.

Chiasakul, Samart *et.al.*, 1989, *Thailand's Economic Development in the 1980's*, Tokyo: Institute of Developing Economies.

Chiengkul, Witayakorn, 1983, *The Effects of Capital Penetration on the Transformation of the Agrarian Structure in the Central Region of Thailand, 1960-80*.

Chiengkul, Witayakorn, 1983, "The Transformation of the Agrarian Structure of Central Thailand", *Journal of Contemporary Asia*, 13, 3, pp.340-60.

Chiengkul, Witayakorn *et.al.*, 1984, *Report on Employment Problems in Thailand*, Bangkok: CUSRI.

Chintayarangsan, Rachain, 1989, "Thailand's Expectation on Reaching NIC Status", in: Prasith-rathsint, S., ed., *Thailand's National Development: Social and Economic Background*, Thai University Research Association, pp.106-48.

Chirapanda, S., 1986, *The Role of Local Organisations in Thai Rural Development Process*, Paper No. 34, Ministry of Agriculture and Cooperatives, Bangkok (in Thai).

Chirathivat S., 1988, *et.al.*, *Effects of the Generalized System of Preference on the Thai Economy*, Geneva: UNCTAD.

Cho, Lee-Jay and J.G. Bauer, 1987, "Population Growth and Urbanization: What Does the Future Hold?", in: R.J. Fuchs *et.al.*, eds, *Urbanization and Urban Policies in Pacific Asia*, Boulder: Westview Press, pp.15-37.

Chongpeerapien, Tienchai, Somthawin Sungsuwan, Phanu Kritiporn, Suree Buranasajja and Resource Management Associates, 1990, *Energy and Environment: Choosing the Right Mix*, Bangkok: TRDI.
Choomchai, Prachoom, 1973, "Thailand's Industrial Development: Rationale Strategy and Prospects", in: Chapman and Ho, eds, *Studies of Contemporary Thailand*, Canberra: ANU.
Choopoh, Deuleu and Marianne Nass, 1994, "Deuleu: A Life-history of an Akha Woman", Unpublished paper.
Chou Ta-Kuan, 1987, *The Customs of Cambodia*, translated by J. G. d'A. Paul from the French translation by Paul Pelliot from the Chinese original, Bangkok: The Siam Society.
Chowdhury A. and S. Kunnoot S., 1992, "Export-oriented Industrialization and Industrial Deepening in Thailand: An Input-Output Perspective", *Economic Bulletin for Asia*, XLIII, 1, Bangkok.
Chunanunthathum, Supote, 1986, *Trade and Industrialization in Thailand.*
Chuta, Enyinna and Carl Liedholm, 1979, *Rural Non-Farm Employment: A Review of the State of the Art*, Michigan State University Rural Development Papers, No. 4.
Chuta, Enyinna and S.V. Sethuraman, 1984, *Rural Small-Scale Industries and Employment in Africa and Asia*, Geneva: International Labour Office.
Clifford James, 1988, *The Predicament of Culture: Twentieth-Century Ethnography, Literature, and Art*, Cambridge: Harvard University Press.
Cohen, Erik, 1979, "The Impact of Tourism on the Hill Tribes of Northern Thailand", *Internationales Asienforum*, 10, 1/2, pp.5-38.
Cohen, Erik, 1982a, "Jungle Guides in Northern Thailand: The Dynamics of a Marginal Occupational Role", *Sociological Review*, 30, pp.234-66.
Cohen, Erik, 1982b, "Marginal Paradises: Bungalow Tourism on the Islands of Southern Thailand", *Annals of Tourism Research*, 9, 2, pp.189-228.
Cohen, Erik, 1983a, "Hill Tribe Tourism", in: J. Mackinnon and W. Bhruksasri, eds, *Highlanders of Thailand*, Kuala Lumpur: Oxford University Press, pp.307-25.
Cohen, Erik, 1983b, "Insiders and Outsiders: The Dynamics of Development of Bungalow Tourism on the Islands of Southern Thailand", *Human Organization*, 42, 2, pp.403-28.
Cohen, Erik, 1988a, "Authenticity and Commoditization in Tourism", *Annals of Tourism Research*, 15, 3, pp.371-86.
Cohen, Erik, 1988b, "From Tribal Costume to Pop Fashion: The Boutiquisation of the Textiles of the Hill Tribes of Northern Thailand", *Studies in Popular Culture*, 11, pp.49-59.
Cohen, Erik, 1989a, "Primitive and Remote: Hill Tribe Trekking in Thailand", *Annals of Tourism Research*, 16, 1, pp.30-61.
Cohen, Erik, 1989b, "International Politics and the Transformation of Folk Crafts: The Hmong (Meo) of Thailand and Laos", *Journal of the Siam Society*, 77, 1, pp.70-82
Cohen, Erik, 1991, *Thai Society in Comparative Perspective: Studies in Contemporary Thailand*, Vol. 1, Bangkok: White Lotus.
Cohen, Erik, 1993, "The Study of Touristic Images of Native People: Mitigating the Stereotype of a Stereotype", in: D.G. Pearl and B.W. Butler, eds, *Tourism Research*, London: Routledge, pp.6-69.

Commission on International Development, 1969, *The Pearson Report: Partners in Development*, London: Report of the Commission on International Development.
Connell, John, 1981, "Remittances and Rural Development: Migration, Dependency and Inequality in the South Pacific", in: G.W. Jones and H.V. Richter, eds, *Population Mobility and Development: Southeast Asia and the Pacific*, Canberra: The Australian National University, Development Studies Centre Monograph No. 27, pp.229-55.
Cooper, R., 1984, *Resource Scarcity and the Hmong Response*, Singapore: Singapore University Press.
Cooper, R.G., 1979, "The Tribal Minorities of Northern Thailand: Problems and Prospects", *Southeast Asian Affairs*, pp.323-32.
Costa, F.J., A.K. Dutt, L.J.C. Ma and A.G. Noble, eds, 1988, *Asian Urbanization: Problems and Processes*, Berlin: Gebruder Borntraeger.
Cook, N.M., 1993, "Democratisation in Thailand", *Asian Studies Review*, 17, 1, pp.126-34.
Cook, Scott, 1984, "Peasant Economy, Rural Industry, and Capitalist Development in the Oaxaca Valley, Mexico", *Journal of Peasant Studies*, 12, 1.
Crick, M., 1985, "Tracing the Anthropological Self: Quizzical Reflections on Field Work, Tourism and the Ludic", *Social Analysis*, 17, pp.71-92.
Crick, M., 1989, "Representation of International Tourism in the Social Sciences: Sun, Sex, Sights, Saving and Servility", *Annual Review of Anthropology*, 18, pp.307-44.
Crone, Donald K., 1988, "State, Social Elites, and Government Capacity in Southeast Asia", *World Politics*, 40, 2.
Crone, Donald K., 1991, "Military Regimes and Social Justice in Indonesia and Thailand", *Journal of Asian and African Studies*, 26, 1-2, pp.96-113.
Crooker, R.A., 1988, "Forces of Change in the Thailand Opium Zone", *The Geographical Review*, 78, pp.241-56.
Crozat, Y., A. Sitthicharoenchai, P. Kaewongsri, S. Pornpinatepong and P. Chitapong, 1986, *The Improvement of Rice Cultivation in Sathing Phra Area, Songkhla Lake Basin*, Publication No. 6, Thai-French Farming Systems Project, Prince of Songkhla University.
Cummings, B., 1987, "The Origins and Developments of Northeast Asian Political Economy: Industrial Sectors, Product Cycles and Political Consequences", in: F.C. Deyo, ed., *The Political Economy of the New Asian Industrialisation*, Ithaca, Cornell University Press, pp.44-83.
Curtis, D., 1991, *Beyond Government: Organisations for Common Benefit*, London and Basingstoke. Macmillan.
Damrongkiattisak, W., 1984, "Communication Effectiveness between Commune Extension Agents and Rice Farmers in Chiang Mai, Thailand", unpublished PhD thesis, Department of Agricultural and Extension Education, Pennsylvania State University.
DANIDA, 1990, *Situations- og Perspektiv Analyse Thailand* (Situation and Perspective Analysis), Copenhagen: DanEduc Consulting for Danish International Development Agency, Ministry of Foreign Affairs.
Dearden, P., 1988, "Tourism in Developing Societies: Some Observations on Trekking in the Highlands of North Thailand", in: L.J. D'Amore and J.

Jafari, eds, *Tourism: A Vital Force for Peace*, Montreal, First Global Conference, pp.207-16.
Dearden, P., 1991, "Tourism and Sustainable Development in Northern Thailand", *The Geographical Review*, 81, pp.400-13.
Dearden, P., 1992, *Integrated Watershed Management Planning and Information Needs in Northern Thailand: A Case Study of the Nam Mae Taeng*, Regions and Resources Study Group Research Report No. 6, University of Victoria.
Dearden, P., 1995a, "Reply to Michaud", *Annals of Tourism Research*, 22 (in press).
Dearden, P., 1995b, "Development and Biocultural Diversity in Northern Thailand", *Applied Geography* (in press).
Dearden, P., 1995c, "Development, the Environment and Social Differentiation", in: J. Rigg, ed., *Counting the Costs: Environmental Growth and Economic Change*, Singapore: ISEAS (in press).
Dearden, P., 1995d, "Ecotourism, Parks and Biocultural Diversity: The Context in Northern Thailand", Plenary Address, International Conference on Ecotourism: Concept, Design and Strategy, Ecotourism Institute, Sri Nakharinwirot University, Bangkok, February, 1995.
Dearden, P. and S. Harron, 1992a, *Trekking in Northern Thailand: Rural Development and Information Needs*, Regions and Resources Study Group Research Report No.3, University of Victoria.
Dearden, P. and S. Harron, 1992b, "Tourism and the hilltribes of Thailand", in: B. Weiler and M. Hall, eds, *Special Interest Tourism*, London: Bellhaven Press, pp.95-104.
Dearden, P. and S. Harron, 1994, "Alternative Tourism and Adaptive Change: Insights from Northern Thailand", *Annals of Tourism Research*, 21, pp.81-102.
Demaine, H., 1986, "*Kanpatthana*: Thai Views of Development", in: M. Hobart and R.H. Taylor, eds, *Context, Meaning and Power in Southeast Asia*, Ithaca: Cornell University Southeast Asia Program, pp.93-114.
Demaine, H. and R.E. Malong, eds, 1987, *Decentralisation: Area Development and Practice in Asia*, Bangkok: Asian Institute of Technology.
Deyo, Frederick, ed., 1987, *The Political Economy of the New Asian Industrialization*, Ithaca: Cornell University Press.
Dhiratayakinant, Kraiyudht, 1982, "A Decade of Nondevelopment in Ayutthaya", *Summary Report: Ayutthaya Project*, Bangkok: CUSRI.
Dhiratayakinant, Kraiyudht, 1990, "Role of the Private Sector in the Thai Economy: Now and in the Future", in: Suchart Prasith-rathsint, ed., *Thailand on the Move: Stumbling Blocks and Breakthroughs*, Bangkok: Thai Universities Research Association.
Dhiravegin, Likhit, 1992, *Demi Democracy*, Singapore: Times Academic Press.
Dhungel, Basundhara and Karl E. Weber, 1988, *Women and Development: Bibliography on the Advancement of Women and Essay on Women's Studies with Focus on South and Southeast Asian Countries*, Bangkok: Asian Institute of Technology, Human Settlements Division.
Dilley, R.S., 1986, "Tourist Brochures and Tourist Images", *The Canadian Geographer*, 30, 1, pp.59-65.

Dixon, C.J., 1976, "Settlement and Environment in North East Thailand", *Journal of Tropical Geography*, 46, pp.1-10.
Dixon, C.J., 1977, "Development, Regional Disparity and Planning: The Experience of Northeast Thailand", *Journal of Southeast Asian Studies* , 8, 2, pp.210-23.
Dixon, C.J., 1979, "Thailand: Economic Survey", *Far East and Australasia*, London: Europa, pp.1067-72.
Dixon, C.J., 1981, "Capitalist Penetration, Uneven Development and Government Response: the Case of Thailand", in: M.B. Gleave, ed., *Societies in Change: Studies of Capitalist Penetration*, Developing Areas Research Group Monograph No. 2, pp.65-92.
Dixon, C.J., ed., 1987, *Rural-Urban Interaction in the Third World*, London: Developing Areas Research Group, Institute of British Geographers.
Dixon, C.J., 1991a, *South East Asia in the World Economy*, Cambridge University Press.
Dixon, C.J., 1991b, "Thailand: Economic Survey", *Far East and Austalasia*, London: Europa, pp.1030-8.
Dixon, C.J., 1993, "The Impact of Structural Adjustment on the Thai Rural Economy", in: J. Dahl, D. Drakakis-Smith and A. Narman, eds, *Land, Food and Basic Needs in Developing Countries*, University of Goteborg Monograph Series B No.83, pp.102-130.
Dixon, C.J., 1995, "Structural Adjustment in Comparative Perspective", in: D. Simon, A. Narmen and C. Dixon, eds, *Global Change, Structural Adjustment and the Struggle for Resources in Sub-Saharan Africa*, London: Pluto Press, pp.202-28.
Dixon, C.J. and M.J.G. Parnwell, 1991, "Thailand: The Legacy of Non-Colonial Rule in South-East Asia", in: C.J. Dixon and M. Heffernan, eds, *Colonialism in the Contemporary World*, London: Mansell, pp.204-16.
Dixon, C., D. Simon and A. Narmen, 1995, "The Nature of Structural Adjustment", in: D. Simon, A. Narmen and C.J. Dixon, eds, *Global Change, Structural Adjustment and the Struggle for Resources in Sub-Saharan Africa*, London: Pluto Press, pp.1-14.
Doner, R.F., 1992, "Limits of State Strength: Towards an Institutionalist View of Economic Development", *World Politics*, 44, 3.
Doner, R.F. and A. Ramsay, 1993, "Post-Imperialism and Development in Thailand", *World Development*, 21, 5, pp.691-704.
Donner, Wolf, 1978, *The Five Faces of Thailand: An Economic Geography* , London: Hurst.
Douglass, M., 1981, "Thailand: Territorial Dissolution and Alternative Regional Development for the Central Plains", in: W.B. Stöhr and D.R.F. Taylor, eds, *Development from Above or Below? The Dialectics of Regional Planning in Developing Countries*, Chichester: Wiley, pp.183-208.
Douglass, M., 1984, *Regional Integration on the Capitalist Periphery: The Central Plains of Thailand*, Research Report No.15, Institute of Social Studies, The Hague.
Douglass, M., 1990, *Regional Inequalities and Regional Policy in Thailand: An International Perspective*, Bangkok: TDRI and NESDB.
Douglass, M., 1990, *Urban and Regional Development Policy for the 7th Five-Year Plan in Thailand*, Bangkok: TRDI.

Douglass, M., 1991, *Uneven Urbanisation in Asia: Towards an Alternative Policy of Endogenous Development for Intermediate Cities*, Honolulu: University of Hawaii.

Douglass, M., 1992, "Global Opportunities and Local Challenges for Regional Economies", *Regional Development Dialogue*, 13, 2, pp.3-21.

Douglass, M. and M. Zoghlin, 1994, "Sustaining Cities at the Grassroots: Livelihood, Environment and Social Networks in Suan Phlu, Bangkok", *Third World Planning Review*, 16, 2, pp.171-200.

Drakakis-Smith, D.W., 1979, "Urban Planning: The Challenge of Alternative Urbanism in South-east Asia", in: R.J. Pryor, ed., *Migration and Development in South-East Asia: A Demographic Perspective*, Kuala Lumpur: Oxford University Press, pp.286-94.

Drakakis-Smith, D.W., 1990, "Urban Essays for Harold Carter", in: C.R. Lewis, ed., *Colonial Urbanisation in Asia and Africa: A Structural Analysis*, Cambria: University of Wales.

Drakakis-Smith, D.W. and P.J. Rimmer, 1982, "Taming the 'Wild City': Managing Southeast Asia's Primate Cities since the 1960s", *Asian Geographer*, 1, 1, pp.17-34.

Duggan, S.J., 1991, "Education and Economic Development in Thailand", *Journal of Contemporary Asia*, 21, 2, pp.141-51.

Duncan, S.S., 1989, "Uneven Development and the Difference that Space Makes", *Geoforum*, 20, 2, pp.131-9.

Durrenberger, E.P., 1983, "The Economy of Sufficiency", in: J. McKinnon and W. Bhruksasri, eds, *Highlanders of Thailand*, Kuala Lumpur: Oxford University Press, pp.87-100.

Durst, P.B., 1987, *Natural History and Nature-Oriented Adventure Travel for Rural Development and Wildlands Management: Diagnosis of Research Needs and Project Opportunities for Thailand*, Southeastern Center for Forest Economics Research, Forest-Private Enterprise Initiative Working Paper No. 12, Research Triangle Park, N.C.

Eberhardt, N. ed., 1988, *Gender, Power and the Construction of the Moral Order: Studies from the Thai Periphery*, University of Wisconsin-Madison, Centre for Southeast Asian Studies, Monograph 4.

Economist, 1989, "Thailand: Of Elephants and Dragons", *Economist*, 21 January 1989 p.94.

Economist, 1993, "The Price of Thailand's Prosperity", *Economist*, May 15th 1993.

Economist Intelligence Unit, 1995, *Country Profile: Thailand and Burma, 1994-5,* London: EIU.

Egan, M.L. and M.Jr. Bendick, 1986, "The Urban-Rural Dimension in National Economic Development", *Journal of Developing Areas*, 20, pp.203-22.

Ekachai, Sanitsuda, 1990, *Behind the Smile: Voices of Thailand*, Bangkok: Thai Development Support Committee.

Ekachai, Sanitsuda, 1994, *Seeds of Hope: Local Initiatives in Thailand*, Bangkok: Thai Development Support Committee.

Elliott, D., 1978, *Thailand: The Origins of Military Rule*, London: Zed.

Elliott, James, 1983, "Politics, Power and Tourism in Thailand", *Annals of Tourism Research*, 10, 3, pp.377-93.

Elliott, S., 1995, "The Wildlife Resources of Doi Inthanon National Park and their Potential as Ecotourist Attractions", Report submitted to "Conservation of Biodiversity in Northern Thailand: the Role of Ecotourism in Protected Areas" Project, Kasetsart University, Bangkok.

Errington, F., and D., Gerwertz, 1989, "Tourism and Anthropology in a Post-Modern World", *Oceania*, 60, 1, pp.37-54.

ESCAP, 1982, *Migration, Urbanization and Development in Thailand*, Comparative Study on Migration, Urbanization and Development in the ESCAP Region, Country Report No.5, Bangkok: United Nations Economic and Social Commission for Asia and the Pacific.

ESCAP, 1983, *Foreign Investment Incentive Schemes*, Bangkok: United Nations Economic and Social Commission for Asia and the Pacific.

ESCAP, 1992, *Migration and Urbanization in Asia and the Pacific: Inter-Relationships with Socio-Economic Development and Evolving Policy Issues*, Bangkok: United Nations Economic and Social Commission for Asia and the Pacific.

ESCAP, 1994, *Economic and Social Survey of Asia and the Pacific, 1993*, New York: United Nations.

Esterik, Penny van, 1994, "Cutting up Culture: Colonizing Costume" in: L. Milgram and P. Van Esterik, eds, *The Transformative Power of Cloth in Southeast Asia*, Toronto: The Museum for Textiles, pp.39-52

Evers, H.D., 1987, "Trade and State Formation in the Early Bangkok Period", *Modern Asian Studies*, 21, 4, pp.751-71.

Ewers, Kirsten, 1994, "Politics of Biodiversity Conservation in Thailand: Global and Local Discourse", *Proceedings of the IIAS/NIAS Workshop on Environmental Movements in Asia*, Leiden, The Netherlands, 27-29 October 1994.

Fairclough, G., 1993, "Missing Class: Problems Loom over Failure to Educate Rural Poor", *Far Eastern Economic Review*, 4 February, pp.25-26.

Falkus, M., 1990, "Economic History and Environment in Southeast Asia", *Asian Studies Review*, 14, 1, pp.65-79.

Falkus, M., 1991, "The Economic History of Thailand", *Australian Economic History Review*, 31, 1, pp.53-71.

FAO, 1990, *Report of the Global Consultation on Agricultural Extension, Rome, Italy, 4-8 December 1989*, Prepared by the Agricultural Education and Extension Service, Human Resources, Institutions and Agrarian Reform Division, with the editorial assistance of B E Swanson. Rome. FAO.

Far Eastern Economic Review, various issues.

Farrington, J., D.J. Lewis, S. Satish and A. Miclat-Teves, eds, 1993, *NGOs and the State in Asia: Rethinking Roles in Sustainable Agricultural Development*, London: Routledge.

Feeny, D., 1982, *The Political Economy of Productivity: Thai Agricultural Development, 1880-1975*, Vancouver: University of British Columbia Press.

Feeny, D., 1990, "The Political Economy of Regional Inequalities in Developing Economies: The Northeast of Thailand", *Proceedings of the 4th International Conference on Thai Studies*, Volume II, pp.81-114.

Flaherty, M. and V. Filipchuk, 1994, "Women in Local Governments in Northern Thailand", *Revue Canadienne D'Etudes Du Developpement - Canadian Journal of Development Studies*, 15, 1, pp.35-54.

Forbes, D.K., 1984, *The Geography of Underdevelopment: A Critical Study*, London: Croom Helm.

Freeman, Donald B. and Glen V. Norcliffe, 1985, *Rural Enterprise in Kenya*, Department of Geography, University of Chicago, Research Paper No. 214.

Friedmann, J. and M. Douglass, 1978, "Agropolitan Development: Towards a New Strategy for Regional Planning in Asia", in: UNCRD, *Growth Pole Strategy and Regional Development Planning in Asia*, Nagoya: UNCRD.

Fuchs, R.J., G.W. Jones and E.M. Pernia, eds, 1987, *Urbanization and Urban Policies in Pacific Asia*, Boulder: Westview Press.

Fuller, T.D., Peerasit Kamnuansilpa, P. Lightfoot and Sawaeng Rathanamongkolmas, 1983, *Migration and Development in Modern Thailand*, Bangkok: Social Science Association of Thailand.

Fuller, T.D., P. Lightfoot and P. Kamnuansilpa, 1985, "Rural-Urban Mobility in Thailand: A Decision-Making Approach", *Demography*, 22, 4, pp.565-79.

Ganjanapan, Anan, 1989, "Conflicts over the Development and Control of Labor in a Northern Thai Village", in: Gillian Hart *et.al.*, eds, *Agrarian Transformations: Local Processes and the State in Southeast Asia*, Berkeley: University of California Press.

Garforth, C., 1982, "Reaching the Rural Poor: A Review of Extension Strategies and Methods", in: M.J. Rolls and G.E. Jones, eds, *Progress in Rural Extension and Community Development: Vol. I, Extension and Relative Advantage*, Chichester: John Wiley and Sons.

Garforth, C., 1990, "RPOs: Why the Fuss? How Rural People's Organisations can Play a Role in Extension", *AERDD Bulletin*, 30, November 1990, pp.3-8.

Garforth, C., 1995, *Guide to Extension Training*, Third Edition, Rome: FAO.

Garforth, C. and M. Munro, 1990, *Rural People's Organisations and Agricultural Development in the Upper North of Thailand*, Agricultural Extension and Rural Development Department, University of Reading.

Garforth, C., N. Patanapongsa and W. Kunaporn, 1993, *Communication for Agricultural Development: the role of Rural People's Organisations in Amphoe Mae Sod, Thailand*, Agricultural Extension and Rural Development Department, University of Reading.

GATT, 1980, *International Trade*, Geneva: GATT.

GATT, 1990, *International Trade*, Geneva: GATT.

Geddes, W.R., 1970, "Opium and the Miao: A Study in Ecological Adjustment, *Oceania*, 41, 1, pp.1-11.

Geddes, W.R., 1976, *Migrants of the Mountains: The Cultural Ecology of the Blue Miao (Hmong Njua) of Thailand*, Clarendon: Oxford University Press.

Geertz, C., 1973, *The Interpretation of Cultures*, New York: Basic Books.

von Geusau, L.A., 1983, "Dialectics of Akhazan", in: J. McKinnon and W Bhruksari, eds, *Highlanders of Thailand*, Kuala Lumpur: Oxford University Press, pp.242-77.

von Geusau, L.A., 1988, "The Interiorization of a Perennial Minority Group", in: J.G. Taylor and A. Turton, eds, *Sociology of 'Developing Societies': Southeast Asia*, Basingstoke: Macmillan, pp.215-29.

von Geusau, L.A., 1992. "Regional Development in Northern Thailand: Its Impact on Highlanders and Documenting and Applying Traditional Environmental Knowledge in Northern Thailand", in: M. Johnson, ed, *LORE: Capturing Traditional Environmental Knowledge*, Ottawa, Canada: Dene Cultural Institute and the International Development Research Centre, pp.141-73.

Ginsburg, N., 1976, "The Great City in South-East Asia", in: Y.M. Yeung and C.P. Low, eds, *Changing South-East Asian Cities: Readings on Urbanization*, Singapore: Oxford University Press.

Ginsburg, N., 1988, "Reflections on Primacy: Cases from Asia", in: F.J. Costa *et.al.*, eds, *Asian Urbanization: Problems and Processes*, Berlin: Gebruder Borntraeger, pp.39-45.

Ginsburg, N., B. Koppel and T.G. McGee, eds, 1991, *The Extended Metropolis: Settlement Transition in Asia*, Honolulu: University of Hawaii Press.

Gilbert, A. and J. Kleinpenning, 1986, "Migration, Regional Inequality and Development in the Third World", Introduction to Special Issue of *Tijdschrift voor Econ. en Soc. Geografie*, 77, 1, pp.2-6.

Girling, J.L., 1981a, *The Bureaucratic Polity in Modernizing Societies*, Singapore: Institute of Southeast Asian Studies.

Girling, J.L., 1981b, *Thailand: Society and Politics*, Ithaca: Cornell University Press.

Girling, J.L., 1994, "Thailand: Twin Peaks, Disturbing Shadows", *Southeast Asian Affairs*, pp.305-19.

Gittinger, Mattiebelle, 1982, *Master Dyers to the World*, Washington: The Textile Museum.

Gittinger, Mattiebelle, 1992a, "An examination of Tai Textile Forms", in: M. Gittinger, and H. L. Lefferts Jr., *Textiles and the Tai Experience in Southeast Asia*, Washington: The Textile Museum, pp.28-57.

Gittinger, Mattiebelle, 1992b, "Textiles in the Service of Kings", in: M. Gittinger and H.L. Lefferts Jr., *Textiles and the Tai Experience in Southeast Asia*, Washington: The Textile Museum, pp.142-176.

Gittinger, Mattiebelle and H. Leedom Lefferts Jr., 1992, *Textiles and the Tai Experience in Southeast Asia*, Washington: The Textile Museum.

Gohlert, E.W., 1990, *Power and Culture: The Struggle Against Poverty in Thailand*, Bangkok: White Lotus.

Goldey, P., 1990, "Thailand: Women's Groups for Rural Extension", *AERDD Bulletin*, 30, pp.15-18.

Goldstein, S., 1987, "Forms of Mobility and Their Policy Implications: Thailand and China Compared", *Social Forces*, 65, pp.915-42.

Goldstein, S. and A. Goldstein, 1986, *Migration in Thailand: a Twenty-Five Year Review*.

Gorton, P., 1988, "Tourism: A Cash Crop that can Hurt the Hilltribes", *Bangkok Post*, February 14.

Gould, W.T.S., 1982, "Rural-Urban Interaction in the Third World", *Area*, 14, p.334.

Goulet, D., 1992, "Development: Creator and Destroyer of Values", *World Development*, 20, pp.467-75.
Governement General de l'Indo-Chine, 1903, "La sericulture au Siam", *Bulletin Economique Indo-Chine*, 2, 20, pp.586-7.
Graburn, Nelson H.H., ed., 1976, *Ethnic and Tourist Arts: Cultural Expressions from the Fourth World*, Berkeley, L.A.: University of California Press.
Graburn, Nelson H.H., 1982, "The Dynamics of Change in Tourist Arts", *Cultural Survival Quarterly*, 6, 2, pp.7-11.
Graburn, Nelson H.H., 1984, "The Evolution of Tourist Arts", *Annals of Tourism Research*, 11, pp.393-419.
Grace, B., 1981, "The Farmers' Federation of Thailand", in: H. Handleman, ed., *The Politics of Agrarian Change in Asia and Latin America*, AUFS Reports, Bloomington: Indiana University Press.
Grandstaff, T.B., 1979, "The Hmong, Opium and the Haw: Speculations on the Origin of their Association", *Journal of the Siam Society*, 67, pp.70-79.
Grandstaff, W. Sumluckrat, 1992, "Income Disparities: What Can Be Done?", *Pacific Viewpoint*, 33, 2.
Grandstaff, W. Sumluckrat, 1990, *The Role of Demand in Provincial Industrialisation*, Bangkok: TDRI.
Gugler, J., 1981, "The Rural-Urban Interface and Migration", in: A. Gilbert and J. Gugler, *Cities, Poverty and Development: Urbanization in the Third World*, Oxford: Oxford University Press.
Gwynne, R., 1992, *Chile to 1994: More Growth Under Democracy*, London, Economist Intelligence Unit.
Hadjimichalis, C., 1987, *Uneven Development and Regionalism: State, Territory and Class in Southern Europe*, London: Croom Helm.
Hafner, J.A., 1980, "Urban Resettlement and Migration in Northeast Thailand: The Spectre of Urban Involution", *Journal of Developing Areas*, 14.
Haggard, Stephan, 1990, *Pathways From the Periphery: The Politics of Growth in the Newly Industrializing Countries*, Ithaca: Cornell University Press.
Haggard, Stephan and Chung-In Moon, 1990, "Institutions and Economic Policy: Theory and a Korean Case Study", *World Politics*, 42, 2.
Haggard, Stephan and Robert Kaufman, 1989, "The Politics of Stabilization and Structural Adjustment" in: Jeffrey Sachs, ed., *Developing Country Debt and Economic Performance: The International Financial System*, Chicago: University of Chicago Press.
Hall, A., 1988, "Community Participation and Development Policy: A Sociological Perspective", in: A. Hall and J. Midgeley, eds, *Development Policies: Sociological Perspectives*, Manchester: Manchester University Press.
Hallett, Holt, 1890, *A Thousand Miles on an Elephant in the Shan States* Edinburgh and London: William Blackwood and Sons.
Hamilton, Clive, 1983, "Capitalist Industrialization in East Asia's Four Little Tigers", *Journal of Contemporary Asia*, 13, 1, pp.35-73.
Handley, P., 1988a, "Ports Clog, Roads Jam", *Far Eastern Economic Review* 29 September, pp.94-96.

Handley, P., 1988b, "Thailand Hits the Wall", *Far Eastern Economic Review,* 29 September, pp.94-95.
Handley, P., 1989, "Seeding the South", *Far Eastern Economic Review*, 30 March, pp.56-57.
Handley, P., 1991, "Growth Without Tears", *Far Eastern Economic Review,* 18 July, pp.34-35.
Handley, P., 1993a, "Watering the Roots", *Far Eastern Economic Review*, 5 August, pp.46-48.
Handley, P., 1993b, "Thought for Food: Thai Farm Policy Faces Long-Term Choices", *Far Eastern Economic Review*, 29 April, pp.46-50.
Hanks, J.R., 1988, "The Power of Akha Women", in: N. Eberhardt, ed, *Gender, Power and the Construction of the Moral Order: Studies from the Thai Periphery*, Centre for Southeast Asian Studies Monograph 4, Madison: University of Wisconsin, pp.13-31.
Hanks, Lucien M., ed., 1965, *Ethnographic Notes on Northern Thailand*, Ithaca: Cornell University, Southeast Asia Program, Data Paper No. 58.
Hansen, N.M., 1981, "Development from Above: The Centre-Down Development Paradigm", in: W.B. Stöhr and D.R.F. Taylor, eds, *Development from Above or Below? The Dialectics of Regional Planning in Developing Countries*, Chichester: Wiley, pp.15-38.
Hantrakul, Sukanya, 1988, "Prostitution in Thailand", in: G. Chandler, N. Sullivan and J. Branson, eds, *Development and Displacement: Women in Southeast Asia*, Clayton: Centre of Southeast Asian Studies, Monash University, pp.115-136.
Hardoy, Jorge E. and David Satterthwaite, 1989, *Squatter Citizen: Life in the Urban Third World*, London: Earthscan.
Hauser, P.M., D.B. Suits and Naohiro Ogawa, eds, 1985, *Urbanization and Migration in ASEAN Development*, Tokyo: National Institute for Research Advancement.
Hayward, J., 1990, "Agricultural Extension: The World Bank's Experience and Approaches", in: B. Swanson, ed., *Global Consultation on Agricultural Extension*, Rome: FAO.
Hewison, Kevin, 1985, "The State and Capitalist Development in Thailand", in: R. Higgott and R. Robison, eds, *South East Asia: Essays in the Political Economy of Structural Change*, London: Routledge and Kegan Paul, pp.266-94.
Hewison, Kevin, 1987, "National Interest and Economic Downturn: Thailand", in: Richard Robison, Kevin Hewison and Richard Higgott, eds, *Southeast Asia in the 1980s: The Politics of Economic Crisis*, Sydney: Allen and Unwin.
Hewison, Kevin, 1988, "Industry Prior to Industrialisation: Thailand", *Journal of Contemporary Asia*, 18, 4, pp.389-411.
Hewison, Kevin, 1989a, *Bankers and Bureaucrats: Capital and the Role of the State in Thailand*, Monograph Series 34, New Haven: Yale Center for International and Area Studies.
Hewison, Kevin, 1989b, *Power and Politics in Thailand: Essays in Political Economy*, Journal of Contemporary Asia Publishers.
Hewison, K. and A. Brown, 1994, "Labour and Unions in an Industrialising Thailand", *Journal of Contemporary Asia*, 24, 4, pp.483-514.

Heyzer, N., ed., 1987, *Women Farmers and Rural Change in Asia: Towards Equal Access and Participation*, Kuala Lumpur: Asian Pacific Development Centre.

Hiemenz, U., 1983, "Growth and Efficiency of Small and Medium Industries in ASEAN Countries", *Asian Development Review*, 1, 1, pp.101-18.

Hindle, T., 1987, "Tropical Balance: A Survey of Thailand", *Economist*, 31 October, pp.1-22.

Hinton, P., 1975, "Karen Subsistence: The Limits of a Swidden Economy", unpublished Ph.D. Thesis, University of Sydney.

Hirsch, Philip, 1987, "Participation, Rural Development and Changing Production Relations in Recently Settled Forest Areas of Thailand", unpublished Ph.D. Thesis, University of London.

Hirsch, Philip, 1989, "Local Contexts of Differentiation and Inequality on the Thai Periphery", *Journal of Contemporary Asia*, 19, 3, pp. 308-23.

Hirsch, Philip, 1990, *Development Dilemmas in Rural Thailand*, Singapore: Oxford University Press, South-East Asia Social Science Monographs.

Hirsch, Philip, 1993, *Political Economy of Environment in Thailand*, Manila: Journal of Contemporary Asia Publishers.

Hirsch, Philip, 1994, "The Thai Countryside in the 1990s", *Southeast Asian Affairs*, pp.320-34.

Hirsch, Philip and Larry Lohmann, 1989, "Contemporary Politics of the Environment in Thailand", *Asian Survey*, XXIX, 4, pp.439-51.

Hitchcock, Michael, Victor T. King and Michael J.G. Parnwell, eds, 1993, *Tourism in South-East Asia*, London: Routledge.

Ho, Samuel P.S., 1986, "Rural Non-Agricultural Development in Asia: Experiences and Issues", in: Yang-Boo Choe and Fu-Chen Lo, eds, *Rural Industrialisation and Non-farm Activities of Asian Farmers*, Kuala Lumpur: Asian and Pacific Development Centre.

Hobart, M. and R. Taylor, eds, *Context, Meaning and Power in South-East Asia*, Ithaca: Cornell University Press.

Holland, S., 1990, "Development and Differentiation in Rural Thailand", unpublished Ph.D. Thesis, University of Oxford.

Holloway, R., ed., 1989, *Doing Development: Governments, NGOs and the Rural Poor in Asia*, London: Earthscan.

Holtsberg, C., 1982, "Rice Pricing Policy", in: P. Richards, ed., *Basic Needs and Government Policies in Thailand*, Singapore: Maruzen Asia, pp.161-81.

Hong, Evelyne, 1985, *See the Third World While it Lasts: The Social and Environmental Impact of Tourism, With Particular Reference to Malaysia*, Penang: Consumers Association of Penang.

Hudson, Ray, 1988, "Uneven Development in Capitalist Societies: Changing Spatial Divisions of Labour, Forms of Spatial Organization of Production and Service Provision, and their Impacts on Localities", *Transactions of the Institute of British Geographers*, N.S.13, pp.484-96.

Hulme, D., 1991, "Agricultural Extension Services as Machines: The Impact of the Training and Visit Approach", in: W.M. Rivera and S.J. Gustafson, eds, *Agricultural Extension: Worldwide Institutional Evolution and Forces for Change*, Amsterdam and London: Elsevier, pp.217-30.

Hussey, A., 1993, "Rapid Industrialization in Thailand, 1986-1991", *Geographical Review*, 83, 1, pp.14-28.
Hutaserani, Suganya, 1990, "The Trends of Income Inequality and Poverty and a Profile of the Urban Poor in Thailand", *TDRI Quarterly Review*, 15, 4 (December 1990).
Hutaserani, Suganya and Pornchai Tapwong, 1990, *Urban Poor Upgrading: Analyses of Poverty Trend and Profile of Urban Poor in Thailand*, Bangkok: TRDI.
Ichaporia, Niloufer, 1982, "Imports and Exportmania", *Cultural Survival Quarterly*, 6, 4, pp.12-14.
Ichikawa, Nobuko, 1991, "Geographic Implication of Foreign Investment in Thailand's Industrialisation", *Southeast Asian Journal of Social Science*, 19, 1/2.
IDRC Reports, 1988, "Artisans of Progress", 17, 2 (April), pp.1-15.
Ikemoto, Yukio, 1988, "An Overview of Thai Economic Growth in the Post-War Period", in: Ikemoto, Yukio and Warin Wonghanchao, 1988, *Economic Development in Thailand: A Historical Review*, Tokyo: Institute of Developing Economies, pp.1-37.
Ikemoto, Yuriko, 1991, *Income Distribution in Thailand: Its Changes, Causes, and Structure*, Tokyo: Institute of Developing Economies.
Ikemoto, Yuriko and K. Limskul, 1987, "Income Inequality and Regional Disparity in Thailand, 1962-81", *Developing Economies*, 25, 3, pp.249-69.
Ikemoto, Yukio and Warin Wonghanchao, 1988, *Economic Development in Thailand: A Historical Review*, Tokyo: Institute of Developing Economies.
Ingram, J.C., 1971, *Economic Change in Thailand, 1850-1970*, Stanford: Stanford University Press.
Isarankun, Chirayu, 1969, "Manufacturing Industries in Thailand", unpublished Ph.D. Dissertation, Australian National University, Canberra.
Isarankura, Watana, 1990, "Emerging Urban-Regional Linkages: The Bangkok Metropolitan Region", *Regional Development Dialogue*, 11, 2.
Islam, Rizwanul, 1983, "Poverty, Income Distribution and Growth in Rural Thailand", in: A.R. Khan and E. Lee, eds, *Poverty in Rural Asia*, Bangkok: International Labour Organisation, Asian Employment Programme [ARTEP], Agricultural Land Reforms Office.
Islam, Rizwanul, ed., 1985, *Strategies for Alleviating Poverty in Rural Asia,* Bangkok: International Labour Organization, Asian Employment Programme.
Islam, Rizwanul, ed., 1987, *Rural Industrialization and Employment in Asia,* New Delhi: International Labour Organization, Asian Employment Programme.
Jacobs, N., 1971, *Modernization Without Development: Thailand as an Asian Case Study*, New York: Praeger.
Jansen, K., 1989, "Financial Development and the Intersectoral Transfer of Resources: The Case of Thailand", *Development and Change*, 20, 1, pp.5-34.
Jansen, K., 1990, *Finance, Growth and Stability: Financing Economic Development in Thailand, 1960-86*, Aldershot: Avebury.
Jansen, K., 1991, "Thailand: The Next NIC?", *Journal of Contemporary Asia*, 21, 1, pp.13-30.

Jitsuchon, Somchai, 1988, "Thailand's Changing Income Distribution Pattern: 1975/76 to 1985/86", *TDRI Quarterly Newsletter*, 3, 3 (September).

Jitsuchion, Somchai, 1989, *Alleviation of Rural Poverty*, Bangkok: Thailand Development Research Institute Foundation.

Jones, G.W., 1988, "Urbanization Trends in Southeast Asia: Some Issues for Policy", *Journal of Southeast Asian Studies*, 19, 1, pp.137-54.

Jones, G.W., 1993, "Industrialization and Urbanization in South-East Asia", in: H. Brookfield and Y. Byron, eds, *South-East Asia's Environmental Future: The Search for Sustainability*, Tokyo: United Nations University Press, pp.47-71.

Johnson, Chalmers, 1982, *MITI and the Japanese Miracle*, California: Stanford University Press.

Johnson, Chalmers, 1986, "The Nonsocialist NICs: East Asia", *International Organization*, 40, 2.

Johnson, Chalmers, 1989, *The Democratization of South Korea: What Role Does Economic Development Play?*, Copenhagen University: Museum Tusculanum Press, No. 4.

Johnson, V.W., 1969, *Agricultural Development of Thailand with Special Reference to Rural Institutions*, Bangkok: Government of Thailand, Division of Land Policy, Department of Land Development.

Justice and Peace Commission, 1984, *Samui in the Time of Changes: The Study of Tourism in Samui Island*, Bangkok: Justice and Peace Commission of Thailand.

Judd, L.C., 1977, *Chao Rai Thai: Dry Rice Farmers in Northern Thailand*, Bangkok: Suriyaban Publishers.

Judd, L.C., 1987, *A Vision to Some - A Case Study of Rural Development Activities by a NGO in Thailand*, Research Report Series no. 18, Payap University Centre for Research and Development, Bangkok: Suriyaban Publishers.

Judd, L.C., 1988, *In Perspective: Trends in Rural Development, Policy and Programmes in Thailand, 1947-1987*, Chiang Mai: Payap University Centre for Research and Development, Research Report No. 41.

Kabilsingh, Chatsumarn, 1991, *Thai Women in Buddhism*, Berkeley: Parallax Press.

Kachondham, Y. and S. Chunharas, 1993, "At the Crossroads: Challenges for Thailand's Health Development", *Health Policy and Planning*, 8, pp.208-16.

de Kadt, E., ed., 1979, *Tourism: Passport to Development? Perspectives on the Social and Cultural Effects in Developing Countries*, New York: Oxford University Press.

Kammerer, C.A., 1986, "Gateway to the Akha World: Kinship, Ritual, and Community among Highlanders of Thailand", unpublished Ph.D. dissertation, University of Chicago.

Kammerer, C.A., 1987, "Minority Identity in the Mountains of Northern Thailand: The Akha Case", in: *Southeast Asian Tribal Groups and Ethnic Minorities*, A Cultural Survival Report, 22, Cambridge.

Kammerer, C.A., 1988, "Shifting Gender Asymmetries among Akha of Northern Thailand", in: N. Eberhardt, ed., *Gender, Power and the Construction of Moral Order: Studies from the Thai Periphery*, Centre fo

Southeast Asian Studies Monograph 4, Madison: University of Wisconsin, pp.33-51.
Kammerer, C.A., 1989, "Territorial Imperatives: Akha Ethnic Identity and Thailand's National Integration", in: J. McKinnon and B. Vienne, eds, *Hilltribes Today: Problems in Change*, Bangkok: White Lotus-Orstom, pp.259-301.
Kammerer, C.A., 1990, "Customs and Christian Conversion among Akha Highlanders of Burma and Thailand", *American Ethnologist*, 17, 2, pp.277-291.
Kampe, K., 1992, "Development, Bureaucracy and Life on the Margins", *Pacific Viewpoint*, 33, 2, pp.159-64.
Kanjanaharitai, Paiboon, 1981, "Bangkok: The City of Angels", in: M. Honjo, ed., *Urbanization and Regional Development*, pp.203-25.
Kanjanawanawan, Suda, 1992, "Feeding Time at the Human Zoo", *The Nation*, 26 March 1992.
Kaojarern, S., G. Trébuil, P. Traimongkonkool and N. Ngernprasertsri, 1992, "Agro-Ecological Zonation and Recent Agroecosystem Transformations in Kanjanaburi Province, Western Thailand: Hypotheses for Improving Farming Systems Sustainability", *Proceedings of the 9th Thailand National Farming Systems Seminar*, Phuket, Thailand, 24-27 March 1992, pp.119-38.
Kaosa-ard, Mingsarn Santikarn and Kitty Israngkura, 1988, "Industrial Policies in Thailand", in: Warin Wonghanchao and Yukio Ikemoto, eds, *Economic Development Policy in Thailand: A Historical Review*, ASEDP No.1, Institute of Developing Economies, Tokyo.
Kaothien, Utis, 1991, "Regional and Urbanization Policy in Thailand - The Tertiary Sector as a Leading Sector in Regional Development", *Urban Studies*, 28, 6, pp.1027-43.
Kaplinsky, Raphael, 1990, *The Economies of Small: Appropriate Technology in a Changing World*, London: Intermediate Technology.
Karnjanauksorn, Teeranat, 1987, "Gender Relations, Sex-Related Services and the Development of the Thai Economy", Paper presented to the Annual Meetings, Association for Asian Studies, Boston, April 1987.
Kathuria, Sanjay, Virginia Miralao and Rebecca Joseph, 1988, *Artisan Industries in Asia: Four Case Studies*, Ottawa: IDRC, Technical Study 60e.
Kaufman, J.C., 1960, *Bangkhaud: a Community Study in Thailand.* Locust Valley: J.J. Augustin.
Keller, C.P., 1987, "Stages of Peripheral Tourism Development - Canada's Northwest Territories", *Tourism Management*, 8, pp.20-32.
Kelley, A.C. and J.G. Williamson, 1987, "What Drives City Growth in the Developing World?", in: G.S. Tolley and V. Thomas, eds, *The Economics of Urbanization and Urban Policies in Developing Countries*, Washington DC: World Bank, pp.32-45.
Keokungwal, Chalerm, 1992, "Current Human Settlement Situation in Thailand and Related Policies", *Regional Development Dialogue*, 13, 4, pp.35-47.
Kerkvliet, B.J.T., 1990, *Everyday Politics in the Philippines: Class and Status Relations in a Central Luzon Village*, Berkeley: University of California Press.

Kesmanee, C. and K. Charoensri, 1994, "The Impact of Tourism on Culture and Environment: A Case Study of the Mae Taeng Trekking Route in Chiang Mai", Bangkok: Report to Office of the National Culture Commission.
Ketudat, Sippanondha, 1990, *The Middle Path for the Future of Thailand: Technology in Harmony with Culture and Environment*, Honolulu: East-West Center/Chiang Mai University: Faculty of Social Sciences.
Keyes, Charles F., 1966, "Peasant and Nation: A Thai-Lao Village in a Thai State", unpublished Ph.D. thesis, Cornell University.
Keyes, Charles F., 1967, *Isan: Regionalism in North-East Thailand,* Cornell University Southeast Asia Program, Data Paper No. 65, Ithaca, New York: Cornell University.
Keyes, Charles F., 1987, *Thailand: Buddhist Kingdom as Modern Nation-State*, Boulder: Westview Press.
Keyes, Charles F., 1989, *Thailand: Buddhist Kingdom as Modern Nation State*, Bangkok: Duang Kamol.
Keyes, Charles F. and P. van den Berghe, eds, 1984, "Tourism and Ethnicity", *Annals of Tourism Research* (special issue), 11, 3, pp.333-501.
Khan, H.U., 1981, "Concentration of Heavy-Metals in Bangkok Metropolitan Area", *Journal of Environmental Science and Health Part A - Environmental Science and Engineering*, 16, 6, pp.637-45.
Khan, Habibullah, 1988, "Development Planning in ASEAN: Lessons of Experience", *Economic Bulletin for Asia and the Pacific*, XXXIX, 2, Bangkok: UNESCAP.
Khoo, Siew-Ean, 1984, "Urbanward Migration and Employment of Women in Southeast and East Asian Cities: Patterns and Policy Issues", in: G. Jones, ed., *Women in the Urban and Industrial Labour Force: Southeast and East Asia*, Canberra: Development Studies Centre Monograph No. 33, Australian National University, pp.277-91.
King, William L., 1977, "Umbrellas Make their Day", *Journal of the National Research Council of Thailand*, 9, 2, pp.1-33.
Kiranandana, Thienchay and Suwanee Surasiengsunk, 1985, *Population Policy Background Paper Study on Economic Consequences of Urbanization in Thailand, 1987-2001*, Bangkok: Thai Development Research Institute.
Klausner, William J., 1981, *Reflections on Thai Culture*, Bangkok: Suksit Siam.
Koizumi, Junko, 1992, "The Commutation of *suai* from Northeast Siam in the Middle of the Nineteenth Century", *Journal of Southeast Asian Studies*, 23, 2, pp.276-307.
Kojima, Kiyoshi, 1977, *Japan and a New World Economic Order*, Tokyo: Charles E. Tuttle.
Komin, Suntaree, 1989, *Social Dimensions of Industrialization in Thailand*, Bangkok: NIDA Research Center.
Komin, Suntaree, 1991, "Social Dimensions of Industrialization in Thailand", *Regional Development Dialogue*, 12, 1.
Korff, R., 1989a, *Bangkok and Modernity*, Bangkok: CUSRI.
Korff, R., 1989b, "Urban or Agrarian? The Modern Thai State", *Sojourn*, 4, 1, pp.44-53.

Krongkaew, Medhi, 1985, "Agricultural Development, Rural Poverty and Income Distribution in Thailand", *The Developing Economies*, XXII, 4, pp.325-46.
Krongkaew, Medhi, 1987a, *Industrialization, Employment, Poverty and Income Distribution of Thai Households*: Bangkok: Thailand Development Research Institute.
Krongkaew, Medhi, 1987b, "The Economic and Social Impact of Thailand's Rural Job Creation Programs", *Philippines Review of Economics and Business*, 14, 3-4, pp.237-72.
Krongkaew, Medhi, 1988, "The Development of Small and Medium-Scale Industries in Thailand", *Asian Development Review,* 6, 2, pp.70-95.
Krongkaew, Medhi, Apichat Chamratrithirong and Varai Woramotri, 1983, *A Study of Low-Income Households in the Northeastern Region of Thailand,* Research Report No.74, Mahidol University, Institute for Population and Social Research.
Krongkaew, Medhi, Pranee Tinakorn and Suphat Suphachalasai, 1990, *Priority Issues and Policy Measures to Alleviate Rural Poverty: The Case of Thailand*, Bangkok: Thammasat University.
Krongkaew, Medhi, Pranee Tinakorn and Suphat Suphachalasai, 1992, "Rural Poverty in Thailand: Policy Issues and Responses", *Asian Development Review*, 10, 1, pp.199-225.
Krongkaew, Medhi and Pawadee Tongudai, 1984, *The Growth of Bangkok: The Economics of Unbalanced Urbanization and Development*, Discussion Paper No. 90, Faculty of Economics, Thammasat University, Bangkok.
Krause, Lawrence B., 1972, "Evolution of Foreign Direct Investment: The United States and Japan" in: Jerome B. Cohen, ed., *Pacific Partnership: United States-Japan Trade*, Japan Society Inc.
Kriedte, Peter, H. Medick and J. Schlumbohm, 1981, *Industrialization before Industrialization: Rural Industry in the Genesis of Capitalism*, New York: Cambridge University Press.
Kritiporn, Phanu, Theodore Panayotou and Krerkpong Charnprateep, 1990, *The Greening of Thai Industry: Producing More and Polluting Less*, Bangkok: TRDI.
Kriengkraipetch, Suvanna and Larry E. Smith, eds, 1992, *Value Conflicts in Thai Society: Agonies of Change Seen in Short Stories*, Honolulu: East-West Center/Bangkok: Chulalongkorn University Social Research Institute.
Kullick, E. and D. Wilson, 1992, *Thailand's Turn: Profile of a New Dragon*, London: Macmillan.
Kukrit Pramoj, M. R., 1981, *Si Phendin (Four Reigns)*, translated by Tulachandra, 2 vols., Bangkok: Editions Duang Kamol.
Kwan, C. H., 1994, *Economic Interdependence in the Asia-Pacific Region*, London: Routledge.
Laothamatas, Anek, 1988, "Business and Politics in Thailand: New Patterns of Influence", *Asian Survey*, 28, 4, pp.451-70.
Laothamatas, Anek, 1989, "From Bureaucratic Polity to Liberal Corporatism: Business Associations and the New Political Economy of Thailand", unpublished Ph.D. thesis, Columbia University.
Laothamatas, Anek, 1991, *Business Associations and the New Political Economy of Thailand*, Boulder: Westview Press.

Laothamatas, Anek, 1992, "The Success of Structural Adjustment in Thailand: A Political Explanation of Economic Success", in: A.J. MacIntyre and Kanishka Jayasuriya, eds, *The Dynamics of Economic Policy Reform in South-east Asia and the South-west Pacific*, Singapore: Oxford University Press, pp.32-49.

Lall, Sanjaya, 1990, *Building Industrial Competitiveness in Developing Countries,* Paris: OECD.

Lea, J., 1988, *Tourism and Development in the Third World*, London: Routledge.

Leelakulthanit, O. and R.L. Day, 1992, "Quality of Life in Thailand", *Social Indicators Research*, 27, 1, pp.41-57.

Lefferts, H. Leedom Jr., 1991, *Research Report: Lao Royal Women's Embroidery*, Paper presented at Annual Meeting, Mid-Atlantic Region/Association for Asian Studies, October 1991.

Lefferts, H. Leedom Jr., 1992a, "Contexts and Meanings in Tai textiles", in: Mattiebelle Gittinger and H. Leedom Lefferts Jr., 1992, *Textiles and the Tai Experience in Southeast Asia*, Washington: The Textile Museum, pp. 58-91.

Lefferts, H. Leedom Jr., 1992b, "Textiles in the Service of Tai Buddhism", in: Mattiebelle Gittinger and H. Leedom Lefferts Jr., 1992, *Textiles and the Tai Experience in Southeast Asia*, Washington: The Textile Museum, pp.94-141.

Lefferts, H. Leedom Jr., 1992c, "Cut and Sewn: The Textiles of Social Organization in Thailand" in: R. Barnes and J. B. Eicher, eds, *The Anthropology of Dress and Gender*, New York: Berg, pp.44-55.

Lefferts, H. Leedom Jr., 1992d, "Woman's Work", Lecture presented at The Textile Museum, Washington, D.C., October 1992.

Lefferts, H. Leedom Jr., 1993, "The Power of Women's Decision: Textiles in Tai Dam and Thai-Lao Theravada Buddhist Funerals", *Southeast Asia Journal of Social Science*, 21, 2, pp.111-29.

Lefferts, H. Leedom Jr., 1994a, "Clothing the Serpent: Transformations of the *Naak* in Thai-Lao Theravada Buddhism", in: L. Milgram and P. Van Esterik, eds, *The Transformative Power of Cloth in Southeast Asia*, Toronto: The Museum for Textiles, pp.19-38.

Lefferts, H. Leedom Jr., 1994b, "Women's Textiles and Men's Crafts in Thai Culture", *1994 Festival of American Folklife*, Washington: Smithsonian Institution, pp.43-46.

Lewis, J.P. and D. Kapur, 1990, "An Updating Country Study: Thailand's Needs and Prospects in the 1990s", *World Development*, 18, 10, pp.1363-78.

Lewis, P. and Lewis, E., 1984, *The Peoples of the Golden Triangle*, London: Thames and Hudson.

Lightfoot, P. and T. Fuller, 1983, "Circular Rural Urban Movement and Development Planning in Northeast Thailand", *Geoforum*, 14, 3, pp.277-87.

Likhit, Dhiravegin, 1978, *The Bureaucratic Elite of Thailand*, Bangkok: Thai Khadi Research Institute.

Lilley, R., 1990, "Afterwords: 'Ethnicity' and Anthropology", in: G. Wijeyewardene, ed., *Ethnic Groups Across National Boundaries in Mainland Southeast Asia*, Singapore: Institute of Southeast Asian Studies.

Lim, Mah Lui and D. Porpora, 1987, "The Political Economic Factors of Migration to Bangkok", *Journal of Contemporary Asia*, 17, 1, pp.76-89.

Lim, Y.C. and P.E. Fong, 1991, *Foreign Direct Investment and Industrialization in Malaysia, Singapore, Taiwan and Thailand*, Paris: Development Centre Studies, OECD.

Lo, F.C., J.S. Edralin and N.T. Dung, eds, 1981, *Rural-Urban Relations and Regional Development*, Singapore: Maruzen.

Loha-unchit, Chesada, 1990, *Policies, Instruments and Institutions for Rural Industrial Development*, Bangkok: TDRI.

London, B., 1980, *Metropolis and Nation in Thailand: The Political Economy of Uneven Development*, Boulder: Westview Press.

London, B., 1981, *Metropolis and Nation: An Ecological Analysis of Primate City-Hinterland Relationships in Thailand*, Ann Arbor: University Microfilms.

London, B., 1986, "Ecological and Political-Economic Analyses of Migration to a Primate City: Bangkok, Thailand c.1970", *Urban Affairs Quarterly*, 21, 4, pp.501-26.

London, B., 1987, "Ending Ecology's Ethnocentrism: Thai Replications and Extensions of Ecological Research", *Rural Sociology*, 52, pp.483-500.

London, B. and K.L. Anderson, 1985, "Population-Density, Elites, and the Distribution of Infrastructural Resources in Thailand", *Sociological Quarterly*, 26, 2, pp.235-49.

Loslier, L. and Y. Porapakkham, 1992, "Environmental Factors and Structural Factors as Determinants of Public Health - Study of the Ubon-Ratchathani Province of Thailand", *Revue Canadienne D'Etudes Du Developpement - Canadian Journal of Development Studies*, 13, 2, pp.181-95.

Lummis, C. Douglas, 1992, "Equality", in: Wolfgang Sachs, ed., *The Development Dictionary: A Guide to Knowledge as Power*, London: Zed Books, pp.38-52.

Mabogunje, A.L., 1980, *The Development Process: A Spatial Perspective*, London: Hutchinson.

Mackie, J.A.C., 1988, "Economic Growth in the ASEAN Region: The Political Underpinnings" in: Helen Hughes, *Achieving Industrialization in East Asia*, Cambridge University Press.

Mainwaring, L., 1991, *Dynamics of Uneven Development*, Aldershot: Edward Elgar.

Manarungsan, Sompop, 1989, *Economic Development of Thailand, 1850-1950: Responses to the Challenge of the World Economy*, Bangkok: Institute of Asian Studies, Chulalongkorn University.

Maneeprasert, M., K. Pokpong and C. Prangkis, 1975, *Reconnaissance Survey of the Impact of Tourism in the Highlands*, Chiang Mai: Tribal Research Centre.

Marcus, G. and M. Fischer, 1986, *Anthropology as Cultural Critique: An Experimental Moment in the Human Sciences*, Chicago and London: The University of Chicago Press.

Marsden, K., 1984, "Services for Small Firms: The Roles of Government Programs and Market Networks in Thailand", *International Labour Review*, 123, 2, pp.235-49.
Martin, B.S. and M. Uysal, 1990, "An Examination of the Relationships Between Carrying Capacity and the Tourism Lifecycle: Management and Policy Implications", *Journal of Environmental Management*, 31, pp.327-33.
Martin, E.D. and M. Yoder, 1987, *Institutions for Irrigation Management in Farmer-Managed Systems: Examples from the Hills of Nepal*, Research Paper No. 5., International Irrigation Management Institute, Sri Lanka.
Maxwell, Robyn, 1990, *Textiles of Southeast Asia: Tradition, Trade, and Transformation,* Australian National Gallery, Canberra; Oxford University Press, Melbourne.
Mazoyer, M., 1981, "Origines et mécanismes de reproduction des inégalites régionales de developpement agricole en Europe", *Congress of the European Association of Agricultural Economists*, Belgrade, Yogoslavia, 31 August-4 September 1981.
Mazoyer, M., 1985, "Preliminary Report to the Agrarian Systems Committee", Paris: Ministry of Research and Technology.
Mazoyer, M., 1988, "Les inégalités de développement agricole dans le monde", *Spring Session of the French Rural Economy Society*, 19-20 April 1988.
MacCannell, D., 1973, "Staged Authenticity: Arrangements of Social Space in Tourist Settings", *American Journal of Sociology*, 79, 3, pp.589-603.
Meer, C. van der, 1981, *Rural Development in Northern Thailand: An Interpretation and Analysis*, Groningen: Rijksuniversiteit te Groningen.
Meesook, O.A., 1978, "Income, Consumption and Poverty in Thailand, 1962/63 to 1975/76", *World Bank Staff Working Paper No.364* (November).
Meesook, O.A. *et.al.*, n.d., *The Political Economy of Thailand's Development: Poverty, Equity and Growth, 1850-1985*, Washington: World Bank.
Mekpaiboon, Sirilert, 1980, "Administrative Reforms for Decentralized Development: Some Experiments in Thailand", in: A.P. Saxena, ed., *Administrative Reforms for Decentralized Development*, Kuala Lumpur: APDAC.
Mekvichai, Banasopit, David Foster, Sopon Chomchan and Phanu Kritiporn, 1990, *Urbanization and Environment: Managing the Conflict*, Bangkok: TRDI.
Meyer, W., 1987, *Beyond the Mask: Toward a Trandisciplinary Approach of Selected Social Problems Related to the Evolution and Context of International Tourism in Thailand*, unpublished Ph.D. thesis, University of Geneva.
Meyer, W., 1988, *Beyond the Mask: Towards a Transdisciplinary Approach of Selected Social Problems Related to the Evolution and Context of International Tourism in Thailand*, Saarbrucken: Breitenbach.
Michaud, J., 1993, "The Social Anchoring of the Trekking Tourist Business in a Hmong Community of Northern Thailand", Paper presented at the Fifth International Conference on Thai Studies, SOAS, University of London, July 1993.

Mies, Maria, 1986, *Patriarchy and Accumulation on a World Scale: Women and the New International Division of Labor*, London: Zed Press.
Milgram, Lynne, 1992, *Considering Cloth as Commodity in Small-Scale Traditional Production in Highland Luzon, Philippines*, Paper presented at AES/CMA Annual Meeting, Santa Fe, New Mexico, April 1992.
Mills, Mary Beth, in press, "Between the Bright City Lights and the Family Hearth: The Dilemma of Village Daughters Working in Bangkok", in: H.P. Phillips, *Being in Bangkok.*
Mingsarn, Santikarn Kaosa-ard and Kitty Israngkura, 1988, "Industrial Policies in Thailand", in: Warin Wonghanchao and Yukio Ikemoto, eds, *Economic Development Policy in Thailand. A Historical Review*, Tokyo: ASEDP No. 1, Institute of Developing Economies.
MacIntyre, Andrew J. and Kanishka Jayasuriya, 1992, *The Dynamics of Economic Policy Reform in South-East Asia and the South-West Pacific*, Singapore: Oxford University Press.
Mirante, E.T., 1990, "Hostages to Tourism", *Cultural Survival Quarterly*, 14, pp.35-38.
Mitchell, D.R. *et.al.*, 1979, "Thailand Sericulture Settlements Project", evaluation presented to the Asia Bureau, USAID, Washington D.C.
Mizoguchi, T., 1985, "Economic Development Policy and Income Distribution: The Experience in East and Southeast Asia", *Developing Economies*, 23, 4, pp.307-24.
McGee, T.G., 1967, *The Southeast Asian City: A Social Geography of the Primate Cities of Southeast Asia*, London: Bell.
McGee, T.G. and C. Greenberg, 1992, "The Emergence of Extended Metropolitan Regions in ASEAN: Towards the Year 2000", *ASEAN Economic Bulletin*, 9, 1, pp.22-44.
McGee, T. G. and Lin, C.S., 1993, "Footprints in Space: Spatial Restructuring in East Asia's NICs", in: C. Dixon and D. Drakakis-Smith, eds, *Economic and Social Development in Pacific Asia*, London: Routledge, pp.152-68.
McKinnon, J. and B. Vienne, eds, 1989, *Hilltribes Today: Problems in Change*, Bangkok: White Lotus-Orstom.
Moerman, M., 1968, *Agricultural Change and Peasant Choice in a Thai Village*, Cambridge University Press.
Moreau, D., 1988, *Cultural Diagnosis on Rice Cropping Systems in Phattalung Province in Southern Thailand*, Publication no. 8, Thai-French Farming Systems Research Project, Prince of Songkhla University.
Mukhopadhay, Swapna and Chee Peng Lim, eds, 1985, *The Rural Non-Farm Sector in Asia*, Kuala Lumpur: Asian and Pacific Development Centre.
Mukhopadhay, Swapna and Chee Peng Lim, eds, 1985, *Development and Diversification of Rural Industries in Asia*, Kuala Lumpur: Asian and Pacific Development Centre.
Mulder, N., 1992, *Inside Thai Society: An Interpretation of Everyday Life*, Bangkok: Editions Duang Kamol.
Muscat, R.J., 1966, *Development Strategy in Thailand*, New York: Praeger.
Muscat, R.J., 1990, *Thailand and The United States: Development, Security and Foreign Aid*, New York: Columbia University Press.
Muscat, R.J., 1994, *The Fifth Tiger: A Study of Thai Development Policy*, Yokyo: United Nations University Press.

McVey, R., ed., 1990, *Industrializing Elites in Southeast Asia*, Ithaca: Cornell University Press.
McVey, R., ed., 1992, *Southeast Asian Capitalists*, Ithaca: Cornell University, Southeast Asia Program.
Nakata, Thinapen and Likhit Dhiravegin, 1989, "Social and Cultural Aspects of Thai Polity", in: Prasith-rathsint, ed., 1989, *Thailand's National Development: Social and Economic Background*, Bangkok: Thai University Research Association, pp.166-96.
Naritoom, C., 1990, "Agrarian System Transformations and Farmer Typology in Tambon Thung Kwang of Kamphaengsaen District for Establishing Applied Research Priorities", *Proceedings of the Seventh Thailand National Farming Systems Seminar*, Surat Thani: Department of Agricultural Extension, Ministry of Agriculture and Co-operatives, 26-29 March 1990.
Naritoom, C., K. Simsiriwong, J.C. Castella, G. Trébuil, P. Saritnirun and J. Jantprasert, 1991, "On-Farm Diagnosis on the Intensification of Vegetable Cropping Systems for Exports to Improve the Sustainability of Small-Scale Farming Systems in Kamphaengsaen Area of Nakhon Pathom Province, Thailand", *Proceedings of the 8th Thailand National Farming Systems Seminar*, Chiang Mai University, 20-22 March 1991.
Nation, various issues.
Neher, C.D., 1988, "Thailand in 1987: Semi-Successful Semi-Democracy", *Asian Survey*, 28, 2, pp.192-201.
Neher, C.D., 1992, "Political Succession in Thailand", *Asian Survey*, 32, 7, pp.585-605.
Neher, C.D. and Budsayamat Bunjaipet, 1989, "Political Interaction in Northern Thailand", *Crossroads*, 4, 2, pp.35-52.
Nemetz, P.N., ed., 1990, *The Pacific Rim: Investment, Development and Trade*, Vancouver: University of British Columbia Press.
Ngernprasertsri, N., P. Traimongkolkool, C. Naritoom and G. Trébuil, 1992, "Agrarian History Zonation: A Case Study of Saiyok, Kanjanaburi", *Proceedings of Kasetsart University 30th Annual Academic Conference*, Bangkok, 29 January-1 February 1992.
NGO Support Project, 1995, *Thai NGOs: The Continuing Struggle for Democracy*, Bangkok: NGO Support Project.
Nolten, Marleen and Gert-Jan Tempelman, 1986, "Handicrafts as a Means of Rural Development: A Case Study from Pahang, Peninsular Malaysia", *Malaysian Journal of Tropical Geography,* 13, pp.37-45.
Noranitipadungkarn, Chakrit, 1981, "Decentralization, Coordination and Development in Thailand" in: G. Shabbir Cheema, ed., 1981, *Institutional Dimensions of Regional Development*, Singapore: Maruzen Asia, pp.117-44.
Oakley, P., *et.al.*, 1991, *Projects with People: The Practice of Participation in Rural Development*, Geneva: ILO.
Ockey, J., 1992, "Business Leaders, Gangsters, and the Middle Class: Societal Groups and Civilian Rule in Thailand", unpublished Ph.D. Dissertation, Cornell University.
Ockey, J., 1993, "Chaopho: Capital Accumulation and Social Welfare in Thailand", *Crossroads* , 8, 1, pp.48-77.

O'Connor, R.A., 1981, "The Southeast Asian Roots of the Primate City", *Southeast Asian Journal of Social Science*, 9, 1-2, pp.127-29.
O'Connor, J., 1989, "Uneven and Combined Development and Ecological Crisis: A Theoretical Introduction", *Race and Class*, 30, pp.1-11.
Odzer, C., 1990, *Patpong Prostitution: Its Relationship to, and Effect on, the Position of Women in Thai Society*, Ann Arbor, Michigan: University Microfilms International.
OECD, 1979, *The Impact of the Newly Industrializing Countries*, Paris: OECD.
OECD, 1992, *Integration of Developing Countries into the International Trading System*, Paris: OECD, Secretary-General's Office.
Ogawa, Naohiro, 1985, "Urbanization and Internal Migration in Selected ASEAN Countries: Trends and Prospects", in: P.M. Hauser, D.B. Suits and Naohiro Ogawa, eds, *Urbanization and Migration in ASEAN Development*, Tokyo: National Institute for Research Advancement.
Omvedt, G., 1986, *Women and Popular Movements: India and Thailand During the Decade of Women*, Geneva: UNRISD.
D'Orleans, Prince Henri, 1894, *Around Tonkin and Siam*, London: Chapman and Hill Co.
Ota, Y., 1993, "Objectification of Culture: The Creation of Culture and Identity in the Tourist World", *The Japanese Journal of Ethnology*, 57, 4, pp.383-410.
Pakkasem, Phisit, 1973, *Thailand's North East Development Planning: A Case Study in Regional Planning*, Bangkok: NESDB.
Pakkasem, Phisit, 1975a, "Development Planning and Implementation in Thailand", in: Prateep Sondysuwan, ed., *Finance, Trade and Economic Development in Thailand*, Bangkok: Sompong Press.
Pakkasem, Phisit, 1975b, "Regional Planning Within a National Framework: The Case of Thailand's Northeast", in: Prateep Sondysuwan, ed., *Finance, Trade and Economic Development in Thailand*, Bangkok: Sompong Press, pp.235-44.
Pakkasem, Phisit, 1976, "Industrialization Strategies and the Growth Pole Approach to South Thailand Regional Planning", in: UNCRD, *Growth Pole Strategy and Regional Development Planning in Asia*, pp.41-53.
Pakkasem, Phisit, 1981a, "Rural-Urban Relations in the Bangkok Metropolitan Dominance Subregion", in: Fu-Chen Lo, ed., *Rural-Urban Relations and Regional Development*, pp. 79-107.
Pakkasem, Phisit, 1981b, "Thailand: Urbanization and Government Policy", in: M. Honjo, ed., *Urbanization and Regional Development*, United Nations: Centre for Regional Development. Regional Development Series No.6, pp.179-99.
Pakkasem, Phisit, 1988, *Leading Issues in Thailand's Development Transformation, 1960-1990*, Bangkok: National Economic and Social Development Board.
Panayotou, T., 1989, "Thailand: The Experience of a Food Exporter", in: T. Sicular, ed., *Food Price Policy in Asia*, Ithaca: Cornell University Press.
Panayotou, T., 1990, "Investing in Rural Industry for Employment and Balanced Growth: The Case of Thailand", in: P.N. Nemetz, ed., *The Pacific Rim: Investment, Development and Trade*, Vancouver: University of British Columbia Press, pp.156-94.

Panayotou, T. and C. Sussangkarn, 1991, *The Debt Crisis, Structural Adjustment and the Environment: The Case of Thailand*, Bangkok: Thailand Development Research Institute Foundation.

Panpiemras, Kosit, ed., 1987, *Rural Industrialization in Thailand,* Bangkok: National Economic and Social Development Board.

Papelka, C.A. and M.A. Littrell, 1991, "Influence of Tourism on Handicraft Evolution", *Annals of Tourism Research*, 18, 3, pp.392-413.

Parnwell, Michael J.G., 1988, "Rural Poverty, Development and the Environment: The Case of North-East Thailand", *Journal of Biogeography,* 15, 1, pp.199-208.

Parnwell, Michael J.G., 1990, *Rural Industrialisation in Thailand*, Hull Papers in Developing Areas, No.1, February 1990, Centre of Developing Area Studies, The University of Hull.

Parnwell, Michael J.G., 1991, "Confronting Uneven Development in Thailand: The Potential Role of Rural Industries", *Malaysian Journal of Tropical Geography*, 22, 1, pp.51-62.

Parnwell, Mike, 1993a, *Population Movements and the Third World*, London: Routledge (Introductions to Development Series).

Parnwell, Michael J.G., 1993b, "Tourism and Rural Handicrafts in Thailand", in: M. Hitchcock, V.T. King and M.J.G. Parnwell, eds, *Tourism in South-East Asia*, London: Routledge, pp.234-57.

Parnwell, Michael J.G., 1993c, "Environmental Issues and Tourism in Thailand", in: M. Hitchcock, V.T. King and M.J.G. Parnwell, eds, *Tourism in South-East Asia*, London: Routledge.

Parnwell, Michael J.G., 1993d, "What's in a Name? Thailand: Asia's Fifth Tiger or a Sheep in Wolf's Clothing?", in: *Thailand: Asia's Fifth Tiger: An Analysis of Thailand's Political, Economic and Social Development and its External Relations in the 1990s*, Brussels: European Institute for South and South-East Asian Studies, pp.53-73; also Annex V.

Parnwell, Michael J.G., 1994, "Rural Industrialisation and Sustainable Development in Thailand", *Quarterly Environment Journal*, 1, 2, pp.24-39, Bangkok: Thailand Environment Institute.

Parnwell, Michael J.G. and Suranart Khamanarong, 1990, "Rural Industrialisation and Development Planning in Thailand", *Southeast Asian Journal of Social Science*, 18, 2, pp.1-28.

Parnwell, Michael J.G. and Jonathan Rigg, in press, "The People of Isan: Missing Out on the Economic Boom?", in: Denis Dwyer and David Drakakis-Smith, eds, *Ethnodevelopment: Concepts and Case Studies*, London: Longman.

Pavinee, Kiatchaipipat, 1994a, "The Textile Industry", *Bangkok Bank Monthly Review*, 35, 5, pp.19-25.

Pavinee, Kiatchaipipat, 1994b, "The Textile Industry in the First Half of 1994 and Future Trends", *Bangkok Bank Monthly Review*, 35, 10, pp.22-24.

Payutto, The Venerable P.A., 1994, *Buddhist Economics: A Middle Way for the Market Place*, Bangkok: Buddhadhamma Foundation (2nd Edition).

Permtanjit, Grit, 1982, *Political Economy of Dependent Capitalist Development: Study on the Limits of the Capacity of the State to Rationalize in Thailand*, Bangkok: Chulalongkorn University, Social Research Institute.

Pernia, E.M., 1988, "Urbanization and Spatial Development in the Asian and Pacific Region: Trends and Issues", *Asian Development Review*, 6, 1, pp.86-105.
Pernia, E.M., 1991, "Aspects of Urbanization and the Environment in Southeast Asia", *Asian Development Review*, 9, 2, pp.113-36.
Phantumvanit, Dhira and Theodore Panayotou, 1990a, *Industrialization and Environmental Quality: Paying the Price*, Bangkok: TRDI.
Phantumvanit, Dhira and Theodore Panayotou, 1990b, *Natural Resources for a Sustainable Future: Spreading the Benefits*, Bangkok: TRDI.
Phélinas, P., 1994, "Rice Entrepreneurs Facing Land Constraints: Some Empirical Evidence", in: Amara Pongsapich, Somchai Ratanakomut, Xavier Oudin, Pascale Phélinas, Jean-Christophe Simon and Jeun-Yves Weigel, eds, *Entrepreneurship and Socio-economic Transformation in Thailand and Southeast Asia*, Bangkok, Chulalongkorn University Social Research Institute/The French Institute for Scientific Research for Development in Cooperation.
Phipatseritham, Krirkkiat and K. Yoshihara, 1989, "Thailand: Industrialization Without Development", *East Asian Cultural Studies*, 28, 1-4, pp.91-100.
Phongpaichit, Pasuk, 1980, *Economic and Social Transformation of Thailand, 1957-1976*, Bangkok: Social Science Institute, Chulalongkorn University.
Phongpaichit, Pasuk, 1982, *From Peasant Girls to Bangkok Masseuses*, Geneva: International Labour Office.
Phongpaichit, Pasuk, 1991, "Transnationalization, the State and the People: The Case of Thailand", *Journal of Southeast Asian Studies*, 22, 2, pp.379-86.
Phongpaichit, Pasuk, 1992a, "Technocrats, Businessmen, and Generals: Democracy and Economic Policy-making in Thailand", in: A.J. MacIntyre and Kanishka Jayasuriya, eds, *The Dynamics of Economic Policy Reform in South-East Asia and the South-West Pacific*, Singapore: Oxford University Press.
Phongpaichit, Pasuk, 1992b, "The Politics of Economic Policy Reform in Thailand", in: David G. Timberman, ed., *The Politics of Economic Reform in Southeast Asia*, Manila: Asian Institute of Management.
Phongpaichit, Pasuk and Sungsidh, 1994, *Corruption and Democracy in Thailand*, Bangkok: Chulalongkorn University, Political Economy Centre.
Piampiti, Suwanlee, 1979, "Thailand: Population Distribution and Development Strategies", in: R.J. Pryor, ed., *Migration and Development in South-East Asia: A Demographic Perspective*, Kuala Lumpur: Oxford University Press, pp.69-75.
Pibunsongkhram, Field Marshall P., 2485 [1942], *Collected Speeches*, Bangkok: Department of Public Relations (in Thai).
Piker, S., 1975, "The Post-Peasant Village in Central Plain Thai Society", in: W.G. Skinner and A.T. Kirsch, eds, *Change and Persistence in Thai Society: Essays in Honour of Lauriston Sharp*, Ithaca: Cornell University Press.
Piker, S., 1983, *A Peasant Community in Changing Thailand*, Arizona: Arizona State University.
Pongsapich, Amara, 1982, "The Unresolved Problems of Ayutthaya", *Summary Report: Ayutthaya Project*, Bangkok: Chulalongkorn University Social Research Institute.

Pongsapich, Amara, ed., 1986, *Women's Issues: Book of Readings*, Chulalongkorn University: Social Research Institute.
Pongsapich, Amara, 1988, *Occasional Papers on Women in Thailand*. Bangkok: Women's Studies Programme, Chulalongkorn University Social Research Institute.
Pongsapich, Amara and Nitaya Kataleeradabhan, 1994, *Philanthropy, NGO Activities and Corporate Funding in Thailand*, Bangkok: Chulalongkorn University Social Research Institute.
Pongsapich, A., C. Banpasirichote, P. Lapthananon and S. Veeravongse, 1993, *Socio-Cultural Change and Political Development in Central Thailand, 1950-1990*, Bangkok: TDRI.
Pongsapich, A., S. Veeravongse and P. Lapthananon, 1993, "Natural Resource Management Policy and Ethnic Minorities: Conflict and Resolutions in the Huay Khakhaeng Buffer Zone", Proceedings of the Seminar on Population and Environmental Protection: A Challenge for the Communication Strategist, December 7-9 1993, Dhurakijpundi Univesity, Bangkok: Asia-Pacific Development Communication Center.
Pongsapich, Amara *et.al.*, eds, 1994, *Entrepreneurship and Socio-economic Transformation in Thailand and Southeast Asia*, Chulalongkorn University Social Research Institute, Bangkok.
Pornchokchai, Sopon, 1992, *Bangkok Slums: Review and Recommendations*, Bangkok: School of Urban Community Research and Actions Agency for Real Estate Affairs.
Porpora, D. and Mah Hui Lim, 1987, "The Political-Economic Factors of Migration to Bangkok", *Journal of Contemporary Asia*, 17, 1, pp.76-89.
Porpora, D., Mah Hui Lim and Usanee Prommas, 1989, "The Role of Women in the International Division of Labour: The Case of Thailand", *Development and Change*, 20, 2, pp.269-94.
Porter, Michael E., 1990, *The Competitive Advantage of Nations*, London: McMillan.
Potter, R.B., 1985, *Urbanisation and Planning in the Third World: Spatial Perceptions and Public Participation*, London: Croom Helm.
Potter, R.B., 1989, "Urban-Rural Interaction, Spatial Polarisation and Development Planning", in: R.B. Potter and T. Unwin, eds, *The Geography of Urban-Rural Interaction in Developing Countries*, London: Routledge.
Pramuanratkarn, Thiravet, 1979, *Impact of Urbanization on a Peripheral Area of Bangkok, Thailand*, Ann Arbor: University Microfilms International.
Prasartsert, Suthy, 1988, "Technological Domination by the Transnational Corporation in Thailand", in: Weizo Teng and N..T. Wang, eds, *Transnational Corporations and China's Open Door*, Lexington: D.C. Heath, pp.145-63.
Prasartset, Suthy, 1990, "Democratic Alternatives to Maldevelopment: The Case of Thailand", Paper submitted to the Conference on Deepening and Globalizing Democracy, Yokohama City, March 17-22.
Prasith-Rathsint, S., ed., 1989, *Thailand's National Development: Policy Issues and Challenges*, Bangkok: Thai University Research Association.
Project for Ecological Recovery, 1992, *The Future of People and Forests in Thailand After the Logging Ban*, Bangkok: Project for Ecological Recovery.

Pryor, R.J., ed., *Migration and Development in South-East Asia: A Demographic Perspective*, Kuala Lumpur: Oxford University Press.
Pubbawesa, Wisarn, 1989, "Review of Economic Development in Thailand", in Prasith-Rathsint, ed., *Thailand's National Development: Social and Economic Background*, Thai University Research Association, pp.16-46.
Punpuing, S., 1993, "Correlates of Commuting Patterns: A Case Study of Bangkok, Thailand", *Urban Studies*, 30, 3, pp.527-46.
Puntasen, Apichai, Somboon Siriprachai and Chaiyuth Punyasavatsut, 1992, "Political Economy of Eucalyptus: Business, Bureaucracy and the Thai Government", *Journal of Contemporary Asia*, 22, 2, pp.187-206.
Putsatee, A.M. *et.al.*, 1992, *Impact of Trekking Tourism on the Environment and Local People*, Faculty of Social Sciences and Humanities, Mahidol Univesity.
Pye, Elwood A., ed., 1988, *Artisans in Economic Development: Evidence from Asia*, Ottawa: IDRC, Research Report 262e.
Radley, H.M., 1986, "Economic Marginalisation and the Ethnic Consciousness of the Green Mong (Moub Ntsuab) of Northwestern Thailand", unpublished Ph.D. dissertation, University of Oxford.
Ramsey, J.A., 1976, "Modernization and Centralization in Northern Thailand", *Journal of South East Asian Studies*, 7, 1, pp.16-32.
Ratanakul, Pinit, 1990, "Reflections on Development and Tradition in Thailand", in: Pinit Ratanakul and U. Kyaw Than, eds, *Development, Modernization, and Tradition in Southeast Asia: Lessons from Thailand*, Bangkok: Mahidol University, pp.259-78.
Ratanakul, Pinit and U. Kyaw Than, eds, 1990, *Development, Modernization and Tradition in Southeast Asia: Lessons from Thailand*, Bangkok: Mahidol University.
Ratanakomut, Somchai, Charuma Ashakul and Thienchay Kirananda, 1994, "Urban Poverty in Thailand: Critical Issues and Policy Measures", *Asian Development Review*, 12, 1, pp.204-24.
Reid, Anthony, 1988, *Southeast Asia in the Age of Commerce 1450-1680, Vol. I, The Lands Below the Winds*, New Haven: Yale University Press.
Resnick, S.A., 1970, "The Decline of Rural Industry Under Export Expansion: A Comparison Among Burma, Philippines and Thailand, 1870-1938", *Journal of Economic History*, 30, pp.51-73.
Richards, P., ed., 1982, *Basic Needs and Government Policies in Thailand*, Singapore: Maruzen Asia, for the International labour Organization.
Richardson, H.W., 1984, "Towards a National Urban Development Strategy for Thailand", in: H.D. Kammeier and P.J. Swan, eds, *Equity with Growth?: Planning Perspectives for Small Towns in Developing Countries*, Bangkok: Asian Institute of Technology.
Richardson, H.W., 1989, "The Big, Bad City: Mega-City Myth?", *Third World Planning Review*, 11, 4, pp.355-72.
Rief, Y.M. and S.H. Cochrane, 1990, "The Off-farm Labour Supply of Farmers: The Case of the Chiang-Mai Valley of Thailand", *Economic Development and Cultural Change*, 38, 4, pp.683-98.
Rigg, Jonathan D., 1985, "The Role of the Environment in Limiting the Adoption of New Rice Technology in Northeast Thailand", *Transactions of the Institute of British Geographers*, 10, 4, pp.481-94.

Rigg, Jonathan D., 1988, "Land Ownership and Land Tenure as Measures of Wealth and Marginalisation: Evidence from Northeast Thailand", *Area*, 20, 4, pp.339-45.
Rigg, Jonathan D., 1991a, *Southeast Asia: A Region in Transition*. London: Unwin Hyman.
Rigg, Jonathan, 1991b, "Grass-roots Development in Rural Thailand: A Lost Cause?", *World Development*, 19, 2-3, pp.199-211.
Rigg, Jonathan D., 1993, "Rice, Water and Land: Strategies of Cultivation on the Khorat Plateau, Thailand", *Southeast Asia Research*, 1, 2, pp.197-221.
Rigg, Jonathan, 1995, "Errors in the Making: Rice, Knowledge, Technological Change and 'Applied' Research in Northeast Thailand", *Malaysian Journal of Tropical Geography*, 26, 1, pp.19-33.
Rigg, Jonathan D. and Philip Scott, 1992, "The Rise of the Naga: The Changing Geography of South-East Asia, 1965-90" in: Graham P. Chapman and Kathleen M. Baker, eds., *The Changing Geography of Asia*, London: Routledge.
Riggs, Fred W., 1966, *Thailand: The Modernization of a Bureaucratic Polity*, Honolulu: East-West Center Press.
Rivera, W.M. and S.J. Gustafson, eds, *Agricultural Extension: Worldwide Institutional Evolution and Forces for Change*, Amsterdam and London: Elsevier.
Robinson, D., Yangho Byeon and Ranjit Teja with Wanda Tseng, 1991, *Thailand: Adjusting to Success: Current Policy Issues*, Washington D.C.: IMF.
Robinson, W.C., 1978, "Economic Policy and Population Change in Thailand", *World Development*, 6, 11-12, pp.1261-69.
Robinson, W.C., 1981, "The Roots of the Southeast Asian Primate City", *Southeast Asian Journal of Social Science*, 9, 1-2, pp.123-26.
Robison, R., R. Higgott and K. Hewison, 1987, "Crisis in Economic Strategy in the 1980s: the Factors at Work", in: Robison, R., R. Higgott and K. Hewison, eds, *South East Asia in the 1980s: The Politics of Economic Crisis*, Sydney: Unwin, pp.1-15.
Rock, M.T., 1994, "Transitional Democracies and the Shift to Export-Led Industrialization: Lessons from Thailand", in: *Studies in Comparative International Development*, 29, 1, pp.18-37.
Rogers, A. and J.G. Williamson, 1984, "Migration, Urbanization and Third World Development: An Overview", in: A. Rogers, ed., *Migration. Urbanization, and Spatial Population Dynamics*, Boulder: Westview Press, pp.261-80.
Rojanaphruk, Pravit, 1993, "Moving Mountains", *The Nation*, 26 September 1993.
Röling, N., 1988, *Extension Science: Information Systems in Agricultural Development*, Cambridge University Press.
Romijn, Hendrika A., 1987, "Employment Generation through Cottage Industries in Rural Thailand: Potentials and Constraints", in: Rizwanul Islam, ed., *Rural Industrialisation and Employment in Asia*, New Delhi International Labour Organization, Asian Employment Programme (ARTEP), pp.211-40.

Rondinelli, D.A., 1983, "Implementing Decentralization Programmes in Asia: A Comparative Analysis", *Public Administration and Development*, 3, 3 July-September.
Rondinelli, D.A., 1990a, "Policies for Balanced Urban Development in Asia: Concepts and Reality", *Regional Development Dialogue*, 11, 1, pp.23-51.
Rondinelli, D.A., 1990b, "Decentralisation, Territorial Power and the State: A Critical Response", *Development and Change*, 21, pp.491-500.
Rondinelli, Dennis A. and K. Ruddle, 1978, *Urbanization and Rural Development: A Spatial Policy for Equitable Growth*, New York: Praeger.
Rutledge, Paul James, 1992, *Central Thai Buddhism and Modernization*, Bangkok: Dhammapradipa Association.
Sahasakul, Chaipat, 1992, *Lessons from the World Bank's Experience of Structural Adjustment Loans (SALs): A Case Study of Thailand*, TDRI Research Monograph No.8, Bangkok.
Saiprasert, P. *et.al.*, 1985, *Paddy Rice Growers Group, San Sai Subdistrict, Prao District, Chiang Mai*, Chiang Mai. Mae Jo Institute of Agricultural Technology.
Sakya, Sapana, 1994, "An Uphill Road to Equality", *Bangkok Post*, 16 April 1994.
Samoff, J., 1990, "Decentralisation: The Politics of Intervention", *Development and Change*, 21, pp.513-30.
Santikarnkaosaard, Mingsarn, 1992, "Manufacturing Growth: A Blessing for All?", Synthesis Report, 1, 2, 1/2-63, Year-End Conference, Thailand Development Research Institute, Bangkok.
Sangvichien, Sud, 1990, "History of Ban Chiang", *Journal of Language and Culture*, 9, 1, pp.15-37 (in Thai).
Sathaanand, S,, 1990, "Religious Movements in Contemporary Thailand: Buddhist Struggle for Modern Relevance", *Asian Survey*, 30, 4, pp.395-408.
Savasdisara, T., 1984, "The Non-Economic Factors in Rural-Urban Migration in Thailand", *Singapore Journal of Tropical Geography*, 5, pp.175-83.
Savasdisara, T., W.E.J. Tips, D. Fordeyn and R. Chaiwut, 1986, "Malnutrition and Basic Needs Surveys in Thailand", *Social Science and Medicine*, 23, 5, pp.485-91.
Schmidt, Johannes Dragsbaek, 1993a, *State Versus Democracy in Thailand: Winners and Losers in a Developmental Context*, Copenhagen Papers in East and Southeast Asian Studies, Museum Tusculanum Press, Copenhagen University, Copenhagen, No.8, pp.71-109.
Schmidt, Johannes Dragsbaek, 1993b, *In the Shadow of the Pacific Century: Comparative Perspectives on Externalities Influence on Economic Policy-Making in Southeast Asian Would-be NICs*, Working Paper No.31, Development Research Series, Aalborg University, Aalborg, Denmark.
Schmitz, Hurbert, 1982, "Growth Constraints on Small-scale Manufacturing in Developing Countries: A Critical Review," *World Development*, 10, 6, pp.430-41.
Schumacher, E.F., 1973, *Small Is Beautiful: Economics As If People Mattered*, New York: Harper and Row.

Scott, A.J., 1987, "The Semi-Conductor Industry in South East Asia: Organisation, Location and International Division of Labour", *Regional Studies*, 21, pp.143-60.
Scott, J.C., 1985, *Weapons of the Weak*, New Haven: Yale University Press.
Seda, Maria, 1993, *Environmental Management in ASEAN: Perspectives on Critical Regional Issues*, Singapore: Institute of Southeast Asian Studies.
Seewuthiwong, D., 1989, "Weddings, Wealth, Pigs and Coca Cola: *farang* Tourists in an Akha Village", in: J. McKinnon and B. Vienne, eds, *Hilltribes Today*, Bangkok: White Lotus-Orstom, pp.409-24.
Sekiguchi, Sueo, 1983, "Japanese Direct Foreign Investment and ASEAN-Japan Relations: A Synthesis" in: Sueo Sekiguchi, ed., *ASEAN-Japan Relations: Investment*, Singapore: ISEAS, Singapore.
Selwyn, T., 1990, "Tourist Brochures as Post-modern Myth", *Problems of Tourism* 13, 3/4, pp.13-26.
Selwyn, T., 1993, "Peter Pan in South-East Asia: Views from the Brochures", in: M. Hitchcock, V.T. King and M.J.G. Parnwell, eds, *Tourism in South-East Asia*, London: Routledge, pp.117-37.
Sen, C.K., 1992, "Effective Methods of Technology Transfer in the Hills of Nepal", unpublished Ph.D. thesis, University of Reading.
Servaes, J., 1990, "Technology Transfer in Thailand: For Whom and For What?", *Journal of Contemporary Asia*, 20, 2, pp.277-87.
Shand, R.T., ed., 1983, *Off-Farm Employment in the Development of Rural Asia*, Vols I and II, National Centre For Development Studies, Australian National University.
Shils, E., 1981, *Tradition*, Chicago: University of Chicago Press.
Shingi, P. and B Mody, 1976, "The Communication Effects Gap", *Communication Research*, 3, 2.
Siamwalla, A., 1987a, *Thailand's Agricultural Future: What are the Questions*, Bangkok: TRDI.
Siamwalla, A., 1987b, "Productivity and Competitiveness in Thai Agriculture", *1987 TDRI Year-End Conference*, Bangkok, 28-29 November 1987.
Siamwalla, A., 1989, *Trade, Exchange Rate and Agricultural Pricing Policies in Thailand*, Washington: World Bank Comparative Studies.
Siamwalla, A., 1993, "The Institutional and Political Bases of Growth-Inducing Policies in Thailand", paper presented at the Fifth International Thai Studies Conference, SOAS, University of London.
Siamwalla, Ammar and Suthad Setboonsarng, 1986, *The Political Economy of Agricultural Pricing Policies in Thailand*, Washington: World Bank.
Siedentopf, H., 1987, "Decentralization for Rural Development: Government Approaches and People's Initiatives in Asia and the Pacific", in: A. Bhatt *et.al.*, *Building from Below: Local Initiatives for Decentralized Development in Asia and Pacific, Vol. I*, Kuala Lumpur: Asian and Pacific Development Centre, pp.1-40.
Siffin, William J., 1966, *The Thai Bureaucracy: Institutional Change and Development*, Honolulu: East-West Center Press.
Silcock, T.H., 1967, "The Promotion of Industry and the Planning Process", in: T.H. Silcock, ed., *Thailand: Social and Economic Studies in Development*, Canberra: Australian National University Press, pp.258-88.

Silcock, T.H., 1967, "The Rice Premium and Agricultural Diversification", in: T.H. Silcock, ed., *Thailand: Social and Economic Studies in Development* Canberra: Australian National University Press, pp. 231-57.
Sill, M., 1987, "Thailand: Not Yet a Newly Industrializing Country", *Geography*, 72, 315, pp.158-62.
Simon J-C and J.R. Chaponniere, 1989, "Les difficultés de la Thaïlande pour devenir un Nouveau Pays Industriel", *Revue Tiers-Monde* , 19, Paris.
Simon J-C, 1993, "Entrepreneurship, Markets and Industrializing Effects: The Case of Textile Industry", in: Amara Pongsapich *et.al.*, eds, *Entrepreneurship and Socio-economic Transformation in Thailand and Southeast Asia*, Chulalongkorn University Social Research Institute, Bangkok.
Singhanetra-Renard, Anchalee, 1987, "Non-farm Employment and Female Labour Mobility in Northern Thailand", in: J.H. Momsen and J.G. Townsend, eds, *Geography of Gender in the Third World*, London: Hutchinson, pp.258-73.
Singhanetra-Renard, Anchalee and Nitaya Prahudhanitisarn, 1992, "Changing Socio-Economic Roles of Thai Women and their Migration", in: S. Chant, ed., *Gender and Migration in Developing Countries*, London and New York: Belhaven Press.
Sinha, Sanjay, 1985, *Planning for Rural Industrialization: A Review of Developing Country Programmes,* Occasional Paper No. 8, London, Intermediate Technology Development Group.
Sippanondha, Ketudat, with R.B. Textor, 1990, *The Middle Path for the Future of Thailand,* East-West Centre and Chiang Mai University.
Sirisambhand, Napat and Alex Gordon, 1987, "Rural Women and Changes in Work Patterns: The Impact of a Reservoir and Transportation Networks on Three Thai Villages", in: N. Heyzer, ed. *Women Farmers and Rural Change in Asia: Towards Equal Access and Participation*, Kuala Lumpur: Asian Pacific Development Centre, pp.313-52.
Siriyuvasak, Ubonrat, 1991, "The Environment and Popular Culture in Thailand", *Southeast Asian Affairs*, pp.298-308.
Sivaramakrishnan, K.C. and L. Green, 1986, *Metropolitan Management: The Asian Experience*, New York: Oxford University Press.
Skrobanek, S., 1986, "Appropriate Technology for Rural Women", in: Amara Pongsapich, ed., *Women's Issues: Book of Readings*, Chulalongkorn University: Social Research Institute, pp.417-41.
Slater, D., 1989, "Territorial Power and the Peripheral State: The Issue of Decentralisation", *Development and Change*, 20, pp.501-31.
Slater, D., 1993, "The Geopolitical Imagination and the Enframing of Development Theory", *Transactions of the Institute of British Geographers*, 18, pp.419-38.
Smith, George Vinal, 1977, *The Dutch in Seventeenth Century Thailand*, Special Report No.16, Northern Illinois University Center for Southeast Asian Studies, DeKalb, Illinois.
Smith, M.E., 1982, "The Process of Sociocultural Continuity", *Current Anthropology,* 23, 2, pp.127-42.
Smith, N., 1986, "On the Necessity of Uneven Development", *International Journal of Urban and Regional Research*, 10, 1, pp.87-103.

Smith, V., ed., 1977, *Hosts and Guests: An Anthropology of Tourism*, Philadelphia: University of Pennsylvania Press.

Somsakdi, Xuto, ed., 1987, *Government and Politics of Thailand*, Oxford University Press.

Sookasame, Kanikar, 1989, "Women's development", in: Suchart Prasith-rathsint, ed., *Thailand's National Development: Social and Economic Background*, pp.197-233.

Sopchokchai, Orapin, Pradinan Sadeewong, Somboon Tanya and Usa Duangsa, 1991, *Women's Organizing Abilities: A Case Study of Sixteen Northeastern Villages in Thailand*, Bangkok: TRDI.

Sternstein, L., 1979, "Thailand: Changing Patterns of Population Movement 1960-1970", in: R.J. Pryor, ed., *Migration and Development in South-East Asia: A Demographic Perspective* Kuala Lumpur: Oxford University Press, pp.19-29.

Sternstein, L., 1984, "The Growth of the World's Pre-Eminent 'Primate City': Bangkok at its Bicentenary", *Journal of Southeast Asian Studies*, 15, 1, pp.43-68.

Stifel, L., 1976, "Technocrats and Modernization in Thailand", *Asian Survey*, 16, pp.1184-96.

Stöhr, W.B. and D.R.F. Taylor, eds, 1981, *Development from Above or Below? The Dialectics of Regional Planning in Developing Countries*, Chichester: Wiley.

Streeten, Paul, 1977, "The Distinctive Features of a Basic Needs Approach to Development", *International Development Review*, 19, pp.8-16.

Suehiro, Akira, 1985, *Capital Accumulation in Thailand, 1855-1985*, Tokyo: Centre for East Asian Cultural Studies.

Suehiro, Akira, 1985, *Capital Accumulation and Industrial Development in Thailand*, Social Research Institute, Chulalongkorn University.

Suehiro, Akira, 1992, "Capitalist Development in Postwar Thailand: Commercial Bankers, Industrial Elite, and Agribusiness Groups", in: R. McVey, ed., *Southeast Asian Capitalists,* Ithaca, New York: Cornell University, Southeast Asia Program, pp. 35-63.

Suphachalasai, Suphat, 1990, "Export Growth of Thai Clothing and Textile", *The World Economy,* 13, 1.

Suphachalasai, Suphat and Direk Patmasiriwat, 1990, "Poverty and Government Policy in Thailand", *Singapore Economic Review*, 35, 2, pp.78-106.

SUPPORT Foundation [2533 (1990)], *Mat Mii May Thai ... Saay Yay Chonnabot (Thai silk ikat ... fine delicate lines from the village)*, in Thai, Bangkok.

Surarerks, V., 1986, *Historical Development and Management of Irrigation Systems in Northern Thailand*, Chiang Mai, Ford Foundation, Thailand, and Department of Geography, Chiang Mai University.

Suthasupa, P., 1987, "Rural Development in Thailand", *Community Development Journal*, 22, pp.81-6.

Suthasupa, P., 1983, *The Role of Contact Farmers in Transferring Agricultural Technology in Training and Visit System of Agricultural Extension in Lamphun, Northern Thailand*, Chiang Mai. Faculty of Agriculture, Chiang Mai University (mimeo).

Suwalai, Dome, 1991, "Joint Move to Curb Trekkers in North: Better Visitors, Image Upgrade Cited as Objectives Behind Three-Way Cooperation", *The Nation*, 9 August 1991.

Suwalai, Dome, 1992, "Heroin Habit Spreads among the Hilltribes: Villages Turn into Havens for Drug", *The Nation*, 6 January 1992.

Suwarnarat, Ksemsan and Watana Luanratana, 1993, "Waste Management and the Need for Public Participation in Bangkok", *Regional Development Dialogue*, 14, 3, pp.67-77.

Swanson, B., ed., 1984, *Agricultural Extension: A Reference Manual*, Rome: FAO.

Swetzoff, Julia B. and Sara Wolf, 1992, "Natural Dyes in Thailand", in: M. Gittinger and H. L. Lefferts Jr., *Textiles and the Tai Experience in Southeast Asia*, Washington: The Textile Museum, pp.243-56.

Swidler, A., 1986, "Culture in Action: Symbols and Strategies", *American Sociological Review*, 51, pp.273-86.

Takaya, Y., 1987, *Agricultural Development of a Tropical Delta: A Study of the Chao Phraya Delta*, Honolulu, University of Hawaii Press.

Tambunlertchai, Somsak, 1983, *Manufactured Exports Promotion: The Case of Thailand,* Tokyo: Institute for Developing Economies.

Tambunlertchai, Somsak, 1989a, "Economic Prospects and External Economic Relations of Thailand", *Asian Development Review*, 7, 2, pp.88-112.

Tambunlertchai, Somsak, 1989b, "Thailand's Industrial Strategy in the Sixth Economic and Social Development Plan", in: Prasith-rathsint, ed., *Thailand's National Development: Social and Economic Background*, Thai University Research Association, pp.47-105.

Tambunlertchai, Somsak, 1990, *A Profile of Provincial Industries*, Bangkok: TDRI.

Tambunlertchai, Somsak and Suthiphand Chirathivat, 1990, "Management of Thailand's International Economic and Trade Relations", in: Suchart Prasith-rathsint, ed., *Thailand on the Move: Stumbling Blocks and Breakthroughs*, Bangkok: Thai University Research Association.

Tambunlertchai, Somsak and Umphon Panachet, 1990, "Foreign Direct Investment in ASEAN" in: Soon Lee Ying, ed., *Foreign Direct Investment in ASEAN*, Kuala Lumpur: Malaysian Economic Association.

Tan-Kim-Yong, U., A. Ganjanapan, S. Ramitanondh and S. Yanasarn, 1988, *Natural Resource Utilisation and Management in Maekhan Basin: Intermediate Zone Crisis*, Chiang Mai: Chiang Mai University.

Tanabe, Shigeharu, 1978, "Peasant Farming Systems in Thailand: A Comparative Study of Rice Cultivation and Agricultural Technology in Chiangmai and Ayutthaya", unpublished. Ph.D. Thesis, University of London.

Tanabe, Shigeharu, 1994, *Ecology and Practical Technology: Peasant Farming Systems in Thailand*, Bangkok: White Lotus.

Tangwisutijit, N., 1990, "Tourism Rot Hits Chiang Rai", *The Nation*, January 3 1990, p.21.

Tantiwiramanond, Darunee and Shashi Pandey, 1987, "The Status and Role of Thai Women in the Pre-Modern Period: A Historical and Cultural Perspective", *Sojourn*, 2, 1, pp.125-49.

Tantiwiramanond, Darunee and Shashi Pandey, 1991, *By Women, For Women: A Study of Women's Organizations in Thailand*, Singapore: Institute of Southeast Asian Studies.

Tasker, R., 1991, "Wedded to Success", *Far Eastern Economic Review*, May 3, pp.49-50.

Taylor, J.L., 1990, "New Buddhist Movements in Thailand: An Individualistic Revolution, Reform and Political Dissonance", *Journal of Southeast Asian Studies*, 21, 1, pp.135-54.

Taylor, J.L., 1993, *Forest Monks and the Nation-State*, Singapore: Institute of Southeast Asian Studies.

Taylor, P. *et.al.*, 1990 "Thailand: Financial Times Survey", *Financial Times*, 5 December, pp.31-36.

Terwiel, B.J., 1989, *Through Travellers' Eyes: An Approach to Early Nineteenth-Century Thai History*, Bangkok: Editions Duang Kamol.

Textor, Robert B., M.L. Bhansoon Ladavalya and Sidthanit Prabudhanitisarn, 1984, *Alternative Sociocultural Futures for Thailand: A Pilot Study Among Academics*, Chiang Mai University, Faculty of Social Sciences.

Thailand: Board of Investment, 1978, *Thailand's Growth Strategy*, Bangkok: BOI.

Thailand: Board of Investment, 1993, *BOI Announcements Nos 1 and 2*, Bangkok: BOI.

Thailand Development Research Institute, 1986, *The Status of Coastal and Marine Resources of Thailand*, Bangkok: TRDI.

Thailand Development Research Institute, 1990, *A Summary Report on Provincial Industries*, Bangkok: TDRI.

Thailand Development Research Institute, 1990, *The Greening of Thai Industry: Producing More and Polluting Less*, Bangkok: TRDI.

Thailand Development Research Institute, 1990, *Industrialization and Environmental Quality: Paying the Price*, Bangkok: TRDI.

Thailand Development Research Institute, 1990, *Urbanization and Environment: Managing the Conflict*, Bangkok: TRDI.

Thailand Development Research Institute, 1990, *Thailand's Economic Structure: Towards Balanced Development*, Bangkok: TRDI.

Thailand Development Research Institute, 1990, *Towards Balanced Development: Sectoral, Spatial and Other Dimensions*, Bangkok: TRDI.

Thailand Development Research Institute, 1990, *Community Integration into Regional Industrial Development*, Bangkok: TRDI.

Thailand Development Research Institute, 1990, *The Making of Modern Bangkok: State, Market and People*, Bangkok: TRDI.

Thailand Development Research Institute, 1990, *Social Inequity: a Source of Conflict in the Future*, Bangkok: TRDI.

Thailand Environment Institute, 1994, "New Solutions for Sustainable Development: Linking Policies with Action", *TEI Quarterly Environment Journal*, 2, 3, July-September 1994.

Thailand Environment Institute, 1994, "Business and Environment", *TEI Quarterly Environment Journal*, 2, 1, January-March 1994.

Thailand: Ministry of Foreign Affairs, 1994, *Thailand Foreign Affairs Newsletter*, July-Sept 1994, Bangkok: Ministry of Foreign Affairs.

Thailand Investment News, 1988, "Getting to Grips with Income Distribution", *Thailand Investment News*, 10 December, pp.3-4.

Thailand: NESDB, 1972, *The Third National Economic and Social Development Plan (1972-1976)*, Bangkok: Office of the Prime Minister, National Economic and Social Development Board.

Thailand: NESDB, 1977, *The Fourth National Economic and Social Development Plan (1977-1981)*, Bangkok: Office of the Prime Minister, National Economic and Social Development Board.

Thailand: NESDB, 1982, *The Fifth National Economic and Social Development Plan (1982-1986)*, Bangkok: Office of the Prime Minister, National Economic and Social Development Board.

Thailand: NESDB, 1984, *Restructuring of Thai Industries*, Bangkok. National Economic and Social Development Board.

Thailand: NESDB, 1986, *Bangkok Metropolitan Regional Development Proposals: Recommended Development Strategies and Investment Programmes for the Sixth Plan.* Bangkok: Office of the Prime Minister, National Economic and Social Development Board.

Thailand: NESDB, 1987, *The Sixth National Economic and Social Development Plan (1987-1991)*, Bangkok: Office of the Prime Minister, National Economic and Social Development Board.

Thailand: NESDB, 1989, *Gross Regional and Provincial Product, 1981-87*, Bangkok: Office of the Prime Minister, National Economic and Social Development Board.

Thailand: NESDB, 1992, *The Seventh National and Economic Development Plan (1992-1996)*, Bangkok: Office of the Prime Minister, National Economic and Social Development Board.

Thailand: NESDB and Industrial Management Co., 1985, *Industrial Restructuring Study,* Bangkok: National Economic and Social Development Board.

Thailand: National Identity Office, 1991, *Thailand in the 1990's*, National Identity Office of the Prime Minister.

Thailand: NSO, 1988, *Statistical Reports of Region: Northeastern Region*, Bangkok: Office of the Prime Minister, National Statistical Office.

Thailand: NSO, 1989, *Survey of Migration into Bangkok Metropolis, 1988*, Bangkok: Office of the Prime Minister, National Statistical Office.

Thailand: NSO, 1992, *Statistical Handbook of Thailand, 1992*, Bangkok: Office of the Prime Minister, National Statistical Office.

Thailand: NSO, 1994, *Statistical Yearbook of Thailand, 1994*, No.41, Bangkok: Office of the Prime Minister, National Statistical Office.

Thai-Australia World Bank Land Development Project, 1985, *Thailand Northern Upland Agriculture*, Chiang Mai: Department of Land Development, Ministry of Agriculture and Co-operatives.

Thammawat, Jaruwan, 1991, *Gemstone-Cutting at Ban Sang Ming*, Thailand: Srinakarinwirot Mahasarakham.

Thandee, Damrong, 1985, *Politics of Policy Implementation: A Case Study of Rural Development in Thailand*, Bangkok: CUSRI.

Thepthong, Phitsanu, 1988, "Opium Use Shows 'Must be Stopped'", *Bangkok Post*, August 3 1988, p.9.

A Bath 1992 Sivaraksa 1990=263

1992 Pederson. The study of Perception of Nature — Towards a sociology of Knowledge about Nature

Thepthong, Phitsanu, 1992, "TAT to Help Boost Chiang Rai Tourism", *Bangkok Post*, 30 July 1992.

Thienthai, Chutta, 1987, *Japanese Management Methods in Thailand,* Bangkok: JICA.

Thorbek, S., 1987, *Voices From the City: Women of Bangkok*, London: Zed Books.

Thrift, Nigel, 1986, "The Geography of International Economic Disorder", in: R.J. Johnston and P. Taylor, eds, *A World in Crisis?*, Oxford: Blackwell, pp.12-67.

Thungwa, S., 1986, "Paupérisation paysanne er crise du système agraire dans la région de Phattalung, sud-Thaïlande", unpublished DEA thesis, INA Paris-Grignon, France.

Tingsabadh, C., 1987, *Thailand: Social and Economic Effects of Petroleum Development,* Geneva: ILO.

Tippenawar, M.B., 1990 "Karnataka, India: Farmer Groups and Water Management", *AERDD Bulletin*, 30, pp.34-37.

Todaro, M.P., 1989, *Economic Development in the Third World*, 4th Edition, London: Longman.

Tongpan, Sopin, Theodore Panayatou, Songpol Jetanavanich, Ketty Faichampa and Charlie Mehl, 1990, *Deforestation and Poverty: Can Commercial and Social Forestry Break the Vicious Circle?*, Bangkok: TRDI.

Tonguthai, Pawadee, 1987, "Implicit Policies Affecting Urbanization in Thailand", in R.J. Fuchs *et.al.*, eds, *Urbanization and Urban Policies in Pacific Asia* Boulder: Westview Press, pp. 183-192.

Tooker, D.E., 1992, "Identity Systems of Highland Burma: 'Belief', Akhazang, and a Critique of Interiorized Notions of Ethno-Religious Identity", *Man*, N.S., 27, 4, pp.799-819.

Tourism Authority of Thailand, 1985, *Master Plan for the Tourism Development of Ko Samui/ Surat Thani*, Bangkok: TAT.

Townsend, J.G. and J.H. Momsen, 1987, "Towards a Geography of Gender in Developing Market Economies", in: J.H. Momsen and J.G. Townsend, eds, *Geography of Gender in the Third World*, London: Hutchinson, pp.27-81.

Toyota, Mika, 1993, "Tourism, Continuity and Change within an Akha Village: Image and Reality", unpublished M.A. Dissertation, University of Hull.

Trébuil, G., 1989, "Research on the Transformations and Differentiation of Regional Agrarian Systems: A Macro Analysis Complementary to Farming Systems Research and Development", *Proceedings of the Sixth Thailand national Farming Systems Seminar*, Khon Kaen, 27-30 March 1989, pp.39-51.

Trébuil, G., 1990, "Croissance agricole et transformations économiques et sociales en Thaïland", *Proceedings of the SOLAGRAL Colloquium on "Comment nourrir le monde? Les Politiques Alimentaires face à la Libéralisation des Économies et des Échanges* , Paris, 26-28 June 1990, pp.203-11.

Trébuil, G., 1992, "Setting Research Priorities with Farmers: Complementarity of Regional, Farm and Plot Diagnoses to Improve the Competitiveness and Sustainability of Thai Production Systems", paper presented to the Second

Asian Farming Systems Symposium on "Sustainable Agriculture: Meeting the Challenge Today", BMICH-Colombo, Sri Lanka, 2-5 November 1992.

Trébuil, G., 1995, "Mécanisation des itinéraires techniques rizico les et changements economiques en Thaïlande", in: CEEMAT/IRAT of CIRAD, ed., *La Mécanisation Rizicole dans le monde*, Paris.

Trébuil, G., forthcoming, "Pioneer Agriculture, Green Revolution and Environmental Costs in Thailand", in: Jonathan Rigg, ed., *Counting the Costs: Economic Growth and Environmental Change in Thailand*, Singapore: Institute of Southeast Asian Studies, forthcoming (1995), pp.58-79.

Trébuil, G. and P. Boonchoo, 1988a, "The Role of the Typology of Agricultural Production Systems in Farming Systems Research and Development", *Proceedings of the Fifth Thailand National Farming Systems Seminar*, NETC, Kasetsart University at Kamphaengsaen Campus, 4-7 April 1988.

Trébuil, G., 1988b, "Principles and Steps of the Method of Diagnosis on Agrarian Systems: A Case Study from Sathing Phra Area, southern Thailand", in: G. Trébuil, ed., *Farming Systems Research and Development in Thailand: Illustrated Methodological Considerations and Recent Advances*, Paris: GRET; Hat Yai: Prince of Songkla University, pp.29-64.

Trébuil, G. *et.al.*, 1990, "A Typology of Farming Systems based on their Functioning and History in Tambon Thung Kwang of Kamphaengsaen District", *Kasetsart Journal (Social Sciences)*, 11, pp.141-50.

Trébuil, G. and M. Dufumier, 1992, "Diagnoses on Regional Agrarian Systems and Sustainability of Agricultural Production Pystems in Thailand", *Journal of the Asian Farming Systems Association*, 1, 4, pp.557-68.

Trébuil, G., S. Kaojarern, P. Traimongkonkool, N. Ngernprasertsri and J.C. Castella, 1994, *Agro-Ecological Zonation and Agricultural Transformations in Kanjanaburi Province: Hypotheses for Improving Farming Systems Sustainability*, Bangkok: Asian Institute of Technology, School of Environmental Resources and Development and Kasetsart University, DORAS Project.

Trébuil, G. and P. Singrat, 1990, "Agrarian Systems Crisis and Improvement of Wood Energy Systems: Applications to the Case of the Small-Scale Palm Sugar Production in Southern Thailand", *FAO Regional Expert Consultation on Wood Based Energy Systems: Rural Industries and Village Applications*, Hat Yai, 12-16 March 1990, pp.59-112.

Trébuil, G., S. Thungwa and I. Patamadit-Trébuil, 1983, *The Present System and Recent Changes in Land Use in Sathing Phra District, Southern Thailand*, publication no. 2, Thai-French Farming Systems Research Project, Prince of Songkhla University.

Turner, Louis and John Ash, 1975, *The Golden Hordes: International Tourism and the Pleasure Periphery*, London: Constable.

Turton, A., 1978, "The Current Situation in the Thai Countryside", in: A. Turton, T. Fast and M. Caldwell, eds, *Thailand: Roots of Conflict*, Nottingham: Spokesman, pp. 104-142.

Turton, A., 1987, *Production, Power and Participation in Rural Thailand*, Geneva: United Nations Research Institute for Social Development.

Turton, A., 1989, "Local Powers and Rural Differentiation", in: Turton, A., G. Hart and B. White, eds, 1989, *Agrarian Transformations: Local Processes and the State in Southeast Asia*, Berkeley: University of California Press.

Turton, A., 1989, "Thailand: Agrarian Bases of State Power", in: Turton, A., G. Hart and B. White, eds, 1989, *Agrarian Transformations: Local Processes and the State in Southeast Asia*, Berkeley: University of California Press.

Tzong-biau Lin and Elwood A. Pye, 1983, *Tourism in Asia: The Economic Impact*, Singapore: Singapore University Press.

Unger, Daniel, 1991, "Politics of the Rising Tide: Riding the Wave of East Asian Capital in Thailand", Annual Meetings, Association of Asian Studies, New Orleans, October 11-14.

United Nations: ESCAP, 1990, *Strategy for Rural Poverty Alleviation: Agriculture-Industry Linkages*, Bangkok: United Nations, Economic and Social Commission for Asia and the Pacific.

United Nations: ESCAP, 1994, *Employment Strategies for the Rural Poor*, New York: United Nations Economic and Social Commission for Asia and the Pacific.

United Nations: ICIRDAP, 1992, *Partners in Rural Poverty Alleviation: NGO Cooperation*, New York: United Nations Interagency Committee on Integrated Rural Development for Asia and the Pacific.

Unwin, T., 1989, "Urban-Rural Interaction in Developing Countries: A Theoretical Perspective", in: R.B. Potter and T. Unwin, eds, *The Geography of Urban-Rural Interaction in Developing Countries*, London: Routledge, pp.11-32.

Uphoff, N.T., 1984, *Analyzing Options for Local Institutional Development*, Ithaca. Rural Development Committee, Cornell University

Vaddhanaphuti, Chayan, 1984, "Cultural and Ideological Reproduction in Northern Thai Society", unpublished Ph.D. thesis, Standford University.

Vichit-Vadakan, V. *et.al.*, 1976, *Urbanization in the Bangkok Central Region*, Bangkok: Thai University Research Associates.

Vienne, B., 1989, "Facing Development in the Highlands: A Challenge for Thai Society", in" J. McKinnon and B. Vienne, eds, *Hill Tribes Today: Problems in Change*, Bangkok: White Lotus-Orstom.

Vorathepputipong, Thavan, 1987, "Decentralization for Rural Development in Thailand", in A. Bhatt *et.al.*, 1987, *Building From Below: Local Initiatives for Decentralized Development in Asia and Pacific*, vol. III, Kuala Lumpur: Asian and Pacific Development Centre, pp.391-425.

Wade, Robert, 1990, *Governing the Market, Economic Theory and the Role of Government in East Asian Industrialisation*, Princeton University Press.

Wahnschafft, Ralph, 1985, "The Role of the State in the Transformation of Thai Seaside Villages into International Tourism Resorts", paper presented to the Third International Thai-European Seminar on "Village and State in Thai Studies", Hua Hin, 9-12 April.

Walker, A.R. and Suvarnabhumi, 1981, *Farmers in the Hills: Upland Peoples of North Thailand.*

Warr, Peter G., ed., 1993, *The Thai Economy in Transition*, Hong-Kong: Oxford University Press.

Warren, William, 1989 [1970], *Jim Thompson: The Legendary American of Thailand*, Bangkok: The Jim Thompson Thai Silk Company.

Wattanasiritham, Wirat, Pak Tongsom, Arkhom Termpittayapaisith and Satien Jirarangsumant, 1988, "Thailand Socio-economic Development Planning", in: Warin Wonghanchao and Yukio Ikemoto, eds, *Economic Development Policy in Thailand: A Historical Review*, Tokyo: ASEDP No. 1 Institute of Developing Economies.

Weatherbee, D.E., 1990, "Thailand: Democracy Ascendant in the Golden Peninsula", *Southeast Asian Affairs*, pp.337-59.

Weber, M., 1977 [1948], *From Max Weber: Essays in Sociology*, London, Routledge and Kegan Paul.

White, B., 1989, "Problems in the Empirical Analysis of Agrarian Transformation", in: Gillian Hart, Andrew Turton, Benjamin White, with Brian Fegan and Lim Teck Ghee, eds, *Agrarian Transformations: Local Processes and the State in Southeast Asia*, London: University of California Press.

White, G., 1988, "Developmental States in East Asia: An Introduction", in G. White, ed., *The Developmental State in East Asia*, London, Macmillan, pp.1-29.

Wijeyewardene, Gehan, ed., 1990, *Ethnic Groups Across National Boundaries in Mainland Southeast Asia*, Singapore: ISEAS.

Williamson, Peter, 1992, "Tourist Developers on Koh Samui, Thailand", *Journal of Cultural Geography*, 12, 2, pp.53-64.

Williamson, Peter, 1993, "Tourist Development and Capitalist Transformation on Koh Samui", unpublished Ph.D. thesis, University of Sydney.

Wilson, David A., 1962, *Politics in Thailand*, Ithaca and London: Cornell University Press.

Wong, S.T. and K.M. Saigol K.M., 1984, "Comparison of the Economic Impacts of Six Growth Centres on their Surrounding Rural Areas in Asia", *Environment and Planning A*, 6, pp.81-94.

Wong Shuang Yann, 1994, "Globalization and Regionalization: The Shaping of New Economic Regions in Asia and the Pacific", *Regional Development Dialogue*, 15, 1, pp.3-17.

Wonghanchao, Warin, 1988, *Thailand in the 21st Century: Economic Prospects*, Bangkok: SEPFU-CUSRI.

Wonghanchao, Warin and Yukio Ikemoto, eds, 1988, *Economic Development Policy in Thailand: A Historical Review*, Tokyo: ASEDP No.1 Institute of Developing Economies.

Wonghanchao, Warin and Jeerasak Pongpissanupichit, 1987, "Contribution of Direct U.S. Investment to the Thai Economy", in: *Asia Pacific Economies: Promises and Challenges. Research in International Business and Management*, 6, Part B, JAI Press Inc.

Wongsupbhasatigul, Ekacit, 1975, *Regional Industrial Development of Thailand: Theory and Practice*, Bangkok: Wacharin Pub.Co.

Wongsekiarrthirat, Watthana, 1991, *Kanplianplaeng Kan Chay Thidin le Raengngan Khong Chumchom Chonabot nay Cangwat Ayutthaya (2512-2532) (Changing Land and Labour Utilisation in Rural Communities in Ayutthaya Province, 1969-1989)*, Bangkok: Chulalongkorn University Social Research Institute.

Wood, Robert E., 1979, "Tourism and Underdevelopment in South-East Asia", *Journal of Contemporary Asia*, 9, 3, pp.274-87.
Wood, Robert E., 1980, "International Tourism and Cultural Change in Southeast Asia", *Economic Development and Cultural Change*, 23, pp.561-81.
Wood, Robert E., 1984, "Ethnic Tourism, the State and Cultural Change in South-East Asia", *Annals of Tourism Research*, 11, 3, pp.353-74.
Wood, Robert E., 1993, "Tourism, Culture and the Sociology of Development", in: M. Hitchcock, V.T. King and M.J.G. Parnwell, eds, *Tourism in South-East Asia*, London: Routledge, pp.48-70.
World Bank, 1980a, *An Industrial Development Strategy for Thailand*, Washington: World Bank, Report No. 2804a-TH.
World Bank, 1980b, *Thailand: Coping with Structural Adjustment*, Washington: World Bank, Report No. 3067a.
World Bank, 1980c, *Thailand: Income Growth and Poverty Alleviation*, Washington: World Bank.
World Bank, 1983a, *Thailand: Rural Growth and Poverty*, Washington: World Bank.
World Bank, 1983b, *Managing Public Resources for Structural Adjustment*, Washington: World Bank.
World Bank, 1984, *Thailand: Managing Public Resources for Structural Adjustment*, Washington: World Bank Country Study.
World Bank, 1986, *Program Performance Audit Report Thailand: First And Second Structural Adjustment Loans*, Washington: World Bank, Report No. 6085.
World Bank, 1990a, *Status of Women: Thailand*, Bangkok: The World Bank.
World Bank, 1990b, *Agricultural Extension: The Next Step*, Policy and Research Series, 13; Agriculture and Rural Development Department, Washington: World Bank.
World Bank, 1991, *Public Policy to Promote Industrialization: The Experience of the East Asian NICs and Lessons for Thailand*, Washington: World Bank.
World Bank, 1993, *The East Asian Miracle Economies*, Washington: World Bank.
World Bank, 1993, "Sustaining Rapid Development, East Asia and the Pacific", *Regional Development Review*, Washington: World Bank: Office of the Vice President.
World Bank, various issues, *World Development Report*, New York: Oxford University Press.
Wright, J.J., 1992, "Thailand's Return to Democracy", *Current History*, December 1992.
Wuliger, Robert, 1992, "A World Economy: Paradigms Lost and Found", *Challenge*, January-February 1992.
Wuttithep, Indhapanya, *et.al.*, 1989, "Distribution and Leakages of Tourism Revenues in Businesses, Hotels, and Tour Agencies", Bangkok: National Institute of Development Administration.
Yoddumnern-Attig, Bencha, Kerry Richter, Amara Soonthorndhada, Chanya Sethaput and Anthony Pramualratana, 1992, *Changing Roles and Statuses*

of Women in Thailand: A Documentary Assessment, Bangkok: Mahodol University, Institute of Population Research.

Yoshikawa, Toshiharu, 2525 [1982], *Japanese Sericulture Experts in the Thai Government During the Reign of King Chulalongkorn*, Paper No.35, Thai Kadii Institute, Thammasat University, Bangkok (in Thai).

Young, G., 1962, *The Hill Tribes of Northern Thailand*, Bangkok: The Siam Society.

Yuen, Ng Chee, Sueo Sudo and Donald Crone, 1992, "The Strategic Dimension of the 'East Asian Developmental States'", *ASEAN Economic Bulletin*, 9, 2.

Index